Robert F. Kenr
and the Shaping oı ~ı⌐ıı
Rights, 1960–1964

ALSO BY PHILIP A. GODUTI, JR.

Kennedy's Kitchen Cabinet and the Pursuit of Peace:
The Shaping of American Foreign Policy, 1961–1963
(McFarland, 2009)

Robert F. Kennedy and the Shaping of Civil Rights, 1960–1964

PHILIP A. GODUTI, JR.

McFarland & Company, Inc., Publishers
Jefferson, North Carolina, and London

LIBRARY OF CONGRESS CATALOGUING-IN-PUBLICATION DATA

Goduti, Philip A., 1974–
Robert F. Kennedy and the shaping of civil rights,
1960–1964 / Philip A. Goduti, Jr.
p.   cm.
Includes bibliographical references and index.

ISBN 978-0-7864-4943-9

softcover : acid free paper ∞

1. Kennedy, Robert F., 1925–1968.   2. African Americans —
Civil rights — History — 20th century.   3. Civil rights
movements — United States — History — 20th century.   4. United
States — Politics and government —1961–1963.   I. Title.

E840.8.K4G58 2013   973.922092 — dc23   2012040187

BRITISH LIBRARY CATALOGUING DATA ARE AVAILABLE

On the cover: photograph showing Attorney General Robert F.
Kennedy speaking to a crowd of African Americans and whites through
a megaphone outside the Justice Department, photographer
Warren K. Leffler June 14, 1963 (Library of Congress)

Manufactured in the United States of America

*McFarland & Company, Inc., Publishers
Box 611, Jefferson, North Carolina 28640
www.mcfarlandpub.com*

For Alyssa, Alex, Olivia and Sam

Table of Contents

Acknowledgments

This book stands on the shoulders of all who have written about the Kennedys and the early sixties. Taylor Branch's *Parting the Waters: America and the King Years, 1954–1963* and David Garrow's *Bearing the Cross: Martin Luther King, Jr., and the Southern Christian Leadership Conference* gave great insight into Martin Luther King, Jr., and his contribution to the movement. Raymond Arsenault's *Freedom Riders: 1961 and the Struggle for Racial Justice* is another book that illuminated the racial divide in the nation. These books are among many that paint a picture of the angst that African Americans felt in those years. I hope I was able to translate those feelings effectively. James Hilty's book *Robert Kennedy: Brother Protector* and Arthur Schlesinger's *Robert Kennedy and His Times* provided insight into the legacy of Robert Kennedy. With him at the center of this study, these two books provided guidance in my quest for the story I was trying to craft. While these are not the only sources this study uses, they deserve special mention.

A special thanks to the staff at the John F. Kennedy Library. Their constant assistance helped me find primary sources for this book. Also, the librarians at the Arnold Bernhard Library at Quinnipiac University have always been helpful with requests for books and other material.

I would not have been able to publish this book without the encouragement of my colleagues. Ronald Heiferman of Quinnipiac University is a wonderful mentor and adviser. His encouragement of my writing has always been something that has driven me. Our mutual friend and colleague, Alex Wellek, passed away while I was writing this book. He and his wife Margorie were kind enough to read parts of the manuscript and offer insight. For that I am grateful. In addition, Leonard J. Kent, my former English professor at Quinnipiac University, also passed away recently. His influence led me to teach and write. I hope I honor that legacy. Professors Heiferman, Kent and Wellek were instrumental in my education in American history as well as writing, and continue to inspire me in my work.

In addition to my colleagues at Quinnipiac University, I gained a great amount of support and encouragement from the faculty and staff at Somers High School. Donna Norige and Carol Black of our Library Media Center showed me various databases and websites to make research easier. A special thanks to the Social Studies Department: Kristen Angelica, Andrew Drummey, Marc Dzicek, Donald Gaston and Matthew Macaluso. I have been blessed with great friends and wonderful colleagues, and this book would not have been possible without their support.

One of the things that helped me understand the brotherly relationship between John and Robert Kennedy, as well as the brother/sisterhood within the civil rights movement, was my relationship with my own brothers, Michael, Mark and Matthew. My experience as an older brother helped me see how important and instrumental it was to have that dynamic in the White House and the movement. I hope I was able to translate the importance of that relationship in my writing.

I could never have written this without the support and patience of my family. I am fortunate to have had wonderful influences that have defined my life. My uncle John Mendes and aunt Sharon Mendes have always supported my endeavors. My mother, Rosemarie Goduti, always taught me to strive for my dreams. My father, Philip A. Goduti, Sr., passed away while I was finishing the manuscript. I read part of the book to him in the hospital, days before he died. I believe that his spirit is in parts of this book.

Finally, this book is dedicated to my wife Alyssa and our three children, Alex, Olivia and Sam. Without their encouragement, patience and sacrifice this book would never have been written. Their support has inspired me and I am fortunate to have such a wonderful family. I write for them more than anyone else.

We few, we happy few, we band of brothers;
For he today that sheds his blood with me
Shall be my brother; be he ne'er so vile,
This day gentle his condition.

William Shakespeare
Henry V
Act IV, scene iii, 60–63

⸺⸻⸺

We know through painful experience that freedom is never voluntarily
given by the oppressor; it must be demanded by the oppressed.

Martin Luther King, Jr.
"Letter from Birmingham Jail"
April 16, 1963

⸺⸻⸺

Not because it is legally the thing that you should do, but because it is
morally the right thing to do, and that we are all brothers and that we
have to live as brothers. I think that as long as you have that, and
understanding of that, and the acceptance of that in the United States
that is where real progress is going to be.

Robert F. Kennedy
June 3, 1963

⸺⸻⸺

We are confronted primarily with a moral issue. It is as old as the
scriptures and is as clear as the American Constitution.... One
hundred years of delay have passed since President Lincoln freed the
slaves, yet their heirs, their grandsons, are not fully free. They are not
yet freed from the bonds of injustice. They are not yet freed from social
and economic oppression. And this nation, for all its hopes and all its
boasts, will not be fully free until all its citizens are free.

John F. Kennedy
June 11, 1963

Preface

The struggle for civil rights in this nation is something that embodies the notion of being an American. At the heart of this story is the courage and determination to realize a dream denied to too many Americans since the founding of the nation. In 1955 Martin Luther King, Jr., became a main protagonist in this story, with many supporting players, including, but not limited to, Rosa Parks, John Lewis, Ralph Abernathy, Diane Nash, James Bevel, Roy Wilkins, A. Philip Randolph and many others. Taylor Branch's book *Parting the Waters: America in the King Years, 1954–1963*, brought me into this world. Upon reading that book I gained a greater appreciation of "the movement" and its place in American history. Branch's book taught me that there were other perspectives to consider, and I left that experience wanting to contribute to that story, which embodied so much of what being an American was about.

While I was writing my first book, I spent a great deal of time researching Robert F. Kennedy. I had always been enthralled with John F. Kennedy and how he confronted the Soviet Union during the Cold War, but through that book I found that Bobby was a significant player in the administration. I had always known he was a main player, but now I saw the elements of that play out on history's grand stage. I went through Robert Kennedy's oral history for my first book. In those histories, he and Burke Marshall, his assistant attorney general in charge of civil rights, were interviewed. They gave testimony in 1964 about how they tried to shape the movement from the Justice Department. I was hoping I could take something from that and offer a new perspective of the Civil Rights movement. The more I looked at Bobby's contributions through primary and secondary sources, the more I realized that he and King were connected, whether they liked it or not, at the crossroads in the movement: the Freedom Rides, Birmingham and the March on Washington.

There are many wonderful accounts of John Kennedy's role in civil rights. Chief among them are Carl Brauer's *John F. Kennedy and the Second Reconstruction* and biographies from Kennedy insiders Arthur Schlesinger and Theodore Sorensen. However, few books focus on Robert Kennedy's role at the center of decision-making in civil rights. President Kennedy made great speeches and called out the National Guard when necessary, but Robert Kennedy was the chief architect who advised the president in these areas. His influence led to great leaps in civil rights. This study highlights how that influence translated into lasting, effective change, paving the way for future generations to build on.

The goal of this book is to provide a history of the civil rights movement from the perspective of Robert Kennedy. James Hilty's book *Robert Kennedy: Brother Protector* offers insight into that world. Robert Kennedy could not have shaped civil rights if it were not for the dedicated individuals in the Justice Department. In another sense, this book is about those "soldiers" who risked themselves to bring justice for Americans. Kennedy needed more than just these "soldiers"; he also needed influence, which came in the form of his brother, President John F. Kennedy. All of these elements combined to give Robert Kennedy a unique opportunity to effect change for African Americans, which would have a lasting place in history.

Finally, the election of Barack Obama to the presidency in 2008 demonstrated that Robert Kennedy's efforts and Martin Luther King's dream were possible. It was not the mere fact that an African American had finally made it to the White House that led me to put pen to paper. The nation's reaction to his candidacy left me realizing that we have not come as far in race relations as most people think in this country. There were many in this nation who struggled with the concept of an African American as president. While watching an HBO documentary, I saw a person, who was clearly not for Obama, carrying around a Curious George doll with the word "Obama" drawn across his shirt.[1] I saw in Obama what I learned in Branch's book. At the heart of his candidacy was something more than other people who ran for that office. President Obama had to know that there would be people who wanted to hurt him, not because he was trying to become president, but because he was black. Obama, like the leaders Branch and others write about, knew it would be difficult to take that office. For the rest of his life he would be in the history books as the first African American president, forever a target for the racist American. On the night Barack Obama was elected, John Lewis was in attendance at the rally where Obama spoke. He was a congressman from Georgia in 2008. In 1961 he was beaten in Montgomery, Alabama, by an angry mob because he was part of the Freedom Rides. Obama's election was a vindication for all the battle scars Lewis had endured as a civil rights warrior. He had seen the fruits of his labors.

This is a book about how the Kennedy brothers, Martin Luther King, James Meredith, John Lewis and others who changed the course of America, setting it on a path to accept Barack Obama as president of the United States. His candidacy took the same courage required of the many men and women of the civil rights movement. This book examines the lengths people will go to do what is right, not what is expedient. Finally, it's a testament to the Kennedy brothers. Despite what some have said, they committed themselves to civil rights. Like Abraham Lincoln and the Emancipation Proclamation, they needed to find the right time to make their stand. Once they were able to find that moment in history, they embraced the movement, setting America on a new path.

Introduction

"What mattered was doing *something."*

John Bartlow Martin, who interviewed Robert Kennedy in 1964, commented during that discussion that John F. Kennedy was the "greatest civil rights president since Lincoln." He said he wanted to make sure that Robert Kennedy included all the major issues that affected civil rights in that interview, and that the former attorney general was an "outward symbol" of that spirit. Robert Kennedy responded, "If the campaign meant anything, if what Jack Kennedy had always stood for meant anything, it meant doing something in this field." He went on to say, "It was never a question of sitting around thinking, 'well, should we do it or shouldn't we do it,' because it was always quite clear that we *would* do it. And *had* to do it."[1] John and Robert Kennedy wanted to change the country. While they were not only thinking in terms of civil rights, they had every intention of making a difference in that aspect of American life. While there were other factors that influenced the work, they were steadfast in their approach. The political climate was not ready for revolutionary change. Like Lincoln in the Civil War, they needed to wait for the right moment. Nevertheless, they intended to take advantage of an opportunity to challenge segregation. However, there are many who argue that the Kennedys did not have that intention and were more considered with Southern politics and their congressional agenda. This was a political reality. The Kennedys were, in fact, civil rights warriors who led the way to incremental change, paving the way for future movements. They were revolutionaries, without using the term, who were pushed by civil rights leaders, evoked change and began a rights movement in which they were the symbols of hope that inspired many to follow and make a difference.

Robert F. Kennedy, Dr. Martin Luther King, Jr., John Lewis and many others found new, innovative ways to confront racial issues in the sixties. Their work led to a different America. This course was set in motion not by rhetorical politicians, nor by old school civil rights leaders, but by four students who decided to challenge segregation at a lunch counter. These students inspired a wave of protest such as this country had never seen before. It was not only the start of major revolution in America with rights at the center, but it also had an immediate impact. The civil rights movement for racial equality in the early sixties influenced movements that shaped a new fabric in America. Those students were the catalyst for a new wave of change, and in their wake came larger change in the nation that involved feminism, free speech and other rights-oriented movements.

Racial issues in America have been cause for controversy since the first slave ship made its way to Virginia's shores in 1619. As Edmund Morgan argued in his book *American Slavery, American Freedom*, without the institution of slavery there would not be American freedom.

This great paradox has plagued American institutions for centuries.[2] Abraham Lincoln's 1863 Emancipation Proclamation laid the groundwork for the 13th Amendment, which abolished slavery in the United States. Despite that milestone, America has struggled with race. Jim Crow laws and segregation were entrenched in the South well into the twentieth century. The Second World War paved the way for a new movement in America. Fresh off battling Nazism in Europe and militarism in Japan, many African Americans believed they had a natural right to equality and were willing to fight for it. In 1944 Swedish economist Gunnar Myrdal's work entitled *An American Dilemma: The Negro Problem and Modern Democracy* exposed the racial divide in the United States from an outsider's perspective, illuminating the problem at various levels of government.[3] Compounding that drive for change, the 1954 *Brown v. Board of Education* Supreme Court decision afforded the legal grounds to challenge segregation. A movement sprang from these events, which culminated in the early 1960s. One of the key people at the center of these events was Robert F. Kennedy.

Robert Kennedy was a reluctant civil rights advocate in 1960. Fearing reprisal from Southern politicians, Robert Kennedy and John F. Kennedy were very careful about how they approached the issue of race in America during the 1960 campaign and at the start of the administration. Martin Luther King, Jr., was not impressed with Senator Kennedy's record on civil rights. Civil rights was not at the forefront of the New Frontier. In fact, Robert Kennedy said on one occasion that he "didn't lie awake nights worrying about it."[4] In addition, it was not even mentioned in the very famous inaugural address; yet when James Meredith risked his life to be the first African American at Ole Miss, he credited JFK's address for the inspiration to do it.[5] Indeed, the Freedom Riders saw the Kennedys as people who would sympathize with their plight. While many historians see the Kennedys as noncommittal in this realm, it seems that they were an inspiration for many to risk their lives and push the movement to a new level.

Robert Kennedy said in 1964 that civil rights was not something that captivated the nation until the Birmingham riots in 1963. Many politicians sent up legislation that was ignored by Congress. "Well, my brother and I thought that that really didn't make any sense, and what mattered was *doing* something."[6] In time, and after an education by fire, the Kennedy brothers were civil rights warriors as passionate as they were cold warriors. They were men of their time, especially President Kennedy, but willing to consider new ideas that would bring America to new heights. Robert Kennedy was the moralist, while John Kennedy was the consummate politician. While it took time to accept their role in this movement, in the end they would contribute a great deal, paving a way for future politicians to continue that mission. At the heart of this direction was Robert Kennedy's determination to uphold justice and do what was right under the Constitution. The idea of sacrifice, embodied in the inaugural address — to make a better and stronger America — may have been all that James Meredith needed to confront segregation. From the experiences of the Freedom Riders to James Meredith to the travails in Birmingham culminating in the March on Washington, Robert Kennedy found his cause in the civil rights movement.

The prologue of this book introduces the reader to the main actors behind change in the sixties. Indeed, these people set in motion forces that, like a chain reaction, sustained themselves for years to come, ushering in great change to American society. This part of the book offers three perspectives on the fight for equal rights. This study aims to see civil rights history from several points of view in hopes of gaining greater insight into the events that had such far reaching affects. The Kennedy brothers, Martin Luther King, Jr., and students like John Lewis were all shaped by their experiences in the fifties. These events molded a different, unique leadership quality in each person that would play a role in the civil rights discourse of the sixties. The combination of these varied leadership styles came together and ushered civil rights issues to the forefront of politics. It also brought greater awareness of the racial divide in the United States. Each of these leaders dealt with different stimuli that shaped their determination and ambition to overcome great obstacles and invoke change.

Dr. King's entrance into the civil rights movement was a momentous, national event, serving as a springboard for other, similar forms of protest. Indeed, his philosophy of non violent protest inspired many young people and challenged the entrenched older leadership. John and Robert Kennedy were working in Congress to distinguish themselves to the world. The "Brothers Kennedy" drew special acclaim when they challenged the labor unions and organized crime before the nation on the floor of the Senate. Finally, John Lewis was an example of a younger, idealistic and morally toughened generation that wanted to embrace Dr. King's notion of non-violent resistance and bring the movement to new levels. Both used that tactic in the hopes that the federal government would get involved, creating a tense situation requiring federal assistance. These individuals lived in extraordinary times shaped by revolutionary notions about challenging the status quo. The rights revolution of the sixties began in the fifties with this new generation of leaders finding their own styles. They eventually discovered their voices in 1960 at the start of a phenomenal decade with major implications for the social structure of the United States.

Part I of this book examines the election of 1960 and how its result shaped a new voice in civil rights that would endure for much of the sixties. The 1960 campaign showcased both the issues and the main people who would play a role in shaping this voice at the start of the decade. The Kennedy brothers were very reluctant to overtly express a position against segregation, though it was clear they did not support it. The political climate of the South made it very difficult for any presidential candidate to embrace civil rights. That said, Senator Kennedy did support the sit-in movement and made a campaign speech at Howard University outlining his views on segregation in the South. In addition, when Dr. King was jailed for participating in the sit-in movement, both Kennedys played a role in his release when the judge attempted to keep him in prison longer than necessary. John Kennedy's phone call to Coretta Scott King had major political reverberations, demonstrating compassion and sincerity. In addition, Robert Kennedy's call to the judge, questioning the decision to deny bail, also had an immediate effect, allegedly contributing to King's subsequent release. While these gestures may seem too little in retrospect, they challenged the status quo in 1960. No other candidate went to those extremes. That said, these actions seemed like mere tokens to some African Americans and even to Dr. King, despite Kennedy's gestures during his incarceration. The Kennedy brothers demonstrated to the black community that they cared enough to risk political alienation from their support in the South to do what was right. The election brought the brothers to the White House with all the hopes and aspirations that came from the campaign.

In 1961 the Kennedys demonstrated how they would confront issues in the new justice department. In addition, the young generation of civil rights leaders wanted to move Kennedy to action. Part II of this book focuses on the actions both of the Kennedys and of civil rights leaders. While the Kennedys did make some headway in civil rights on their own, the real difference started with the Freedom Rides, originally started by Congress of Racial Equality (CORE) and then taken over by Student Nonviolent Coordinating Committee (SNCC). The Freedom Riders demonstrated the passion, zeal and determination of that young, new generation of Americans to vanquish Jim Crow. Robert Kennedy, with the support of his brother, took greater strides than any other attorney general thus far in United States history to dismantle Jim Crow. RFK believed that the law, above all, would confront and defeat injustice. It was this concept that he leaned on to evoke such change.

While the Kennedys focused on strengthening voting rights and desegregating schools for the rest of 1961, the next greatest civil rights challenge came from the University of Mississippi in 1962. James Meredith and the NAACP attempted to integrate the Mississippi school system at the highest, most cherished level in the state. The challenge to "Ole Miss" had both symbolic and legal importance for the movement. Part III explores the civil rights movement by examining the Kennedy White House in the midst of a national crisis. How did the Kennedy brothers react to Meredith's actions? JFK had just installed a tape recording system in the Oval Office and the cabinet room. The tapes caught the various strategy sessions held in the White House to address these issues, as well as some of the phone conversations with Ross Barnett and others in the Mississippi government. These tapes illuminate how the Kennedys navigated through this tense period with sound leadership in the face of the unknown. Though the Kennedys sent marshals to Montgomery during the Freedom Rides, their use of the military in Mississippi is highly controversial and remains one of the few times in American history when the president had to use such powers. This overt act was another step to Kennedy's gradual acceptance that the executive needed to take a lead role in integration. It was clear that the Kennedy brothers were committed to upholding the law and willing to do whatever necessary to maintain order.

The Freedom Rides and the Ole Miss episodes shed light on the race issues in America not only for the privileged Kennedy brothers, but also for the rest of the nation. Part IV of this study explores the issues surrounding the climactic confrontation in Alabama in 1963. Particular attention is paid to the issues in Birmingham, wherein Dr. King and others attempted to desegregate one of the worst cities in America. The events that transpired in Birmingham brought Kennedy further along in his views on integration. Martin Luther King, Jr.'s leadership in that crisis ultimately challenged Bull Connor, bringing race issues to the American people and forcing Kennedy to see this no longer as a political issue, but as a moral issue, "as old as the scriptures." In addition to the issues in Birmingham, Kennedy confronted George Wallace over the integration of the University of Alabama and introduced a civil rights bill to Congress. These events and Kennedy's leadership led to the great March on Washington for Jobs and Freedom on August 22, 1963.

For the race issue in America, 1963 was a watershed year. Only months after the March on Washington, Kennedy was gunned down by Lee Harvey Oswald in Dealey Plaza, leaving the legacy of civil rights to his successor, Lyndon Johnson. Robert Kennedy no longer had the same authority as he did under his brother and slowly moved away from pushing civil rights as attorney general. Instead, he ran for the senate and picked up a seat in New York in 1964. However, it was another young senator from Massachusetts who chose to make his maiden speech in the Senate an endorsement of John Kennedy's civil rights initiative. Edward M. Kennedy, youngest brother of the slain president, made his cause one with his brother's, ushering in a new era in politics for the Kennedys.

John and Robert Kennedy could not overtly challenge segregation. Like Abraham Lincoln in the civil war, they needed to tread lightly with regard to the status quo in the South. Lincoln needed the border states to maintain the integrity of the union; John Kennedy needed the Southern states for the legislation he hoped to pass in Congress and to get re-elected in 1964. When Abraham Lincoln issued the Emancipation Proclamation, he did it at a time he felt was appropriate. He did not force it on the country, as he knew the country would reject it. Despite the strong abolitionist movement, Lincoln was realistic in his approach. Unlike Lincoln, Robert Kennedy's hand was forced by civil rights advocates who wanted rights immediately. As attorney general and the brother of the president, RFK had a great deal of latitude to confront civil rights as he believed necessary. As I've argued in my previous book, *Kennedy's Kitchen Cabinet and the Pursuit of Peace*, JFK wanted to be his own secretary of state, and was very concerned with foreign affairs — especially the issues that involved the Soviet Union.[7] Civil rights issues were linked to America's prestige abroad, something JFK was acutely aware of. While President Kennedy utilized his brother in his pursuit of strong foreign policy, he also relied on him to handle civil rights in America. There is no historical precedent for two brothers having so much control of the political discourse in America. The Kennedy brothers had a direct impact on the civil rights movement and changed the nation's direction on the racial issues. Their leadership inspired people to challenge the status quo, setting up a new climate for future politicians and Americans.

The Kennedys were part of a larger story. John, Robert and Edward have a place in the history books. This is largely the story of brotherhood and how that relationship translated into the national discourse over civil rights. Indeed, Edward Kennedy made it his cause, while Bobby's run for higher political office was tragically short lived, ended by Sirhan Sirhan in 1968. In addition to the Kennedy brothers, this story includes members of the old school elite looking to change the country while ushering in a new age of leadership, while the SNCC and others struggled to find a role for themselves and their children. This movement was at a critical mass and leadership was important to help define the outcome not only of that decade, but for decades to come. Much like the pervasive Cold War, civil rights galvanized the United States. The movement shaped a new world that would elect Barack Obama, an African American, as president of the United States in 2008.

Prologue: 1950s —
"A New Generation of Americans"

The Reverend King

"Well, if you think I can render some service, I will."

On May 17, 1954, the Supreme Court made a ruling in the case of *Brown v. Board of Education* that would change America forever. The decision desegregated the education system in America. It told Southern schools that white boys and girls had to attend school with African American boys and girls. It was a revolutionary act, one that still reverberates in the twenty-first century. Most importantly, the Supreme Court repudiated the previous doctrine handed down from *Plessy v. Ferguson*, which stated the "separate but equal" doctrine in American law. That 1896 decision legalized most, if not all, forms of segregation in the South. The *Brown* decision not only ensured equal education under the law, it also emboldened African Americans to challenge segregation. This, combined with the great victory of World War II, which African Americans played a part in, started a new movement in America. In 1954, no one would have ever dreamt that this movement would come to fruition under the leadership of a young minister who preached from Montgomery, Alabama.

The Rev. Dr. Martin Luther King, Jr.'s entrance to the civil rights movement came when he was twenty-six years old. He had just finished his dissertation, earning a Ph.D. from Boston University. Dr. King was exposed to racism at a very young age, and it left an indelible mark. He had a childhood companion who was white; when they started attending separate schools, the child's father did not want his son playing with King anymore. "This was not my desire but his," King said later. "I will never forget what a great shock this was to me." King asked his parents about why such things happened, and they discussed it around the dinner table that night. King remembered that it was then "I was made aware of the existence of a race problem. I had never been conscious of it before."[1] King had an important revelation at a young age. This, however, was not unique to King. Life in the segregated system shaped the childhood of many from his generation. This experience for many African Americans influenced how they saw the world and focused their lives on challenging this system of hate and prejudice, and sowing great change. King eventually attended Morehouse College, skipping ninth and tenth grades. Though King struggled with his grades, earning a 2.48 GPA at Morehouse, he was accepted at Crozer Theological to further his education in divinity.[2]

At Crozer, King started to develop his philosophical views and took his studies more seriously than he did at Morehouse. Indeed, the young King was already pondering different ways to look at life. David Garrow writes that King was exposed to Reinhold Niebuhr, who said, "Disproportion of power in society is the real root of social injustice." King said years later that Niebuhr's realism demonstrated "the complexity of human motives and the reality of sin on every level of man's existence."[3] He would change his views on this over the years. Garrow points out that this was an early period in King's thinking. He did not always believe that love and non violent protest was the path to great change. At Boston University, King worked on his Ph.D. in divinity and challenged some of his own assertions from Crozer, which eventually led to his own philosophy on how to evoke change. He started to believe that the "balanced Christian" had to embrace both love and realism. He made distinctions between one-on-one relationships and larger social groups.[4] It was at Boston University that he met Coretta Scott. The two eventually married before he was done at Boston University. Soon after his marriage, there was a position at Dexter Baptist Church in Montgomery, Alabama.

King's development was important because it revealed his ability to embrace realistic goals while at the same time continuing idealistic, philosophical notions about life. Instead of using Niebuhr's argument as his main thesis for the movement, the genius of King is that he challenged that thinking, which led to a novel approach in the fight against segregation. In addition, his experience at Boston University further emphasized the need for realism in life, something that kept him grounded, looking within himself for each challenge that the movement presented over the years. The mere fact that he met and fell in love with Coretta Scott during this period in his life had its own effect on King's ability to find strength within himself. Scott was the rock that King needed to recognize his potential and create a realistic foundation. All of these events culminated in an interview at Dexter Baptist Church.

King went to interview for the Dexter Baptist position in 1954. He preached his favorite sermon, "The Three Dimensions of a Complete Life."[5] In this sermon King said, "Life at its best and life as it should be is the life that is complete on all sides." He said that life should consist of three things: length, breadth and height. The length of life has to do with achieving personal goals and ambitions. Breadth of life is the "outward concern for the welfare [of] others." Finally, the height of life is the upward reach toward God. In King's notes from the sermon, he quotes John Donne: "No man is an island," which was something he did in other speeches during the movement to reinforce how we are connected and need to remain concerned with one another. This sermon demonstrated that King was already trying to help others through his words and connecting that work through God, which would be one of the principle goals of the not yet formed Southern Christian Leadership Coalition (SCLC). It also shows how he categorized ideas, making it easier for people to understand his thesis. Ultimately, the sermon speaks to balance in life. King wrote, "The tragedy of much of modern life is that in quest of our [personal?] and social goals we have unconsciously forgotten God. We have pursued the length and breadth of life and neglected the height. And so we find ourselves living a disorganized, incomplete and disconnected life."[6] In short, King looked to God first in the hopes of achieving balance in life. That was how he lived his life, and he tried to promote change.

King's sermon reveals the moral basis of his philosophy. The teachings of Jesus Christ played a big role in how King confronted major crises in his life. Prayer and non violence are at the core of Christ's teachings, and they played an integral role in King's own work. The spiritual search for the balance that King preached was an aspect of the movement. Indeed it drove him and others to sacrifice for what they believed was God's will. This sermon also spoke to the realism within his philosophy and served as a precursor to his acceptance of non violence as a valid tool to combat racism. The teachings of Gandhi and Henry David Thoreau helped King develop a realistic method to confront segregated governments that had extreme power over the people. King used those ideas and combined them with Christianity, forming a new, revolutionary form of protest. King got the position at Dexter Baptist and brought himself and Coretta to Montgomery, Alabama, where they would start their family.

On December 1, 1955, Rosa Parks refused to move from her seat for a white person. This act started a series of events that ultimately led to a desegregation of the public transportation system in Montgomery. History has proven time and time again that the smallest gestures can have the largest reverberations. Her action not only challenged segregation, but also catapulted Martin Luther King, Jr., into the national spotlight. The new pastor became inexorably involved in what started as a small, grassroots movement. When the African American community in Montgomery was looking for leadership for a boycott of the buses, King did not think he was going to be chosen. In fact, he was apprehensive at taking the presidency of the local NAACP. Despite that hesitation, they held the first meeting that would lead to the formation of the Montgomery Improvement Association (MIA) in his church. So disorganized was this first meeting that people tried to leave. King stopped one person, saying, "I'd like to go too, but it's my church."[7] The leadership, as it was, decided on a boycott of the buses for a day to see how it went. It was successful, and they looked for someone who could offer greater leadership than the small group of people who met at Dexter Baptist.

Rufus Lewis, one of the leaders of this boycott, said that Martin Luther King, Jr., looked "more like a boy than a man." That said, King was educated and articulate, and would appeal to many.[8] The MIA met at Mt. Zion AME church to outline their goals for the organization. A smaller group met in the pastor's study. P.E. Conley nominated King as the president of the MIA. His nomination was seconded immediately. Ralph Abernathy, fellow minister, and soon to be King's lieutenant in the movement, thought his friend was going to decline. Much to his surprise, after a moment of silence, in the wake of the nomination, King said, "Well if you think I can render some service, I will."[9] In that small room, King started his journey to national prominence as the foremost leader of the civil rights movement until his untimely death in 1968. David Garrow writes, "When the MIA's presidency unexpectedly was thrust upon him on December 5, King was uncertain of his ability to lead a community he had lived in so briefly, but he was able to draw upon the same strong conviction that had inspired his leadership at Dexter."[10] When introduced to the community as the president of the MIA, King electrified the crowd, instilling hope and inspiration into the boycott's cause.

"He who lives by the sword will perish by the sword"

The boycott would prove to be a monumental success. King was challenged physically, emotionally and spiritually by those who tried to stymie his efforts through intimidation. His house was bombed and he was harassed on the phone almost daily. He was arrested and put in prison for the first time during the movement. When asked about the overarching impact of the boycott, King responded, "It is part of a world-wide movement. Look at just about any place in the world and the exploited people are rising up against their exploiters. This seems to be the outstanding characteristic of our generation."[11] Indeed, this generation would pave the way for subsequent generations who would invoke their rights under the

Constitution, leading into the twenty-first century. The Montgomery Bus Boycott not only brought King to national recognition; it also revealed the ugliness behind the racial problem in America. This was the first major challenge to the system of segregation since *Brown v. Board of Education*. The success of the boycott was a testament to the path that the *Brown* decision blazed for subsequent generations. King's leadership was important because this new aspect of the movement hinged on his success. The only way for the future of the movement to embrace this new form of protest would be on the coattails of King's success in Montgomery.

The greatest affirmation of King's importance to the movement came very early in the protest. King valued his family, and they served as a major foundation for why he risked his life for the cause. Any real threat to them should have pushed him away from the leadership role he was asked to take. His devotion to the cause and to make the world better for his children and future generations made him a true leader. As the boycott moved into new stages, the MIA looked for drivers to help with the effort and keep up the demonstration. King was one of those drivers. As a result of his efforts, on January 26, 1956, he was arrested for going thirty miles per hour in a twenty-five mile per hour zone. He was sent to jail for the first time in his life. David Garrow writes, "The emotional trauma of the arrest heightened the growing personal tensions King was feeling. He had not wanted to be the focal point of the protest in the first place."[12] As King was led to his cell, the jailer opened the door, saying, "All right, get on in there with all the others."[13] Ralph Abernathy came to bail him out, but met resistance from the jailer. It took a large group of African Americans outside the building for the jailer, with fear of reprisals from the crowd, to release King on his own signature.[14] King's arrest made it clear that no person affiliated with the movement was untouchable — not even a young preacher. Indeed it also demonstrated to the people of the community King's importance to the movement, which made him even more of a target. King came from a prominent family in Atlanta, and being jailed was traumatic. Instead of running from this burden of leadership, he labored on.

In the wake of King's arrest he was spiritually challenged by the events and the stress that the boycott was putting on himself and his family. "I felt myself faltering and growing in fear," King said.[15] He was constantly being harassed over the phone, but one night a phone call went too far — shaking King to his core. He worked hard the day after his jailing with the MIA to get things moving again. The mere fact that he jumped back into his work so quickly is evidence of his determination, strength and resolve to lead. He got home late that night and could not sleep, so he went downstairs to make a cup of coffee in the hopes that it would settle his nerves. Around midnight he received a phone call from what he called an "ugly voice." The caller said, "Nigger we are tired of you and your mess now. And if you aren't out of this town in three days, we're going to blow your brains out and blow up your house."[16] The threat to his family was a watershed moment for King spiritually. King thought of his little girl, who was only two months old, sleeping in her crib. He thought of his wife and how they were both in danger because of his efforts.

King looked to the cup of coffee he had made to calm his nerves. He brought his hands together and prayed. "Lord. I'm down here trying to do what's right. I think I'm right. I think the cause that we represent is right. But Lord," he went on, "I must confess that I'm weak now. I'm faltering. I'm losing my courage." King recalled having a spiritual awakening. "And it seemed at that moment that I could hear an inner voice saying to me 'Martin Luther, stand up for righteousness. Stand up for justice. Stand up for truth. And lo I will be with you, even until the end of the world.'" He finished, saying, "I heard the voice of Jesus saying 'still fight on.'"[17] Indeed, this spiritual experience gave King a new strength and drive to continue his work. It was a revelation that moved him to shut out the fear. Taylor Branch writes, "It was for King the first transcendent religious experience of his life.... For King, the moment awakened and confirmed his belief that the essence of religion was not a grand metaphysical idea but something personal, grounded in experience."[18] In a matter of days, King had two experiences that established how he would cope with similar situations throughout his career. He would be arrested again. He would be threatened again. In fact, in 1958 he was stabbed in New York City during a book signing, just grazing an artery. The phone call in 1956 coupled with his previous arrest were influential moments for this young civil rights leader. King was going to need this new spiritual strength in the days that followed. The true test of his beliefs threatened not him, but his family.

Four days after King's arrest he attended the Monday night mass meeting for the MIA. He was at that meeting when his wife Coretta and a friend heard a strange noise sounding like footsteps outside King's house. They made their way to a back bedroom, near the nursery where two-month-old Yoki was sleeping. A bomb exploded suddenly and ferociously, spreading glass and smoke everywhere, destroying the front porch.[19] King was still at the mass meeting and noticed some commotion. Ralph Abernathy went to him saying, "Your house has been bombed." King immediately asked, "Are Coretta and the baby all right?" They did not know.[20] The threat to his family was the final piece that drove him to embrace his role as leader and his philosophy of non violence. This moment, more than any other, prepared him for the trials that lay ahead. The threat to the most important aspect of his life empowered King to willingly risk his own life on their behalf. A crowd had formed around King's house in response to the incident. They wanted payback for such a violent act against King and his family. When King arrived the police and fire chief were there inspecting the debris by the front porch. The crowd grew contentious and after he was sure that Coretta and Yoki were ok, he went out to address them.

> Don't get panicky. Don't do anything panicky. Don't get your weapons. If you have weapons, take them home. He who lives by the sword will perish by the sword. Remember that is what Jesus said. We are not advocating violence. We want to love our enemies. Be good to them. This is what we must live by. We must meet hate with love.[21]

King's speech, in the wake of such a personal, traumatic experience, is evidence that he was committed to his cause, believing he was justified. This was the greatest example of King's commitment to non violence. In the wake of a mortal threat to his family, King responded with love, not hate. He made it clear to anyone there that they were supposed to love their enemy and not seek retribution. King said later, "My religious experience a few nights before had given me the strength to face it."[22] King's response is one of the greatest moments in the movement. The man proved to everyone that he truly believed in his cause and his method of non violence. It also set the tone for the rest of the boycott.

King's arrest, his spiritual awakening at midnight, and the bombing of his home remained formative experiences in his role as a leader of the civil rights movement. He found strength through his faith in the wake of tragedy. That would prepare him for any obstacle he would face. The Montgomery Bus Boycott brought civil rights issues to the national stage and King came with that exposure. The boycott would last for 381 days and involve controversial civil rights leader Bayard Rustin, a person committed to non violent action, as well as mass indictments of all its leaders. In the end, public transportation would be desegregated with a federal ruling on the matter by the Supreme Court. King was ready to lead the movement beyond Montgomery and into the national spotlight. However, lacking federal help, the movement was stymied in the fifties. It needed leadership outside of the movement and support from the mainstream to bring broader, far sweeping change to America. It especially needed help from law makers in Washington, D.C.

Brothers Kennedy

"He's the only one who doesn't stick knives in my back."

While King was coming of age in Montgomery, Robert F. Kennedy entered the national stage with his older brother, Senator John F. Kennedy. The Kennedys did not have to endure the ridicule and threat of violence that King did in Montgomery. They were part of another world in America. Their privileged background gave them opportunities that many, black or white, did not have. The Kennedys came from a legendary family that grabbed the interest of the nation in the forties. Jack and Bobby would do more to catapult them into the history books. John Kennedy rose through the House of Representatives to the Senate. He was a World War II hero, taking the place of his fallen brother Joseph Kennedy, Jr., as the political heir apparent. Robert Kennedy would eventually rise to the office of attorney general and deal with civil rights issues for much of his time in that office, laying the groundwork for future politicians. However, before Robert Kennedy could make a difference at that level, he needed to develop his own philosophy.

The "Brothers Kennedy" discovered their potential as a team around the same time as King. Where King was finding his philosophical method on combating segregation through non violence, the Kennedys were learning to work politics in the Senate, eventually leading to the White House. They were a formidable team. During this time the Kennedy brothers strengthened their bond. If there was going to be great change in America, it was just as imperative that these brothers learn how to work politics as it was for King to discover Gandhi's methods of protest. The civil rights movement needed leaders at all levels in order to succeed. John and Robert Kennedy were just as important as the leadership that King and others contributed to the movement.

The brothers also had to find their own moral and spiritual foundation. Robert Kennedy was extremely driven by a righteous spirit, more than any other Kennedy. Bobby chose each cause carefully and embraced it with vigor to do what was just under the law. Indeed his vigilant pursuit in each of his undertakings contributed to his growth, resulting in novel, unique leadership qualities that even his famous brother did not possess. In many ways he was exactly like King. His righteous spirit and willingness to sacrifice are all in line with King's most endearing leadership qualities. For example, when he was at Harvard, Robert Kennedy challenged the Catholic priest Father Leonard Feeny. RFK believed him a bigot and anti–Semite. Despite misgivings from his father, he wrote the cardinal saying that the priest should be removed.[23] This little episode in Robert Kennedy's undergraduate experience is evidence that he had a moral compass and was willing to question authority on the righteousness of different issues. In addition, going against his famous father was something that served him well later in life.

Robert Kennedy graduated from Harvard in 1948 and decided on the University of Virginia Law School for his next stop on his way to making a difference in the world. Bobby Kennedy's venture to study law was a natural progression for him on two levels. One, it served the familial purpose of continuing to do something that mattered. There was a great deal of pressure on all of the Kennedys to contribute to the world at large. Second, on a more personal note, Bobby continued to explore that moral righteousness that was so much a part of him through the law. This experience gave him a sound foundation for making moral and just decisions as attorney general. It especially made a difference when addressing the racial issues in the United States. When Robert Kennedy was in law school at the University of Virginia, he invited Ralph Bunche, a U.N. peace negotiator who won the Nobel Peace Prize, to speak. Bunche, an African American, refused to speak to a segregated audience. When leaders questioned whether Bunche should speak, Kennedy spoke his mind.[24] The student council voted to ban Ralph Bunche from speaking. RFK called the decision "morally indefensible," saying they were all "gutless" at the meeting.[25] Indeed, his social conscience may have started to develop, looking for ways to help others and striving for social justice and equality. These were small, yet telling examples of where Bobby Kennedy was headed.

After Robert Kennedy graduated from law school he went on a trip with his brother John abroad. Congressman Kennedy thought that his younger brother would be a "pain in the ass."[26] In the end the elder Kennedy was glad that Bobby came along. On their way to Korea John Kennedy became very ill, due to Addison's disease, a condition where the adrenal glands produce insufficient steroid hormones. With his temperature reaching 106 degrees, "Everybody just expected him to die," Robert Kennedy recalled.[27] The brothers found a new respect and understanding for each other as result of this episode. It was an important moment in Bobby Kennedy's life, as much of his own legacy is tied to his brothers. It seems that through pure happenstance the brothers' experience on this trip fostered a stronger, lasting relationship in which John Kennedy trusted Robert Kennedy even more. That trust eventually played a role when the brothers reached the White House. It also illuminated Bobby's role as a protector for his older brother, one which would move with them to the Senate and the White House. In fact, not long after the trip, the younger Kennedy was called to the political arena.

Robert Kennedy took a job with the Justice Department after graduating from law school. He worked in the New York office investigating income-tax evasion.[28] The job was short-lived as Kenny O'Donnell, one of Bobby's close friends and his roommate from Harvard, called and asked him to join John Kennedy's senate campaign as manager. At first Robert resisted, saying, "I'll just screw it up." He called back within a week and said, "Okay I guess I have to do it."[29] His response of "having" to do it pointed to how the family consistently put pressure on each other to commit themselves to one another's cause, making it a family affair. This constant obligation to do the right thing for the family was always a part of Bobby's life. In fact, it would be a similar pressure that brought him into the attorney general position. Historian James Hilty writes, "Robert acted as a buffer between his brother and father." Joseph P. Kennedy, former British ambassador and father of John and Robert, had a lot to say about how the brothers should be running the campaign. Bobby would take phone calls from him, saying, "Yes, Dad. Yes, Dad."[30] Robert Kennedy took over as campaign manager, bringing the two brothers even closer. Robert took an interest in John's well being, constantly protecting him from different issues. James Hilty writes that Bobby "ferociously defended his brother's interests, sometimes losing himself in his zeal."[31] Indeed, the younger Kennedy became known for his blunt way of dealing with issues head on, giving him the reputation as the "ruthless one."

On one occasion Robert Kennedy was introduced as "the candidate's brother." He shrugged, saying, "I don't care if anyone around here likes me as long as they like Jack."[32] RFK remembered, "People didn't like me. But it never bothered me." His brother defended the younger sibling's efforts, saying, "Oh bullshit, everybody bitches about Bobby, and I'm getting sick and Goddamn tired of it. He's the only one who doesn't stick knives in my back, the only one I can count on when it comes down to it."[33] Indeed, they started to foster a stronger relationship. John Kennedy trusted his younger brother and looked to him for advice in his gravest hours. While they were not as close in childhood, their bond formed differently as adults, rooted in respect for each other, becoming a unified force within politics. John Kennedy went on to win the Senate seat. Many people, including his father, credited Robert Kennedy's steadfast determination as campaign manager as a key factor in this victory.[34] Bobby's growing social conscience during his education at Harvard and the University of Virginia Law School, and his new relationship with his older brother, pointed to a new avenue in his life that developed further through his role in the Senate, until the 1960 campaign.

"...No real research was ever done."

Moving into the next phase of his career, Bobby worked for Senator Joe McCarthy. After his brother's win in the 1952 election, Kennedy wanted to be lead counsel for McCarthy, going after what was perceived to be a growing threat to America: communism. The move to work on this team was more evidence that Robert Kennedy always tried to do what was, in his mind, the righteous pursuit for justice. In this sense, there were some similarities with Martin Luther King, Jr., in that they were both very passionate about the morality of their actions. However, instead of Robert Kennedy, Joe McCarthy chose Roy Cohn, the young attorney famous for prosecuting the Rosenbergs, for the role of chief counsel.[35] Kennedy joined McCarthy's team at a difficult time. In many ways, the younger Kennedy differed with McCarthy's methods of gathering information and investigating these alleged communists. In fact RFK "disagreed with the way that the committee was being run." He went on to say, "The way they were preceding I thought it was headed for disaster."[36] Kennedy recalled, "With two exceptions no real research was ever done. Most of the investigations were instituted on the basis of some preconceived notion by [Cohn] or his staff members and not on the basis of any information that had been developed." Kennedy said, "I thought Senator McCarthy made a mistake in allowing the committee to operate in such a fashion, told him so and resigned."[37]

Kennedy's resignation from the McCarthy committee saved the family from political embarrassment when the infamous senator fell from the grace of the American people. Indeed, Bobby struggled in the period that followed his decision to leave McCarthy. While he disagreed with how they proceeded, he did believe that the war against communism was just and that it should be in the forefront for all Americans. Hilty writes, "The period from July 1953 to January 1954 marked a professional and personal nadir, a time of anger, confusion, depression, and disorientation, for Robert Kennedy."[38] In that time, the young Kennedy found himself adrift, without purpose. For someone so dedicated to proving himself to his family and resolved to seek out his place in the world, Robert Kennedy must have been bothered with this turn of events. He was determined to do something that mattered. It was the Kennedy family mantra. In his memoir, *True Compass*, Edward Kennedy recalled something his father said to him: "You can have a serious life or a non-serious life, Teddy. I'll still love you whichever choice you make. But if you decide to have a non-serious life, I won't have much time for you. You make up your mind. There are too many children here who are doing things that are interesting for me to do much with you."[39] Indeed all the Kennedys looked to do something "interesting." This also speaks to why the three Kennedy brothers held such a unique place in American history. They already had money and power. The fact that so many of them devoted their time and energy to public service was a testament to their willingness to sacrifice. Indeed, some of the Kennedys would pay with the ultimate sacrifice. Bobby would not have to wait long to find the next assignment that would help define his national reputation.

Robert Kennedy's disdain toward Roy Cohn reared its head during the Army-McCarthy hearings in 1954. McCarthy alleged that the United States Army had been covering up dealings with communists among its ranks. These hearings, in the wake of the armistice with Korea, demonstrated for the nation how unethical and wrong McCarthy's tactics were, exposing him and his dastardly methods. Robert Kennedy was now working for the subcommittee investigating McCarthy. The fact that he switched to the other side was evidence that RFK did not agree with the methods of his previous boss and wanted to be on the right side of history. Some historians, however, see it as his way at going after Cohn, who took the job that Kennedy wanted in the first place. In fact, Roy Cohn recalled that Kennedy "came back not to fight McCarthy, but to fight me."[40] It all came to a head on June 11, 1954, when Roy Cohn noticed that Robert Kennedy was snickering with other Democratic senators poised to attack him. At the recess, Cohn came up to Bobby. The *New York Times* reported that when Cohn threatened Democratic senator Henry Jackson after a line of questioning, Kennedy jumped at him, saying, "Don't you make any warnings to us about Democratic Senators." Cohn responded by saying, "I'll make any warnings to you that I want to — any-time, anywhere." Cohn then asked, "Do you want to fight right here?" The article said that Cohn did not want Kennedy involved in the hearings due to his "hatred for one of the principals." Kennedy replied that if there was a "dislike" for anyone involved in the hearings he was "certain that it was justified."[41]

Despite his issues with Cohn and the subcommittee's methods, Kennedy stood by McCarthy until his death in 1957. His brother, John, controversially did not vote on the senator's censure in December later that year. This episode is evidence not only of the loyalty that Robert Kennedy had for people who believed in him, but also the fierce commitment he had to a cause when he became involved. That loyalty served as a big part of how John and Robert Kennedy bonded in that first year of the administration. That same loyalty, however, would also get Robert in trouble from time to time. Nevertheless, it was that quality that emboldened him to make civil rights a cause for himself and the administration.

Before his next venture, Robert Kennedy and the entire Kennedy clan were committed to getting Jack the nomination as vice president on the 1956 democratic ticket when Adlai Stevenson put it up to the convention. Robert Kennedy played a similar role as he did in the 1952 Senate campaign as the person who dealt with their father. Joseph P. Kennedy did not want John Kennedy involved in being vice president, but JFK said to his brother from the convention: "Tell him I'm going for it." Robert Kennedy hung up the phone, saying, "Whew, is he mad."[42] Though they tried, the brothers would come up short, and Senator Estes Kefauver would serve on the ballot instead of JFK. Hilty argues that John Kennedy's concession speech launched his campaign of 1960. In fact, Robert Kennedy stated as they left the convention, "You're going to be candidate the next time."[43] The bond between the brothers was growing. Soon, they would be in front of cameras not as individuals, but as the Kennedy brothers.

"I thought only little girls giggled, Mr. Giancana."

The next episode in Robert Kennedy's development prior to the election of 1960 was announced on Christmas Day, 1956. While Martin Luther King, Jr., and the MIA were celebrating their victory over segregation, Robert Kennedy told his family that he was going after organized crime's influence on labor unions. His father was furious. No one could change his mind. Hilty writes, "Not only was Robert determined at last to do something of consequence on his own, he believed that the proposed investigation would bring enormous political returns, more than worth alienating unsavory elements in the union movement."[44] While RFK wanted to distinguish himself within his family, he realized that he would need his older brother on the venture. Indeed, the author of the recently published *Profiles in Courage*, as well as a young, rising senator, would lend a great deal of credibility to Bobby's efforts.

On a larger level it was also a great opportunity for the older Kennedy to get press while fighting crime. The press would play well in the 1960 election. John and Robert Kennedy were determined to make a name for themselves and challenge the status quo. In addition to the political gain, Robert Kennedy's competent investigation of the labor unions demonstrated to his older brother that he could handle difficult problems. It was also his way to show Cohn and others from McCarthy's camp how to handle such matters. Indeed, these hearings left an impression on the future president and may have played a role in giving Bobby such a great deal of independence as attorney general.

Beginning in 1957 Robert Kennedy joined Senator McClellan's committee as chief counsel. The committee investigated organized crime's role in labor unions. It was dubbed the "Rackets Committee" by the press. Bobby took the lead in questioning, with his brother, who also served on the committee, right by his side. James Hilty writes, "Rather than concern himself with protecting the constitutional rights of the accused, Robert Kennedy was absorbed with uncovering wrongdoing and bringing it to light."[45] Robert Kennedy's determined approach became his trademark, and he would use a similar approach in the White House. Indeed, RFK was scrutinized by many on his line of questioning and the fact that the people who came before the committee were considered guilty. Hilty also wrote that while the committee was "Robert's show," many people saw it as a "Kennedy brothers production."[46] Robert Kennedy's tough questioning coupled with John Kennedy's political prowess cultivated a growing perception among Americans that these brothers were the future of the nation. It was a poignant political move on the part of brothers resulting in great rewards.

U.S. News and World Report published an article entitled "The Kennedy Brothers: Off to a Fast Start." The article started by saying, "The tousle-haired brothers from Boston are catching attention in Washington just now as young men who may have big careers ahead." The article discussed how John Kennedy had narrowly missed the vice presidential nod on the 1956 democratic ticket. The article said that JFK "at 39 has plenty of time left to realize his ambitions." It went on to say, "The other brother, Robert F. Kennedy, 31, is a mainspring of the current investigation of racketeering in the labor management field." The nation was introduced to the "Kennedy Brothers" through the Rackets Committee. "The Two Kennedys share an appealing air of boyish earnestness and a capacity for hard, painstaking work." The article ended by saying, "The impression that these two have made upon Washington is such that most expect to hear much of them in the years ahead."[47] While it was clear from the article that the older Kennedy looked to the White House, it was also clear that Robert

Kennedy was still figuring out what he wanted to pursue. This impression is exactly what they wanted to exude to the American people.

Arthur Schlesinger writes that when Robert Kennedy started working for the McClellan Committee, "the labor movement itself was in a time of stagnation. The idealism generated in the great organizing battles of the 1930s was largely spent, except in the United Automobile Workers and a few other unions."[48] The labor movement's malaise in the wake of World War II allowed organized crime to creep into its ranks. Robert Kennedy embraced his role as chief counsel on the Rackets Committee in the same tenacious, determined, passionate way that he did everything else. John Kennedy said, "Bobby wanted me on that committee in order to keep it more balanced. He asked me to come and give him support or the committee would be too conservative and would have seemed anti-labor."[49]

The brothers were making a splash on the Washington scene together. Not only were they featured in the *U.S. News and World Report* article, but they also had an eight page article in *Look* magazine entitled "The Rise of the Brothers Kennedy" and an article in the *Saturday Evening Post* entitled "The Amazing Kennedys."[50] In fact, one person wrote to Joseph and Rose Kennedy to tell them "what a wonderful job you have done in raising your children. I am now watching your son Bob on T.V. [during the Senate hearings] and you both must have a good warm feeling of accomplishment."[51] In that *Saturday Evening Post* article, the author, Harold Martin, wrote that the admirers of the Kennedys "confidently look forward to the day when Jack will be in the White House, Bobby will serve in the cabinet as Attorney General, and Teddy will be the Senator from Massachusetts."[52]

The Rackets Committee had successfully exposed David Beck, the president of the Teamsters, for income tax evasion and grand larceny.[53] In the wake of this conviction, James Riddle Hoffa took on the role as president of the Teamsters' union, becoming RFK's next target. "My biggest problem as counsel is to keep my temper," Robert Kennedy said. "To see people sit in front of us and lie and evade makes me boil inside. But you can't lose your temper — if you do, the witness has gotten the best of you."[54] Bobby's famous temper was something he brought with him to the White House. His impatience contributed to this, making it difficult to slowly question witnesses, leading to overarching points. Instead, Robert Kennedy fired questions at people, and even reacted when someone gave him an answer that made him "boil inside." Jimmy Hoffa was a person who did that to Kennedy. That said, the Rackets Committee prepared Robert Kennedy for the many challenges of being attorney general. Many who challenged integration at the government level were evading their responsibility and oath to uphold the law and contribute to the larger federal system of government. Robert Kennedy needed the experience to learn how to keep his cool in the face of such hypocrisy and defiance.

Kennedy and Hoffa met for the first time at Edward T. Cheyfitz's home. Cheyfitz worked for the Teamsters, but was also friendly with Bobby. On February 19, 1957, Hoffa and Kennedy were dinner guests. Kennedy had found out that Hoffa tried to plant someone on the committee to send information back to him.[55] Cheyfitz was hoping to show Robert Kennedy that Hoffa was unlike Beck and genuinely wanted to help the Teamsters.[56] It did not work. RFK wrote later in his book *The Enemy Within* that when Hoffa and Cheyfitz met him at the door Hoffa gave him "a strong, firm handshake." Kennedy wrote that Hoffa maintained a consistent theme throughout the night of "I do to others what they do to me, only worse." Kennedy remarked at one point, "Maybe I should have worn my bulletproof vest."[57] Hoffa and Kennedy hated each other after the meeting. Hoffa thought that Kennedy's questions over dinner were condescending, remarking when Kennedy went home that he was "a damned spoiled jerk." Ethel Kennedy called at 9:30. Bobby answered, saying, "I'm still alive, dear. If you hear a big explosion, I probably won't be." It was snowing pretty badly and a driver had smashed into a tree near their home at Hickory Hill. The driver was in Kennedy's living room, shaken. Kennedy decided to go home to assist Ethel.[58] As RFK left Hoffa commented, "Tell your wife I'm not as bad as everyone thinks I am." Kennedy laughed. Writing later, Kennedy remarked, "In view of all I already knew, I felt that he was worse than anybody said he was. In the next two and half years, nothing happened to change my opinion."[59] Kennedy was obsessed with bringing down Hoffa not only because of the Teamster president's arrogance but also because of the fact that he threatened justice and the American way of life. Kennedy's righteousness was something that often took over his personality, detaching him from the realities of situations. In addition, Kennedy saw this as a political opportunity to move up the ranks.

That first encounter with Hoffa offered a glimpse into two important facets of Bobby Kennedy. First, he was too self righteous to ever identify with Hoffa, as Cheyfitz had hoped. This part of Kennedy's personality helped propel him into the civil rights movement, throwing off pragmatism and embracing a just and righteous cause, rooted in morality and not politics. The fact that Hoffa was trying to plant a spy in the committee only made it more difficult. Burton Hersh writes, "Almost from the start, Hoffa incarnated the evil Kennedy took it as his mission to vanquish in America."[60] Robert Kennedy honestly believed he was doing the right thing by going after the unions and organized crime. The country meant a great deal to him, and he was willing to sacrifice almost anything to see its ideals preserved. Second, Robert Kennedy had a dark sense of humor that many could not identify with. His remark about the bullet proof vest and telling Ethel that he was "still alive" are examples of this sense of humor, which he used in stressful situations. These types of comments in tension filled moments were often misconstrued. He would have a similar exchange with Dr. King during the Freedom Rides episode when the group was surrounded by an angry mob at the First Baptist Church in Montgomery, Alabama.

In the summer of 1957 Hoffa was brought up on charges of bribery and conspiracy by the FBI in a sting operation orchestrated by Robert Kennedy. Kennedy arrived at the federal courthouse to personally see Hoffa. "He stared at me for three minutes with complete hatred in his eyes," Kennedy remembered. Hoffa challenged Kennedy to see who could do the most push-ups. Finally he looked at RFK, saying, "Listen, Bobby, you run your business and I'll run mine. You go home and go to bed, I'll take care of things. Let's don't have no problems." Kennedy later joked with a reporter that he'd "jump off the capital" if Hoffa was acquitted.[61] It would turn out to be an embarrassing comment. When Hoffa was acquitted of all the charges his lawyer, Edward Bennett Williams, and friend of Kennedy, said, "I'm going to send Bobby Kennedy a parachute."[62] This was a tough turn of events for Kennedy, but he still labored on.

In an effort to continue the fight against corruption, Pierre Salinger made his way to Detroit, serving members of the Teamsters subpoenas. They started their investigation of Hoffa in earnest, going through his records. Hoffa appeared before the committee on August 20, 1957. After a series of questions, Hoffa answered on one occasion: "To the best of my recollection, I must recall on my memory, I cannot remember." Kennedy repeated his answer back, saying, "Is that your answer?" When asked about a telephone call that the committee played for him, Hoffa said that he couldn't remember the "facts together concerning what it pertains to." Kennedy responded, "You have had the worst case of amnesia in the last 2 days I have ever heard of."[63] Kennedy struggled with the Hoffa hearings, ultimately writing in September 1958 that he was "mentally fatigued — more than any other hearing."[64] However, his work on this committee proved to him that organized crime played a role in the unions, and he was determined to prevail over it.

Kennedy moved on to the mafia bosses in his quest for justice. Among those men was Chicago crime boss Momo Salvatore Giancana. Giancana inherited Al Capone's territory, and was just the person that Robert Kennedy believed was a threat to American values. When Giancana came before the committee he pled the Fifth Amendment thirty-three times. Kennedy finally asked, "Would you tell us anything about your operations or will you just giggle every time I ask you a question?" Giancana responded, "I decline to answer because I honestly believe my answer might tend to incriminate me." Kennedy quickly said, "I thought only little girls giggled, Mr. Giancana."[65] Kennedy did not shy away from confrontation with some of the most dangerous men. It's a testament to his commitment and passion for his cause. James Hilty writes, "Clearly, Robert Kennedy became chief counsel of the McClellan Committee not to satisfy some sinister agenda of his father's ... but to gain a sense of his own worth, to establish himself within his family, and to respond to his compulsion embedded since early childhood to do the right and the moral thing."[66] Kennedy made an impression on the nation. The next move was to get his brother elected to the White House. Both brothers would work together to bring a "new generation of Americans" into leadership roles, defining a "New Frontier" for American politics and culture.

Lewis

"The voice held me right from the start."

While Martin Luther King, Jr., and Robert Kennedy were coming of age, John Robert Lewis was working to move beyond the three room house where he grew up in Troy, Alabama. He yearned to do more with his life than work in a field picking cotton, like so many generations before. His parents were sharecroppers, descendants of slaves. Lewis remembers hearing stories of the slave days when he was a child. He was told these stories because his great-grandfather on his mother's side was born into slavery.[67] Discovering his own voice at a young age, Lewis preached to the chickens on his family farm. "I preached to my birds just about every night," Lewis remembered in his memoir, *Walking with the Wind.* "I would get them all in the henhouse, settle them onto their roosts, and then stand in the doorway and speak to them, reciting pieces of the Bible, the same verses I memorized in Sunday school."[68] Lewis did not want the same life his parents had. Unlike the Kennedy brothers and, to some extent, Dr. King, Lewis had a great many obstacles to overcome in order to make his way in the world. He told his parents that sharecropping was "gambling." His mother responded, "What else are we going to do? You got to work to make a living." Lewis replied, "Nobody should have to work like this."[69]

John Lewis looked to education to find a way out of the hard life he and his parents had to endure. His first encounter with school was in a one room schoolhouse, with one teacher for three grades. He wrote: "I loved school, loved everything about it, no matter how good or bad I was at it."[70] Education became an escape from the life that he had to endure. The cotton fields his family had worked in since before the Civil War were miles away from him while he learned to read and write. Lewis dove into topics ranging from reading literature to exploring history. "Most of all, though, I loved reading, especially about real people and the real world," wrote Lewis. He struggled at times with his family when it came to prioritizing his education over work in the fields. "My parents knew education was important, and it was clear to them how hungry I was for it.... But when there was work to be done in the fields, that came first."[71] Beyond formal schooling, Lewis would be educated in other, powerful ways. When he visited Troy, Alabama, he experienced the ugliness of segregation. That experience left a deep impression on the young boy.

Being the son of sharecroppers empowered Lewis in many ways. That struggle was something that may have hurt many others, who succumbed to the circumstances that life dealt them. Instead of accepting his place, Lewis is an example of the American dream. He worked hard and moved to higher levels in society, making a difference in the nation. Indeed, his quest would pave the way for a new America. Lewis remembered Troy having separate bathrooms marked "White" and "Colored." Perhaps even more affecting was his rejection at the public library. "That killed me," he remembered. "The idea that this was a public library.... I was supposedly a U.S. Citizen, but I wasn't allowed in."[72] The experiences in Troy and other places near his home brought the horrible reality to the awareness of the young, aspiring boy, who wanted nothing more than to learn. Lewis writes, "By the turn of the 1950s, the lines between black and white in the place where I lived were becoming painfully clear to me." In 1951, Lewis went north, experiencing a different world, where there was no segregation and African Americans lived near white Americans. When he returned home, he was even more agitated. "The signs of segregation that had perplexed me up till then now outright angered me."[73] That anger turned into determination, as Lewis's coming of age inexorably led him to work with King and the Kennedy administration to confront segregation in the South.

Lewis started junior high school in the fall of 1951. He noticed the disparities between the white and black society. He remembered driving by prison work gangs, mostly African American, while in the background, other African Americans were "chopping or picking cotton."[74] Lewis's experience in the North, combined with his insatiable appetite for knowledge, were formative forces in his young adult life. "By then," he writes, "I was absolutely committed to giving everything I had to bettering myself in the classroom. I had no doubt that there was a way out of the world I saw around me and this was the way."[75] So determined was Lewis to do well in school that he hid from parents during harvest time and went to school instead.[76] These experiences gave Lewis a drive and conviction for change. In 1955, he would experience another formative, life altering event.

On a Sunday morning in 1955, Lewis turned on radio station WRMA from Montgomery. A young preacher from Atlanta was giving a sermon. Lewis missed the name at the start of the broadcast, but he writes, "The voice held me right from the start."[77] Martin Luther King, Jr., was preaching his sermon entitled "Paul's letter to the American Christians." Lewis remembered that King talked about how schools, stores and other parts of American society belonged to African Americans as much as to whites. "I was on fire with the words I was hearing. I felt this man ... was speaking directly to me."[78] Little did Lewis know that he would be working with this preacher someday, realizing their dreams for America. That same year, 14-year-old Emmett Till was killed for saying "Bye, baby," to a white woman as she left a local store. Subsequent to that comment Till was beaten and killed. His mutilated body was found in a nearby river. Lewis remembered, "I was shaken to the core by the killing of Emmett Till. I was fifteen, black, at the edge of my own manhood, just like him."[79] Not long after the Till murder, the Montgomery Bus Boycott began in earnest, propelling that young preacher Lewis heard on the radio to new heights.

Lewis started action against segregation before his college years. After being turned away from the segregated Pace County Library, he wrote a petition, had his friends sign it and mailed it to the library. He believed that a library should be open to all tax paying individuals. Though nothing came of it, the act was the first step in an education where Lewis would stand up for his rights — trying to evoke change in the process. In addition to that, his second action was joining the NAACP.[80] These instances were a testament to his commitment for change. They also signify an awakening in Lewis that formed part of his social conscience. That moment was an important step for Lewis. He represented a new generation of leadership with new ideas to combat racism and segregation in the South. How he came to find his social voice was important, because it fed his core values that played such a significant role in the movement. In 1957, Lewis turned his attention to college. He wanted to attend Morehouse College, like Dr. King, but could not afford it. He found out that he could work off his tuition at American Baptist Theological (ABT) Seminary. ABT was in Nashville, Tennessee. He applied, was accepted and decided that was where he would pursue the next step in his education.[81]

At Nashville, Lewis met many people who would shape the movement. James Bevel, from Mississippi, became a force in Lewis's experience in the first year. In his second year, Lewis met James Lawson. Lawson studied Gandhian methods of non violent resistance and would impart his knowledge to his classmates during a crucial stage in the civil rights movement. Also, Lewis continued to be influenced by Martin Luther King, Jr. He attempted to start a chapter of the NAACP at ABT in his first year, but was denied. In an effort to propel himself into the throes of the civil rights movement, Lewis wrote King about trying to integrate Troy State College. At the end of his first year, Lewis heard from attorney Fred Gray, King's associate. He met Dr. King with the Rev. Ralph Abernathy and Fred Gray in the spring of 1958. King called Lewis "the boy from Troy" when they met. King said, "If you really want to go to Troy State, we will do what we can to help you. We will get the money to fight the legal battle. All that will be taken care of." King went on to say, "If you really want to do it.... We will see you through." Lewis left the meeting feeling "exhilarated."[82] However, he needed his parents' permission to venture into this battle for equal rights. While at first they were supportive and willing to sign, they changed their minds. Lewis had to tell King that he could not do it. Lewis went back to Nashville. He was destined to play a part in this movement in another way.

Lewis's venture to desegregate Troy University was an important turning point for him. First, it brought him face to face with a man whom he respected and who was an inspiration to play a larger role in the movement. Despite the fact that he was unable to desegregate the university, this was significant. Second, he was taken seriously by serious people. He was driven to make a difference in the movement. Very few students his age were willing to risk their lives in an effort to desegregate the South. While Lewis was not alone in this endeavor, his work was representative of a handful of exceptional students who challenged the social structure of the South at the risk of death. Lewis was not the only student in the movement, but he represents the type of person that made this movement possible. Each of these students who challenged Jim Crow had a certain moral aptitude and an unwillingness to quit.

Howard Zinn writes that Lewis was among a special group of individuals. Indeed, John Lewis had the moral courage to put his life on the line. This special group brought passion and zeal to the movement — reigniting the fervor in others and shaping new leadership. The movement would not be successful without such people in their ranks. Lewis met James Lawson at the start of that second year. Lawson brought non violent resistance to ABT. Eventually, Lewis, Lawson and James Bevel would contribute to the formation of the Student

Non violent Coordinating Committee (SNCC). Zinn argues that the people who formed this group "came right out of the Black Belt and, even though they tasted college, they had nowhere to go but back towards danger and freedom."[83] Lewis was among this group of Americans who shaped the nation, throwing off the vestiges of the old world, combating racism and the country better for themselves and future generations. Like the framers of the nation in 1787, these students knew that a lot was at stake. They were at a crossroads in history that had the potential of changing the nation for themselves and future generations. That said, these young leaders could not do it alone. They needed leaders in government and civil rights leaders to embrace their passion, their vision. Together they challenged the status quo and ushered change to the United States.

Martin Luther King, Jr., the Kennedy brothers and John Lewis came into their moral and spiritual beliefs at about the same time. They all had a passion for what they were doing and a common feeling of righteousness. They all wanted to change the nation, making a better place that realized the dream of the founders — a place of equality for all. That said, they all had a difficult time relating to each other. The Kennedys were pragmatic at first about civil rights, taking time to realize that King and Lewis were just and right in their actions. In contrast, King's unwillingness to acknowledge the complex political ramifications put his quest in jeopardy. Ironically, he and Lewis would have differing opinions that revolved around a similar tension. However, they all needed each other to become the force of change that they were. The Kennedys needed King to challenge them. The morally tough, justice seeking attorney general would prove to be an ally for the civil rights movement. However, he needed to be challenged by King and Lewis and others to act in accordance with his own beliefs, despite the political fallout. These men were a new generation of Americans who would work with each other in trying times, evoking change and challenging the status quo. Indeed, they all set the stage for a subsequent movement that surrounded rights. They were the founders of the rights revolution of the sixties. Though they did not always agree, they needed each other.

PART I : 1960—FINDING A VOICE
The Campaign

1. Sit-Ins, the Kennedys and King

"American students have come of age."

At the start of 1960 America was ready for another great change. The 1940s brought a world war, the end of a depression and a leading role in world politics. The 1950s served as a jumping board for rock and roll, popular trends and an affluent society. America was complacent with what it accomplished and its future in the world. No one in the country was ready for what the sixties would bring. The 1960s challenged the fabric of American society, forcing many to reexamine their lives and place within their respective communities. It brought historic politicians, people and events that would shape the nation for subsequent generations. The '60s was a watershed period in American history.

The rights revolution of this decade remains one of the most society-changing events of the twentieth century. While this revolution would involve many groups, at the heart of the movement were African Americans, both young and old. They were trying to throw off the vestiges of the Civil War, battling segregation throughout the South using any method possible. The men and women of this movement challenged a system that was entrenched in Southern society, serving as a great paradox for what America was supposed to stand for to the rest of the world. Indeed, the existence of this racist policy not only threatened the daily activities of many in the South, but also America's place as leader of the free world. It served as fodder for the Soviet Union as it threatened to discredit the notion of American freedom and democracy. Politicians were especially afraid to confront such issues, as it could potentially cost them Southern votes in national elections and Congressional votes for the presidential agendas. While the civil rights movement had been raging since the days of Booker T. Washington and W.E.B. Dubois, a new energy came to the scene in 1960. That story began in Greensboro, North Carolina, with four students, eventually including pastors, presidents and many others for years to follow.

On February 1, 1960, four college freshmen in Greensboro, North Carolina, entered a local Woolworth's, sat down and waited to be served. This would normally not have been a problem, except they were African American and it was a segregated counter. This was not a planned event so there was no press. This was not thought out as a part of a grand scheme to bring down the local segregation laws as in Montgomery, Alabama, in 1955 or in Little Rock in 1957. Taylor Branch writes: "Greensboro helped define the new decade."[1] The very essence of this new turn in the civil rights movement was epitomized by these four young men. The sit-ins acted on the nonviolent method of protest utilized by Gandhi in the '40s and Dr. King in 1955. These four students ratcheted up the issue of civil rights, highlighting not only the tragic inequality within American democracy but also the tactic of nonviolence.

The largest difference between the sit-ins and King's bus boycott was that it was led and contrived by students, without any organization, fueled by a naiveté that became a strength in the movement. This simple act gave birth to a new, innovative, society-changing way to fight segregation. These four students set the example for the rest of America as the nation entered a new decade. Their actions had far reaching effects beyond the black civil rights movement. This young, energized approach paved the way for feminism, the free speech movement and other movements of the sixties. The four seats those students occupied are now located in the Smithsonian Museum of American History in Washington, D.C.

The decade ahead would be fraught with some of the most tension filled, stressful issues in the history of the American republic. Indeed the students were on the brink of a revolution, which had reaching effects and motivated others to join the cause. Taylor Branch went on to say, "Almost certainly the lack of planning helped create the initial euphoria. Because the four students at Woolworth's had no plan, they began with no self imposed limitations." That euphoric feeling had the potential to foster new ideas and leadership. Branch went on to write, "The surprised discovery of defensiveness within the segregated white world turned their fear into elation."[2]

After Montgomery and Little Rock the movement had struggled for another momentous victory in civil rights, looking for a catalyst to propel it to the next level. These four students created the momentum that the movement yearned for. That happened on a Monday. The students kept going back and by Wednesday there were eighty-five demonstrators.[3] The sit-ins represented a new awakening in America. These four students demonstrated that it was easy to make a point, challenging a system entrenched in the South, with a single act. Further, their action had far reaching results on several levels. First, it invested the nation's youth in the movement. These young leaders had a forum to express their ideas and used it for years to come. Second, it challenged both civil rights leaders and national politicians to reexamine their position on the race issue. The sit-ins at the start of 1960 gave pause to established, respected voices across the divide in politics and the movement itself.

While the civil rights movement was at an ideological crossroads, so was American politics. The Greensboro sit-ins thrusted civil rights into the spotlight during an election year, and the candidates needed to respond. John F. Kennedy was one of those people who sought the presidency. Kennedy's candidacy for the presidency was beginning to gain momentum in those early months of 1960. This young, energetic candidate gave new hope to many Americans, but the black community was a little apprehensive. The strong Democratic South that Kennedy was courting represented the segregated system these civil rights leaders hoped to change. The sit-in movement illuminated the racial issue during the campaign. Historically, each side was cautious in its approach to civil rights. Neither Kennedy nor his opponents took a definitive position on the issue. In 1960 civil rights was the "third rail" in politics. JFK was a politician and careful about how he handled race relations in the campaign. His brother and campaign manager, Robert Kennedy, was equally cautious.

Civil rights was something that both Kennedys acknowledged as a potentially dangerous issue for their campaign. They needed support from the South to win this election. The pragmatic, political brothers were deliberate in the primaries, avoiding any direct answer to the race question. However, both Kennedys gained a new perspective on the race issue in the general election, thus beginning the transition to a new approach. In the subsequent administration John and Robert Kennedy would move the civil rights issues from a political issue to a moral issue. All administrations prior to them had handled civil rights politically. In fact, most politicians did their best to distance themselves from the issues in the South.

JFK and RFK moved the discourse in a new direction, creating new avenues for the nation and future politicians. Lyndon Johnson's gesture, saying, "We shall overcome" at a session of Congress, while dealing with the issue at Selma bridge in 1965, was a much Kennedy's triumph as his own. For it was Kennedy's actions from 1961 to 1963 that moved the nation closer to embracing Johnson's act in 1965. No Democrat, including Johnson, attempted to make that gesture in the 1960 election.

The four students jump-started an ailing movement and added a new thread led by college students and the philosophy of Martin Luther King, Jr. King was called by Fred Shuttlesworth to comment on what would be known as the "sit-in movement." He said in his address to a crowd of students on February 16, 1960, that people around the world were tired of dealing with oppression: "Formerly oppressed people are making it palpably clear that they are determined to be free." He went on to say,

> You students of North Carolina have captured this dynamic idea in a marvelous manner. You have taken the undying and passionate yearning for freedom and filtered it into your own soul and fashioned it to a creative protest that is destined to be one of the glowing epics of our time.[4]

King's endorsement of these students' actions demonstrates how he, like the movement, was evolving with the times. "You have taken hold of the tradition of resolute nonviolent resistance," King said, "and you are carrying it forward toward the end of bringing us all closer to the day of full freedom."[5] King also said, "What is fresh, what is new in your fight is the fact that it was initiated, led, and sustained by students. What is new is that American students have come of age. You now take your honored places in the worldwide struggle for freedom."[6]

Martin Luther King, Jr., served as a bridge of leadership within the civil rights movement. He appealed to young and old members of the movement and his endorsement of the student sit-in movement paved the way for the old guard to respect this new, vibrant approach. Without the leadership of King this movement had the potential to fail. The young students might have been disregarded by the old establishment that have been fighting Jim Crow since before the Second World War. In fact, King and some of these young students disagreed on several occasions during the movement, from the March on Washington to the bridge at Selma. King's presence during these critical junctures in history was the final piece that brought both sides together. The Greensboro sit-ins lit a fire under civil rights organizers, giving birth not only to a new method of protest, but also to student-led organizations. It also gave those wanting to maintain the status quo of segregation a new reason to fear change — making them even more dangerous.

While civil rights organizers wanted to capitalize on the sit-in movement, so did the candidates of the presidential election. Taylor Branch argues, "Race played a large role in the campaign, less because of the civil rights movement than because the polls were showing the Negro vote to be divided and volatile."[7] John Kennedy and Richard Nixon looked for any way they could thwart the other. However, it was difficult not to alienate some of the white vote while they campaigned. Branch continued his argument, saying, "The candidates competed intensely for the Negro votes, but they tried to do so in ways that would generate as little controversy as possible among whites."[8] In the wake of the sit-in movement candidates looked for counsel from African American leaders, in the hopes of gaining a greater understanding between political and civil rights leaders at a time when there needed to be such an alliance to bring great change. No candidate fully embraced a strong, vigilant civil rights platform. Indeed, many white Southern Democrats who supported segregation could hurt not only a presidential campaign, but also any agenda that an administration would pursue. All the candidates, both Democrat and Republican, looked to the segregated South to secure their nomination, eventual election to the presidency, and ability to put forward an ambitious domestic agenda once in office.

In light of the power of the Southern vote, the race just got more interesting. With the sit-in movement taking on steam and the polls indicating that the black vote was divided, candidates could capitalize on this in a very tight race. While it might cost them votes in the South, it still could potentially pay out for them in the end. With such a tight race, the Kennedy camp looked for any way to appear sympathetic to the movement. Also, Kennedy educated himself on the issue of race. His privileged background offered little exposure to racism in America. Therefore, empathy was something he lacked in this area. In May 1960, John Kennedy met with Harry Belafonte about a number of issues, ranging from Jackie Robinson's endorsement of Nixon to the possibility of "organizing Negro stars" in favor of JFK. Belafonte told Kennedy to establish a "close relationship" with Martin Luther King, Jr., Kennedy asked, "Why do you see him as so important?" He went on, "What can he do?" Belafonte responded, "Forget me — forget Jackie Robinson and everybody else we've been talking about. If you can join the cause of King, and be counseled by him, then you'll have an alliance. That will make a difference."[9] Belafonte's comments pointed toward King's definitive role in this new era of civil rights. His contemporaries saw him as the moral leader for the movement. Politics, not moral outrage, played a role in this meeting with Belafonte. Kennedy was looking for ways to get the black vote that polls were showing as divided. Belafonte wanted him to consider King because he knew that in the long run, King would be the leader for the black community and one that Kennedy should embrace as an advisor. The campaign, and not long term change, was on JFK's mind. Despite the campaign and his need for immediate results, he met with King in an effort to follow Belafonte's advice. Harris Wofford, a civil rights advisor to Kennedy, played a role getting JFK and King together. On June 23 they met in Joseph Kennedy's New York apartment.

David Garrow writes that Martin Luther King, Jr., remembered that Senator John Kennedy did not side with black leadership on the Civil Rights Act of 1957. King believed that Kennedy was too preoccupied with ambition, compromising "basic principles to become President." With that in mind, King was not enthusiastic about the prospects of a Kennedy presidency. The meeting changed his mind.[10] When Kennedy met King he emphasized "strong presidential leadership" and "initiatives to protect the right to vote." Kennedy agreed especially with the role that the president should play in these matters. King wrote a letter the next day about the meeting. In it he said that the meeting was "fruitful and rewarding." He also said, "I have no doubt that he would do the right thing on this issue if he were elected President."[11] However, King also reportedly said that Kennedy lacked a "depthed understanding" of civil rights. Despite that, shortly after the meeting Kennedy remarked to African diplomats, "It is the American tradition to stand up for one's rights — even if the new way to stand up for one's rights was to sit down."[12] Kennedy's meeting with King represents his willingness to explore any avenue to reach out to the black vote. He assured Dr. King privately that he wanted "no compromise of the basic principles — no evasion of basic controversies — and no second class citizenship for any American anywhere in this country."[13] Kennedy followed through on that statement, before he became president, with a simple phone call.

"Love alone is radical."

No group embodied the spirit of this new generation more than the Student Non violent Coordinating Committee (SNCC). The members of this group showed how the philosophical notions of nonviolence could be embraced and utilized on a larger scale. It also showcased the sheer power and determination of the young men and women who refused to give up on the notion of equality under the law, demonstrating not only to the nation but to the world how important one person's voice can be. Howard Zinn wrote in 1964 that the SNCC was

> ...more of a movement than an organization, for no bureaucratized structure can contain their spirit, no printed program capture the fierce and elusive quality of their thinking. And while they have no famous leaders, very little money, no inner access to the seats of national authority, they are clearly the frontline of the negro assault on the moral comfort of white America.[14]

This was a new kind of revolution. Howard Zinn's assessment of the SNCC was prophetic as he wrote in 1964. The SNCC would serve to be the catalyst that turned the civil rights movement in a new direction. However, since they had no principal members who could give them the limelight they needed, after the election the Kennedy brothers would have to work with them in order for their voices to be heard. Dr. King would have to embrace them in order for them to achieve real status among the black community. It was the dawn of new leadership, something that would last into the 21st century. "For the first time in our history," Zinn wrote, "a major social movement, shaking the nation to its bones, was being led by youngsters."[15] These youngsters were even younger than the "new generation of Americans" Kennedy would eventually speak of in his inaugural address.

Zinn goes on to say, "All Americans owe them a debt for — if nothing else — releasing the idealism locked so long inside a nation that has not recently tasted the drama of social upheaval."[16] He went on, "Theirs was a silent generation until they spoke, the complacent generation until they marched and sang, the money-seeking generation until they renounced comfort and security to fight for justice in the dark and dangerous hamlets of the black belt." Zinn called this group "the new abolitionists."[17] For the civil rights movement to be successful it needed strong leadership. Leadership came in different ways from within and outside the movement. The SNCC represented a shift from the old, traditional approach — ushering in a revitalization to the movement. There was not one leader. Instead, they were a force of people, moving and challenging segregation laws. Martin Luther King, Jr., in his own way, was like the SNCC; he also offered new ideas for the movement and challenged the older generation of leadership who held the reins in the wake of World War II. This youthful approach gave the movement the moral compass and tools they needed to destroy Jim Crow. The SNCC was inspired by King and the philosophy he offered the movement from the Montgomery Bus Boycott.

King's embracement of the SNCC served as a watershed moment in the movement — bringing a young, energized group in tune with a new style of leadership. The Kennedys, however, offered a different type of leadership. In Washington, they could pave the way by supporting the initiatives of King, the SNCC and others who challenged segregation at a legal and moral level. Indeed, without this dynamic the civil rights movement would have failed. It was, however, a strained relationship that did not always agree and even came close to collapsing on a few occasions. The SNCC and King did not always agree on tactics privately. Publicly, however, they demonstrated resolve. In fact, Robert Kennedy's Justice Department also differed with both groups on the timing and tactics of their demonstrations. Their alliance was not obvious in their time, but looking back on events it is clear that all three needed each other to leave a lasting legacy.

Howard Zinn, who while teaching at Spelman College got to know some of these young men and women, went on to characterize these young leaders: "They are happy warriors, a refreshing contrast to the revolutionaries of old. They smile and wave while they are being taken off in the paddy wagons; they laugh and sing behind bars."[18] Indeed, this was a new way to protest. The SNCC wore their time in prison on their shirts like a badge of honor. Though incarceration was a frightening prospect, they saw it as a necessary step on the journey to freedom. This new way to embrace the movement was something that took many civil rights leaders by surprise—paving the way for larger, profound change. It was a time for the youth to show their elders that they would not wait for change, they would instead go out and take it. Like the progressives of the nineteenth century, civil rights organizers were exposing the ills of the South and trying to force the government to support basic rights for all. Also, like the progressives from the nineteenth century, civil rights leaders needed the government to play a role in this transition. They needed a progressive president like Theodore Roosevelt or Woodrow Wilson. Eisenhower did not approach civil rights in a revolutionary way. Without a president willing to reach beyond the standard rhetoric of the time, the civil rights movement would fail. The SNCC challenged politicians to confront the racial issues in America.

Jane Stembridge, one of the white members of the SNCC, said of the group,

> It all boils down to human relationships. It is the question of whether we ... whether I shall go on living in isolation or whether there shall be a we. The student movement is not a cause ... it is a collision between this one person and that one person. It is I am going to sit beside you.... Love alone is radical. Political statements are not; programs are not; even going to jail is not.[19]

Stembridge's emphasis on love and solidarity—two important concepts that brought the movement to new levels—linked their effort to something larger than themselves. The emotion and symbolism behind such an act was, in itself, a powerful motivator for the students within the movement. Further it showed the world that this new generation of leaders would look to constants within humanity, something that could not be challenged, as part of their plight for equality. In addition it fostered a new notion of brotherhood and sisterhood, which was at the basis for almost every successful grassroots movement in history.

What was so daring about this group was that they not only challenged each others courage, but also told politicians that rhetoric meant nothing. Action was the way to force change. Zinn said, "They come themselves from the ranks of the victims, not just because they are mostly Negroes, but because for the most part their fathers are janitors and laborers, their mothers maids and factory workers."[20] Clearly the SNCC was different. They wanted to shape the future, because they owned the future and wanted it to be better for themselves and their children. They wanted to inspire, because they needed inspiration—not only from black leaders, but from themselves. They wanted commitment to the cause. These men and women were not looking for any reward other than the freedom their government had promised since the end of the Civil War.

John Lewis was one of the students King was referring to in his speech at North Carolina. John Lewis writes in his memoir, *Walking with the Wind,* "The term 'movement' was beginning to look as if it might actually apply to American society at large, to the nation's attitude about the response to the struggle for racial equality."[21] Lewis, one of the principal people in SNCC out of Nashville, was taken with the efforts of his fellow students in Greensboro. He wanted to keep the change moving. He writes, "Forces were gathering in this country in terms of civil rights—there was a general sense that momentum might be beginning to mount—but we weren't about to sit on the sidelines to see what happened."[22] Lewis wrote about how students in Nashville, Tennessee, were getting ready to demonstrate against Jim Crow. Just on the cusp of that intervention, those four students sat down in Greensboro. Lewis remembered, "And then ... as fate — or the spirit of history — would have it, someone else made the move for us."[23] He went on to say, "It happened so spontaneously, so suddenly, that the next morning's newspapers contained no accounts of the incident."[24] The Greensboro sit-ins were inspirational, leading to many other demonstrations across the country exhibiting similar leadership and courage in an effort to vanquish Jim Crow. Perhaps the best example of how this solidarity strengthened the bonds of these civil rights warriors was that their own actions prompted others to build on the success. From this new hope sprang the belief that it was time for a change in America. John Lewis would play an integral role in this change.

John Lewis contributed strong leadership, helping others get the movement going in Nashville, Tennessee. Lewis prepared students for their acts of courage. "We spent the next week," he remembered, "in daily gatherings, briefing everyone who could attend on the essentials of sitting in, on the behavior that would be demanded as they entered those downtown stores. No aggression. No retaliation. No loud conversations, no talking of any kind with anyone other than ourselves."[25] John Lewis wrote on a piece of paper the following for each person to remember: "Remember the teachings of Jesus, Gandhi, Thoreau, and Martin Luther King, Jr."[26] Each student carried this with them, knowing that they might be arrested, beaten or threatened. The Nashville and Greensboro sit-ins showed that racial issues dominated American society in the 1960s. It was something presidential hopefuls should have discussed and debated, yet they shied away from it. These sit-ins demonstrated that all generations of African Americans embraced the quest for equality under the law. These heroes of the movement challenged the notion that it was only a political issue, which was an idea that dominated the period after the Civil War. Reconstruction and the carnage of the Civil War forced law makers to treat the race issue as a political problem, with solutions that addressed it as such. In the age of the Cold War and modernization, it became a moral issue — and one that could not be ignored by any leader in the United States.

Lewis went on to contribute to a series of sit-ins based out of the First Baptist Church in Nashville. The first day of the sit-ins was easy. In fact when Lewis returned to the church later that evening, he wrote, "It was like New Year's Eve." The excitement was pervasive and many thought they were on their way. On Thursday, February 18, Lewis set out again. This time it was to W.T. Grants. In many of these cases the owners of the establishments closed lunch counters in an attempt to stop any possible confrontation. "White Nashville just was not ready for this. It had never had to deal with black people this way," wrote Lewis.[27] This was the beginning of a new era in the movement. Arthur Schlesinger writes in *Robert F. Kennedy and His Times*: "The white south's customs were rooted in a bitter history. The Supreme Court's law came on them as a threat to tradition, womanhood and social order. Southern blacks, awakening after so many years to their constitutional rights, were growing as militant for federal law as whites were for local custom."[28] Lewis and others were ecstatic over the success of the Greensboro and early Nashville sit-ins. It was the start of a new decade. Martin Luther King, Jr., empowered many young African Americans with a speech in Durham, North Carolina. Things looked like they were moving again. However, subsequent events would challenge those feelings of triumph and elation. Lewis set off on February 27, 1960, ready for another planned sit-in.

On the day John Lewis was arrested for the first time in his life he heard white men shouting "Go home, nigger," and "Go back to Africa."[29] This future congressman of the

United States was hit and belittled, enduring great humiliation. He stood up to hate and violence differently than people were used to. He said, "We weren't playing by those rules, of course, and that infuriated them even further." After he took his seat at Woolworth's, he was hit in the ribs and knocked to the ground. He watched a white man put the stub of his cigarette out on a fellow demonstrator's back. He made his way back to his seat. The police came in to arrest him and others for disorderly conduct. As they were led out of the store they sang, "We shall overcome." Lewis wrote: "I felt no shame or disgrace.... I felt exhilarated."[30] It wasn't a jail cell as much as it was a place of honor, a place where Gandhi, Jesus Christ, Martin Luther King and Henry David Thoreau had all been. This was the start of a new kind of protest that would not only propel civil rights to the forefront of the national discourse, but also inspire many African Americans to confront racism and segregation.

2. The New Frontier

"The moral imperative behind the laws which the Congress has passed."

On October 7, 1960, Senator John F. Kennedy finished one of his famous televised debates and then made his way to two college campuses for campaign speeches. He talked for five minutes at American University, moving on to Howard University, a predominantly black university. Four hundred cramped people waited in the university chapel, while more students listened from outside to the candidate's address on civil rights.[1] Kennedy started the speech by saying that a political campaign was an important time

> because it gives the American people an opportunity to make a judgment as to which course of action they want to follow, which leadership, which viewpoint, which political philosophy, and it is also an important time for political parties, because it does give the political party an opportunity not merely to live off its past successes, but also consider where it is going in the future, what contribution it can make.[2]

Kennedy emphasized that the issues were great and the problem that the nation faced was the greatest "since the administration of Franklin Roosevelt, and in many ways transcends any that we have faced since the administration of Lincoln one hundred years ago."[3] Kennedy's allusion to these presidents was no mistake, as many African Americans saw both presidents as champions for their cause.

In his grand way Kennedy said that the great question for them was, "Can we make freedom work here and around the world. Can we sustain it? Can we demonstrate over a long period of time that our system represents the best means of organizing human society?" He went further and asked if the United States could create a strong, lasting freedom that would "not only endure but prevail over a Communist system." Kennedy was a cold warrior, equating success with triumph over a system that challenged basic democratic beliefs. While the United States needed to uphold freedom, it also needed to vanquish communism in the process. To that end, Kennedy alluded to the lack of freedom currently affecting African Americans and how he wanted to change it. "In order to maintain our freedom, to meet our commitments, to the Constitution, to the great moral principles enunciated by this country's leaders," he said, "we have to as I say tonight set a high example ... in the early days of the 1960's, to move this country closer toward that example."[4]

The issue of race was not something that either Kennedy or Nixon had fully addressed. Kennedy struggled to find his voice on this issue, consulting Harry Belafonte, Martin Luther King, Jr., and others. Kennedy came out and highlighted the issues surrounding statistics of African American children versus white children:

The prospects, percentage-wise, of a Negro child getting through high school, of that child getting to college, of that child becoming a professional man, of that child when it is born owning its house ... and now we have only one that is a Negro out of some 200, the chances of that child getting through high school are about a third. The same percent getting through college is one quarter of a white baby being born in the house next door, the chance of owning his house is far less of a percentage, and the chances of being unemployed are far greater.

Kennedy went on to say, "I think we cannot afford in 1960 to waste any talent which we have. It is a matter of our national survival as well as a matter of national principle."[5] By highlighting these statistics Kennedy tried to empower the audience, the way his rhetoric did time and time again. In addition the fact that the candidate took five minutes with a group of 3,000 at American University and presented a much longer, in depth speech to four hundred, mostly black, students at Howard University is evidence that he wanted to connect with this group.

Kennedy followed up his statistics with a pledge of sorts to the crowd, saying, "I believe that the President of the United States must take the leadership in setting the moral tone, the unfinished business, in setting the sights of Americans to the goal realizing the talents in an equal way of every American." With his mention of a "moral tone," Kennedy moved his rhetoric in a new direction regarding civil rights. His lofty ideals set a new goal that would be carried on beyond his assassination. In perhaps one of the strongest assertions of equality under law, John Kennedy said that while every person in America might not finish school or college or even own a home, "that should be on the basis of his contribution to society, his energy, his vitality, his intelligence, his motivations, not based on the color of his skin. That is the goal of the society which I think we should work towards in the 1960s."[6] The crowd erupted in applause.

Kennedy's speech was representative of his response to the race issue in America. It was different than any other and offered hope to this new generation of leaders. It was meant to inspire and force change. Indeed there were many that saw Kennedy as the leader of such change. In fact, as a demonstration of strong leadership to promote such change, Kennedy said,

> I believe if the President of the United States indicates his strong support of the extension of equal constitutional rights to all Americans wherever they may live, if he stands strongly behind the principles of equality of opportunity of education and employment, I believe this country will then recognize the moral imperative behind the laws which the Congress has passed, or which the Constitution promotes.[7]

While these were words in an election filled with strong rhetoric on both sides, they were words that very few candidates had emphasized in such a climate that the sit-ins created. That is what made Kennedy stand out on civil rights—his vision and his audacity to take risks.

Kennedy went on to indicate his notions of equality under law, solidifying his platform on civil rights to the packed chapel. He said that the previous one hundred and fifty years of world history has been a course toward freedom, alluding to how he disagreed with colonialism and the policies of the Eisenhower administration. "Man's desire to be free," he said, "is the strongest force not only in this country but around the world. We should associate ourselves with it." By linking America's domestic policy to the prestige abroad, Kennedy was giving a great deal of power to the plight of African Americans, which was a big reason why he saw civil rights and equality as something that the U.S. needed to address if it was truly going to be the leader of the free world.

One of Kennedy's last lines was meant to empower the audience, thereby strengthening his position as a candidate and future leader of the United States. He addressed voting rights, saying, "There is no need for providing the right to vote in some states where Negroes are denied the vote unless they vote to the fullest." As the applause started up at this point, Kennedy used that energy from the crowd to further his point.

> Unless in those communities where they are given their rights to participate in the political process they do it as free individuals, not part of some great organization or other, but speaking as individuals giving their considered judgment on what is best for their country and what is best for themselves and what is best for the cause of freedom.[8]

Kennedy's idealistic, grandiose language was meant to inspire these young African American students. It was also meant to distinguish his candidacy from that of Nixon, who was mute on the topic, in an attempt to show a deeper understanding of and empathy for the race issue. So excited was the crowd that Kennedy had to fight his way through it to make his way to the next campaign spot.

Kennedy's Howard University speech was evidence that he wanted to demonstrate to the African American community that he cared and was willing to look at the issue of race and equality in a different light. That said, the speech was only words and while it had grandiose language, it lacked action. Kennedy needed to make some gesture to the black community that would distinguish him even further from the usual political discourse over racial issues. The *New York Times* reported Kennedy saying that Nixon "likes to repeat that 'everybody is aware of the strong convictions he has on this issue.'" Kennedy went on to say that he was unable to find a statement in any of Nixon speeches that described his "convictions." According to Kennedy, Nixon failed to discuss the inequality that African Americans had to deal with in the South, telling crowds that it was a Southern issue and they had to deal with it, which is in contrast to Kennedy, who frequently praised the sit-in movement. The *Times* article goes on to say that, while in the House, Nixon "voted several times against an enforceable fair employment practice bill. The Democratic platform pledges such legislation by name, while the Republican plank does not mention it."[9] Kennedy tried to demonstrate to the black community that he was different. He would not have to wait long to put action behind his rhetoric.

"I was thinking of you and Dr. King."

In March 1965, Harris Wofford and others were making the famous march from Selma to Montgomery. Coretta Scott King saw Wofford on Highway 80. When the group stopped to rest, Coretta Scott King moved toward him, welcomed him back to Alabama and said, "They say that his call to me made the difference, that it elected him President. I like to think so. He was beginning to do so much, he and his brother."[10] James Hilty argues, "Two telephone calls from the Kennedy brothers changed the outcome of the 1960 election."[11] The mere fact that a presidential candidate looked to aid an African American in distress was a very powerful symbol.

The 1960 election was very close, and one event such as that could have had an impact on the whole outcome. The country moved to embrace the new energy these student sit-ins infused into the movement. Seeing an opportunity, Martin Luther King, Jr., wanted to contribute to this spirit. On October 18, 1960, several students, including Julian Bond, contacted King to participate in the sit-in movement. They targeted Richard H. Rich's store in downtown Atlanta. Lonnie King, one of the other student leaders, said, "Martin, you've got to come with us." Lonnie King insisted that King needed to go to jail if he intended to be the leader of this movement. The next morning King and thirty-five others were arrested when they refused to leave Rich's restaurant.[12] When it looked as though King was going to be released, Judge Oscar Mitchell issued a bench warrant for the unrelated charge of driving without a Georgia driving license. Mitchell sentenced King to four months' hard labor with a road gang, which James Hilty argued was "an outrageously harsh sentence and clearly racially motivated."[13] King's incarceration had reverberations throughout the movement, bringing the Kennedys full force into the race issues that infected the nation.

While the Kennedys were always reluctant to get involved in civil rights issues, their journey toward a new realization began with the jailing of King during the election. In many ways it was the first civil rights crisis they had to confront. While it did not have the larger implications of other crises, it did give them a taste of the injustice in the Southern system. That said, they needed the South in the election and didn't want to jeopardize any endorsement. Evan Thomas writes, "The strains of genuine decency and hardheaded pragmatism met in arguably the most important moment of the campaign, the effort to get Martin Luther King, Jr., out of jail.... Just two phone calls — one by JFK, one by RFK — decided the outcome of the election and the course of racial politics for decades to come."[14]

When King was arrested for sitting in at a lunch counter, King's wife Coretta called Harris Wofford. Wofford suggested that Kennedy phone Coretta, who was six months pregnant and worried about her husband. "All he's got to do is show a little heart," Wofford said. Sargent Shriver, Kennedy's brother-in-law and advisor, played a role after other political advisors left the room, saying, "Negroes don't expect everything will change tomorrow, no matter who's elected, but they do want to know whether you care. If you telephone Mrs. King, they will know you support a pregnant woman who is afraid her husband will be killed."[15] The mere fact that the Kennedy camp considered some gesture is evidence that they were thinking in different terms than previous candidates, wanting to embrace civil rights initiatives as a part of their platform not only as a token gesture, but with action.

One of JFK's strengths was his ability to empathize with others, or at least demonstrate it. It was empathy that staved off war with the Soviet Union during the missile crisis in 1962, and it was empathy, coupled with compassion, that led him to make the phone call to Mrs. King. When Sargent Shriver suggested to Kennedy that he call Mrs. King, he replied, "That's a good idea. Why not? Do you have her number? Get her on the phone."[16] When Wofford talked to Mrs. King later that day she said that she was "very moved, and grateful." According to King, Kennedy said:

> I want to express to you my concern about your husband. I know this must be very hard for you. I understand you are expecting a baby, and I just wanted you to know that I was thinking about you and Dr. King. If there is anything I can do to help, please feel free to call on me.[17]

Kennedy's gesture to King had far reaching effects. Also, it was uncommon at the time for any politician to embrace a civil rights leader in such a thoughtful, personal way. Though some may have seen it as a token attempt to get the black vote, it clearly meant a great deal to Coretta Scott King. Despite Kennedy's gesture it did very little to get King out of jail. It did, however, demonstrate solidarity with King and his cause. That, combined with the lofty rhetoric of the Howard University speech just days earlier, gave a small glimpse into how JFK would handle the races issue when president. His compassion helped move the issue from political to a moral imperative, rooted in what was righteous.

Not long after the news got out, John Seigenthaler called on behalf of Robert Kennedy, saying, "Bob wants to see you bomb throwers right away."[18] RFK's first reaction was one of outrage at who asked JFK to make the call. As campaign manager, he saw this as a problem that might prove fatal to the election. He even went so far as to say to the men who advised his brother to make the call, "Do you know that three southern governors told us that if Jack supported Jimmy Hoffa, Nikita Khrushchev, or Martin Luther King they would throw their states to Nixon? Do you know that this election may be razor close and you have probably just lost it for us?"[19] Robert Kennedy was always loyal to his brother first and foremost, especially in the days of the campaign. He was not only letting his brother down if they lost, but also his family, which was something he held dear. It was a momentous occasion for the Kennedy family and would lay the groundwork for future family members to play a role in politics and history for decades after the election.

After the initial reaction and scolding of the men, RFK started to change his position. The younger Kennedy was known for his impetuous approach when confronted with issues or backed into a corner. However, after some reflection, Robert Kennedy returned to his righteous attitude, focusing on the legalities behind the act of the judge and how injustice played a role in the incident. It was the first step for Robert Kennedy that would challenge his beliefs and make him embrace a new, daring view of race in America. With the die being cast, he looked for a way to control or even influence the situation. While flying to New York, not too long after the altercation with Wofford and Shriver, he kept thinking about the treatment of King.[20] When RFK was told that the judge had denied King bail, RFK responded, "How could they do that? You can't deny bail on a misdemeanor."[21] Immediately Robert Kennedy thought of the law, not the emotion or the political ramifications behind the issue. It was his natural response to think in that manner. His political prowess was more a result of how his father drove the Kennedys to the top of the political echelon. Robert Kennedy had a quick legal wit, founded in righteousness. In the future, this would serve him well in fostering change. John Seigenthaler, who drove Robert Kennedy to the airport that day for his trip to New York, told him not to get involved.

Robert Kennedy hoped to take some of the heat away from his brother, which was something he did often. At first RFK agreed not to get involved. However, on the plane to New York the incident resonated with him. Robert Kennedy said, "I thought about it and I kept thinking it was so outrageous. When I got off the airplane, I'd made up my mind that somebody had to talk to that judge." He went on to say, "It made me so damned angry to think of that bastard sentencing a citizen to four months of hard labor for a minor traffic offense and screwing up my brother's campaign and making our country look ridiculous before the world."[22] From this account, it seemed clear that Robert Kennedy was more concerned about a violation of the law than of civil rights. While the phone call to the judge is evidence that Robert Kennedy cared about civil rights, it is also evidence that he would consider abiding by the rule of law for justice on racial matters.

This experience awakened Robert Kennedy to the race issue. As he acknowledged later, when interviewed for the oral history, he did not lie awake at night thinking about civil rights. His morally minded social conscience took hold when he saw a U.S. citizen being mistreated. Kennedy always wanted to be on the right side of history. That was why he pursued communists under McCarthy and the rackets in the Senate. His departure from the pragmatic politician was not only about the racial issue, he also didn't want his or JFK's legacy to be tied to something that was so blatantly wrong. While this may have been one of his motivators at the start of the administration, over time he discovered the moral and ethical reasons to oppose segregation, pushing for greater change. This was a moment where RFK equated the injustices of the South to JFK's campaign. It was a moment where he made it plain, without mentioning color, that he was outraged that a "citizen" was mistreated. This was the essence of how he handled issues in the justice department; he always looked to the law as a means to make his point clear. It was a strong foundation on which to base such stances. However, RFK's phone call to the judge was not politically calculated; it was based on raw emotion and anger over the injustice of the situation.

Robert Kennedy said to the judge: "Are you American? Do you know what it means to be an American? You get King out of jail." After Bobby told Louis Martin, a civil rights advisor with the campaign, that he had called the judge, Martin called him "an honorary brother."[23] The phone call to the judge speaks to RFK's need to control the situation as well as his new awareness of the injustice in the South. James Hilty argues, "Robert Kennedy's phone call to Judge Mitchell, some thought, marked the awakening of his social conscience."[24] Years later, Kennedy changed his story somewhat, claiming he simply asked, "Will he get out on bail?" Mitchell responded, "Bob it's nice to talk to you. I don't have any objection to doing that." Kennedy concluded, "Whatever I said, he got him out."[25] Perhaps he changed his story for political reasons at the time of the interview or, perhaps, however unlikely, for modesty. Nevertheless, at the time of the incident his action had a significant effect in the black community. He and JFK demonstrated resolve for African Americans.

Evan Thomas goes on to argue another side of the story, one of "realpolitik" rather than moral outrage. He says that when King was arrested, "Jack and Bobby Kennedy discussed the political ramifications of getting him out of jail."[26] They were concerned that the Republicans would use this against them. JFK called Georgia governor Ernest Vandiver who said that being a segregationist, he would be looking for cover and could not do anything. Vandiver did reach the judge through an intermediary, only to get the same response. Judge Mitchell would release King, but he also needed political cover. According to Thomas, "Judge Mitchell had to be able to say that he let King out of jail only after being called on the phone by Senator Kennedy or his brother."[27] While there is still speculation about which story is correct, the fact that John and Robert Kennedy chose to get involved in this situation demonstrates their willingness to back the civil rights movement. If Thomas's version is true, it represents the type of cat-and-mouse game that Southern politicians played with the Kennedys. These actions were more than any other presidential candidate undertook. The Kennedys did not have the power of the White House, nor that of Congress. They were paving new roads in race relations — trying to be the young progressives that they hoped to be in the White House. While it may have been a political plight for both Kennedys, it turned out to be an important, effective, moral move as well.

Evan Thomas writes that all of Mitchell's comments were relayed to JFK: "Kennedy, in turn, instructed Bobby to call the judge." Most interesting about Thomas's assertion was that "RFK was not operating on his own initiative. He was carrying out his brother's orders."[28] If Robert Kennedy was, in fact, carrying out his brother's order, then this was not the watershed moment many historians argue. That said, Robert Kennedy had a great deal of influence over his brother in circumstances like this. JFK's record on civil rights was nothing to brag about. Bobby, on the other hand, was the more moralist of the two. While one could never determine definitively who influenced who or who gave orders, it was clear that John and Robert Kennedy were getting in the thick of a civil rights war that had been raging since Appomattox.

The whole incident illuminates a few pieces of JFK's policy on civil rights — as well as how the two would handle civil rights in the future. The Kennedy brothers worked in tandem to evoke change. However, JFK looked for cover by using his brother to make the jump into politically sensitive areas. That said, RFK was upset over the social injustice of the situation. He clearly wanted to stand up for what was morally right. If he felt otherwise, he would have told JFK that he shouldn't get involved any further than the phone call to Coretta Scott King. Other candidates would have left it alone, as did Nixon, in such a tight race. The Kennedy brothers, however, chose to get involved in the hopes of changing politics and government. This coalition was how they would do it.

After being released, Martin Luther King said, "I am deeply indebted to Senator Kennedy, who served as a great force in making my release possible. For him to be that courageous shows the he is really acting upon principle and not expediency."[29] King stopped short of endorsing Kennedy, as he realized that he needed to work with whoever made it to the White House. Despite King's reluctance to endorse Kennedy, his father said, "I'll take a catholic or the devil himself if he'll wipe the tears from my daughter-in-law's eyes." Ralph Abernathy, King's lieutenant, told a crowd to "take off your Nixon buttons."[30] The issue of race relations was very pervasive in the election. The decade started with the sit-in movement, which would eventually affect the election in the arrest of King. The two phone calls demonstrate that the Kennedys were ready to address segregation, or at least the injustice behind it, paving the way toward greater change in America. Though there were many issues to confront, this was one that needed both leaders and soldiers, which was why Robert Kennedy's choice for people in the justice department was so important and history changing.

Evan Thomas argued, "Nowhere was the Kennedy calculus on moral pragmatism more evident than in the campaign's courtship for the black vote." He went on to say, "In 1960, the segregated south was still solidly democratic. John and Robert Kennedy had to be careful not to offend local sensibilities." Thomas also says, "To the happy surprise of liberal activists, Bobby took a hard line in favor of a pro–civil rights platform at the convention." Robert Kennedy said to those in charge, "Don't fuzz it up."[31] Robert Kennedy had his hands tied with civil rights. John Kennedy may have wanted to make an impact; however, like Lincoln, he needed a realistic, pragmatic approach for eventual change. This was important, lest he be positioned as too much of a radical on segregation. Bobby on the other hand could be a vital asset in this plight. RFK did nothing in a vacuum and sought advice from his brother on all matters often. Therefore, as RFK reached out to civil rights leaders, so did JFK.

James Hilty argues, "Robert Kennedy played a more prominent role influencing the perception of this brother by African Americans. Before the 1960s the Kennedys were, in Arthur Schlesinger's charitable words, 'only intermittently sensitive to racial injustice.'" The matter of race and the problems faced by African Americans, RFK said, "was not a particular issue in our house."[32] John and Robert Kennedy were afraid of what taking a stand in civil rights would do to them politically. Hilty writes, "The Kennedys' quest to win the African American votes in the pivotal urban-industrial centers was tempered by their fear of alienating white Southerners, which precluded not only an overt alliance with the civil rights movement but even a close public identification with African American politicians."[33] Indeed the whole issue speaks to the politics and history within the South. These issues also demonstrated that when Kennedy did embrace the plight of civil rights workers, it came with a political cost. Hilty went on to write, "Southern Democrats reacted angrily to news of the Kennedy's involvement in King's release, exaggerating the impact of the two telephone calls and predicting a costly southern reaction."[34] This speaks to not only the issues the Kennedys faced in the campaign, but also what was in store for them when they reached office.

John Kennedy won the election of 1960 by one of the slimmest margins in the history of the United States. In the critical state of Illinois, JFK garnered approximately 250,000 African-American votes, carrying Chicago's predominately black areas.[35] President Eisenhower had remarked that Nixon lost because of "a couple of phone calls."[36] Theodore Sorensen wrote that JFK was "jubilant about his victory. At the same time he was deeply touched by it."[37] This was an extraordinary time, where an Irish-Catholic was elected to the White House for the first time in history. Though "razor close," as Bobby predicted, this election demonstrated that things were changing in America. While Kennedy would be confronted with threats from the Soviet Union, civil rights would remain at the center of his domestic policy. He needed cabinet members who would challenge the status quo, much like he did by running for election as the first Irish-Catholic, confronting segregation, creating a different America. He would not have to look very far to find them. This group of individuals would begin to realize the New Frontier rhetoric that was so prominent throughout the campaign.

3. "We Few, We Happy Few"

"We're going to have to change the climate in this country."

Immediately after the election, John Kennedy worked to fill cabinet positions with the "best and the brightest" that the nation had to offer. Keeping up with his role from the campaign, Robert Kennedy played an integral part in choosing Robert McNamara as secretary of defense and Dean Rusk as secretary of state. These positions were important for the travails that the administration would have to face down the road. Equally important was the role of attorney general. That office would combat the civil rights struggle that America was facing. Kennedy had made it clear in his Howard University speech that he would give the attorney general the ability to carry out suits as he saw fit against the voting disparities in the South. John Kennedy wanted his brother to be a part of his cabinet. In Hyannis Port, the day after the election, Robert Kennedy and John Kennedy discussed what role his younger brother would play in the administration. Robert Kennedy remembered in 1964 that JFK "asked me if I wanted to be attorney general. I said I didn't want to be attorney general." Robert Kennedy believed that "nepotism was a problem." He also thought that he had "been chasing bad men for three years" and did not want to devote his entire life to that endeavor. He believed that he could achieve things outside of the Department of Justice. RFK said that he could go after the Teamsters "where the cases hadn't been adequately handled," and he also had, fascinatingly enough, an "interest in civil rights."[1] Perhaps the episode involving King made him realize the need for such action.

Robert Kennedy also said that another reason why he did not want to do it was "the fact that I had been working with my brother for a long time, and I thought maybe I'd go off by myself." Another chief advocate for Bobby to take the attorney general position was his father, Joseph Kennedy. "He wouldn't hear of anything else," Robert Kennedy said. Joseph Kennedy believed that RFK should have a cabinet position in the hopes of being "involved in all the major decisions that were made." Their father also thought that "Jack should have somebody that was close to him, and had been close a long period of time when he went into this job."[2] RFK said in 1964 that after the campaign "I didn't know what I was going to do, but I wasn't going to do that."[3] Bobby called his brother to tell him no, but JFK stopped him short, saying, "Well, don't tell me no now. I want to have breakfast with you in the morning. Come to the house on N Street [in Georgetown]."[4]

It was early, cold, and the snow lay thick on the ground as Robert Kennedy went with John Seigenthaler for breakfast in Georgetown, where the president-elect made decisions for his cabinet. Seigenthaler remembered,

A few reporters were outside when we went in. The president was upstairs. Bob went up, and within about two or three minutes they came down. We had breakfast in the little breakfast nook about halfway back in the house—bacon and eggs. The president began to tell us about his selection of members of the Cabinet.[5]

Bobby finally said, "Johnny, can we talk about my situation?"[6] Robert Kennedy remembered JFK saying that he did not know all of these people in his government. RFK said that his brother "thought it would make a difference to have somebody that he could talk to over some of these problems, and so he thought it was important that I become attorney general." Seigenthaler remembered JFK saying,

I know full well these are going to be difficult years in many areas, and I'm going to have great problems, and I'm going to need to rely on many people. But I'm in a difficult position because in this Cabinet there really is no person with whom I have been intimately connected over the years. I need to know that when problems arise, I'm going to have somebody who's going to tell me the unvarnished truth, no matter what he thinks, and Bobby will do that. And so I need him.[7]

JFK also alluded to the issues with civil rights, saying, "I don't want somebody who is going to be fainthearted. I want somebody who is going to be strong; who will join with me in taking whatever risks." It is unclear whether JFK was saying this for Seigenthaler's benefit or not. Nevertheless, civil rights was clearly on John Kennedy's mind as he embarked on this new, historic role.

John Kennedy went on about civil rights, saying, "We're going to have to change the climate in this country. And if my administration does the things I want it to do, I'm going to have to be able to have someone as attorney general to carry these things out on whom I can rely completely. I can do that with Bobby."[8] Indeed, having Robert Kennedy in that role would lend more credibility to the use of the Justice Department in matters of civil rights. JFK said, "When these civil rights problems come up, if my Administration takes the rap for it, I want to know why we took the rap for it if there's a rap to take. And with Bobby there I can count on him completely."[9] JFK then turned to his brother, saying, "You know that, Bobby. You remember that." Despite Robert Kennedy's insistence on thinking about it further, JFK said to his thirty-four-year-old brother, "Well, let's go out and announce it."[10]

Since the issue of nepotism was an obvious concern, Ben Bradlee of *Newsweek* asked how President-elect Kennedy was going to make the announcement about his brother being attorney general. Kennedy replied, "Well, I think I'll open the front door of the Georgetown house some morning about 2:00 A.M., look up and down the street, and if there's no one there, I'll whisper 'It's Bobby.'"[11] Robert Kennedy left and came back to the N Street home later in the day, and the announcement was made at noon. Before they went outside the older Kennedy asked Bobby to brush his hair.[12] On the porch of the apartment, with the sun glaring off the snowy landscape, John Kennedy announced that he had made his younger brother attorney general.[13] Robert Kennedy remembered his brother saying to him as they went outside, "Don't smile too much, or they'll think we're happy about the appointment."[14] It was unprecedented in United States for a brother to serve a president in a cabinet position. Robert Kennedy took on a role that would define his place within history.

After being thrust into the role of attorney general, Robert Kennedy needed to address the growing issues in American domestic policy. With regard to civil rights, RFK had a great deal of license to do whatever he thought was necessary to uphold the law. RFK was quoted in a *Look* magazine article from March 1961, saying, "My fundamental belief was that all people are created equal. Logically it follows that integration should take place today everywhere." He went on to say, "Other people have grown up with totally different backgrounds and mores, which we can't change overnight."[15] This pragmatic approach was typical of the Kennedy style in government. It was the same realpolitik that JFK used in foreign affairs. It helped the Cabinet see the issues as they were, not as they thought they should be. That was an effective tool when dealing with racism and segregation. If Kennedy wanted to make real change — not a token gesture — he needed to acknowledge the views of others. However, he also needed to challenge those social norms. RFK was the person who JFK hoped could usher in this change. They hoped it would protect him in the South for the 1964 election. However, as the administration progressed many in the South saw them as the Kennedy brothers, not making a distinction between the two, which made it difficult for John Kennedy to distance himself from any legislation in the South.

Much like the Rackets Committee, John and Robert Kennedy were seen as a united force in domestic issues. Robert Kennedy said,

> I suppose in 19—1962 or end of 1962 or 1963, instead of talking about Robert Kennedy, they started talking about the Kennedy brothers, which he used to point out to me frequently; that it was no longer the ... attorney general, but now they were talking about the Kennedy brothers.... By 1963 it was focused on the both of us, and that caused a lot of problems politically as we got ready for the election."[16]

Politics was at the heart of the civil rights movement, but as the Kennedys looked to shape a new world in the South and elsewhere, they became entwined with the movement, changing it to a moral issue. This association by 1963 made it difficult for them to work with the deep Southern Democrats within the party, paving the way to larger issues that they would have to confront in the election of 1964. The Kennedy brothers relied on each other to do the right thing politically and morally. Unfortunately, throughout American history, those things were not always synonymous.

Despite the political pressure, President Kennedy was committed to civil rights. "I would say, as I just have to keep going back to the point, that there was a good deal of feeling on the part of President Kennedy about helping those who were helpless," Robert Kennedy said.[17] It seems that Robert Kennedy argued JFK had always intended to make a difference in civil rights. However, the Kennedy brothers knew that if they came in with a strong liberal agenda and immediately tried to integrate the South, they would fall short. They needed to wait for the right time. Eventually Birmingham gave them that chance in 1963. But from 1961 to that point, they needed to be careful about how they approached this topic. In short, the Kennedys had every intention to make an impact on civil rights; they just needed the right event to propel their ideas to the nation.

John F. Kennedy was hands off in his approach to civil rights, giving Bobby a lot of power to develop his own policy: "[JFK] could reach his own conclusion." According to Robert Kennedy, "He didn't have to have the attorney general call and tell him what was bad and what was good."[18] John and Robert Kennedy pushed the envelope for change in this country. They helped each other in different ways, John Kennedy gave his brother political capital unlike any other attorney general in history. Robert Kennedy gave his brother some political cover, with his reputation for impetuous decisions. In an effort to usher in change, both wanted to challenge the old school of thought. Their relationship was a part of the political maneuvering necessary for such change.

While politics remained an obstacle for strong civil rights legislation, the Kennedys were committed to navigating such legislation through those impediments, not to change the system overnight, but to lay the foundation for future endeavors. Arthur Schlesinger argues that RFK "saw civil rights in 1961 as an issue in the middle distance, morally invincible but filled for the moment with operational difficulty." Schlesinger went on to say that RFK "did not see racial injustice as the urgent American problem, as the contradiction, now at last intolerable, between the theory and the practice of the republic."[19] At first, this was not at the top of the list of issues the Justice Department was battling. The approach was limited in those early days to voting and judicial appointments. Further, RFK would eventually become deeply involved in foreign policy.

The Bay of Pigs brought Robert Kennedy even closer to the decision making process. There is a lot to consider when looking at the Kennedys and civil rights. How did they view it in political terms versus natural rights? Theoretically, the Constitution and the Declaration of Independence were crafted to establish an egalitarian society, predicated upon the idea that all Americans had equal chances at social mobility. That was not the case in 1961, nor has it ever necessarily been the case. Schlesinger goes on to argue, "The Kennedys were abstractly in favor of equal opportunity. But it took presidential policies to involve them with the movement; and then the prospect of responsibility to think about the problem."[20] In fact, while the Kennedys were somewhat reactive to different crises, they were setting the stage for larger gains in civil rights. Their methods were deceptive in foreign affairs, utilizing back-channels and unorthodox methods when trying to solve problems. With civil rights, however, there were issues to contemplate other than prestige abroad. The issue of race had been at the heart of American history since the first slave ship docked at Jamestown in 1619. The sit-in movement made it clear that things needed to change in America. African Americans were inspired by themselves and the lofty rhetoric of the New Frontier.

Robert Kennedy took a clear, direct leadership role in civil rights. While he was given a great deal of autonomy, he still answered to his brother. "I must have kept him advised," Robert Kennedy said, "but I think that it was just understood by us, which was always understood, that I have ... my area of responsibility, and then I'd do it. And if there was a problem where he should be kept advised, then I'd let him know — or where I have to have his ideas of which way to proceed."[21] Robert Kennedy had the implicit trust of his brother on domestic matters. While JFK would eventually look to his brother for advice on foreign policy, it was always in conjunction with others. JFK wanted to be his own secretary of state. However, Bobby had a virtual blank check when dealing with issues like civil rights. He shaped the policy in his brother's name, and had great power over the outcome.

James Hilty argued that Robert Kennedy had a greater respect and determination for the civil rights cause than his brother. "Robert ... conveyed a greater, more genuine sense of indignation and moral outrage over America's social problems while his brother was still alive, and he later broke new ground for the Kennedys by directly advocating for causes of the disadvantaged and underrepresented."[22] Over time, Robert Kennedy found his voice and used his office to help the oppressed. In addition, Kennedy had the great benefit of events unfolding around him, spawned by some of his rhetoric, that shaped the remainder of the century. However, without the rights-conscious people of the 1960s, the Kennedys would not have been able to make such lofty strides in civil rights, nor would the leaders of the movement have gotten such tolerance from Americans as they pursued their agendas.

Robert Kennedy's success was partially owed to the American people. That said, the Kennedys, King and others cultivated an atmosphere where anything was possible and people remained open to change. Hilty argues, "Robert Kennedy left a remarkably distinguished record as attorney general, especially considering the criticisms he and his brother endured over the appointment and the many responsibilities he accepted."[23] Hilty went further and argued, "His direct involvement in advocating (reluctantly at first) the moral and legal dimensions of the civil rights movement molded the course of events in the 1960s."[24] RFK did a great deal in making the plight of civil rights workers known to the nation. Hilty's argument speaks to the evolution of Kennedy's social conscience and how that evolution played a role in civil rights.

Evan Thomas argues that Robert Kennedy "was not the spoiled rich boy he might have been. Rather he showed a genuine curiosity about, and nascent concern for the less fortunate. More easily than his princely siblings, he could identify with working people."[25] Robert Kennedy evolved differently than JFK. In some ways he needed to prove himself not only to his family but also to himself. His cause was one of empathy and moral integrity. Despite constant criticism from those Kennedy was trying to help, he truly wanted to make a difference for those who did not have the same advantages that he had. His reaction in the Bunche episode, while in law school, for example, is consistent with how he reacted to King's denial of bail. Though reluctant at first, Robert Kennedy was very concerned with leaving a lasting legacy. His work on the McCarthy and Rackets committees showed that he was committed to causes, giving his best efforts amidst criticism from his family, peers and the press. He was the perfect person to lead this movement for change. In addition to his tenacious spirit and staunch determination, Robert Kennedy's choices for the Justice Department demonstrated that he was ready to confront any obstacles with as many legal tools as possible.

"I think he had in mind bringing in the best people possible."

Robert Kennedy needed people to help him "change the climate" of the nation, as his brother said the morning he pushed for Bobby to take the office of attorney general. There were many people at the Department of Justice who made a difference in the civil rights movement. Byron White, future justice of the Supreme Court, had a huge influence on these appointees. Through the Rackets Committee, Robert Kennedy met Edwin Guthman (his future press aide), Pierre Salinger (future press secretary to his brother) and John Seigenthaler. Thomas writes, "Robert Kennedy first impressed lawyer and civil rights activist Harris Wofford as 'an arrogant, narrow, rude young man.' In a word 'insufferable.'"[26] RFK took time to discover his place in the administration, and his actions to protect his brother may have caused some issues among others who served JFK. Wofford's description was not the only one that portrayed him in a bad light. However, this characterization spoke of only one facet of his personality and not a deeper understanding of the man.

Robert Kennedy's fierce loyalty to his brother coupled with his competitive nature brought out a ruthless, unnatural quality. He was unwilling to hurt his brother in any way. This aspect of his personality and an unwillingness to back down in the face of adversity was something that would prove to be a major asset in the civil rights movement. While Robert Kennedy had Kenny O'Donnell, Guthman and Salinger, who helped with the campaign, and was comfortable with them, he recognized that he needed experts in law and civil rights to make a difference.

John Seigenthaler, a Southerner and reporter for the *Tennessean*, had known Robert Kennedy for some time. Seigenthaler's presence at that breakfast is evidence of Kennedy's comfort with him and also speaks to the trust both Kennedys had in the man. He would serve as administrative assistant to the attorney general in 1961, at the outset of the administration. Burke Marshall, a lawyer suggested by Byron White, would be appointed assistant attorney general in 1961, serving Robert Kennedy for the duration of his time in the Justice Department. Harris Wofford, friend and counsel to Dr. Martin Luther King, Jr., had played a role in focusing the message for the campaign with regard to civil rights. He was appointed as special assistant to the president on civil rights. Though Wofford did not serve Robert Kennedy, he did play a role in civil rights issues in 1961, only to go on and assist with the creation and implementation of the Peace Corps. These three men gave considerable insight into the inner workings of the administration when it came to civil rights issues. Their actions and advice in that first year paved the foundation for other difficult issues that the administration would confront.

Seigenthaler said in 1966 that Robert Kennedy planned to change things in the Justice Department: "I don't think it was clearly defined or spelled out, but I think he had in mind bringing in the best people possible."[27] Robert Kennedy remarked later, "Harris Wofford was very emotionally involved in all of these matters and was rather, as I say, was rather in some areas a slight madman."[28] Like the civil rights leaders, Wofford wanted change quickly. He did not want to practice the realpolitik that the Kennedys were famous for. Moreover, he needed to maintain strong relationships with civil rights leaders and any acquiescence would be tantamount to failure, losing him credibility. That said, it hurt what role he would play in the administration. The pragmatic Kennedy did not want an emotional civil rights zealot running the show. He wanted level headed, legally minded people to promote his agenda.

Robert Kennedy said of Wofford: "I didn't want to have someone in the civil rights division who was dealing not from fact but was dealing from emotion ... and who wasn't going to give what was in the best interest of President Kennedy."[29] Wofford in RFK's opinion was not rational enough to lead the civil rights division of the Justice Department. To be successful in this endeavor, Robert Kennedy intended to use the letter of the law in supporting the efforts of civil rights leaders. He may have been furious with Sargent Shriver for suggesting that JFK call Coretta Scott King, but when he looked at the facts of the case and applied his legal mind, Robert Kennedy recognized the injustice within the situation and went on to correct it. This mentality was at the heart of his approach to civil rights issues. He looked for others with the same sensible, legal approach to these problems. Byron White suggested Burke Marshall head the civil right division. RFK said that he "wanted a very good lawyer and somebody also who had some feeling about this and knew something about it."[30] Burke Marshall would play a large role in the formation of civil rights policy for the Kennedy White House. He was, in many ways, one of the foot soldiers who put himself on the line to make a difference in the war against racism. Seigenthaler said that Burke Marshall "was a man of steel. He had more guts and more ingenuity than any man I met in the Kennedy Administration — and extremely good judgment."[31]

Burke Marshall graduated from Yale Law School in 1951. He worked for the law firm of Covington and Burling out of Washington, specializing in antitrust law. Carl Brauer writes, "Personally he was very interested in civil rights problems."[32] Brauer writes that at first, Kennedy almost rejected Marshall in that role: "The soft spoken, taciturn corporate lawyer had failed to make a favorable impression on the equally reticent Kennedy."[33] Seigenthaler remembered, "Burke Marshall was terribly nervous. I thought he was nervous. He kept getting up and walking around."[34] Despite his nervousness, Marshall got the job. Robert Kennedy and Burke Marshall had a friendship that would last until Kennedy's death in 1968. They worked together, tirelessly, to confront violations of civil rights law. Marshall and Seigenthaler were joined by others as foot soldiers for the Justice Department. In his oral history interview John Seigenthaler was asked about a drawing of the Justice Department, which hung over his door, with an inscription from Robert Kennedy. It said, "We happy few." Robert Kennedy had given it to members of the Justice Department as a Christmas gift in 1963, the year his brother was assassinated. It pointed to a passage in Shakespeare's *Henry V*, "We few, we happy few, we band of brothers." Seigenthaler remembered, "It was the feeling, I thought, and not just in the Justice Department. It was the feeling, really, throughout the Administration among those who really were a part, felt a part."[35] This feeling was a pervasive factor not only in the Justice Department; it also played a role in the student movements as well as other, similar movements during the sixties.

"...he intends to use the weight of his office..."

As the Justice Department found its voice and direction under the leadership of Robert Kennedy, Martin Luther King, Jr., and SNCC were forming an alliance that would change the civil rights movement. King's efforts to embrace the sit-in movement had a huge impact on how people saw the SNCC. In addition, like the Justice Department, there were people coming of age from obscure places that would soon be household names, shaping a new political discourse surrounding civil rights. Two days before the election, King was interviewed on the radio and said, "My only concern is that we solve this problem of racial injustice, which, to my mind, is one of the most difficult, if not the most difficult, problems facing our nation today."[36] He goes to say, "I don't think President Eisenhower has given the leadership that this great problem demands. I am absolutely convinced that if we had had a very strong man in the White House on this issue many of the problems and even the tensions that we face in the South at this time would not exist."[37] When asked about John Kennedy, King responded,

> I don't know how much Senator Kennedy would do, but I'm sure he would take a pretty forthright position. I have talked with Senator Kennedy twice since the nomination about civil rights, and I was very impressed with his intelligence and, on this problem, his understanding of the problem and his honesty in discussing it, and I think he would take a pretty forthright position. He doesn't hide it; he's made it clear in the campaign that there is a great deal that the president can do and that he intends to use the weight of his office to get behind the struggle for civil rights and to mobilize forces in the nation for implementation of the Supreme Court's decision on desegregation.[38]

King's reference to his meetings with Kennedy and the rhetoric of the campaign demonstrates just how much Kennedy worked at maintaining an image and perception that he was a champion of civil rights. King thought that he would take a "forthright position" using the "weight of his office." King was not one to pay any politician lip service. Kennedy's call to Coretta and his efforts to assist King's release had clearly made an impression. King expected Kennedy to take a stand and pave the way for new civil rights legislation. Based on his remarks, King was not happy with Eisenhower's efforts in civil rights. He did not say too much about Nixon, which implied that he was not as interested or impressed with him. Also, given the fact that he was so unimpressed with Eisenhower, one can assume that he felt the same about his vice president.

On November 13, 1960, in the wake of the election, King took questions at Cornell University discussing the results of the election. "I have spoken to Senator Kennedy and I am very impressed with his grasp of the problem," King said when asked whether there would be an impact on the south. "I will be very disappointed if he does not take a forthright stand in this field. I am sure that we will have stronger action in his administration than we have had in the past eight years."[39] King believed that Kennedy was going to act and was hopeful on the prospects of what could happen in the south: "I think that desegregation, which is not necessarily integration, will be a reality in most of the South, certainly the urban areas, in less than ten or twelve years. And by desegregation I mean a breakdown of all legal barriers."[40] Clearly King saw this as a watershed moment. It was, in fact, a true test of character for both leaders. King put his trust in the Kennedys. He had not done that with any other political leader. These are important comments. King was not trying to *work* with who was in office, he *believed* in the person who held the office. Kennedy, on the other hand, needed to move on these issues. Inaction would only damage the trust King had in the president. If JFK was going to change the climate of the nation he needed King. Conversely, Kennedy was King's greatest opportunity to challenge the status quo. King was poised to use his new organization, the Southern Christian Leadership Conference (SCLC) as a way to push for change in America.

The SCLC was born from the turmoil that followed the Montgomery Bus Boycott. King was dealing with a great many issues including dissension in the ranks of the Montgomery Improvement Association (MIA). Some in the group, especially E.D. Nixon, felt that King was getting too much praise. Nixon even considered resigning from his post.[41] Bayard Rustin wanted to get a larger group together. He hoped that the momentum from the boycott would carry over into a larger movement, involving many from the South. King's leadership evolved, becoming a major force in the nation. He said that if anyone had asked him to lead this movement a year before, he "would have run a mile to get away from it." He went on to say that when he was involved in the boycott, he "realized that the choice leaves your own hands. People expect you to give them leadership ... you can't decide whether to stay in it or get out of it, you must stay in it."[42] The Southern Negro Leaders Conference on Transportation and Nonviolent Integration (as it was originally called) came from the Montgomery Bus Boycott in the hopes of continuing solid leadership in the South. However, the conference, which met in January 1957, was interrupted when King and Abernathy were recalled to Montgomery to address bombings in the community, which had destroyed much of Abernathy's church. King and Abernathy's lack of influence, due to their absence, hurt the conference's aims. However, they returned toward the end and spoke with the press, saying that they would continue to meet.[43]

There was more violence against King as well as internal conflict. Ultimately, King adopted the name Southern Christian Leadership Conference by the end of the third meeting. During this meeting, held in Montgomery in August 1957, the group determined the new name and started what they called the Crusade for Citizenship. The effort was a plan for large scale voter registration. This operation would cost $200,000, taking up a great deal of time and energy. Roy Wilkins, the president of the NAACP, was upset when he heard of the initiative, telling many in the organization not to participate in the project.[44] It is another example of the tension within the movement over what was the best way to push for integration. Also, it illuminates how many African American leaders struggled to accept King as the new leader for his generation. By the end of 1959, King realized that he needed to streamline how he would be involved in the movement. He moved to Atlanta and worked to bring the SCLC into the national spotlight.

"Through nonviolence, courage displaces fear; love transforms hate."

The SNCC came of age while many students were trying to find their voice in the rights protests of 1960. On April 16, 1960, members of the group met in Raleigh, North

Carolina. This conference was meant to craft the message and infrastructure of the organization. Clayborne Carson argues that Ella Baker, an executive director of the SCLC, and the person who called the conference, "understood the psychological need of student activists to remain independent of adult control [and] resisted efforts to subvert their autonomy."[45] According to Carson, Baker figured that these new, young leaders had little preparation to take on the roles and responsibilities that were suddenly a big part of their lives.[46] The purpose of the meeting, according to Baker, was to achieve "a more unified sense of direction for the training and action of nonviolent resistance." The conference attracted approximately 120 students from 56 different college and high schools. The SCLC and the Congress of Racial Equality (CORE) were among the many other groups in attendance.[47] Perhaps the strongest link between the SCLC and the rise of the SNCC was the presence of Dr. King. King was highly respected among the students in attendance. Beyond his physical attendance, King's philosophy reverberated throughout the SNCC and became a pervasive force in its core ideology. His presence, however, also contributed to the tension between the two organizations, as there was pressure to determine what role the SCLC would play in the leadership of this student led movement.

It was at the Raleigh convention that the "Boy from Troy," as King once called Lewis, was thrown into the leadership role he wanted so badly. The Nashville delegation was the largest group there. In addition to Lewis, James Lawson and James Bevel were among this delegation. Diane Nash and Marion Barry came from Fisk University, also located in Nashville. All of them would play a large role in the years to come in influencing how the movement would progress. Jane Stembridge, who was recruited by Baker, said of the conference, "The most inspiring moment for me was the first time I heard the students sing 'We Shall Overcome.' It was inspiring because it was the beginning, and because in a sense, it was the purest moment."[48] These students were asserting to themselves and the rest of the world that they had a voice and intended to use it for change. They were not always embraced by the leaders of the movement, but there were some leaders already among them who would stand up and set forth their own, distinct philosophy. The Kennedy brothers responded to the young voices when pressured to act in various situations. These students, in turn, were empowered by Kennedy's rhetoric of hope and change. Whether they intended to or not, the Kennedys were partially responsible for movements that would continue beyond their time in the White House.

Despite the fact that a very influential thirty-one-year-old Martin Luther King, Jr., was at the conference, in many ways it was James Lawson who stole the show. Clayborne Carson writes, "Lawson expressed a visionary set of ideas that distinguished the student activists both from the rest of society and from more moderate civil rights leaders." Lawson stressed the moral and spiritual issues behind the protests, further strengthening SNCC's distinction in the movement. In fact, he criticized the NAACP for their focus on fund raising and legal action.[49] The SNCC's statement of purpose is evidence of Lawson's influence within the organization. The first line of the statement reads: "We affirm the philosophical or religious ideal of nonviolence as the foundation of our purpose, the presupposition of our faith, and the manner of our action." Embracing nonviolence as a tactic not only demonstrated their commitment to that tactic, but also paid respect to King's efforts in Montgomery. His acceptance of that tactic speaks to King's overwhelming influence on the movement. The statement went on to say, "Through nonviolence, courage displaces fear; love transforms hate. Acceptance dissipates prejudice; hope ends despair. Peace dominates war; faith reconciles doubt."[50]

It went on to focus on love, saying, "Love is the central motif of nonviolence. Love is the force by which God binds man to Himself and man to man." Love was at the heart of Dr. King's message on his porch after his house was bombed in the midst of the bus boycott. Love was an important ideal in this war, and it served not only the SNCC but also the SCLC. In many ways it was the motif that bound the two organizations together philosophically. The statement of purpose ended with the following: "By appealing to conscience and standing on the moral nature of human existence, nonviolence nurtures the atmosphere in which reconciliation and justice become actual possibilities."[51] Lawson's ideas were now the philosophical foundation for the group. The Nashville delegation maintained its influence as Marion Barry was elected as the first chair of the organization. Carson writes, "The Raleigh conference represented the peak of influence within the SNCC for Lawson and his Nashville group."[52] These students were starting a new form of protest that would have overwhelming effects on the rest of the decade.

The SCLC and the SNCC were kindred spirits in how they wanted to fight segregation. They both embraced nonviolence and Judeo-Christian traditions as a weapon to fight hate. In addition, the concept of love was the heart of where their energy came from. They linked this concept of love to God, creating a deeper, more meaningful type of love that was divine in its influence. That was a powerful motivator for young students who had cigarette butts put out on their backs while sitting at lunch counters. That said, there was tension between the two organizations. Howard Zinn writes that the cause for that tension was whether the SNCC was going to have an official connection to the SCLC. Despite their common approach and King's embracing of the student's work, the SNCC decided to remain independent but maintain a friendly relationship with the SCLC.[53] The major difference between the organizations was that the SNCC had a different perspective as students. They were inspired by men like Martin Luther King, Jr., but in a larger sense wanted to distinguish themselves to the world and carve out their own place in the movement. That was the largest dividing issue and, perhaps, the group's greatest strength, for that drive to demonstrate to the world that they were a force in this movement would not only reap great benefits for themselves, but also inspire other groups to make similar contributions as the truculent decade marched on into other rights issues and Vietnam.

As 1960 came to a close, all the major players in this struggle for equality were ready to test whether their ideology would triumph. The Kennedys put the finishing touches on the administration that would enact New Frontier ideals. King created a group distinct from the Montgomery Improvement Association, embraced a new president-elect and started to show the world that he was the leader of the civil rights movement. Finally, students of the age organized in a cohesive unit with a clear, thought-out philosophy. All three groups were ready for change. None of them were ready for what was about to happen. Nineteen sixty-one would prove to be a year of action by civil rights leaders, and the United States government had no choice but to respond with subsequent action to maintain equality under the law. These instances played a role in setting up the rest of the Kennedy presidency and how the Kennedys would reply to other civil rights issues during their tenure in the Oval Office. The Kennedys were getting ready to promote their agenda to Congress, King was preparing to push his initiatives forward, and the SNCC worked with another civil rights group, which had been challenging the system since the end of World War II, paving the way for a movement on the roads of America. Nineteen sixty was a year when the people who would push for a new America found their voice, leading to inevitable action on the part of all of them.

PART II : 1961— ACTION
Freedom Rides and the Vote

4. Soldiers for Justice

"...unwilling to witness or permit the slow undoing of those human rights..."

John Kennedy made an indelible mark on history with his inaugural address. Theodore Sorensen's prose coupled with JFK's delivery created what has been lauded by many as one of the greatest addresses in modern times. The speech spoke to grand ideas and lofty goals for this Boston Brahim and his Irish Mafia, as they were called. Theodore Sorensen wrote, "JFK's inaugural helped to change America." While Sorensen was the main architect of the rhetoric and his opinion is somewhat biased, Kennedy's speech did have a tone that set the stage for the issues the nation was about to confront. "The inaugural," wrote Sorensen, "fulfilled Kennedy's purpose and hopes, transforming the perception of him from a young president elected by the narrowest possible margin to a confident leader hailed by world statesmen and by elders of his own party."[1] However, one thing was missing from the epic speech. With all its hope and grandeur, there was no outright mention of civil rights. The speech was inspiring and led many Americans to embrace the ideals embodied within it. Parts of it are often quoted by politicians and leaders around the world. It was mainly a speech about foreign policy and the Cold War, which was what Kennedy wanted to confront. The largest domestic problem at the time was civil rights, so there should have been something to demonstrate to the people what Kennedy planned to do about the issue.

If Kennedy planned on changing the "climate" of the nation, as he said to Robert Kennedy, it would have made sense to outline how he planned to do that in the inaugural address. In fact, Kennedy wanted to focus on foreign policy due to the partisanship and divisiveness so pervasive in domestic policy.[2] On January 20, 1961, Kennedy looked out at the crowd on the cold, brisk day and said,

> Let the word go forth from this time and place, to friend and foe alike, that the torch has been passed to a new generation of Americans — born in this century, tempered by war, disciplined by a hard and bitter peace, proud of our ancient heritage — and unwilling to witness or permit the slow undoing of those human rights to which this nation has always been committed, and to which we are committed today at home and around the world.

This line in Kennedy's inaugural speaks to two very important themes relevant to the civil rights movement. First, when Kennedy mentioned "human rights" it was Harris Wofford and Louis Martin who were able to get the phrase "at home and around the world" put into the speech.[3] It was essential that Kennedy recognize the need to address human rights violations in the South, but he also needed to stay focused and avoid the partisanship that came with domestic issues to start his administration. Second, his reference of passing the torch to "a new generation of Americans" had a great deal of symbolism that many in the country defined as their own. In fact many in the civil rights movement took that line as a reference to their cause. The next line invoked a theme of liberty and freedom that this "new generation of Americans" was meant to maintain.

After applause Kennedy continued with his historic speech. In the very next line after discussing human rights, Kennedy said, "Let every nation know, whether it wishes us well or ill, that we shall pay any price, bear any burden, meet any hardship, support any friend, oppose any foe to assure the survival and the success of liberty." While it was meant to strike a chord on the Cold War front, it also had reverberations at home. The themes of freedom and liberty were where many civil rights leaders found solace and proof that Kennedy was going to promote these ideas. In fact, Fred Shuttlesworth said from the pulpit of St. James Baptist Church in segregated Birmingham, "What a wonderful President we have now!"[4] John Lewis remembered watching that inaugural address with a "great sense of hope." He said,

> Here was this young, vibrant man who seemed to represent the future just by his energy and age. He didn't mention race or civil rights in his speech, but I assumed that it was simply a matter of political expediency. I believed that he believed in what we all believed in — the Beloved Community.[5]

The speech meant a great deal to the nation and history. It spoke to the future, enlightening Americans, helping others see JFK's vision. It became a lightning rod for many in the civil rights movement despite the fact that it did not mention civil rights directly.

Kennedy's inaugural address was an important jumping board for the change that would come in the sixties. The pressures of the Cold War forced Kennedy's hand in those thousand days in office. On the domestic front it gave people a mission statement for how the government planned to lead. JFK was different than previous presidents. Despite his extreme wealth many Americans related to the president and listened to his call to service. That difference helped Americans envision a new America, which led to stronger leadership at all levels of society. Kennedy wanted to keep the initiatives, ideas and aspirations moving, so he followed up the inaugural with a very strong State of the Union address on January 30, 1961. In that speech JFK states that there were many problems that the nation needed to fix. He said, "I speak today in an hour of national peril and national opportunity. Before my term has ended, we shall have to test anew whether a nation organized and governed such as ours can endure." He invoked the Gettysburg address, implying that the issues they feared were as great those during as the Civil War. He emphasized the importance of his job as president and that he was going to need Congress to act and fix the issues that the United States was presented with. Among the many items that he brought to the discourse, JFK acknowledged that there was a racial disparity in the United States. "The denial of constitutional rights to some of our fellow Americans on account of race — at the ballot box and elsewhere," he said, "disturbs the national conscience, and subjects us to the charge of world opinion that our democracy is not equal to the high promise of our heritage."[6]

While it was not the far-reaching policy that many civil rights advocates clamored for, it was a start to discuss these issues. It was also JFK's way to signal to Americans that change was on the horizon. Kennedy linked the racial issues of the country to world prestige. Indeed, that had a pervasive and powerful tone to combat this issue and get people on board for change. In fact, he argued, it was linked to the survival of what the founders had intended America to become.

By invoking national heritage and listing racial discrimination among the ailments of the republic, JFK propelled the racial issues of the nation into the national spotlight. Further, he emboldened civil rights leaders throughout the nation to take action. While these are small pieces of two larger speeches, they represent how Kennedy planned to attack the racial issue. Like Lincoln, the Kennedys knew that if they tried to attack civil rights at the outset they could lose the support of the people. Incremental change was the only way to approach such a heated and difficult topic in American history. These speeches, however, in those first ten days of the administration, were not going to be the way JFK would affect the racial divide in the country. He needed people in the field to lead the way. He needed soldiers.

"And then one day I got a telephone call from Mr. Kennedy."

On March 6, 1961, John Kennedy signed Executive Order 10925, establishing the president's committee on Equal Employment Opportunity. This was the precursor to what is commonly referred to as affirmative action.[7] In the wake of a contentious election, Kennedy had the hopes of many African Americans riding on the aspirations of his administration. Hugh Davis Graham argues, "The emotional core of the long campaign lay not in the cold war abstractions and alleged missile gaps, but in the newly explosive issue of civil rights."[8] James Giglio argues that no domestic issue occupied the presidency more than civil rights, but that "Kennedy had intended to effect racial advances gradually, smoothly, and with a minimum of conflict." Civil rights leaders had another idea and wanted Kennedy to engage immediately. Giglio writes that Kennedy's responses to the civil rights issues he was confronted with "disappointed many civil rights activists and latter-day scholars, but he went beyond Truman's program in helping usher in what C. Vann Woodward and others have labeled the Second Reconstruction."[9] This was an extraordinary time in American history where there was an opportunity to banish Jim Crow from the South. Kennedy had intended to play a role in that transformation, but it was not an easy task.

This executive order, at the time, was not the splash that many African American leaders wanted, nor was it the "stroke of the pen" Kennedy claimed he would make for housing during the campaign. In the 1960 campaign Kennedy told crowds that he would eliminate discrimination in federal housing with an executive order. This was not in line with his campaign rhetoric. Nevertheless, it was evidence that the administration was acknowledging a way to make a difference. However, Graham argues that this gesture was weak considering the momentous issue of civil rights in the early sixties. He writes, "It appeared to be little more than a sincere but weak gesture by a president who believed he could not get any significant civil rights legislation through the congress, and who therefore was unwilling even to try, lest he roil the congress and threaten his higher priorities."[10] While it may have been a "weak gesture," Kennedy was a president who in that first year acknowledged that he was elected without a majority of the electorate. However, Kennedy sent someone who could get things done in congress to head this commission.

To show he meant what he said, Kennedy assigned Vice President Lyndon Johnson to the committee. Johnson had a reputation for getting legislation passed through Congress. Despite that talent, Johnson tried on several occasions to get out of the commission, knowing that there could be political ramifications. In February 1961, before the order was signed, Johnson had his staff draft a letter to the president explaining that his office was not equipped to handle the matter.[11] It is interesting that Johnson gets a good deal of credit for the passage of the Civil Rights Act of 1964 from many historians. His reluctance to take on the commission points not only to his evolution within this aspect of politics, but also the Kennedy brothers' determination to make it a relevant topic. In fact Johnson was afraid of civil rights in 1961 and wanted to distance himself from any civil rights initiative. Only after the Kennedys took a stand on several instances was the political climate such that politicians like Johnson could take such a risk in front of the nation.

Nicholas deBelleville Katzenbach, who would play a large role in civil rights, was working for the Office of Legal Counsel for the Justice Department. He had spent a great deal of time working on the Equal Employment Opportunity executive order and brought it to Robert Kennedy, who was having dinner at his house on Hickory Hill with the president and Lem Billings. Katzenbach gave the order to Robert Kennedy and said, "You've got to sign this and give it to the President." The younger Kennedy was unaware of the order, but the president interrupted and asked Katzenbach, "Did you get that Section, 305 I think it is, worked out with the Vice President? Is that satisfactory to him now?" Since he was going to play such a prominent role in the order, Johnson took some interest in its language. Robert Kennedy had not been informed about his role in this and said to John Kennedy, "Well, I don't know [why] the hell I sign this thing and give it to you. Why don't you sign it and give it to me?"[12] Though it may have been a "weak" gesture in some ways, the order did pave the way for future change in civil rights.

Beyond taking executive action, Kennedy needed to pursue lawsuits to investigate civil rights violations. He needed people in the field who could accomplish this task. Burke Marshall was one of those soldiers Kennedy needed and was ready to make a difference in the civil rights movement. Marshall had a respect for the law and understood that in order to broker change of any magnitude he needed to base those changes on something with precedent. This acute, logical legal mind was exactly what Bobby Kennedy was looking for to combat the racial strife in the nation, which was why he stayed away from the emotionally invested Wofford. Robert Kennedy and Marshall were on the same page for what needed to be done to change the nation. Marshall remembered, "I had a meeting with him and we went over this problem [of racial issues], and it was apparent within five minutes after you got in this office there hadn't been any effort made to enforce the voting laws by that time."[13] The lack of action by Eisenhower was a big problem for the New Frontier.

Desegregation of the school system in the South was a paramount issue when Bobby Kennedy started in the Justice Department. The foundation for most civil rights action was the *Brown v. Board of Education* decision. It was important that the Justice Department maintain a strong position on that decision. If they were going to use the law, then they needed to acknowledge past precedent and force the South to do the same. Kennedy looked to New Orleans as a test case to challenge Jim Crow laws. Judge Skelly Wright had made his own decision on how to desegregate a school in New Orleans, which was in contrast to other districts in Louisiana as well as other states in the South. In an interview in 1964 Marshall said that the situation gave black children the chance in the first grade to choose whether they wanted to go to a closer school or one they would be assigned to. Wright then asked for assistance from the U.S. Marshals in enforcing the order. The main issue before RFK was whether the Department of Justice was going to enforce desegregation. According to Marshall: "The fact is, it never had before."[14] By challenging the climate in the South the Kennedy administration was already different, even radical, setting the foundation for future leaders and movements. These leaders were courageous as they risked their political reputations when very few, if any at all, were doing the same. Instead many, including Johnson, looked for cover from potential political harm. This seems to be the essence of where the Kennedys made a difference in civil rights law. They were treading into uncharted territory, laying the groundwork for future generations.

According to Robert Kennedy, when it came to confronting desegregation there was no cabinet meeting or grand scheme: "It's just the logical thing to do. The United States government couldn't back down." With regard to the Louisiana case, the main discussion centered around putting people in jail for contempt. It doesn't seem that Robert Kennedy and John Kennedy went into the situation without any thought of backing down. The brothers were pragmatic to a point. They really wanted to challenge the status quo and force systemic change. In fact, they surrounded themselves with people who would look at these issues logically — determining the fair use of the law in each circumstance. RFK said in his interview: "I remember there were a lot of different questions as we went along.... And then, eventually, it worked out, and these people backed down. But it was a difficult period, and, I think, rather an interesting period."[15] It was also a very dangerous period, fraught with people who were violent and steadfast in maintaining their position in the tiered society that had had its foundation in the wake of the Civil War. Resolve and perseverance played a role with both the civil rights leaders and the Justice Department. Each side needed to be able to look down dangerous, ignorant people in the hopes of surviving to make the nation better for all its people.

John Kennedy was very supportive of the Justice Department in its efforts to desegregate the schools in New Orleans. Marshall remembered, "It was a matter of a lot of public discussion not only in Louisiana, but up here in Washington at the time, and so [RFK] must have discussed it with the president. In any event he didn't hesitate, and therefore I assumed, and I'm sure rightly, that the president didn't have any hesitation about what should be done."[16] If Kennedy was so worried about the political ramifications of standing up to segregation, it was not evident given his position on the desegregation issue in New Orleans. Part of John Kennedy's support came from wanting to do the morally right thing for the nation. The other aspect centered on the trust that he had in his brother to make the right decisions, as he had during the campaign and other times in their lives.

John and Robert Kennedy had a strong relationship that contributed to the administration's policy on civil rights. Robert Kennedy had the trust of his brother to implement whatever change he felt necessary in this realm of domestic affairs. This relationship served the Justice Department well, as it became an important arm for both the presidency and the people who needed the administration's support. The brothers' bond was not made in childhood. The trip to Europe helped them see each other in a new light, serving as a defining moment in their lives. That experience had reverberations, leading to Bobby's serving as a campaign manager for Jack's Senate seat and again for the 1960 campaign. Their bond was solidified in adulthood and entwined with politics. The two men would talk in short speak, almost code-like, in front of others. Burke Marshall recognized this special relationship between the brothers and its impact on the office of the attorney general. He argued:

> One of the essential ingredients of what's been done in this area of the past three and a half years, was the fact that the President and the Attorney General were so close that the Attorney General did not have to worry, as another Attorney General might have had to do, about checking everything out with the President and dealing with this immensely difficult, politically difficult, emotionally difficult problem, with complete confidence that he'd be backed by the White House.[17]

John and Robert Kennedy worked in tandem on domestic issues at the start of the administration. John Kennedy wanted to focus on foreign policy, which left issues like civil rights to the attorney general. Eventually Bobby would be brought in on the foreign policy issues, ushering in policies like counterinsurgency to oust Fidel Castro and weighing in during the Cuban Missile Crisis in 1962.

The difference between the two men was that JFK had other members of his advisory team to help him on foreign affairs, which demonstrates both the importance and the need to have other minds in on that battle. In addition, John Kennedy was more of a politician, while Bobby was one to consider the implication in a situation. At the Justice Department, Bobby was commander-in-chief, crafting a response-team of lawyers and advisors to address various issues. Civil rights was chief among those concerns and would be the issue that defined Bobby most while in office. He organized his group to tackle these issues. They were akin to soldiers following RFK's orders. Marshall was the second in command who pointed the soldiers toward injustice. They would make a difference in the movement that had as lasting an impact as the foreign policy issues.

John Kennedy was committed to change in America. His lofty rhetoric throughout the campaign and in the inaugural were at the heart of his policies. Many historians devalue the fact that Kennedy created a climate where change could occur. He has been lambasted as reactionary and unwilling to sacrifice political capital for broad, sweeping change in the civil rights law. One piece of evidence of John Kennedy's commitment early on in the administration is a letter he wrote to the Commission on Civil Rights on February 24, 1961. In it President Kennedy wrote, "Let me here pay tribute to these educators — principals, officers of school boards, and public school teachers. The Constitutional requirement of desegregation has presented them with many new responsibilities and hard challenges."[18]

Kennedy acknowledged the people in the trenches and how their contributions made a difference in following through with the law. In fact, his support for the actions that Burke Marshall and his brother had already taken is evident in this letter: "In New Orleans today, as in many other places represented in your three conferences, these loyal citizens and educators are meeting these responsibilities and challenges with quiet intelligence and true courage." In the same perilous tone that he had used in the State of the Union address less than a month prior, Kennedy wrote, "The whole country is in their debt for our public school system must be preserved and improved. Our very survival as a free nation depends upon it." Kennedy continued, "This is no time for schools to close for any reason, and certainly no time for schools to be closed in the name of racial discrimination. If we are to give the leadership the world requires of us, we must be true to the great principles of our Constitution — the very principles which distinguish us from our adversaries in the world."[19] Kennedy used similar imagery in the January 30 State of the Union address, which demonstrated not only his commitment to change but also his resolve to make such ideas reality. Further, it is clear from Marshall's recollections that RFK was at the forefront of this racial battle in the United States. Marshall was willing to confront the Southern status quo and wanted to make a difference in the nation. Marshall was not alone in this endeavor.

John Seigenthaler was among that group, serving the Kennedys during the campaign and the first year in the White House. He was an important asset to the administration. As a reporter for the *Nashville Tennessean* in 1956, Seigenthaler was involved in a series of articles about the Teamsters' union in Tennessee. Knowing the work of the McClellan committee and the publicized hearings that John and Robert Kennedy were involved in, Seigenthaler wanted to get them interested in his stories. In April 1957 he "went up to Columbia [University] to a seminar on investigative reporting that was held at the American Press Institute for about three weeks. And before I left there was an industrialist here in Nashville who had been at Yale with Sarge Shriver.... He, through Sarge, arranged for me to have an appointment with Bob Kennedy while I was in New York." Seigenthaler made an appointment with RFK to tell him about what the Teamsters were doing in Tennessee. He went to the appointment, received a "cool reception," and was told that Kennedy was "busy." He waited for some time until Robert Kennedy came out, greeted him and said, "How are you? I'm glad to see you. I understand you've got a bad problem down there in Tennessee."[20] Kennedy introduced Seigenthaler to his assistant and had him tell the assistant what was going on in Tennessee.

Seigenthaler went back and forth with Kennedy's assistant. He was unable to get any real time with Robert Kennedy. Kennedy's assistant kept asking for memos on the situations in Tennessee, but there was no follow up. Seigenthaler said in 1964, "I became more and more disgusted and more and more despondent about whether we were going to get the McClellan Committee involved and interested." He finally took matters a step further and contacted Senator McClellan through a mutual friend. He met with McClellan, who in turn brought Robert Kennedy to the meeting. Seigenthaler, once again, was asked to put all his information in a memo for the investigative committee. At that point it seemed that he was not going to get his story to the committee. "And then," he said, "one day I got a telephone call from Mr. Kennedy." Kennedy sent some of his men down to see Seigenthaler. "We got into the Teamsters investigation [in Tennessee]." This was where Seigenthaler developed a strong working relationship with Robert Kennedy. "After an extensive and exhaustive investigation of a period of a month we had hearings in Washington," he remembered. "And during the period of that investigation and during the hearings in Washington I got to know Bob Kennedy better and better." Those hearings brought the impeachment of a judge and dismissal of a district attorney, among others. It was a huge success and brought not only Robert Kennedy and Seigenthaler closer, but also Senator Kennedy.[21]

As the years progressed Seigenthaler got to know the Kennedys, slowly becoming a part of the inner circle. On one occasion Robert Kennedy asked Seigenthaler to bring his family and stay with the Kennedys in Washington.[22] Seigenthaler covered the Massachusetts senatorial election in 1958, while on a fellowship at Harvard. Eventually he came and worked out of Washington for the presidential campaign. "I stayed right there, operated largely by telephone with Bob. I was a clearing house for any information between Bob as he went out and made speeches and the President as he was making speeches somewhere else," he remembered.[23] Once the election was over, Seigenthaler went to work full time for Robert Kennedy as an administrative assistant to the attorney general. He remembered, "When he asked me to go to the Justice Department, again he wanted to disassociate himself from politics, insofar as he could. He wanted to put that business behind him and devote his interests and energies to being a good Attorney General."[24] Seigenthaler played a role in making sure that RFK was a good attorney general. Seigenthaler's role was an example of the Kennedy way of doing things. They brought people into their circle, developing a long lasting, familial relationship.

Both Burke Marshall and John Seigenthaler were among a group of individuals that put their lives on the line to maintain the law. At the heart of this movement was the fact that the law was being violated and it was their duty to make it right. While there were moral issues in the civil rights movement, these men did not pass judgment in that vein. Instead they used the law to confront segregation. Over time, however, it became clear that there were larger issues than the illegality behind Southern attitudes toward race. Unlike Wofford, these two men were handpicked by RFK and were a part of his entourage. They both confronted segregation in the hopes of making America a better place. Their efforts exposed the wicked aspects of Southern culture to the rest of the nation. They were committed, highly educated and loyal to the Kennedy brothers. These "new generation of Americans" were about to be tested in many ways.

"We know that if one man's rights are denied, the rights of all are endangered."

The Kennedys dealt with a great deal of turmoil in those early days of the administration. Chief among those issues was Cuba and the Bay of Pigs. John Kennedy agreed to a planned invasion of Cuba in an effort to use Cuban revolutionaries as a means to over throw Fidel Castro. The invasion took place from April 17 to 19, 1961. The Joint Chiefs of Staff, led by Chairman Lyman Lemnitzer, and the CIA, led by Director Allen Dulles, enthusiastically endorsed this operation. When it was clear that the revolutionaries would not succeed, JFK refused to give air support. Robert Kennedy had little, if any, role in the planning of this attack on Cuba. JFK originally had no intention on bringing his brother into the discussions on foreign policy. The Bay of Pigs brought him even closer to his brother. John Kennedy did not trust the principal advisors who led him into the Bay of Pigs. They were mostly men who had served his predecessor. From that point on, JFK relied on his brother and other core members of his advisory team to deal with foreign policy issues.

Like others of his generation, Robert Kennedy understood that America needed to not only preach freedom and equality but also demonstrate strong resolve in the face of injustice. The segregation policies of the South did not look good to America's enemies and were often used against them in the heated rhetoric so pervasive to the debate over communism and capitalism. Bobby Kennedy outlined not only the domestic policy of the country, but also its foreign policy. He was one of the president's closest advisors after the Bay of Pigs, serving on a Kitchen Cabinet of advisors who were close to John Kennedy.

Robert Kennedy had an enormous influence on history. His role in advising on foreign policy matters coupled with his independent handling of the Justice Department made Robert Kennedy the second most powerful man in Washington. He had a great deal of political capital, which was beneficial to any cause he felt was worthy in the civil rights movement. John Kennedy wanted to leave his mark on history through his foreign policy efforts. Robert Kennedy was given a great deal of autonomy to shape his message through the Justice Department. Anything from Bobby was considered to come from the top office.

Robert Kennedy wanted to change the nature of politics in Washington. He wanted to go outside the status quo and usher in a new era of equality. In a May 2, 1961, letter to Father Robert Drinan of the Boston College School of Law, Robert Kennedy acknowledged the lack of African American lawyers in the Justice Department. Kennedy wrote that "ability is the primary consideration." That said he went on to write, "I am anxious to take some steps to break down the barrier which apparently has existed." RFK wanted names of "qualified negro attorneys" who might want to work in the Justice Department.[25] While it may have been a small gesture, it is evidence of his willingness to go outside the normal everyday operations of the Justice Department. Kennedy wanted to make it known that he was going to change the climate of the country. He took the first opportunity to do that in one of his first speeches about the law.

In his first speech as attorney general, Robert Kennedy addressed the University of Georgia Law School on May 6, 1961—less than one month after a major foreign policy disaster and a day after the first bus of freedom riders made its way to the South, challenging segregation. The topic for RFK was Law Day. He started by saying that when JFK had proclaimed this day, he "emphasized two thoughts. He pointed out that to remain free, the people must 'cherish their freedoms, understand the responsibilities they entail, and nurture the will to preserve them.'" RFK went on to say, "The law is the strongest link between man and freedom."[26] When the founders were moved to create the United States, a government of laws was chief on their minds. Nothing less than that could avoid the tyranny they had endured from monarchy in England, thus protecting American rights and freedom. This was an important point that Kennedy made, because the law became the mainstay of how he confronted segregation in the south. At the beginning he did not try to make or create new laws. Instead, Robert Kennedy enforced the ones already in existence. It was a divergence from previous administrations.

Kennedy continued, "We know too that throughout the long history of mankind, man has had to struggle to create a system of law and of government in which fundamental freedoms would be linked with the enforcement of justice." He went on, "We know that if one man's rights are denied, the rights of all are endangered." RFK also emphasized that the courts' decisions played an integral role in maintaining these rights and freedoms. He also said that if people challenged these decisions then they "challenge the foundations of our society." This was tough talk from an attorney general, in the deep South, a place that does not like federal intervention in their affairs. Unbeknownst to Kennedy, the Freedom Rides had already begun to make the move to challenge that system and he would have an opportunity to make good on these assertions. Kennedy was using this speech to outline his goals for the Justice Department. He could not have known that he would have an opportunity to live up to it so soon. He even went so far as to link his efforts in civil rights to the Cold War saying, "The challenge which international communism hurls against the rule of law is very great."[27]

It was extraordinary that the attorney general of the United States played such a prominent role in both foreign and domestic policy. Further, it was noteworthy that this person was the thirty-six-year-old brother of the sitting president he served, had barely practiced law and was given opportunities others never had been. Kennedy said that there were three major areas within the Justice Department that "sap our national strength, that weaken our people, that require our immediate attention." The first issue he mentioned was organized crime, which he argued "knows no state laws" and "drains off millions of dollars of our national wealth." The second issue was businesses who fixed prices and cheated on taxes, "defrauding their customers and even in some instances cheat[ing] their own government."[28] He argued that if capitalism was not working properly it would serve as evidence for American enemies — most notably the Soviet Union. The third and final issue was civil rights.

Kennedy spent the majority of the time talking about civil rights. Since he was giving the speech in Georgia, a segregated system, it seemed he wanted to stress this the most of all three issues. He continued with his emphasis on the authority of the court by asserting the 1954 *Brown v. Board of Education* decision, "which required difficult local adjustments." Kennedy said that his dealings in Congress with Southern representatives made him believe that they would respect and respond to "candor and plain talk." Robert Kennedy prided himself on being "straight" with people and hoped it would serve him well here. His discussion of civil rights set the tone for how the administration would handle that issue. In every circumstance where the Kennedy administration had to respond to a civil rights issues, they used the law to support any action they decided was necessary. He said he would be candid about how the Justice Department planned on handling civil rights issues.

Already challenging the status quo and attempting to change the climate of the country, as JFK said he planned to do when they discussed Robert Kennedy becoming attorney general, RFK said, "The time has long since arrived when loyal Americans must measure the impact of their actions beyond the limits of their town or status." He said that fifty percent of the countries around the world were not white and that "people whose skins are a different color than ours are on the move to gain their measure of freedom and liberty." Bobby Kennedy invoked the plights of others around the world because it was important that the United States set the standard as the so-called leader of the free world. If other nations were throwing off the vestiges of oppression then America should be leading the way if it truly wanted to be the leader of the free world. America needed to abolish the segregation system, making it the example for others. The segregated system was not only a domestic, but also a foreign policy issue. He said, "In the United Nations we are striving to establish a rule of law instead of a rule of force. In that forum and elsewhere around the world our deeds will speak for us."[29]

In the areas of school desegregation, RFK made it clear, "We are upholding the law." He went on, "The Department of Justice will act. We will not stand by or be aloof. We will move." At the core of his thinking on any of these matters was the law. It was at the backbone of his philosophy. Even in the episode when Martin Luther King, Jr., was arrested, he was more incensed with the injustice of denying bail than he was anything else. Kennedy wasn't supporting the movement when he called the judge as much as he was questioning the justice of the situation. He wanted the law upheld first and any issue with civil rights came second. The law was a big piece of what RFK believed in, and he began his journey to embracing the movement through that. Indeed, he was a moral and just man who looked to the righteous method to solve issues. He did not want to argue anything that did not have a backing in law. If it was law, than it was clearly the right thing to do, according to Robert Kennedy. While he started with school desegregation, he quickly moved to another tenet in his philosophy on how to invoke change through securing voting rights throughout the nation.

Robert Kennedy was looking for some common ground with the South, and this was the perfect place to express those ideas. He said, "The decision in 1954 required action of the most difficult, delicate and complex nature, going to the heart of Southern institutions." He tried to empathize with them, saying, "I know a little of this. I live in Virginia. I studied law at the University of Virginia." His speech went on to say that he knew many Southerners who had "enriched our national life." He acknowledged, however, that his knowledge of the South was nothing compared to his audience. Kennedy asserted, "We are maintaining the orders of the courts. We are doing nothing more or less." RFK had not planned on doing anything other than upholding the law, but he made it very clear that the Department of Justice would act in situations that challenged the courts' decisions.

Robert Kennedy told the audience that he believed that the 1954 decision was right. This was something that he chose to express. He wanted people to see where he stood, enforcing his belief system and making it part of his policy. However, he said that his belief did not matter; "It is the law." It was not his opinion. The courts had been clear and set a precedent, Kennedy's stated reason for upholding the law. He went on to voting rights, a key component of his philosophy of civil rights. "The spirit of our democracy, the letter of our Constitution and our laws require that there be no delay in the achievement of full freedom to vote for all. Our system depends upon the fullest participation of all its citizens."[30] Robert Kennedy invaded the South. His beliefs were contrary to the segregation law so pervasive in that part of the nation. He argued that the fate of the nation hung in balance on this question. He said, "If we are to be truly great as a nation, then we must make sure that nobody is denied an opportunity because of race, creed or color." He was there to "advocate reason and the rule of law." That would be the basis for his actions as attorney general. This speech laid out his philosophy on justice and race. In addition, it serves as evidence as to what role the Justice Department would play in future issues. Kennedy said, "For this generation of Americans falls the full burden of proving to the world that we really mean it when we say all men are created free and equal before the law."[31]

In 1961 the citizens of the United States were not "free and equal" before the law. RFK was a pioneer in trying to gain equal rights for every American. While the notion of natural rights expressed by John Locke maintained that everyone was equal in the eyes of God, there was no clear legal definition of equality. Arguably the Fourteenth Amendment makes some headway into this area, but it was ignored by the South. There were plenty of civil rights laws to use in favor of the movement, but those laws were only as good as they were enforced. No president or Congress had been able to define those rights effectively enough to make a difference in race relations up that point. Robert Kennedy was setting a tone early in his tenure. He planned to confront segregation and uphold any court order, because it was the law. Robert Kennedy was a serious man. He always took his task to heart. With great passion and diligence he planned to administer his office in a responsible way that helped the people.

Robert Kennedy finished the speech by quoting Henry W. Grady saying, "We stand for human liberty." While the road to upholding the law might be fraught with adversity, he welcomed the challenge. "I pledge my best effort," he said, "all I have in material things and physical strength and spirit to see that freedom shall advance and that our children will grow old under the rule of law."[32]

5. CORE and the Freedom Rides

"Oh, my God, they're going to burn us up!"

In the wake of the Bay of Pigs it was important that the Kennedy brothers did not have another situation where they looked inadequate. That event, more than anything else, set the tone for how the administration would respond to issues. The Bay of Pigs not only brought Robert Kennedy closer to the president, it also taught President Kennedy that he needed a core group of advisors that he could trust to help him craft the administration's policies. Robert Kennedy took a similar approach in the Justice Department, surrounding himself with people he trusted to change the climate of the nation. John Kennedy's youthful vigor and high minded rhetoric gave many African Americans hope that this administration was looking for change. The civil rights leaders saw this period as a great opportunity to challenge the segregation laws in the country.

The Greensboro sit-ins provided the momentum necessary to get the movement going again. Civil rights leaders saw this as an opportunity to continue that progression. The sit-ins were organized by students, but there were others who had tried to challenge the system through nonviolent action in the past. The nation had not been ready for these movements as they came after World War II, when Americans were concerned with getting their lives on track after the prolonged conflict. Nevertheless, in the 1940s the Congress of Racial Equality (CORE), led by Bayard Rustin, James Peck and James Farmer, proposed what it called the Journey of Reconciliation of 1947. This protest was rooted in nonviolent direct action and challenged the segregation laws in the South by riding buses into the South that had both white and black riders aboard, disobeying the segregation laws. It was largely in response to the case involving Irene Morgan, who defied the segregation laws and refused to give up her seat in 1944.[1] The spirit of the sit-ins inspired CORE to attempt this movement with these young warriors at their sides. It was an opportunity for the old leadership to share the stage with the student movement in the hopes of leading to further cooperation. However, what started out as a movement led by CORE soon evolved into another student-driven effort, culminating in the support of Dr. King. Members of CORE and the SNCC rekindled this idea in the early sixties, calling it the Freedom Rides. Diane McWhorter writes in *Carry Me Home*, "CORE's Freedom Ride would be a departure from the student sit-ins' civil disobedience against state segregation ordinances. Though the Freedom Riders were not breaking the law, they were indeed, as white southerners liked to point out, looking for trouble."[2]

The sit-ins gave students a new voice, and they wanted to use this forum to invoke further change. This was an important aspect of the movement, as it serves as evidence that the students of the sixties were finding not only a voice, but strong leadership on the issues they faced. The Freedom Rides were an important factor in taking these students seriously. In December 1960, the Supreme Court overturned the conviction of Bruce Boynton, a Howard University student who tried to desegregate a Trailways terminal in Richmond, Virginia. The *Boynton* decision, coupled with the *Morgan* decision years prior, gave CORE a reason to challenge the system in the South.[3] In the spring of 1961 CORE was, once again, intending to use the rides into the South as a way to challenge the segregation laws. They sent out fliers and recruited people to ride the buses. The plan was to leave Washington, D.C., on May 4 and arrive in New Orleans on May 17, the seventh anniversary of the *Brown* decision.

Tom Gaither, of CORE, looked for students willing to make the journey into the South. James Farmer saw this as his opportunity to solidify his place in the history of the movement, so he and James Peck took an active interest in the progress of the rides.[4] Farmer and Peck had missed the opportunity in the forties. They were unable to affect the national discourse on the race issue. This was an opportunity to make that difference. The Kennedy brothers inspired them to rekindle that effort. It was clear that neither Truman or Eisenhower had given them any indication that they would support such a venture. The Kennedys gave many people, despite their inaction in office in those early months, a feeling that they were going to change the nation. With that feeling of hope and renewal came action.

On the heels of the Bay of Pigs, these rides had the potential to cause further political damage to the president. John Lewis was among those chosen to make the trip into the South. He recalled that this was a much different trip than the one in 1947. "Fourteen years had passed since then," he wrote. "It was late April 1961, and I had packed my bags for a far different and deadlier trip."[5] Lewis would not make the whole journey. After enduring a slight confrontation at the bus terminal in South Carolina that left him with some scrapes and bruises, he was tracked down by the Foreign Service and told he had an interview in Philadelphia for a possible job. Lewis left the rides, hoping to rejoin them in Birmingham.[6] While he did not make it to Birmingham in time, he would eventually play a role in this historic story.

Non violent direct action was at the heart of this trip to the South. It was important that these students understood the concept. This venture had the potential to get dangerous. Two buses left Washington on May 4, 1961, two days before Robert Kennedy spoke at the University of Georgia. The buses were filled with CORE members and reporters. These rides were in the same spirit as the sit-ins, lending the same spontaneity and power to the movement. The people on-board were courageous, as they understood the danger. It was their time to show America and the world that they wouldn't bow to oppression and racism.

In the days after RFK's speech to the University of Georgia, the Freedom Riders tested his resoluteness to uphold the law. *Jet Magazine* reporter Simeon Booker, who was traveling with the group to write about the event, said that Robert Kennedy was made aware of the Freedom Rules. Alledgedly, RFK was "absorbed" with the fallout of the Bay of Pigs and the University of Georgia speech, and he did not see the possible outcomes such an act might have.[7] On Sunday, May 14, 1961, the Freedom Rides ran into some trouble in Anniston, Alabama. It was Mother's Day. When one of the buses pulled into the Greyhound station, O.T. Jones, the driver of that bus, allegedly greeted Ku Klux Klan members who were waiting, saying, "Well, boys, here they are. I brought you some niggers and nigger-lovers."[8] The Klan members, led by William Chappell, tried to board the bus, but the riders were able to jam the door. As a result, the mob smashed the windows and battered the bus, hoping to get at the riders. When the police finally came, the bus had suffered a great deal of damage, but was operational enough to drive to the city limits with a police escort.

When the police escort left them, they were surrounded by cars and forced to the side of the road, where they were at the mercy of the white mob once again. The angry white mob, some dressed in their Sunday best as they came from church, assaulted the bus, slashed the tires, detonated a firebomb and then tried to barricade the passengers on the bus, yelling, "Burn them alive" and "Fry the goddamn niggers." Freedom Rider Genevieve Hughes yelled, "Oh, my God, they're going to burn us up!"[9] Some of the riders escaped through a broken window. An exploding gas tank scared the mob away, letting the other riders make their way off the bus to safety. State troopers arrived at the scene, cleared away the mob and drove the injured to the hospital. Black smoke filled the sky as the charred bus was left on the side of the road with bloodied, almost asphyxiated Freedom Riders lying around it.

As the crisis unfolded, another bus made its way to the Anniston Trailways station. This bus had James Peck, the middle aged CORE leader who was determined to make a difference in this movement. James Farmer did not make the trip. Simeon Booker, with other reporters, was on this bus. They pulled into the station an hour after the Greyhound bus had made its fateful stop. Once in the station the riders went to get food in the waiting area. When they returned back to bus they found the driver, John Olan Patterson, flanked by other men. Patterson said, "We've received word that a bus has been burned to the ground and the passengers are being carried to the hospital by the carloads." He went on to say that a similar mob was waiting for them if they did not "get these niggers off the front seats."[10] The men who flanked Patterson went after the black riders on the bus saying, "Niggers get back. You ain't up north. You're in Alabama, and niggers ain't nothing here." As they attacked two black riders, Peck and Walter Bergman went to the riders' aid. The black riders adhered strictly to the nonviolent tactics they were taught and suffering a major beating. Peck and Bergman were struck down ferociously, hitting the floor of the bus, spilling blood everywhere and eventually losing consciousness.[11]

The bus driver returned with a police officer, who claimed to see nothing and told the group to move along. As the bus left the station, five Klan members stayed on the bus. One took out a gun to show the group, while another held a steel pipe. Another man yelled out to the riders, "Just tell Bobby [Kennedy] and we'll do him in too."[12] It bears mention that the man thought of Robert Kennedy as someone who would intervene on the behalf of the riders. Just over three months after the inauguration, Kennedy was already seen in that light. His voice was heard on both sides of the fight, serving as a beacon for both hope and hate. The riders were on their way to Birmingham, where there was another mob waiting for them. Raymond Arsenault writes that Birmingham was unlike other cities in the deep South. The Freedom Riders had "no inkling of how far the ultra-segregationists of the south would go to protect the sanctity of Jim Crow." He contended, "There was a close collaboration between the Ku Klux Klan and law enforcement officials." In fact there was an FBI informant in the ranks of the Klan. The FBI knew that the Klan, in collusion with Eugene "Bull" Connor, a vicious, racist public safety official, planned to attack the bus at the Birmingham Trailways station. In fact, Gary Thomas Rowe, the FBI informant, was integral in getting the Klan in position to "welcome" these riders.[13] As the bus pulled into the station, two hours after the altercation in Anniston, there were no visible police officers, yet there were many in the terminal who wanted to kill the passengers of that bus.

The mentality in Birmingham was another example at how out of control the racial strife was in America. The fact that people believed they could assault and possibly kill others in front of reporters and witnesses speaks to the lawlessness of the South. Indeed, these instances point to how much the nation had evolved in the preceding years. It was also evidence that the justice officials who intervened in these early demonstrations were true soldiers of freedom. They confronted racism, but did so under threat of physical harm. Once the bus pulled into the Birmingham terminal, the Klansmen aboard ran off and disappeared into the crowd. James Peck, caked with blood, and Charles Person, another rider, made their way off the bus and took their luggage. One of the men in the terminal saw Peck's face and said that Person should die for attacking a white man. Peck exclaimed, "You'll have to kill me before you hurt him."[14] With that comment, a riot broke out in the Greyhound terminal.

The violence made its way out onto the streets, and many of the Freedom Riders, as well as innocent civilians, were hurt in the melee. While the riot was over in about twenty minutes, the injured Freedom Riders found refuge in several places. The press, however, was able to get the story, and it was on the front page of the newspaper the next morning. This situation had the potential to cause further political damage to the Kennedy brothers. Still licking their wounds from the Bay of Pigs, John and Robert Kennedy needed to respond to these vicious, racist and violent acts against the Freedom Riders.

"I never knew they were traveling down there."

JFK was hands off in his approach to civil rights, giving Bobby a lot of power to develop his own policy. "[JFK] could reach his own conclusion." According to Robert Kennedy, "He didn't have to have the attorney general call and tell him what was bad and what was good."[15] According to Burke Marshall, it appeared that if the Alabama government did not shift its position, "The Federal government would have to do something in order to correct the situation."[16] President Kennedy found out about the Freedom Rides on May 15 in the *New York Times*. He saw a photo of the Greyhound bus burning in Anniston. Richard Reeves writes that the picture and the story angered Kennedy. He knew that this was what the Soviets would use to attack him at Vienna. He was also mad because he did not know about the rides or the people on the buses.[17] John Kennedy, after seeing the Monday morning headlines, told Wofford to tell the Freedom Riders to "call it off." He said, "Can't you get your goddamn friends off those buses?" Kennedy was about to make a trip to Europe. He did not want any issues at home while he was meeting with Khrushchev and de Gaulle in Europe. The racial strife in America weakened his position abroad. The Soviet Union could capitalize on it. The French would also point to the issues as evidence of inexperience on Kennedy's part. He wanted this summit with Khrushchev to succeed, and anything that threatened that needed to be stopped. Wofford told JFK, "I don't think anybody's going to stop them right now."[18] The White House buzzed with the effects this initiative would cause for Kennedy at home and abroad.

In response to the Freedom Rides, John Kennedy decided to have Robert Kennedy appear on NBC. When asked abut the Freedom Riders, he said, "They performed a service bringing the problem to attention, now it's before the courts." He went on, "Are we going to let this be settled in the streets instead of the courts?" Kennedy concluded that violence was not a viable option: "I have no sympathy with segregationists, but segregation is far better than having it decided in the streets, with beatings."[19]

While CORE was trying to find a way out of Birmingham, Robert Kennedy and his office sprang into action. Despite the assertion that *Jet* reporter Simeon Booker had mentioned something to RFK and that CORE had released a letter to the Justice Department before the rides, Robert Kennedy remarked later, "I never knew they were traveling down there."[20] Kennedy said that he read about it in the paper the day after it happened. "There were things going on that shouldn't be going on, and that we had to figure out some way of becoming involved in it, or otherwise the situation was going to get worse." Kennedy acknowledged, "We had to discover some new way of being of some help." RFK said that he did discuss this instance with JFK, but more along the lines of "I'd call and say 'this is what we're going to do.' Or if I had a problem about alternative steps, I'd call him."[21] In the midst of all this confusion, Marshall and Kennedy found out that there was another group getting ready to leave from Nashville to continue the Freedom Ride. Marshall remembered, "It kept getting, from our point of view, worse and worse and worse."[22]

Robert Kennedy and Burke Marshall provided strong leadership. Without that guidance the movement would not have been as successful. While Robert Kennedy had dealt with some of these issues during the campaign, it was Marshall's first crisis. It was most certainly the gravest domestic crisis up to that point in the administration. If Kennedy hope to get reelected he needed to show the people of the nation that he understood their needs and was willing to commit some of his political capital to those efforts. To that end, Robert Kennedy and Marshall sent John Seigenthaler down to Birmingham to get involved immediately.

Robert Kennedy took full command of the Justice Department, built bonds among those men and crafted a brotherhood where they were willing to do anything for him. James Hilty writes, "Gradually it became apparent to all that the attorney general held exclusive strategic and operational responsibility over civil rights. When he acted, everyone understood that it was with the direct authority of the president."[23] Moreover, Hilty argued that the Kennedys not only wanted to assist these leaders, but thought their control "should extend beyond the government and into the movement itself, that their timing should dictate when the civil rights leadership should act."[24]

From Robert Kennedy's perspective, the movement would have to wait until his brother was done in Europe meeting with Khrushchev and de Gaulle. Only after success in France and Vienna did they think that they could tackle these issues. It's clear that Robert Kennedy wanted to make a difference in this aspect of American culture. His speech to the University of Georgia is evidence of that. In addition, committing Seigenthaler to the cause by sending him to the South was another act that demonstrated his desire to get involved in the movement. The Freedom Rides was the first domestic test of Kennedy's New Frontier. It was important, on the eve of the Vienna Summit with Khrushchev and the Bay of Pigs weighing down their political capital, that the Kennedy brothers demonstrate, not only for America, but the world, that they would stand up to segregation in a country that professed freedom and equality. The sixties was a time where new ideas found a way to break into the mainstream consciousness of the age. Despite Robert Kennedy's political pragmatism, which most likely came from his father's involvement in the campaign, he was a young idealist hoping to affect the world. At only thirty-six years old he was still at the beginning of what seemed to be a promising career in government.

To show his support of CORE's efforts and solidarity with the movement, Kennedy phoned some of the Freedom Riders who were beaten during the attacks. Fred Shuttlesworth, the Birmingham preacher, spoke to Kennedy and told his congregation, "Bob told me 'if you can't get me at my office, just call me at the White House."[25] Shuttlesworth was not expecting to use that number as soon as he did. After speaking with the riders and realizing the severity of the situation not only for the movement but also for the safety of Americans,

Robert Kennedy wanted to get the Freedom Riders out of there. He also wanted to use the bus system, continuing the Freedom Ride, if possible. The fact that Kennedy wanted to continue the Freedom Ride is evidence that he was willing to risk political capital to do what he saw was right under the law. He truly believed that these men and women had a right to the service that they purchased. After Kennedy's call to the Freedom Riders, he attempted to contact Governor John Patterson to restore order in Birmingham, guaranteeing free passage for the Freedom Riders.

Raymond Arsenault argued that Robert Kennedy "felt confident ... that he could convince Patterson that protecting the Freedom Riders from violent assaults was essential, not only from a legal and moral perspective but also as a deterrent to federal intervention." With that in mind, Robert Kennedy was both "surprised and disappointed" that Patterson would not cooperate.[26] Eventually the Justice Department got a weak promise to "maintain public order."[27] Robert Kennedy looked to Governor Patterson for help. The Alabama governor was a strong supporter of Kennedy during the election and they expected that he would step in and provide the necessary support for these rides that were taking the nation by storm.

Kennedy saw civil rights as more than just a political issue. The phone call to Patterson demonstrated his determination, to some extent, and even his solidarity with the riders. However, it was more a reflection of how he hoped these types of demonstrations would take shape. The local authorities, not federal action, should handle such matters. The Freedom Riders wanted federal intervention, and expected these responses from local authorities. The riders were determined and believed that Bobby Kennedy could find a way to work with the local officials. However, Robert Kennedy was still a pragmatic politician trying to protect his brother's legacy and the administration's agenda. He risked political capital and his brother's Congressional agenda by intervening in this affair. The civil rights movement needed Bobby Kennedy. They needed the righteous, young activist who was present at the McClellan hearings. If the movement could get Kennedy on its side he would be a strong supporter.

RFK wanted to provide an equal opportunity for the Freedom Riders to continue their effort. He did not tell them to stop, nor did he use the power of his office to file an injunction against their actions, as others had in the past. This points not only to his duty as the attorney general, but also a part of his own personality that shaped his time in office. He believed in doing the "right" thing. This is especially relevant with past choices in his career. He joined McCarthy because he thought it was the right thing to do. He joined the Rackets Committee because it was the right thing to do, despite a great deal of criticism from his father. He stood up to the students at the University of Virginia because they were wrong not to let Ralph Bunche speak. Robert Kennedy wanted to help the civil rights movement. When asked about the sit-ins later in March 1961 Kennedy said, "My sympathy is with them morally."[28] He was not the typical 1961 politician. He was a new generation of American.

"Surely somebody in the damn bus company can drive a bus, can't they?"

The Freedom Riders made their way to the Greyhound station, hoping to get protection and passage out of Birmingham. It seemed that the ordeal was almost at an end. There were reporters in the terminal to see the event. At this point the story had been on the front cover of the *New York Times* and the *Washington Post*. It was international news. James Peck said to one reporter, "It's been rough, but I am getting on that bus to Montgomery." He was determined, as were the other members of CORE, to continue the ride. It seemed they would have an opportunity to do that. While they were waiting to board the bus, however, the tide changed rather quickly. The radio reported that Governor Patterson could not protect the Freedom Riders. "The citizens of the state are so enraged that I cannot guarantee protection for this bunch of rabble rousers," he said on the radio. In addition to the radio report the state police informed the riders that there were mobs ready to interrupt the bus route. Patterson said he would escort the group to the Birmingham line, but not to Montgomery.[29] It was time for Shuttlesworth to use the number that Robert Kennedy gave him.

Upon hearing that Patterson had reneged on their agreement, Robert Kennedy started making phone calls. He called Burke Marshall, who was recovering from the mumps, and preceded to call Alabama officials, dealing with one issue after another. At 3:15 P.M. on May 15, Robert Kennedy phoned George Cruit, the superintendent of the Birmingham branch of the Greyhound Bus Company, to get a driver for the Freedom Riders. He was told by Cruit that no one would drive the bus from Birmingham to Montgomery. Kennedy said, "Well, hell, you can look for one can't you? After all these people have tickets and are entitled to transportation to continue the trip or project to Montgomery." Kennedy's use of the entitlement with regard to the ticket points to how he viewed the law in this circumstance. While it could have been the famous Kennedy bravado that was unwilling to give up, it is more likely that Robert Kennedy wanted to see these people succeed. He abhorred the fact that there were forces trying to stop people from exercising their rights under the law. That was not his idea of America. Indeed, his frustration came through when he lost his temper in the exchange, showing a very passionate, determined Kennedy.

What got him in trouble were statements such as, "We have gone to a lot of trouble to see that they get to this trip and I am most concerned to see that it is accomplished."[30] His true sentiments may have been revealed or his patience was spent. Nevertheless his comment linked him to the riders. What Kennedy did not know was that the conversation was being recorded, and it seemed that he was behind the rides or at least in support of them, which was a problem in Southern politics. Burke Marshall reiterated that Robert Kennedy did not know about the rides until the violence in Birmingham and Anniston. Marshall remembered in 1964, "It was obviously intolerable for the country that the bus couldn't move because of the lack of police protection. But the references in that conversation, which was recorded, were widely used in Alabama and in the South and I think were widely accepted as showing that the attorney general had inspired this entire incident."[31] As the phone conversation continued, it seemed that Kennedy's patience grew very thin.

Kennedy went on with Cruit, asking if he could get a "colored" bus driver, but the superintendent said no. The exasperated Kennedy said, "Surely somebody in the damn bus company can drive a bus, can't they?" He went on to say that Cruit "had better be getting in touch with Mr. Greyhound or whoever Greyhound is and somebody better give us an answer to this question." Kennedy continued, "I am — the government — is going to be very much upset if this group does not get to continue their trip." Kennedy said, "Under the law they are entitled to transportation provided by Greyhound and we are looking for you to get them on their way." When Cruit said, "I shall be glad to do what I can," Kennedy responded, "I will be glad to talk with your people and somebody better get in the damn bus and get it going and get these people on their way."[32] Despite the fact that Kennedy was adamant about getting assistance for the riders, they did not leave Birmingham by bus. Kennedy even considered sending an Air Force plane to pick them up.[33] Simeon Booker called John Seigenthaler, saying, "It's pretty bad down here, and we don't think we're going to get out. Bull Connor ... and his people are pretty tough, and I don't think there's any bus that's going to take us out of here."[34] Robert Kennedy sent Seigenthaler to Birmingham in the hopes of getting them out by plane.

Seigenthaler remembered arriving in Birmingham, finding Booker and others waiting for him at the airport. "They were scared," he said. He went to find the official for the airline to get the riders out of Birmingham. He said to the official, "I'm from the federal government. I've flown down here on instructions of the attorney general. We want to get these people out of here and on their way. It's going to be better for you if you do that." The official told him that there were bomb threats and they could not get the flight out of the airport. Seigenthaler said, "They're not going to blow up any airplane. Couldn't you just ignore it?" Despite the fact that the official said he could not, they were able to get a plane out of Birmingham and into the safety of New Orleans.[35] Once off the plane, Burke Marshall got in touch with Seigenthaler, asking him if he knew Diane Nash. Seigenthaler said yes. "Well, she's getting ready to lead a group to Birmingham to take up where the other group left off. Could you call her and ask her not to do that?"[36] Diane and the SNCC gathered the energy and money to mount their own Freedom Ride into the South. Although the Kennedy brothers believed that their troubles were over with the CORE ride safely in New Orleans, they suddenly had to redirect their efforts at securing the safe passage of a new, young batch of riders that would challenge the segregation laws of the South.

While the Justice Department would have liked to control the events surrounding the Freedom Rides, it was clear that the young idealistic students of SNCC and veteran CORE members were forcing the administration to acknowledge and act on the segregation issues of the South. This situation was the Kennedy brothers' maiden voyage into the realm of civil rights issues. They were not able to navigate as well as they would have liked. Robert Kennedy was more concerned with providing political cover for his brother than with coming up with real solutions to potential problems. Most importantly, the Kennedy brothers still saw civil rights as a political issue. The Freedom Rides started to make it clearer to Robert Kennedy that this was larger than politics and involved human life and equality. It served as an important factor in his evolution as a civil rights advocate.

The righteous minded Kennedy brother was being exposed to this mistreatment under the law for the first time in his life. He realized very quickly that he was in a unique position to influence history. He started to move his beliefs from political to moral. He made that journey before his politically minded brother. In fact, Robert Kennedy helped John Kennedy see that he needed to show some leadership in this issue. Robert Kennedy was intimately involved in the civil rights movement. The close relationship he had with his brother helped him bring the president to embrace the same ideals as Bobby. However, they were still at the beginning of this crisis.

6. SNCC: Getting to Montgomery

"You better get back up there."

The Nashville contingent of the SNCC paid close attention as the situation unfolded with CORE's Freedom Ride into the South. John Lewis, who left the Freedom Rides in South Carolina, was in Nashville instead of Birmingham and among the students who wanted to see the buses continue their run into the South. James Bevel, Diane Nash and others listened to the events in Anniston and Birmingham that Sunday and Monday. Nash and Lewis believed that the civil rights movement had reached a critical juncture. The students understood that this was a unique opportunity for the movement. The nation watched the events unfold. The time had come to make a stand.

John Lewis had come a long way from the letter he sent the library to take out books like the white citizens. Raymond Arsenault writes, "If the movement allowed segregationist thugs to destroy the Freedom Ride, white supremacist extremists would gain new life, violent attacks on civil rights activists would multiply, and attracting new recruits to the nonviolent cause would become much more difficult."[1] Lewis and the Nashville group needed to do something to keep the momentum. Since the nation was enthralled with the story it was an opportune time for these civil rights leaders to make their case to the American people. The media could have an impact on the movement the way that Harriet Beecher Stowe's *Uncle Tom's Cabin* had on the abolition movement. If the civil rights leaders could expose Jim Crow for what it was, then the nation would fall in behind the movement. They still, however, had a long way to go.

The young group decided that the rides needed reinforcements and that they would try to continue the effort. Lewis, Nash and Bevel were the voice of this young generation that would not only forced the Kennedys to intervene on behalf of civil rights leaders, but also change the direction of the veteran leaders. When word came that the CORE riders had been flown to New Orleans, the young leaders were appalled. John Lewis said, "I couldn't believe it. I understood the thinking behind this decision, but it defied one of the most basic tenets of nonviolent action — that is, that there can be no surrender in the face of brute force or any form of violent opposition."[2] Much to the dismay of the Kennedy brothers, Lewis and others planned for a trip into the South. The group in Nashville intended not only to challenge Robert Kennedy's efforts to stop the violence but also to confront CORE with not following through on their commitment to continue the rides. While that showed some level of arrogance on their part, it also pointed to their resolve. Lewis, Nash and Bevel wanted to change the direction of the nation. They knew if they did not seize the moment it would be gone. Thus their hopes to create a different world would be dashed.

SNCC leaders were upset with CORE and felt that they could challenge the Kennedy administration to act further. Robert Kennedy's phone call to Greyhound was a step in the right direction, but these student leaders wanted more, challenging not only Kennedy to make a stand, but also CORE for backing down.

Seigenthaler was Kennedy's man on the ground. He had his marching orders from Washington and played a good soldier. He was from Nashville and the hope was that he would be able to reason with SNCC. Robert Kennedy wanted to avoid bloodshed. The SNCC was determined to push for it so that the nation would see Jim Crow at its worst. Seigenthaler contacted a lawyer who gave him Nash's number. He remembered in 1966 that Nash said she was not going on the trip, but there was, in fact, a group going to Birmingham to continue the trip. Seigenthaler replied, "You know, they're going to kill them." Nash responded, "They don't care. They think this is important. If they kill them, we'll just have that many more down there, and sooner or later we'll get somebody through." Nash's response is consistent with the notion that students were willing to continue this momentum under threat of death. In fact when presented with such an outcome it only produced greater resolve. This attitude is what drove the movement. Such defiance had never been seen and it was having an impact on the nature of the movement. Much to Seigenthaler's dismay he took down her number and the number of the Reverend Ralph Abernathy, who was a contact for SNCC. He called Robert Kennedy the next day, saying, "Well, they're on their way, and there's nothing we can do." Kennedy responded, "You better get back up there."[3] With that Seigenthaler traveled to Birmingham for the second act of the Freedom Rides.

Kennedy wanted Seigenthaler involved not only because of political issues, but also because he wanted to maintain the law. In another way he also wanted the Freedom Riders to see that they were not alone and the U.S. government was on their side. As he said to Cruit, these citizens had a legal right to continue their journey. Marshall remembered in 1964 in an interview with Robert Kennedy that Seigenthaler "went down there so that we'd have somebody there on the scene to tell [them] what was going on."[4] At this point, Governor Patterson had completely cut off all communication with the White House. Sending Seigenthaler into the South, to assist the Freedom Riders, without letting the state and local authorities know, was already a truculent act on the part of Robert Kennedy. The South did not want the federal government involved in its affairs, equating it to the Civil War and Northern aggression. On Tuesday Nash called Shuttlesworth to let him know that the Nashville students were on their way. Lewis boarded a bus the next day with five black men, two black women and two white students, one male, one female. This time he was headed for Birmingham.[5] As the Nashville students prepared to continue the rides, Kennedy's soldier would eventually put himself in harm's way for the cause.

The events that transpired after the new Freedom Riders left Nashville galvanized the movement and forced Kennedy to make a real commitment. Lewis and others were on their way to Birmingham. Before they got to the terminal the bus was intercepted by the police. All but one of the riders were identified by the police and the bus was escorted back to the station, with newspaper over the windows to hide what was happening on the bus. While two were sent to prison, an undetected Freedom Rider made a call to Nash, who called Burke Marshall.[6] The Justice Department, however, was limited in the role they could play in Birmingham. In addition, they wanted to maintain the integrity of federalism, with the local authorities handling their own problems. Governor Patterson refused to grant protection to this new group of Freedom Riders. Bull Connor took these Freedom Riders into custody, "for their own protection," and carted them off the jail. Once in prison the SNCC utilized Gandhian tactics of nonviolence and refused to eat, despite the fact that they had not eaten since that morning. In addition, the group decided that instead of sleeping they would sing to pass the time.[7]

Meanwhile the Justice Department struggled with how to handle this new crisis in Alabama. It was at a dinner party that Wednesday night, while the Freedom Riders spent the night in prison, that Deputy Attorney General Byron "Whizzer" White, future justice of the Supreme Court, suggested that the administration had "to get those people out of there and keep them moving somehow."[8] Whether White was more concerned about their safety or the momentum of the movement is debatable. Given the ineffectiveness of Southern law enforcement, White suggested the use of federal troops as a means of securing the riders' safety. It was Louis Oberdorfer, a Birmingham native and head of the tax division, who suggested a civilian force of marshals to protect the riders. The main issue was to avoid a situation similar to Little Rock in 1957, where Eisenhower sent in the 101st Airborne Division to Central High School. That would have had larger political ramifications and the South would have seen it as tantamount to invasion. In fact, on the cusp of the Little Rock episode, Eisenhower had commented that they could be looking at another civil war.[9] At this point in the presidency, Robert Kennedy was unwilling to risk the political capital. That said, it was clear enough that something needed to be done. Robert Kennedy and Burke Marshall felt so strongly about it that they held an emergency meeting at the president's breakfast table Thursday morning, while JFK was still in his pajamas. His breakfast was never eaten.

Robert Kennedy outlined the situation in Alabama for his brother. Marshall remembered, "The purpose of the breakfast was to inform the president of the gravity of the situation and of the plans which we had decided had to be made to deal with it by direct federal police action if there was no other way."[10] President Kennedy had been informed of the situation prior to the meeting by his brother. Marshall remembered, "It had become serious enough so that a presidential decision was required. It was beyond what could be dealt with just by the Department of Justice."[11] This was the first time that Marshall had met with the president on official business. "The breakfast was in a sort of a sitting room outside the president's bedroom in the mansion.... It was the first time that the president had had this problem of serious racial disorder."[12] Robert Kennedy went over "the possible steps that might have to be taken and what [they] were planning to do and what action would be required by him in the event that different things happened during the next two or three days."[13] Those steps included the marshals that White and Oberdorfer had discussed the night before. White's plan involved the army as a transport for the marshals into the South. His notion was create a "credible force that would convince Patterson that the threat of federal intervention was real."[14] Marshall went on to discuss some of the legal measures the group planned to take.

Burke Marshall was at the forefront of decision making for this civil rights crisis. He not only had the president's ear, but also had the trust and confidence of the attorney general. Marshall told the president that they intended to file a suit against the Klan in Alabama. They "had evidence that the Klan groups were behind the riots in Birmingham and the bus burning in Anniston — from interfering with interstate movement and [the suit] also would enjoin the police from failing to protect interstate travelers."[15] Marshall believed that there was very little precedent despite the fact that the government had, in the past, filed an injunction against Eugene Debs. He said later that he believed it would grant President Kennedy two powers he could use in the crisis:

> One would be the enforcement of a court order directly, we could probably do without a proclamation; and the other would be to make a finding that there was a breakdown of law and order

such that the right to travel interstate was not being protected and he could act on that basis independently of the court order.[16]

President Kennedy took in this information. In the midst of foreign policy turmoil over the Bay of Pigs and with the Vienna Summit on the horizon, JFK was confronted with his greatest racial crisis so far.

John Kennedy did not want to use a civilian force in Alabama. In fact, he was hoping that Patterson would intervene instead. Marshall remembered in 1964 that their "recommendation to the president was that he should not use troops unless it was unavoidable."[17] Kennedy was not taking this situation lightly. On the contrary, he was very much in tune with the crisis. "The president was a very good listener," Marshall remembered.

> My first impression of him from that meeting was just of a tuned-in intelligence, I mean a real intelligence at work on gathering all this data and understanding it, weighing it, and accepting it. I mean not complaining about the governor or complaining about the mob or complaining about the biracial group or the situation, but simply taking it all in and accepting it as the facts that he had to face.[18]

JFK had foreign policy issues and did not want to get into a race war in the South. John Kennedy asked the White House operator to get Patterson on the phone. The operator told the president that the governor was out fishing. Governor John Patterson would not take President Kennedy's call for at least twenty-four hours. As a result of Patterson's absence John Kennedy ordered Marshall and White to begin preparations for the marshals. However, he wanted them to tread lightly.[19] Kennedy hoped to not involve the federal government, a reluctance typical of any politician in 1961. That said, his preparations are evidence that he was willing to at least attempt to change the climate. It is clear that he recognized the reality of the situation and wanted to be ready in case more blood was spilled over Jim Crow — as there would be. Marshall and White were perfect examples of the new generation of Americans. They were innovative and looked for different solutions so the president was never backed into a corner. The Justice Department was very active in securing the rights of the Freedom Riders, and Robert Kennedy used the law to help them. In the meantime, the Freedom Riders were under the "protection" of Bull Connor.

Bull Connor wanted to go after Shuttlesworth for bringing the Freedom Riders into Birmingham. Since it was Shuttlesworth who helped organize the bus ride with Diane Nash, Connor looked at charging him with inciting a riot, which was in addition to interfering with the police when the Freedom Riders were initially arrested at the Greyhound terminal.[20] Shuttlesworth met with SCLC members. While others in the group wanted to negotiate with the city, Shuttlesworth understood the reality that there could be no agreement yet with Birmingham and wanted to stress their support of the students. Shuttlesworth told the press, "These students came here to ride out on a regularly scheduled bus and that's what they hope to do. This is our irrevocable position. The challenge has to be made."[21] In addition to Shuttlesworth, CBS newsman Howard K. Smith told the nation about the violence on Mother's Day and how the CORE riders flew to New Orleans. He ended the broadcast by criticizing Connor's tactics, saying, "Fear and hatred did stalk Birmingham's streets yesterday."[22] There would be action in the wake of Smith's broadcast, but it was not the Kennedy brothers, Shuttlesworth or Patterson who would act.

Bull Connor came into the jail cell and told the Freedom Riders that he was going to get them out of Alabama. Yelling through the bars at them, he said, "You people came in here from Tennessee on a bus. I'm taking you back to Tennessee in five minutes under police protection." There were two unmarked cars waiting for the riders. While they refused to cooperate, letting their bodies go limp, the students were still loaded into the car and taken to the Tennessee border.[23] "This was strange. A midnight ride in the Deep South with a man like Bull Connor?" Lewis wrote later. Once in the car, "He tried being friendly, making small talk as we drove through dark empty streets and out of the city." The group was taken to the Tennessee line and let out in the small town of Ardmore. Connor turned to the riders and said, "This is where you'll be getting out." He went on to say, "Y'all can catch a train home from here." With a chuckle he added, "Or maybe a bus." Lewis also remembered that Ardmore was Klan territory. The small, quiet town in the Deep South was not where they wanted to be. They ventured through the train tracks and found a couple that let them use the phone, where they called Diane Nash. Nash sent a driver to pick them up and they proceeded to Birmingham, where they joined with eleven other riders and made the trip to Montgomery.[24]

"You're just making speeches at me. You're not talking to me."

Once back in Birmingham the riders made an attempt to board the Greyhound buses and make the ride into Montgomery. They were met with a great deal of opposition at the terminal and from the Alabama government. John Lewis remembered, "It was a surprise to see a crowd waiting for us at the Greyhound station." He went on to say, "The crowd, which was larger than any I'd seen so far — estimates later put it at three thousand — was loud and angry. They pushed in at us as we entered the terminal, but no one touched us." Greyhound officials canceled the trip, saying there was no one to drive the bus. Lewis remembered that as the day turned to night the situation grew even more ominous. "With darkness the mob grew bolder and more violent. We could see them through the glass doors and street side windows, gesturing at us and shouting."[25] Meanwhile, the Justice Department was working behind the scenes to make sure that these riders were safely escorted out of Birmingham.

Robert Kennedy was in a Cabinet meeting when the elusive Alabama governor finally got a hold of the president. Since every attempt to get the governor on the phone had failed, the Kennedy brothers intimated that they would have to use federal intervention if he continued to ignore the president. This brought Governor John Patterson magically to the phone.[26] Burke Marshall remembered the phone call to Governor Patterson, "but those conversations had not resulted at that time in any agreement." He went on to say, "The points made by the attorney general were that the situation was intolerable, that the country could not stand for a bus not being able to move, therefore the bus had to be protected, and that it was up to the governor to do that."[27] The governor started to lecture Kennedy and Marshall on the roles of the federal government and the Supreme Court and their relationships with the states. He even went so far as to bring up the Civil War. Bobby Kennedy responded, "Now, John, you don't have to make speeches to me. You're just making speeches at me. You're not talking to me."[28] Robert Kennedy hoped that reason would overcome the violence, but Patterson just sent more rhetoric his way. They were at a point where people could be hurt. Many had already been.

Robert Kennedy remembered: "And then the president said that [Patterson] would have John Seigenthaler, who was going to be [President Kennedy's] representative as well as my administrative assistant, talk to him."[29] Seigenthaler was already in Birmingham. Kennedy called Seigenthaler and he made the trip to Montgomery to meet with Patterson. Seigenthaler said, "I had talked with Bob and with [Byron White] at length the night before, before going in, and we had outlined pretty well what our position was going to be."[30] Sending in Seigenthaler is significant because it demonstrated that the Kennedy brothers were exhausting all avenues before they involved any kind of military or police force. In a larger sense Seigenthaler's involvement was another means for the Kennedys to get an idea of what they were dealing with in Montgomery. In addition, it was clear the JFK was more concerned with issues overseas, giving Robert Kennedy more latitude to make decisions for domestic policy.

When Patterson met Seigenthaler on that Friday evening, the governor greeted him by saying, "There's nobody in the whole country that's got the spine to stand up to the goddamned niggers except me."[31] Sitting at a conference table in the capitol building, Patterson continued with a tirade about the stand he was taking. "I'll tell you," he said to Seigenthaler, "I've got a stack of letters over there in my desk, and I am more popular today in the United States — not only with the people of Alabama, but with people all across the country — for the stand I've taken against these people than Jack Kennedy ever will be. And it just makes me sick to see this happen." Seigenthaler remembers that Patterson went on for almost fifteen minutes, attacking Robert Kennedy and finally saying, "By God, I'm telling you if federal marshals come in to Alabama, there'll be blood in the streets. You'd better not send federal marshals into Alabama."[32] Being from the South, Seigenthaler was used to this reaction.

John Seigenthaler gently disagreed with the governor — using diplomacy and his Southern perspective to diffuse the situation. Seigenthaler remembered: "I said that I appreciated everything he said; although I didn't agree with everything he said, I respected his right to say it; that I too was a Southerner; and that as a Southerner, I respected his position because I knew a lot of people felt the same way." He went on to say, "Speaking for myself, I didn't agree with him; that my position was, personally, that these people had a right to travel the highways; but more importantly the position of the United States government was that these people had a right to travel the highways."[33] Seigenthaler was integral in trying to find a solution to this crisis. By clearly stating his position to Patterson, he was speaking as a Southerner, but in full agreement with Robert Kennedy's position as attorney general. This was important because the Kennedys knew that they had to be careful who they sent into this situation. Choosing Seigenthaler was brilliant, because Patterson would be less guarded and would be willing to work with him. If Robert Kennedy had made his way to the South he would not have been so welcomed.

Seigenthaler said to Patterson, "The United States government was going to make sure, if necessary, that people had the right to safe travel and free access on public conveyances and on public highways; and that if [the governor] was not capable or willing to provide safety to travelers that we would provide it in any way that we could."[34] This was something that Southern politicians did not want and Patterson was furious that the Kennedy brothers suggested that they might send federal troops to the South. Despite the hard rhetoric, Patterson and Seigenthaler were able to come to an agreement. Patterson told Seigenthaler, "The state of Alabama will provide safe travel for all who travel the highways, including visitors, on the highways and elsewhere while they're in this state." He finished, saying, "You can tell the Attorney General I said that." Seigenthaler acknowledged his statement as a "firm commitment" to protect the riders. However, Patterson said, "Now I'm not going to say I'm going to protect a bunch of goddamn foreign troublemakers who come in here to stir up trouble. I can't say that. But I am going to say this: that we have the means and the desire to protect on the highways and elsewhere citizens and visitors, and we will provide them safety."[35]

Kennedy trusted Seigenthaler, and without that trust the situation could have gotten worse. If Kennedy was not such a superb delegator, and had tried to handle the situation on his own, then an already difficult situation could have gotten worse. It was important that the White House not only chose someone to go into the South to work the problem, but that they also chose the right person. Seigenthaler was the right person. What Seigenthaler did not know, however, was that after Patterson left the meeting he inquired on how to obtain an injunction against the riders, making them outlaws in the state of Alabama. It seemed at every inch of the way both the Justice Department and the riders were stymied by Patterson and the white mobs. Floyd Mann, the Alabama director of safety, guaranteed that the Freedom Riders would have safe passage. Meanwhile Patterson conferred with the state's attorney general, MacDonald Gallion, to find a judge to issue the injunction.[36]

Robert Kennedy called Fred Shuttlesworth in an effort to stop the riders from making the journey further. RFK wanted the riders to fly to New Orleans, like the CORE members days before. Kennedy went on to say that Alabama was dangerous. But Mississippi, the next stop, was even worse. Trying to appeal to Shuttlesworth's religious convictions, which RFK shared, the attorney general said, "The Lord hasn't ... been to Mississippi in a long time." The minister responded, "But we think the Lord should go to Mississippi, and we want to get Him there." Kennedy also asked him if he planned to take the trip with the riders. "I'm a battlefield general," Shuttlesworth responded. "I lead troops into battle. Yes sir, I'm going to ride the bus."[37] The situation rapidly moved out of Robert Kennedy's control, which was not how he planned to deal with this crisis. His chief concern was to get protection for the riders, and that was becoming a very daunting task for the second most powerful person in the nation.

At 6:05 the next morning Joe Caverno arrived to drive the Freedom Riders to Montgomery. He looked at the riders and said, "I don't have but one life to give. And I don't intend to give it to CORE or the NAACP." Caverno left the platform. The riders, hoping to lighten the mood and their spirits broke into song.[38] They were not leaving the platform until someone came to drive them to Montgomery. When he found out about the Freedom Riders huddled at the platform, Seigenthaler called Greyhound to get a driver. Officials at the company promised that someone would drive the bus, and Caverno made his way back to the platform. As the Freedom Riders boarded the bus, Shuttlesworth was stopped by the police and told that he could not go with them, despite the fact that he had a ticket. Shuttlesworth refused to stop and was arrested for disobeying a police officer. The convoy pulled out of the station, headed for Montgomery, the scene of the famous boycott that had enthralled the nation in 1955. Raymond Arsenault writes, "The Freedom Riders departure from Birmingham resembled a staged Hollywood scene."[39] This movement had all the drama of a Hollywood blockbuster. They were finally on their way to the next stop. What the Freedom Riders did not know was that they were riding into a very dangerous situation.

As the Freedom Riders made their way to Montgomery forces were mounting to meet them at the terminal. John Seigenthaler and John Doar made their way to the Federal Building in Montgomery, hoping to meet the riders at the terminal around 11:00, when they were scheduled to get in. However, the bus skipped a few scheduled stops and arrived at the terminal at 10:23. Seigenthaler dropped off Doar and circled around the block to find a parking space. While he did this, the bus arrived and was met by an ambush.[40]

The bus made its way to the terminal and the Freedom Riders made their way to reporters who were waiting for them. John Lewis had just been asked a question by one of them when the melee began. While the group tried to maintain their nonviolent protocol, it was very difficult with the oncoming wave of white rioters. "They carried every makeshift weapon imaginable," Lewis remembered. "Baseball bats, wooden boards, bricks, chains, tire irons, pipes, even garden tools — hoes and rakes. One group had women in front, their faces twisted in anger, screaming. *'Git them niggers, GIT them niggers!'*"[41] John Seigenthaler was trying to park his car when all this was going on and unexpectedly ran into the riot.

As the crowd chose their targets and the bloodshed commenced, Seigenthaler realized that a riot had broken out as he passed the terminal. Seigenthaler remembered in 1966:

> As I started up the street on the back side of the bus terminal, I looked across and saw that crowds had gathered. And as I drove slowly up, I saw suitcases and bags being hurled into the air, and people started shouting. I drove slowly on up, realizing then that the bus had come early and that there was trouble.[42]

Seigenthaler went on to move his car into the riot in an effort to quell some of the violence. He noticed several Freedom Riders who were getting beaten by the white mob. "I came on down the front side, really, of the terminal and looked over, and I could see in the area where the bus had parked that some people were getting beaten. Just in front of me, maybe twenty yards, a girl was walking around with a circle of people around her taunting her. She was a white girl." Seigenthaler was looking for a place to intervene.

He found a place where the curb changed to a drive way and moved his car to protect a girl who was getting beaten. He got out of the car and went over to her in an effort to help her. He remembered:

> I took her by the arm and said, "Are you hurt?" She was bleeding a little bit from the mouth. She said no. I pulled her around to the door and started to put her into the car.... I then noticed that the other girl had gotten into the car on the other side, and I yelled over, "Who are you?" She said, "I'm with her." I said to her, "Get into the car." She was dazed, and she said, "Mister, get away. Leave me alone. You're going to get hurt. You're only going to get killed. This is not your fight." I said to her, "Get into the car," and I began to push her. She grabbed a hold of the car door and began to resist. At that time some man in khaki clothes said to me, "Who the hell are you?" I said, "Get back, get back. I'm a federal man." I turned back to her, and got it over the left ear.[43]

As Seigenthaler announced he was a federal man a third man came from behind and hit him in the head with a pipe. Seigenthaler fell to the ground unconscious, and was kicked in the ribs and pushed under his car. He was discovered by a reporter twenty-five minutes later.[44]

Jim Zwerg, a white Freedom Rider, was especially punished by the mob. Calling him a "communist" and "nigger lover," they knocked him down to the ground. His arms were pinned back and they took turns beating him, eventually tossing his limp body over a railing.[45] The crowd then turned on the other riders, which included John Lewis. He remembered "this sea of people, more than one hundred of them, shouting and screaming, men swinging fists and weapons, women swinging heavy purses, little children clawing with their fingernails at the faces of anyone they could reach."[46] Lewis watched Jim Zwerg hit the ground. Someone grabbed Lewis's briefcase from him, ripping it from his fingers. He remembered, "At that instant I felt a thud against my head. I could feel my knees collapse and then nothing. Everything turned white for an instant, then black."[47]

Floyd Mann made his way to the chaos, trying to make good on his promise to protect the riders, and fired shots into the air. John Doar watched from the third floor of the federal building. He called Burke Marshall, saying, "Oh, there are fists punching.... A bunch of men led by a guy with a bleeding face are beating them. There are no cops." He was frantic, describing the scene as "awful."[48]

John Seigenthaler was one of the new type of government officials who represented the New Frontier. They were willing to get in the middle of the fight if right was on their side. His willingness to put himself in harm's way without thought for his own wellbeing was something that was lacking in the government's response to race issues. Many politicians were unwilling to risk political power to stand firm on what was right. Seigenthaler remembered waking up for a brief moment after being hit on the head. He was sitting in a car with a police officer who had his notebook with names like Nash, Abernathy and Shuttlesworth.

> I was pretty groggy, and I said, "What happened?" He said, "You've been hurt. You better sit still." I said, "You'd better call Mr. Kennedy." He said, "What Mr. Kennedy?" and I said, "Robert Kennedy." He said, "Why? Who are you?" I said, "I work for him. I'm with the Department of Justice." So it scared him. He opened the door of the car and said, "Get out." I got out, and as soon as I got on my feet, I passed out again.[49]

The next time Seigenthaler woke up he was in the hospital. Byron White was on the phone and said to Seigenthaler, "Look, stay there. Bob's not here. He'll be back in a little bit, but you're going to have to stay there over night." Seigenthaler responded, "This is going to cause an awful mess." White told him, "It already has. Don't worry about it. Everything's all right. It's probably the best thing that could have happened."[50] Seigenthaler was moved and they put guards by his door. He was now an active member of this fight for equality and a casualty of the hatred that had engulfed the South since the last shots were fired.

7. First Baptist Church

"Well, the marshals are on their way."

Having just come back from horseback riding and an FBI baseball game, Robert Kennedy was still in shirtsleeves and a baseball cap when he had heard about the attack on John Seigenthaler. In the wake of that attack, Kennedy sent a telegram to Governor Patterson telling him, "Deeds not words would be appreciated."[1] Kennedy was angry that the governor could not make good on his word to protect the riders. This would be a continual issue with Southern politicians. "The agreement was that they'd get out of Birmingham and get out of the state of Alabama," Kennedy remembered. He went on to say that they were "just sitting in Birmingham as a festering sore," and he believed that the Justice Department had "avoided a problem."[2] Kennedy needed to regroup and approach this issue more directly.

It seemed that the Freedom Riders would have been able to continue their protest, with the help of the Justice Department. "All they said they had to do was to get on the bus and keep going. So that was important to us." Kennedy went on to stress that he was able to secure all this without federal intervention, so they "wouldn't have to send marshals or troops or any other federal presence, and it would be behind us."[3] It seemed clear that Kennedy was behind the riders in that he wanted to see them carry on their right to protest. It wasn't that he wanted to be a part of the movement, though in many ways he was an active participant; Robert Kennedy wanted to see American ideals upheld. His righteous spirit drove John Seigenthaler and others to put themselves in the same line of fire as the Freedom Riders. That made them a part of the movement. The young attorney general was dealing with a very explosive situation, which now garnered a response from the president and further action on the part of the federal government.

On May 20, 1961, John Kennedy made a statement about the Freedom Riders. While he stopped short of sending troops, he did make it clear that the federal government would respond if there was further violence: "The situation which has developed in Alabama is a source of the deepest concern to me as it must be to the vast majority of the citizens of Alabama and other Americans. I have instructed the Justice Department to take all necessary steps based on their investigations and information." While President Kennedy always looked to his brother to handle these matters, he also made it clear to the nation that RFK was in command and had the authority to do what was necessary to maintain order. In addition, JFK put the responsibility to keep the peace on the states themselves: "I call upon the governor and other responsible state officials in Alabama as well as the mayors of Birmingham and Montgomery to exercise their lawful authority to prevent any further outbreaks of violence." He finished by saying, "I hope that state and local officials in Alabama will meet their responsibilities. The United States government intends to meet its."[4] The federal government, under RFK's leadership, worked to get some level of assistance to the Freedom Riders. It was clear that the South could not stop the riots and ensure the safety of these riders.

While Robert Kennedy and the Justice Department wanted to avoid sending troops, like Eisenhower in Little Rock, he needed to do something in response to the violence. Kennedy spoke with Seigenthaler after his attack. "How are you? How do you feel?" RFK said to Seigenthaler. He responded, "All right. I've got a small headache." In an attempt at using humor in the tense situation, Robert Kennedy said to Seigenthaler, "Let me give you some advice.... Never run for governor of Alabama. You couldn't get elected." Kennedy reassured his soldier, saying, "There was nothing else you could do. I think you did what was right." Seigenthaler said, "It's going to create an awful stink." Kennedy said, "Well, the marshals are on their way." Seigenthaler, a Southerner, understood the implication behind such an action and said he regretted that action and hated it, saying, "It's sort of like an invasion." Kennedy reassured him, however, saying, "Well, sooner or later something had to happen. This is what triggered it. You did the right thing. You did what you had to do. I talked to the president about it. He feels very strongly about it. We're moving in the proper direction."[5] Kennedy's support and decisive action in the wake of violence was a new direction for the federal government. In the past the federal government would have tread lightly, but Bobby believed two important things that would move him to act. First, this was the right thing to do, which he emphasized to Seigenthaler. He believed that something was going to happen eventually to confront segregation. Second, the law was clear and these riders had a right to travel on the interstate highways. Kennedy did not want a denial of rights while he was in office.

Politics was at the heart of decision making in the Kennedy White House, but there was also foreign policy to consider as the administration prepared for its trip to Europe. Raymond Arsenault writes, "Robert Kennedy did not like the idea of alienating voters of a state that had just given his brother five electoral votes, but he was running out of patience — and options." Arsenault argues that it was risky to rely on state and local authorities and that RFK would do whatever possible to minimize political fallout. "With the summit on Vienna less that two weeks away, he simply could not allow the image and moral authority of the United States to be undercut by a mob of racist vigilantes, or, for that matter, by a band of headstrong students determined to provoke them."[6] Robert Kennedy followed up his brother's statement with a wire to Governor Patterson and released it to the press.

In his wire to the governor, Robert Kennedy laid out his reasoning for action in Montgomery. It was a complicated venture, justified by acts from the nineteenth century and Supreme Court cases that ruled in favor of federal intervention in such instances. Kennedy's wire, as well as the public release of it, was meant to demonstrate that these actions were justified and necessary to secure the rights and freedom of American citizens. It was as much a political maneuver as it was a statement of federal authority. Kennedy said that he had made it very clear that this was an issue that he was "deeply concerned" about. In addition he had had "numerous conversations" with Governor Patterson. Kennedy went through the timeline of events, which included the Mother's Day attack, the unanswered phone calls to Patterson, President Kennedy hoping that the state could handle these issues by themselves, and Patterson's request for a "personal representative" to meet with him. The statement portrayed a very accommodating federal government and a Governor Patterson unwilling to meet those accommodations. Kennedy went into the situation at Montgomery, saying that Patterson had guaranteed their safety and that it had been under that assumption that the bus left Birmingham and went to Montgomery.

Kennedy did a brilliant job of setting up the events for the press, not only for the citizens of Alabama who would see this as an invasion, but also the neighboring states in the South that would construe this as an attack by the federal government. Kennedy said that despite all this preparation and assurances from the governor, the Freedom Riders "arrived in Montgomery and were attacked and beaten by a mob." He went on to say that the federal government even involved the FBI, who notified the Montgomery police department that the students were coming. "As a matter of fact, no police were present. However, an armed mob was. Several of the travelers were beaten. The president's personal representative ... was knocked to the ground and left unconscious in the street." The two brothers used each other's comments and sent a message to the South and the nation. The president made a short, terse statement about the issue and left it to Bobby to handle. It was exactly what they had talked about at John Kennedy's apartment before the appointment to attorney general. Their actions were supportive and public. They were trying to change the climate of the nation, and many people were not happy about it.

Robert Kennedy finished the wire on a strong note, saying that he had tried to contact Patterson, but that, once again, he was unavailable. He went on to state the following:

> Therefore, although I strongly believe that law enforcement matters should be handled by local authorities whenever possible, now not being even able to reach you to learn what steps you intend to take we have no alternative but to order the following action.

Kennedy laid out for the nation three points. First, he asked the United States court in Montgomery to "enjoin the Ku Klux Klan, the National States Rights Party, certain individuals and all persons acting in concert with them, from interfering with peaceful interstate travel by buses." Second, Kennedy said that the FBI would investigate the incident in Montgomery and all other incidents from the preceding week. Finally, he said that Deputy Attorney General Byron White would lead a group of United States officers who would "begin to assist state and local authorities in the protection of persons and property."[7] His actions, coupled with the JFK's strong statement and faith in his brother, demonstrated that they were willing to risk political capital to maintain the right course. In addition, their reluctance to use troops speaks not to Robert Kennedy's fear of being ostracized in the South but to his respect for the rights of American citizens and the law, which does not permit the use of the military except in extreme circumstances. That said, the brothers were willing to use the army if necessary.

Raymond Arsenault writes that Kennedy received a call from Patterson before his telegram was sent, expressing a concern that federal intervention might be on the horizon. Kennedy challenged the governor, saying, "why don't you call out the national guard and make it unnecessary for us to take federal action?" Patterson responded that that would be an "embarrassment" prompting him to defend himself "politically."[8] Burke Marshall remembered that the debate over whether the president was going to use troops was one that they contemplated.

> The military didn't want to get into it. That was one factor. I mean in the terms of using trucks or something like that, they didn't want army trucks used. They didn't want army equipment. They didn't want army planes if it could be avoided. Anything that looked like the army, they didn't want, because if you're going to get the army in at all you might as well have the soldiers.[9]

Marshall said that they were trying to avoid another Little Rock, but there was a proclamation ready for the president to sign if they needed it.

"Let's clean the niggers out of here!"

While they debated the next course of action the Freedom Riders made their way to
First Baptist Church, where Martin Luther King, Jr., flew in to meet them. King brought
more tension to the situation and had the potential to bring even more press to the South.
Diane Nash worked behind the scenes to get King to Montgomery. King's presence galvanized the people in Montgomery and solidified SNCC's place in the civil rights movement.
Nash wanted all their efforts to be forefront in the media, and King had the star power to
make that happen. She was determined to show "solidarity" and "commitment" from the
SCLC.[10] Robert Kennedy "nearly exploded" when he found out that King was on his way
to Montgomery. He was going to great lengths to provide safe passage for these freedom
riders. Kennedy and Marshall tried to convince King to stay in Chicago, but he felt that
his place was with the riders at the First Baptist Church. Bobby Kennedy was even more
certain now that he would get no help from the local authorities.[11] King's presence made it
a forgone conclusion that troops needed to intervene. Bobby established a command center
out of his office and had a direct line to his brother, who was in Virginia at the time of the
crisis. The fact that President Kennedy was not even in Washington is evidence of his confidence in his brother's leadership. Byron White and Louis Oberdorfer boarded a plane to
Montgomery to be on-site for Robert Kennedy. Meanwhile, John Doar looked for a judge
who would sign a restraining order for the Klan. He found Judge Frank Johnson, who
signed a "limited order" and then found protection for fear of reprisal for his act.[12]

In all these situations Kennedy's soldiers mobilized and started to take on the race
issue. While many historians criticize Kennedy's handling of the race issue, saying that he
and his brother hid behind politics and their own agenda instead of tackling it head on,
the opposite seems evident in this crisis. The Kennedys confronted the racist South with
various legal tools. Robert Kennedy's frustration that King went to the South is not because
he disagreed with the cause. In fact, it's evidence to the contrary. He wanted the cause to
succeed. Many in the South accused him of being involved anyway. If King made the situation worse it could set the movement back even further. Robert Kennedy wanted to
control the situation and use the justice system to pick away at segregation in the South.
By sending justice officials into the situation, Robert Kennedy sent a message that the Justice
Department would follow through on its promise to uphold the law. He was not afraid of
conflict. The McClellan committee and his work with Joe McCarthy were a testament to
his commitment and determination to pursue what he believed was the just course, not the
easy one.

Byron White was on the ground in Alabama to confront Governor Patterson. White,
however, was a politically ambitious person and considered the ramifications of his stand.
Patterson wanted a meeting with White that would be viewed by the press. It took place
at the capitol. "We consider you interlopers," Patterson said. White defended the Freedom
Riders and said that they had the right to travel anywhere in the United States. Patterson,
however, knew that there was an injunction and a warrant out on the Freedom Riders and
asked White if he knew that and if so would the marshals help apprehend them. White did
not know of the arrest warrant. He said that the marshals would not help Patterson in
apprehending the riders. After the meeting, White considered a withdrawal of the marshals.
Motivated by politics, he went above Robert Kennedy and called President Kennedy instead

to seek advice. Supporting his brother, JFK told him to stay the course. White went back to leading the charge for the freedom riders and escorted King and others to the First Baptist Church.[13] The fact that White did not consult Robert Kennedy and instead looked to the president is evidence that Bobby was relentless with this crisis and wanted the Freedom Rides to succeed. Perhaps White was hoping that Kennedy would be more pragmatic. True to form, however, President Kennedy deferred to his brother and wanted White to help the riders.

The marshals stood outside the church wearing yellow arm bands to distinguish themselves from others. Confederate flags were flying and people were ready to start a war and preserve their way of life. Raymond Arsenault writes that the Kennedys and White were "reticent to do anything beyond the minimum effort needed to forestall disaster." The situation at Maxwell Field, where the marshals were deployed from, was characterized as "chaotic." The administration would only use more marshals if they needed to, and thus they sent a very small unit to the church.[14] While the administration's efforts were minimal, it was still more than other presidents had done for the movement.

The situation at the church got dangerous very quickly. King went to the basement to try to finish a speech that he had started on the plane, but the chaos began and people banged on the door. The marshals used tear gas to keep the rioters off the property. The mob got restless and there were chants of "Let's clean the niggers out of here!"[15] Robert Kennedy had taken to his office, crafting a command center where he would be informed of everything that transpired at First Baptist Church. He was committed to seeing that the civil rights demonstrators were protected. While he wanted to avoid the military, he was ready to deploy them if needed. The situation became even more dangerous when the crowd started to throw Molotov cocktails and makeshift bombs at the church.[16]

It was clear from that point that the administration made the right decision to send the marshals to the South. Robert Kennedy remembered, "The reason we sent marshals was to avoid the idea of sending troops. Now, we thought that marshals would be much more accepted in the South and that you could get away from the idea of a military occupation — and we had to do something." In fact JFK believed that situations like this "should be headed off before a showdown so that wouldn't be necessary."[17] The notion of sending any troops to the South was a tough one for the South to handle. However, the administration had troops on alert in Birmingham, sitting in planes in Birmingham. RFK recalled, "They were doing that almost every crisis we had." This, however, was the first such crisis where it was necessary.[18] Bobby Kennedy deployed four hundred marshals from Marshall Field to stop the carnage that was taking place at First Baptist Church.[19]

The use of troops was always in the background and almost a reality, which could have caused larger problems politically for John Kennedy. Burke Marshall said, "It was very close at one point on that Sunday night. The troops were on alert." RFK also said, "You didn't know how the marshals were going to react. But nobody knew whether they were going to be able to stand, and they'd never been subjected to this kind of test before, and there was a big crowd, and they were all mad and angry."[20] The use of troops would have made King and those in the church at ease, feeling that the federal government came down forcibly on their side, hence proving, from their perspective, that civil rights were important to Kennedy. However, it was important that Kennedy use troops cautiously and be careful how the federal government interfered with state power. This issue was at the heart of the civil rights movement. Indeed, this was something that Kennedy and many other presidents prior had to contend with — especially in the realm of civil rights.

"It's more important that these people survive than for us to survive politically."

Wyatt Walker called Kennedy when people were about to break down the door to the church. Kennedy told him that there were more marshals on the way and said, "We are doing everything we can."[21] Kennedy asked to speak with Dr. King. RFK recalled the events that took place the Sunday that King was in the First Baptist Church.

> Martin Luther King was concerned about whether he was going to live and whether his people were going to live. And I was concerned about whether the place was going to be burned down. He kept getting these reports that the crowds were moving in and that they were going to burn the church down and shoot the Negroes as they ran out of the church.[22]

This was a serious juncture in this episode of the movement. Kennedy and his staff were worried that there would be bloodshed. In the past there had been. If history was any indicator, there would be bloodshed once again. If Kennedy did not do something, King and the people in First Baptist could have been killed.

Once on the phone with King, Kennedy asked if they should consider a cooling off period. King was noncommittal, and there was a great deal of tension between the two leaders. In an effort to relieve some of the tension, Kennedy made a joke that King did not appreciate. Robert Kennedy remembered his conversation with King, saying, "There were our people down there, and as long as he was in church, he might say a prayer for us." Kennedy remembered, "He didn't think that was very humorous." Kennedy said that King "rather berated me for what was happening to him at the time. And I said to him that I didn't think that he'd be alive if it wasn't for us, and that we were going to keep him alive, and that the marshals would keep the church from burning down." King reminded Kennedy that the mob was getting closer. If they did not do something to hold them off, "they were going to have a bloody confrontation," he said to Kennedy. The reinforcements arrived while the two were on the phone.[23] Kennedy's humor was often times misplaced, but it was an indicator that he was determined to get those people out alive. King was in a situation that could cost him his life. King brought the notion of a cooling off period to James Farmer, supporting the notion himself, and it was rejected. Farmer said, "Please tell the attorney general that we've been cooling off for 350 years. If we cool off any more, we will be in a deep freeze. The freedom ride will go on."[24] Perhaps King's response to Robert Kennedy was out of fear and uncertainty. The fact that he agreed with Kennedy demonstrates a solidarity on that issue that they did not acknowledge. The two leaders, however, had a strained relationship. King would talk to Bobby Kennedy again.

The standoff at the church was getting to the point where the attorney general needed to consider options other than the marshals. Rocks were going through windows with shards of glass falling on parishioners and small children. Despite the marshals' best efforts their attempt to move the crowd back with tear gas backfired as the wind change and it drifted into the church.[25] Robert Kennedy asked the Pentagon to put units at Fort Benning, in Georgia, on high alert in case he had to deploy them to Montgomery. Sending in the army seemed the next logical step to take. Since the state was unwilling to make the commitment to protect its citizens, the federal government needed to intervene to maintain domestic tranquility. Was John Kennedy ignoring the preamble of the Constitution in an effort to maintain state sovereignty over its issues? There is a time where the president needs to intervene and the time had passed in Montgomery. The marshals had met resistance and were not as effective as Robert Kennedy had hoped. Robert Kennedy was ready to make a larger commitment.

Governor Patterson was very aware of the communication between Kennedy, White and Doar. He was eavesdropping on all the phone calls through a telephone company operator. Patterson knew that Kennedy was about to make a commitment of military forces in Montgomery. Before Robert Kennedy could get his brother's signature, Patterson acted and declared martial law in Montgomery.[26] Kennedy wanted this outcome and even took an interview with *Time* magazine about how the state and federal government worked together to stop the crisis from escalating.[27] If Patterson had not acted, Kennedy was willing to send in the military to stop the bloodshed. That moment points to an awakening in Kennedy that had not been there prior to this crisis. Kennedy had experienced the harsh circumstances in the South. The Freedom Riders and the other civil rights leaders had made an impression on the righteous Kennedy brother. The Freedom Rides were the first step to seeing the civil rights movement as a moral, not a political, issue. At 10:00 P.M. Patterson made the declaration and by 10:05 the Alabama National Guard had surrounded the church.

Kennedy's actions staved off calamity on a lot of levels. The Freedom Riders were protected and the state saved face, making it easier to deal with them in the future. Though civil rights leaders wanted more, it was imperative that Kennedy put the lives of the people first and the politics second. He knew that if he brought in the troops it would cause issues with future altercations in the South, resulting in violence. They had troops ready in case the marshals could not handle the situation, and would have sent them in if the situation gotten to the point where death seemed imminent. RFK kept in communication with the president: "I just kept him advised as to what was going on. I don't remember where he was. But, again, there wasn't any decision that he could make at the moment, at that time."[28] If one follows the letter of the law, as RFK always did in this and other situations, it is important to not disrupt the relationship between the state and the federal government, unless it is extremely necessary. Federalism played as large a role in the civil rights movement as the segregation laws in the South. RFK wanted the Freedom Riders to slow down at this point. "I thought that people were going to get killed, and they had made their point. What was the purpose of continuing with it?" Kennedy said.[29] Was this politically motivated or was Kennedy truly worried that they would not be as lucky as they were in Alabama?

Kennedy withdrew the marshals, and the National Guard took control of the situation. General Henry Graham stated that he had everything under control and did not need the marshals any longer. The mob, however, was much more difficult to move away from the church. The night was not over. Dr. King addressed the crowd, upholding law and empowering the people who were trapped in the church.

While King spoke to the church, the situation outside grew worse. After the speech they headed for the exits, but were stopped by the Guard. The situation had turned into something different, where the group was not allowed to leave the church. They were now held captive for their own safety. King made another call to Kennedy. King continued to push RFK for more help and assistance. Kennedy shot back that King would be "as dead as Kelsey's nuts if it weren't for the marshals and the effects that we'd made."[30] King was unaware of the old Irish saying but understood that Kennedy was on edge. He handed the phone to Shuttlesworth, who had similar concerns. Kennedy shot back, "You look after your end, Reverend, and I'll look after mine."[31] Patterson called Kennedy not long after the conversation with King. "Now you've got what you want," Patterson started in on Kennedy. "You've got yourself a fight. And you've got the National Guard called out, and martial law, and that's what you wanted." Patterson said that Kennedy could get all forces out of the state. Kennedy asked Patterson how he planned to evacuate the church and protect the people. Patterson said that everyone in the church would be protected except King. "I don't believe that," Kennedy shot back: "Have General Graham call me. I want to hear a general of the United States Army say he can't protect Martin Luther King."[32] Patterson admitted that the situation with King was more about him surviving politically. RFK's response was, "Now John, don't tell me that. It's more important that these people survive than for us to survive politically."[33] Patterson and Kennedy left the conversation without any guarantee that the people in the church would be protected.

King and Kennedy did a lot to empower the cause. King's leadership in the church became a trumpet call to the people that some laws were meant to be broken. Similarly, Kennedy's insistence that protection be given to all Americans stood in the face of Southern segregation law. Bobby Kennedy showed strong leadership in this situation. That leadership was evidence that he was evolving. However, he believed that it was better if the state handled these matters. Kennedy sent William Orrick, a Justice Department official, to negotiate with the National Guard. When Orrick went to talk to General Graham, he recalled, "There wasn't a sign of an American flag ... just the Confederate flags."[34] Orrick had to threaten more federal intervention if Graham could not guarantee a peaceful solution. They both agreed to get the people out of the church and the next morning several convoys brought them out of the situation.

8. Mississippi

"Everyone should have the right to protection."

The morning after the Freedom Riders were out of the church, Robert Kennedy went to the White House to brief the president on the developments from the prior weekend. Raymond Arsenault argues that the Kennedy brothers planned "a graceful retreat without weakening the integrity of federal authority or appearing to abandon the Freedom Riders." Robert Kennedy especially did not want to stand by while the Freedom Riders went to an Alabama prison. The White House did not have a plan to get their people or the riders out of Alabama safely.[1] One thing that did help the administration was the arrest of the men who had burned the bus in Anniston. The four Klansmen were arrested by the FBI. J. Edgar Hoover called Robert Kennedy himself to tell him the news.[2]

After safely leaving the church, John Lewis and the other Freedom Riders spent time at Dr. Dean Harris's house. It was there that they waited for some resolution to this standoff. Lewis remembered that they decided to go to court and challenge the injunction that was filed against the Freedom Riders. He would testify. The NAACP lawyers and King's friend Fred Gray had brought the issue before a judge. The presiding judge, Frank Johnson, was under marshal protection because he had signed the restraining order against the Klan. Lewis went before Johnson, where he testified for the first time in court. Johnson asked Lewis what he had experienced and why they wanted to carry on these rides. "I was nervous," he remembered. "This was a courtroom, the seat of the law, and it was the law itself, come down from the Supreme Court in Washington, that was the issue of this day. That was how I answered the judge's question, by stating that we had begun this ride to see that the law was carried out, and we wanted to continue it for the same reason."[3] As a result of Lewis's testimony and the efforts of the lawyers, the judge lifted the injunction and the Freedom Riders were allowed to continue their journey. The big question was whether the rest of the group would continue and how Robert Kennedy would be able to find protection for them.

Martin Luther King, Jr., was very involved at this point in what was going on in Montgomery. His solidarity with the riders gave many hope that he would join them as they prepared to continue the journey. Nash had suggested this already, but now it was an important juncture in this relationship. King said that he was on probation, and if he were arrested it could mean as long as six months in prison. Lewis remembered that others in the group said, "I'm on probation, too," and "me too."[4] King and others believed that he was too valuable a leader for the movement to be imprisoned. When pushed further, King stayed firm on his position. He excused himself from the room, speaking with Wyatt Walker separately. Walker came back to the group and said that King would not accompany them and the matter not up for discussion. This episode hurt King's standing with these students, prompt-ing jibes at him such as "De Lawd," a way to mock King's assumption of Christ-like standing in the movement.[5] That Tuesday afternoon the group held a press conference in Ralph Abernathy's back yard, telling the nation that they would continue the rides to Jackson, Mississippi.[6] At this meeting Martin Luther King told reporters, "Freedom Riders must develop the quiet courage of dying for a cause." He went on, "We would not like to see anyone die ... but we are well aware that we may have some casualties." He finished, saying, "I'm sure these students are willing to face death if necessary."[7]

As the Freedom Riders arranged for their trip to Mississippi, Robert Kennedy was in talks with Mississippi senator James Eastland and Mississippi governor Ross Barnett to secure the safe passage of the Freedom Riders into Mississippi. Barnett had made it clear through other leaders in the state as well as his own statement that law and order would be maintained. While it may have been a hollow promise, since he could not control every person in the state, it was more than Patterson had done. A larger drama unfolded in the conversations that Robert Kennedy, Governor Ross Barnett and Senator Eastland had.

On May 22, 1961, Burke Marshall contacted Attorney General Joseph Patterson of Mis-sissippi to prepare for the coming of the Freedom Riders. This was one of the first gestures on the part of the administration to find a way to help the Freedom Riders and avoid blood-shed. It was Robert Kennedy's attempt at a back channel response to the crisis. Marshall started the conversation, saying, "I am calling because of the situation that has developed in Alabama because of the possibilities that the press seems to reveal that there may be a situation created in Mississippi." Marshall went on to say that the authorities in Alabama had been unsuccessful at stopping the bloodshed. "I was calling you General Patterson in order to find out what the attitude of the state government in Mississippi is."[8] The phone call was a part of a large effort by Kennedy and Marshall to secure the safe passage of the Freedom Riders through Mississippi. Kennedy spoke with Senator Eastland seven times on May 24. Marshall started with Patterson to see what the state had planned for the Freedom Riders.

Patterson responded to Marshall, saying, "We should be realistic — we are going to be realistic and I am assuming that you and Mr. Kennedy will be. What right do 14 wild-eyed fanatics have to go into a state for the purpose of creating what they did in Alabama?" Mar-shall shot back, "I think if we are going to be realistic we have to face the situation as it exists. If these students just like any other citizens buy bus tickets to go across the state they have a perfect right to do it." Marshall would not have gone out on limb like that if he did not have Robert Kennedy's support. Patterson replied, "But if they get off the bus and make trouble they will have to suffer the consequences."[9] Both leaders took a stand in this con-versation. Marshall went further to assert himself as the conversation progressed.

Patterson said that if the Freedom Riders went through Mississippi without any "fanfare and forewarning," then they should be ok. Marshall said, "I am assuming there will be no trouble. I am also assuming that it will be known who they are. You said we have to be realistic — those assumptions we have to make." Patterson did not appreciate the tone in Marshall's point that he assumed that there would be trouble. The conversation started to take on a different direction when Patterson said, "In order to be frank with you, it is incon-ceivable to me that the U.S. Government will throw its prestige behind 12 radicals and demoralize a state of 2 million people." He went on to say, "It is inconceivable that we have reached this point in America." Marshall wanted to stick to the issue of safety and responded by saying, "We are talking about if these people are going to have police protection in the state of Mississippi."[10] That was at the heart of the Kennedy strategy — using the law to protect citizens who were standing up for their rights. Marshall and Robert Kennedy agreed that the Freedom Riders had the right to use those bus terminals and they were trying to uphold the law as they saw it.

Patterson was concerned that Robert Kennedy would hear about this conversation, and Marshall assured him that he would indeed let the attorney general know. "This is a call," Marshall said, "because I wanted to find out what your feeling is about what position the state of Mississippi will take." The Justice Department knew, after Alabama, that they had to be proactive and see how the riders were going to protected. Marshals were not a good idea and the administration was hard-pressed to use them again, especially in Mississippi. "Mississippi is quiet and peaceful today," Patterson said to Marshall. He went on to say that he wouldn't advise the governor to let "12 wild-eyed radicals in here to have them spit in the faces of the people of Mississippi." Marshall stayed on point and asked, "What would you do?" Patterson was firm and replied, "If they think they are going to get off the bus and swagger around the cafes and bus stations with police protection, we will not do it."[11] Marshall had a much more realistic tone in his questions and reasoning with Patterson. He told him that they could not do anything about whether these riders wanted to ride the bus.

Patterson said that the federal government was too involved in these rides and should not interfere with state and local law. Marshal responded, "The federal government would not have had to do anything in Alabama and would not do anything in your state if the law enforcement officials of the state itself, which we agree has the responsibility for matters within the state, afford protection, but in Alabama they did not and my purpose is to find out whether they will in Mississippi." Marshall, once again, wanted to get a answer from the attorney general. He was consistent in saying that the travelers deserved protection under the law. Patterson disagreed and said, "They want to come in here and want to make the state give police protection so they can spit in the faces of the people of our state. I think they ought to go home and quit their darned Communist conduct." He finished, "They got no business in Mississippi." Patterson was still resistant, which was the usual response from the Southern states when it came to enforcing Jim Crow laws and the role that the federal government would play in these matters. Perhaps the larger issue here was the power between the federal and state governments and how that power is used in situations like this. This has been a controversial issue since the Whiskey Rebellion and continued with the nullification crisis right into the Civil War. These were difficult questions that evolved in the twentieth century.

Marshall was steadfast in his interpretation of the law, saying, "General Patterson, everyone — and I believe everyone — communists and fascists, who want to get on a bus can't be stopped to ride on a bus. We've got to start from that starting point." He continued, "I recognize why the people of Mississippi do not like this but it's a serious law enforcement situation." A major disconnect with the Southern states and the federal government was this presumption that some laws did not apply to their states. Marshall was clear that these riders had the right to travel into the South as the Supreme Court had decided years prior. Marshall's point to Patterson that they needed to start from that idea was important, in that it was a firm commitment by the federal government to enforce all law decided by the courts, which would have further implications for other decisions that protected the rights of the people of the United States. Patterson said that if these riders were coming down there to start trouble then why should they be protected. Marshall's reply was, "Everyone should have the right to protection." The phone call ended with Patterson saying that he was only being "absolutely frank."[12]

"Now I was here, and it was unsettling."

Robert Kennedy was worried that the Freedom Riders would not survive Mississippi. Burke Marshall felt the same way about their prospects. The two leaders were looking for a way to protect the Freedom Riders and save face. Indeed, Robert Kennedy was impressed with the Freedom Riders, admiring their courage and saying that they had "succeeded in moving the nation's conscience."[13] Marshall remembered, "We had a great deal of advice that they could be killed in Mississippi." He was unsure if he could trust Governor Ross Barnett and Mississippi Senator James Eastland, who both were in contact with the Justice Department regarding the Freedom Riders' inevitable trip to Jackson.[14] Robert Kennedy utilized back-channel communication to ensure the safety of the riders as they attempted to make the trip to Mississippi.

The White House had decided that it was too risky to use federal marshals as the group moved in to Mississippi. Many who advised Kennedy said that they could not trust Barnett and they should consider other options. Robert Kennedy turned to Senator James O. Eastland. Eastland had been a supporter during RFK's confirmation hearings. He trusted him. Arsenault writes, "Over the course of three days and several dozen phone conversations, this trust deepened as Eastland convinced the young attorney general that he would see to it that Mississippi's response to the Freedom Rides served the best interest of the nation."[15]

This was an important piece for Robert Kennedy. While he wanted to ensure safe passage for the riders, he was also preoccupied by his brother's trip to Vienna. Just on the heels of the Bay of Pigs invasion, it was important that the Kennedys had a victory somewhere. Keeping the peace in the South was tantamount to such success. In addition, the notion of back-channel communication between him and Eastland was appealing and would serve as a tool for Kennedy when it came to working with the Soviet Union. Later in 1961 he established a similar relationship with Georgi Bolshakov, Khrushchev's emissary, in an attempt to work with the Kremlin behind the scenes.

Robert Kennedy took a different approach as the Freedom Riders made their way to Mississippi. Eastland said to Kennedy that if the group tried to violate the segregation laws it would result in their arrest. Kennedy did not want to push Eastland and said that the federal government's "primary interest was that they weren't beaten up." Raymond Arsenault writes, "The rioting in Alabama had convinced the Kennedy brothers, along with White and Marshall, that almost anything was preferable to mob violence—including unconstitutional arrests of interstate travelers.... Ironically, a tentative show of force in one state had undercut federal authority in a second."[16]

While Kennedy lost some leverage in Mississippi, he hoped to diffuse the situation through his back-channel agreement with Eastland and a legal approach, which he preferred. Many in the administration acknowledged later that acquiescing to Eastland's and Barnett's demands was a mistake.[17] That said, given the circumstances it was important that the administration move on and confront the situation in a way that did not threaten lives. If the riders were jailed it would give Kennedy time to approach it from a new perspective that did not back him into a corner. Further, many civil rights leaders failed to see that it was important that the state get an opportunity to take care of the situation without federal intervention, which would lead to other legal problems for the administration. However, the fact remained that Freedom Riders would be jailed for exercising their right to travel as dictated by the Supreme Court. Kennedy would follow through on exploring the legal means to protect travel. Until that time, the Freedom Riders boarded buses and made their way to Mississippi.

Robert Kennedy remembered that Eastland had said, "They'd all be arrested. And I said to him my primary interest was that they weren't beaten up." Kennedy went on to say that he "didn't have any control" of whether they were arrested. Marshall recalled in the same interview that many told them that the riders "could be killed in Mississippi." Marshall went on to say that James P. Coleman, the former governor, said that the Kennedys "couldn't trust Barnett, and that the riders would never reach Jackson; they'd be killed."[18] While the situation was not as acutely dangerous as Alabama, there was potential for missteps and violence that could harm the Freedom Riders and further damage the international prestige of the United States. Kennedy and Marshall considered these aspects as the Freedom Rides moved into Mississippi.

Robert Kennedy remembered, "Jim Eastland really took a responsibility for it." He went on to say that he trusted Eastland; "I mean, the assurances that he gave me that this was what was going to happen: that they'd get there, they'd be protected, and then they'd be locked up."[19] The Kennedys struggled on how to handle this issue. There were no real precedents other than the Little Rock episode to guide the brothers. Perhaps the greatest example was Lincoln and how he dealt with the South. Many other presidents had been confronted with similar states' rights issues, from Jefferson to Jackson to Lincoln. There was no textbook way to handle it. Each president had put his own signature on it. The Kennedys used the federal marshals to avoid the idea of military intervention, something that John Kennedy had criticized Eisenhower for during the campaign. Now he was confronted with a similar issue. The administration was not confident in the marshals' ability to maintain peace. It was time to consider other options. This deal with Barnett and Eastland was it.

As the Freedom Riders left Dr. Harris's house they knew nothing of the plan to protect them as they made their journey into Mississippi. Once at the terminal, they saw five hundred armed national guardsmen. The Kennedy administration was letting the state handle its own issues, but they were cautious not to leave them completely in charge. In the crowd there were several plainclothes FBI agents.[20] General Graham gave orders to allow only the Freedom Riders on the buses. Nobody else would be making the trip to Jackson that morning. The bus was already filled with reporters as the Freedom Riders took their seats. General Graham came on board, telling them that they were about to embark on a "hazardous journey." However, he reassured them, "We have taken every precaution to protect you." He went on to say, "I sincerely wish you all a safe journey." Six guardsmen stayed on the bus and the group started their journey to Jackson. King waved goodbye to them as they left for Mississippi.[21]

Kennedy's efforts with Eastland and Barnett were unknown to the riders. Kennedy wanted to ensure that there was no bloodshed in Mississippi. With that in mind they made similar preparations. While it may seem that Robert Kennedy was not involved in this operation, the opposite was true. His negotiations were coupled with a steadfast watch on the situation as it developed. He was determined to avoid violence and was ready to act if necessary. If the Freedom Riders had not had Robert Kennedy's support they would not have gotten as far as they had. Further, there could have been larger tragedies than the beatings at Montgomery.

On the border of Mississippi were National Guardsmen and highway patrolmen. General Pat Wilson led the Mississippi guard. Before the riders even made it into the state there were several reports of threats that had guardsmen searching the woods. Once over the line

General Graham relinquished control of the convoy to Mississippi officials, General Wilson and the commissioner of public safety, T.B. Birdsong. They put six Mississippi guards on the bus and further down the road they switched drivers.[22] At that point, it seemed that the Freedom Riders were going to make the trip to Jackson without any issue. While some of the guardsmen were short with the riders, they provided protection, and that was more than the riders had gotten in previous attempts to desegregate the South. On the heels of the first bus was another group of Freedom Riders, which included John Lewis. Similar precautions were being taken for this group, as it was always CORE's intention to have two buses filled with people. This bus did not have the same feeling of a military motorcade, but they were protected and had a similar exchange at the border.[23]

In the wake of the violence from First Baptist Church the Freedom Riders prepared to make the journey to their next destination. Reporters and photographers were aboard the bus before the riders, in the hopes of gaining some newsworthy information. John Lewis remembered that the group was "escorted by a convoy of national guard jeeps and trucks, highway patrol cruisers and carloads of reporters — forty-two vehicles in all, plus two helicopter spotters and three U.S. Border Patrol airplanes flying overhead to check bridges and trouble spots ahead of the bus for signs of booby traps, bombs or snipers."[24] There was a military presence there that day as Freedom Riders made their way into Mississippi. The problem was not Alabama, which had been sufficiently tamed in the wake of all that violence starting with the first Freedom Rides. Robert Kennedy and his Justice Department had made sure that the riders would make it out of Alabama safely. Mississippi was another issue. Since there was less military support for the second bus there was a great deal of trepidation among the riders about what they would encounter in Mississippi. Lewis recalled, "All my life I had heard unbelievably horrible things about the place, stories of murders and lynchings, bodies dumped in rivers.... Now I was here, and it was unsettling seeing crowds of onlookers standing by the roadside, held back by those armed troops."[25]

"Ours is a way out—creative, moral and nonviolent."

Robert Kennedy's attempt to control the situation was not working. No sooner did the second bus leave the terminal than there was word of a third bus departing Atlanta. The ride originated in New Haven, Connecticut, with Yale University chaplain William Sloane Coffin, Jr., at the helm. Robert Kennedy was looking into this third bus when the first bus arrived at Jackson.[26] Once in Montgomery and safe, Coffin debated on continuing with the third bus full of Freedom Riders. In an effort to gain more support from the Kennedy administration, Coffin attempted to contact fellow Yale graduate McGeorge Bundy, Kennedy's national security advisor. Coffin was hoping for a statement that denounced racism, making this a moral issue for the nation. The administration was preparing for the summit in Vienna while dealing with this national crisis and Bundy was especially preoccupied. Coffin moved on to Wofford, but got nowhere with him.[27]

The Kennedy administration focused on the summit in Vienna, leaving the brunt of decision-making in this crisis to Bobby and the Justice Department. The administration's reluctance to embrace the third group of riders was contrary to New Frontier ideology. In fact it directly opposed Robert Kennedy's Law Day speech. Raymond Arsenault argues that there were several factors leading to Kennedy's determination to stop the Freedom Rides. The administration's most "pressing concern was the apparent polarization of the struggle over racial segregation." The rides had attracted extremists from "both ends of the political spectrum." The American Nazi Party was in New Orleans protesting the movement, affirming support for the Klan's members who had attacked the buses in Anniston and Montgomery.[28]

As the riders tried to challenge the segregation law in Jackson, Mississippi Police captain J.L. Ray warned them to "move on" from the whites-only waiting room. When the riders did not, Ray arrested all twelve that were on the bus. The police put them in a paddy wagon and sent them off to jail.[29] Arsenault argues that in Washington, Montgomery and Jackson, "pure emotion seemed to be driving much of the official reaction to the Freedom Riders' exasperating commitment to nonviolent direct action. Although Robert Kennedy was angry at Ross Barnett for allowing the Jackson police to put the Trailways group in jail, he was even angrier at the obstinacy of the Riders themselves."[30]

Robert Kennedy liked to control the outcome of situations. In the back of his thinking was his brother's presidency, which he felt a responsibility to protect. In addition, he was learning about the injustice that existed in the South and wanted to do something about it. However, he recognized that federal intervention was the only way to do it. He was in a situation to make a difference yet. From his perspective he needed time to find the proper laws and get things moving. Bobby was a pragmatic idealist. In many ways so was King. Despite the fact that King pushed Kennedy on many fronts, an example of his pragmatism was the fact that he chose not to accompany the Freedom Riders on the journey to Jackson. The rides were important to the movement, but there were other aspects that King needed to attend to, and being in jail would not help the movement.

Robert Kennedy was very concerned about what could potentially happen to the students in Mississippi. "I thought that people were going to get killed, and they had made their point," he recalled later.[31] Nevertheless, he was highly criticized by people in the movement for asking the Freedom Rides to stop. The morning statement said that the administration had been in contact with the officials from Alabama and Mississippi and had been told that they "fully intend to see that law and order is maintained." Further, this statement made it clear that the marshals would not accompany the bus anywhere else. He reinforced the idea that the federal government's responsibility was only if the state and local officials could not protect interstate travelers. There was no reason to assume that the citizens of Mississippi would act unlawfully in this situation, according to the statement. What bothered some people was that Robert Kennedy referred to the upcoming meeting with Nikita Khrushchev in Vienna, saying, "I think we should all keep in mind that the President is about to embark on a mission of great importance. Whatever we do in the United States at this time which brings or causes discredit on our country can be harmful to his mission."[32] While that may have irked many, challenging their patriotism in the press, the afternoon release added further insult to the Freedom Riders' efforts.

Kennedy said in his other release that he was very concerned about the situation in Mississippi and Alabama. He was afraid that innocent people would be harmed. "A mob asks no questions." He boldly asserted, "A cooling off period is needed. It would be wise for those traveling through these two states to delay their trips until the present state of confusion and danger has passed and an atmosphere of reason and normalcy has been restored."[33] Kennedy was also concerned about others coming to the South looking for publicity, and he wanted that all to stop. "So my response to that," he said later, "was that I was interested in preserving the peace, not having somebody killed."[34] Kennedy's concern was warranted, as he received a telegram from Governor Ross Barnett telling him, "You will do a great disservice to the agitators and the people of the United States if you do not advise the agitators to stay out of Mississippi."[35]

The first group of Freedom Riders declined bail and planned on spending time in jail. The NAACP offered to pay, but the riders chose to spend time in jail instead. This added to the tension with Robert Kennedy.[36] To make matters worse for the attorney general, the second bus arrived at Jackson and the fifteen riders were arrested in the same fashion as the first. They too declined bail and chose to spend time in prison until their trial date. Robert Kennedy wanted the Freedom Riders out of prison and sent Marshall and White to see of any of them would reconsider their decision. They came up short, and Robert Kennedy decided to call King directly.[37] Kennedy admired the Freedom Riders, but he felt that they had made their point. Further he believed that he had done all that the federal government could do up that point. He needed time to take action legally, which was how he planned to tackle these issues. It was also likely that Kennedy was annoyed that this crisis was taking him away from helping his brother plan for the meeting with Khrushchev, which, in the wake of the Bay of Pigs, was very important for American prestige abroad.

Robert Kennedy wanted to get the Freedom Riders out of jail. Despite the fact that he went to Eastland and Barnett to make a deal, he was concerned for their safety in a Southern jail. When Martin Luther King called him, he was surprised by what he had to say. King said that they would stay in prison. "It's a matter of conscience and morality. They must use their bodies to right a wrong," King said to Kennedy over the phone. Hoping to reason with King and get the riders out of prison, Bobby responded, "This is not going to have the slightest effect on what the government is going to do in this field or any other." He went on, "The fact that they stay in jail is not going to have the slightest effect on me."[38] Kennedy's response is representative of how he handled different situations. He did not like to be threatened, nor did he appreciate being backed into a corner. The exchange between him and King grew even more tense when it was clear that the standoff in the church would not push Bobby to make a stronger stand in this instance.

Hoping that Robert Kennedy would do more to embrace the riders, King said, "Perhaps it would help if students came down here by the hundreds — by the hundreds of thousands." Kennedy responded, "The country belongs to you as much as to me. You can determine what's best just as well as I can, but don't make statements that sound like a threat. That's not the way to deal with us." There was a silence on the other end of the line. King continued with a philosophical attitude on how to move on, trying to reason with Kennedy: "It's difficult to understand the position of oppressed people. Ours is a way out — creative, moral and nonviolent. It is not tied to black supremacy or Communism, but to the plight of the oppressed." King continued, saying that the movement could "save the soul of America," and that only pressure had reaped gains.[39] King hoped to persuade Kennedy to do more. From Kennedy's point of view, he had done more than any other attorney general in the history of the United States, and he was right to think that. However, the nation was on the cusp of revolution, and Kennedy was not fully prepared to embrace that revolution. Instead, he was planning to chip away at the problem with the power of the federal government.

Kennedy responded to King's points, saying, "But the problem won't be settled in Jackson, Mississippi, but by strong federal action." History had proven that the federal government could make a difference in situations such as this, but it took time and resolve on the part of everyone involved. "I'm deeply appreciative of what the administration is doing," King said. "I see a ray of hope, but I am different than my father. I feel the need to be free now!" Kennedy repeated one last time. "Well, it all depends on what you and the people in jail decide. If they want to get out, we can get them out." King responded, "They'll stay."[40] The exchange between Kennedy and King shows two leaders who believed that what they were doing was righteous. Robert Kennedy was a moral person. Martin Luther King was a moral person. They were both politicians, becoming experts within their communities, and they were both young — only four years apart, with Kennedy as the elder. This episode is evidence of the effect that they would have on history. Bobby, with his penchant for using the power of the government to evoke change. Martin Luther King, with his moral and conscientious approach to bring pressure on the government. Ironically, they both wanted the same things, yet could not see that in the midst of the crisis.

After their conversation Robert Kennedy called Harris Wofford. "This is too much," he said. "I wonder whether they have the best interest of their country at heart. Do you know that one of them is against the atom bomb."[41] Kennedy saw his country first and everything else second. From his point of view the Freedom Riders had made their point, gaining heavy media attention and exposing the ugliness of Jim Crow in the South. There was no need to take it to another level. Kennedy was concerned about foreign policy. Both brothers saw that as the greatest issue that the administration would face, which was why they were so impatient with civil rights. Nevertheless, this issues was as defining as foreign affairs for the Kennedys. Bobby even remarked to Wofford, "The president is going abroad and this is all embarrassing to him."[42]

"In the foreseeable future a Negro can achieve the same position that my brother has."

In Montgomery, King came back to Abernathy's living room after the conversation and said, "You know they don't understand the social revolution going on in the world, and therefore they don't understand what we're doing." When other Freedom Riders made their way to Mississippi, Kennedy showed his anger by stating to the *Washington Post*, "It took a lot of guts for the first group to go but not much for the others." Kennedy even went as far to say that the Freedom Riders who remained in jail were "good propaganda for America's enemies."[43] Both Kennedy and King were right in their assessment of the situation. The Freedom Riders had made their point, and Kennedy did what he could to support them in Alabama. As a result of that movement, Kennedy led an effort to end segregation in interstate travel. Therefore from Bobby's perspective he was doing his job as attorney general. He saw any other rider from this point on as trying to gain a piece of the spotlight. King, on the other hand, was also right. There was a revolution in the world that had not yet extended to the United States. Ironically, the nation that supported freedom and equality was the antithesis of that in the Southern states.

In the midst of the Freedom Rides President Kennedy delivered a second State of the Union to Congress on May 25, 1961. He started by saying, "These are extraordinary times. And we face an extraordinary challenge. Our strength as well as our convictions have imposed upon this nation the role of leader in freedom's cause." He went on, "No role in history could be more difficult or more important. We stand for freedom. That is our conviction for ourselves — that is our only commitment to others. No friend, no neutral and no adversary should think otherwise. We are not against any man — or any nation — or any system — except as it is hostile to freedom. Nor am I here to present a new military doctrine, bearing any one name or aimed at any one area." Kennedy had various reasons for this speech. "I am here to promote the freedom doctrine."[44] Kennedy wanted to talk about this "freedom doctrine" that America was committed to, but he failed to mention the issues in the South. At that point in his administration he was short sighted. Robert and John Kennedy were still learning about the issues in the South. In addition, there were larger political issues that forced them to take their time addressing the racial divide in the country. But this speech was mostly about freedom abroad and not in America.

In fact, Kennedy said, "The first and basic task confronting this nation this year was to turn recession into recovery. An affirmative anti-recession program, initiated with your cooperation, supported the natural forces in the private sector; and our economy is now enjoying renewed confidence and energy. The recession has been halted. Recovery is under way." First and foremost he saw the economy as a pervasive issue in the nation. Without a strong economy America could not lead in Latin America and other nations where American business was important to growth.[45] Kennedy went on to propose legislation to strengthen our foreign policy and help other nations while in turn helping America's goals. Nowhere in the speech were the Freedom Rides, nor was there any mention of the civil rights struggles that plagued the nation. This speech is evidence that Kennedy saw the foreign policy issues as paramount in his administration. Further, it serves as a reminder that the president would not play a direct role in that movement. His brother, however, was another matter. It was understood by the Kennedy brothers that they had their areas that they wanted to concentrate their efforts on.

The day after President Kennedy's speech to Congress, Robert Kennedy commented on the issues in the South in a *Voice of America* radio broadcast. The May 26, 1961, broadcast started by saying, "I think the whole world, as well as all the people of our own country, are aware of what has happened in Alabama over the last two weeks. It is a matter of great concern to all of us." He went on, "It is disturbing in particular to the United States Government."[46] It is no coincidence that Kennedy commented the day after his brother. Once again, they had their areas that they wanted to address. Robert Kennedy's was domestic issues. He was not yet fully invested in foreign policy. At the outset of the administration John Kennedy had clear ideas where he wanted his advisors. Robert Kennedy wanted to distinguish himself in his own right. As the administration proceeded, the Kennedys evolved further, bringing Bobby and Jack together as partners in the administration.

Kennedy said: "We are disturbed about the fact that beatings took place and about the fact that people's rights were not being protected. Police and police officials of states and cities in this area were not properly guarding the people because of color. We sent 500 representatives of the U.S. Government to help and assist these people."[47] In a sense Robert Kennedy sounded defensive, but at the same time he asserted the power of the federal government, saying, "Prejudice exists in the United States and we have many problems and difficulties like that. The United States government has taken steps to make sure that the Constitution of the United States applies to all individuals." This was a message for United States citizens as well as nations abroad.

Kennedy went further, saying that African Americans had achieved posts in the government and that the nation was making progress. He said, "We are not going to gain ground against prejudice by just passing laws. Because prejudice exists with people throughout the world—not with people of this country. But we have tried to make progress and we are making progress. That is what is so important. We are not going to accept the status quo." He said that the U.S. government would not accept the riots and will continue to be vigilant to stop them: "We are working hard at this problem."[48] The most interesting part of the commentary came at the end, when Kennedy talked about his ancestry:

> My grandfather came to this country many years ago. He was brought up in Boston and when he went out to look for a job there were signs on many stores that no Irish were wanted. Now after 40 or 50 years, an Irish Catholic is President of the United States. That progress has been made

over the last fifty years. And we feel that the same kind of progress will be made for the Negroes. There is no question about it. In the foreseeable future a Negro can achieve the same position that my brother has.[49]

He finished by saying, "We will make progress in the country."

Kennedy's interview was as much a show of support and solidarity with the civil rights movement as it was a call for them to recognize that change takes time. Kennedy also wanted his acts made known to the world. The United States, from his perspective, had been doing all that it could to maintain peace and order while recognizing the rights of the Freedom Riders. His greatest show of support, however, was when he looked to the law to make change. Edwin Guthman, Robert Kennedy's press advisor, wrote, "In 1961 [Robert Kennedy] recognized that the country had been too slow and too intractable in redressing the Negroes' historic grievances, and he had acted within the government to accelerate that pace." Guthman goes on to say that Kennedy thought in the "cliches of the times. He did not regard the incipient black rebellion as the gravest threat to American society." RFK believed that there was still time for "steady, rational progress."[50] In this sense Robert Kennedy is seen as a pragmatic politician. However, he still recognized that there was a need for change. Very much like Lincoln and slavery, Kennedy wanted to wait for the right time to address the issue.

Guthman remembered, "Bob was confident that resolute leadership by the federal government and the good sense of the American people would overcome centuries of prejudice and white insensitivity to the human aspirations of those who were not white."[51] Kennedy wanted to foster civil rights change and, in many ways, had a revelation during the Freedom Rides. It was one that started with the campaign and the unjust imprisonment of Dr. King. Guthman wrote that Kennedy's "road to full recognition of what was behind the black rebellion and its crucial implications for the future of the nation, however, lay not only in discharging his official duties but in frequent walks through ghetto neighborhoods, in many visits to ghetto schools, particularly in Washington and in countless conversations — some of them acrimonious confrontations — with black leaders."[52]

Carl Brauer writes, "Robert Kennedy had at the outset defined his department's civil rights role: it would promote racial progress through mediation and, when necessary, through legal enforcement of existing statutes, particularly those related to voting rights.... This definition comported not only with the Attorney General's perceptions of his moral and legal obligations but also with his brother's political welfare."[53] In addition, Brauer writes that Burke Marshall and Robert Kennedy believed that civil rights, in the wake of the Civil War, had failed and it was important that they get it right this time around. In fact, the federal force in the South had made it very difficult for systemic change to take root. The rights of freed slaves were diminished, leading to Jim Crow. Kennedy and Marshall, Brauer writes, "hoped to see civil rights take root this time and were therefore determined to make the absolute minimal use of federal force."[54]

From Kennedy's perspective it was important that federalism remain a part of the national discourse and the states maintain their sovereignty in situations like the Freedom Riders in the South. That power is outlined in the Constitution as well, and there was a great deal riding on protecting the integrity of those powers if the United States was going to continue as the founders had intended. From that point of view the Freedom Rides and Kennedy's response were successes. Kennedy maintained a federal presence during the crisis and the South eventually took hold of the situation without further bloodshed.[55]

On May 29, 1961, Robert Kennedy took action and filed a petition with the Interstate

Commerce Commission to adopt stricter measures to enforce the November 1955 decision that directed interstate bus companies to cease the practice of segregation. Further, he used the Freedom Riders as evidence that current practice had contributed to the violence in the South. He had always said that the law and voter registration were the best way to fight racism in the South.[56] Justice Department attorney Robert Saloscin had the notion of a petition, and Kennedy acted on it. The petition read, "Just as our constitution is color blind, and neither knows nor tolerates classes among citizens so too is the Interstate Commerce Act. The time has come for this commission, in administering that act, to declare unequivocally by regulation that a Negro passenger is free to travel the length and breadth of this country in the same manner as any other passenger." Arsenault writes that despite his impatience with the Freedom Riders, Robert Kennedy was "ideologically and emotionally committed to racial equality."[57]

Harris Wofford wrote that there was a great deal of public sentiment against continuing the rides. A Gallup Poll in June said that 63 percent of the people questioned disapproved of the rides, while 70 percent approved of how Kennedy handled the situation, with 50 percent polled in the South. "It would be inaccurate, however," Wofford remembered, "to conclude that the rides and the jail-going were having no constructive effect." He attributed the ICC petition directly to these protests, which did invoke systemic change in the South. In a larger sense, however, the Freedom Rides failed to get the president speak out in "moral terms" on the issues in the South.[58] Robert Kennedy was the moral compass of the administration. While he was committed to civil rights gains, he was not yet able to convince his older brother that it was in his best interest to make such statements. In the end political pragmatism still ruled the day. However, the Freedom Rides brought Robert Kennedy closer to the movement and may have even invested him more than any other episode up to that point. It was a journey for the young Kennedy, and there was still much to consider as they were confronted with new challenges in the wake of the rides.

Arsenault argues that the ICC petition was not evidence that Kennedy acted on ideals. Instead it was a short-term solution for the problem. RFK hoped to "take some of the steam out of the movement," but if that was his intention, it was a "clear sign, for all his good intentions, the attorney general did not understand the depth of feeling that was driving young Americans, black and white, onto the freedom buses."[59] At the very least, however, the petition is evidence that Kennedy was looking at ways to support the movement. Further, he was doing it the way that he had always wanted — through the law and the federal government.

James Giglio has a different perspective on Robert Kennedy and the rides. He argues, "In many ways the Freedom Rides represented a frustrating experience for the Kennedys. It revealed, first of all, their underestimation of the depth of the problem. Civil rights was not merely a political matter that could be easily orchestrated from the White House by pulling the right strings with business, political, educational, and judicial leaders." Robert Kennedy had more of an emotional reaction to the Freedom Rides. If he were a private citizen, he would have participated in the rides, but as the attorney general and member of the Kennedy administration, he wanted them to stop so it would help his brother. He believed that this embarrassed the president in the eyes of other nations and hurt him in foreign relations.[60] Giglio argues that Robert Kennedy handled the crisis "reasonably well." Kennedy had protected the constitutional rights of interstate travelers, satisfying both Northern and Southern politicians.[61]

The *New York Times* reported, "Mr. Kennedy made clear that his move [to petition the ICC] was inspired by the recent turmoil over the bi-racial Freedom Riders in the south."[62] In an editorial the *Times* wrote, "Attorney General Kennedy's proposal for rigorous rules against segregation in interstate bus facilities shows a refreshingly imaginative approach to the law." The piece went on to say that it was "heartening to see the department look beyond the immediate emergency to establish orderly, enforceable rules against bus segregation in the future."[63] Kennedy's ideas were meant to look at the problem and create a long-term solution that supported civil rights. In this sense Kennedy was doing more than his predecessors. He took the crisis and went further to evoke larger, systemic change. Robert Kennedy was finding his voice in civil rights. His statements in the Law Day speech were idealistic and even naïve, in that he was trying to scare the South into believing that he would enforce the law. Further, his actions in Birmingham and Montgomery show that he was willing to act in the midst of a crisis to enforce the law and protect American citizens. However, his petition to the ICC demonstrated that he was willing to use the force of the federal government to foster change and would put his brother's political capital behind such legislation.

The *Times* piece affirms that Kennedy looked outside the status quo, as he had said on numerous occasions. It went on to say that the "draft rules proposed by the Attorney General would make it plain to everyone ... that there can be no segregation on buses or in waiting rooms, rest rooms or terminal restaurants."[64] Kennedy finally seemed to be making headway in the civil rights movement. He listened to the civil rights leaders, but always emphasized that the law was the most important element of this fight with segregation. Some argue that his use of the ICC was desperate and not in line with the spirit of the movement. It wasn't Kennedy's job to get sucked into the movement. He was meant to police the states and find a legal way to enforce justice. Once he was able to find such a way, he pursued it vigorously. If there was a legal solution, Robert Kennedy would not shy away from a fight, nor would he let any citizen's rights be trampled on by racist ideas.

Once the notion to petition the ICC had surfaced, the Justice Department wasted no time researching and writing the document. They had it ready for Robert Kennedy's signature on the same day it was conceived. There was a renewed sense of commitment to civil rights. However, the Kennedy team, according to Taylor Branch, "had telescoped the process that normally took years — even if the commissioners liked the proposal, which in this case they did not — into less than four months." Branch writes that after the early Freedom Rides, the Justice Department pursued civil rights with a "vengeance."[65]

Robert Kennedy remembered the debate over trying to work out a solution on the Freedom Rides situation, saying, "We then had a lot of conversations with the ICC to see what could be done ... to destroy the color bars that existed in interstate commerce. I suppose it comes down, fundamentally, [to] what authority you have, and that's the conflict between us and I guess some of the civil rights groups: their feeling that we had more authority and our feeling that we didn't have any more authority than we exercised, and we did everything that could be done under the circumstances."[66] Kennedy wanted to see the South take control of its own situation. His comment on authority pointed to his philosophy on what he had the legal responsibility and means to do. Ultimately, the situation came down to power — power for the segregationists and how they asserted that over the civil rights leaders; power of the federal government and how they asserted it over the states. This is a fundamental issue throughout history, plaguing any real chance of change — going from smallest localities to the great rooms of Congress.

The ICC returned a favorable ruling for the attorney general only four months later, in September. All the interstate terminals were desegregated and signs were taken down that made the distinction of "White" and "Colored." Marshall and others made overtures to the commission to make sure that this happened in a timely manner. In 1964 he remembered using "informal" and "unofficial" channels to work with the members of the commission. He goes to state: "I think on the whole it was really rather incredible for anyone that had experience with the commission that the commission came out unanimously with the rules that were suggested by the Department of Justice which was a very explosive.... It was not done just by the force of argument in the situation."[67] This was an important victory for the Freedom Riders, the president and Robert Kennedy's Justice Department. In fact, Robert Kennedy and Burke Marshall were emboldened and looked to other avenues to affect civil rights law.

"It's the very best way to proceed."

Many in the civil rights struggle wanted President Kennedy to speak out against segregation, making the issue a moral and not political issue for the administration. In fact, Harris Wofford told President Kennedy, "What Eisenhower never did was to give clear moral expression to the issues involved." Wofford went on, "The only effective time for such moral leadership is during an occasion of moral crisis. This is the time when your words mean most."[68] John Kennedy's team was stellar, often setting a new standard in politics, at using lofty rhetoric to lift the spirits of the American people. He had proved that during the campaign and in his famous inaugural address. Wofford said to the president, "Negro leaders feel sorely the absence of any such statement."[69] The Kennedys felt that their actions with the marshals, the state taking control of the protection for the riders and the petition to the ICC were sufficient in maintaining their philosophy. A "moral statement" as Wofford asked or declaring a second Emancipation Proclamation, as King asked for, would not have the effect that the Kennedys wanted in this situation.

Clayborne Carson writes, "The significance of the freedom rides was not merely that they led to desegregation of southern transportation facilities. The riders also contributed to the development of a self-consciously radical southern student movement prepared to direct its militancy to toward other concerns." Carson goes on to argue that the group had a larger impact on the nation than the sit-in movement, which involved many more people compared to the hundred involved in the Freedom Rides.[70] There were reverberations from the Freedom Rides. While the students were empowered with their new sense of worth and ability to move the nation, the Kennedys started to see the movement not as a political problem, but as a moral issue that the nation needed to address.

The Freedom Rides had far-reaching implications that moved the administration to reconsider its civil rights policy. The riders were infused with a spirit that would continue through the Kennedy years. Carson argues, "For the freedom riders, the experiences of the spring and summer transformed their own attitudes and produced a new sense of group identity." He argues that the experience in the jails led to a "rapid process of political education for student activists who encountered persons from different backgrounds with a variety of political beliefs."[71] This change was widespread and would lead to greater growth and solidarity in the movement, culminating with the March on Washington in 1963. Despite what some historians say about John and Robert Kennedy's intent and inability to act on civil rights issues, they played an important role in this evolution from a nation that tolerated the racial divide in the South to a nation that came together to fight it. The mere fact that the Kennedy brothers supported these movements at the outset of the administration was enough to bring the nation further along.

Although civil rights leaders wanted the Kennedys to do more, RFK and JFK were looking for ways to legally help them. Robert Kennedy said that John Kennedy "was very concerned ... about what could be done, and what steps we could take. He wanted to, obviously, know what authority he had or what authority we had to deal with the problem. And then we could make the a decision as to what should be done under that authority.... Our authority was limited in my judgment, and in Burke [Marshall's] judgment, and having conversations with Byron White and Nick Katzenbach, there wasn't really any disagreement within the Department of Justice as to how far our authority would go." Kennedy went on:

> And, so what we did was to outline what our authority was, and we went to the maximum of what we felt we could do constitutionally. So there was never ... I mean, if I said to him that I thought we could do something beyond that or give protection, then he would have had to make the decision whether we really wanted to do that. But my conversations with him were the fact that, really, we didn't have the authority to do that. The only authority we had was what I outlined for him, and we went to — and used that authority to the maximum.[72]

President Kennedy and Robert Kennedy looked for a way to help the Freedom Riders within the realm of the law — specifically the Constitution. Their efforts helped not only other administrations, but also themselves when they were confronted with the Ole Miss and University of Alabama crises in subsequent years.

When asked if the authority for law enforcement should be changed from the state and local to the federal government, Robert Kennedy replied, "No." He went on to say,

> I still think it's wise. I think that for periods of time that it's very, very difficult. I'm just looking at it from over a period of a hundred years or fifty years or even a shorter period of time that I think it's a wise way to proceed. Because I just wouldn't want that much authority, much more authority, in the hands of, whether it's the Federal Bureau of Investigation or the Department of Justice or the president of the United States. And I think that it's well that it's not centered, all of that great power is not centered in Washington with the federal government. I think it causes great difficulty.[73]

Bobby saw this issue as a fundamental aspect of his role as attorney general, not only in the case of the civil rights movement, but also for the precedent that it set. Furthermore it strengthened federalism, which helped maintain the integrity of the Constitution. Once he left office, others could build on his use of federal power and cause harm to the fabric of the republic. He needed to tread lightly not only for political issues, but also because he respected his office.

Robert Kennedy was concerned about precedent and adhering to the law. That meant that there needed to be limits on how he confronted civil rights issues. A broad, sweeping act would not have the same strength as something that was rooted in the law and set the standard for future issues that the nation would confront. Moreover he was concerned that that type of act would not take root in the South, which had larger, long lasting implications. Kennedy said, "I think you can, at any time, you can say that it would be much better if we could have sent people, in large numbers perhaps, down to Mississippi and be able to protect that group down there. But I think that it comes back to haunt you at a later time. And I think that these matters should be decided over a long range of history, not on a temporary basis or under the stress of a particular crisis."[74] If anything, this crisis illuminated how Robert Kennedy looked to use the Department of Justice in the fairest and most legal way possible. Speaking in 1964, Kennedy said, "In my judgment, Mississippi is going to work itself out, and Alabama is. Now maybe it's going to take a decade and maybe a lot of people are going to be killed in the meantime, and I think that's unfortunate. But in the long run, I think it's for the health of the country and the stability of the system. It's the very best way to proceed."[75]

Burke Marshall believed that the Freedom Riders were an extension of a larger movement that took place during the Kennedy era: "But I think that the Freedom Rides were a continuation of something that had started in 1960 and which progressed and became a major element of the history of the country during President Kennedy's administration." He said that this movement continued as

> protests, demonstrations to show conditions that existed that were beyond the limits of permissibility of federal law all over the South — bus stations were one condition; there were many others — and really demonstrated to the country and opened the eyes of the country for the first time to the caste system that of course everyone knows the South was already acquainted with, but which the rest of the country didn't know much about.[76]

Indeed, these rides were the just the start of a larger movement that would continue to gain momentum and usher in a new American culture.

9. Striving for Full Equality

"Martin Luther King and I didn't see eye to eye."

Robert Kennedy took time at the start of the administration to identify clear, legal ways for the Justice Department to influence civil rights. He didn't want to expand federal authority. He felt that there were sufficient laws already in place that he could use to challenge segregation. Arthur Schlesinger wrote, "Education and transportation were important; but voting rights remained the primary target."[1] Robert Kennedy saw these rights as the most important because they could make the difference in the fight against racism, while at the same time reinforcing the America system of democracy to Cold War enemies. Robert Kennedy recalled in 1964 how important he believed the right for African Americans to vote to be, saying, "I thought a good deal more needed to be done, and I thought that ... this was the area in which we had the greatest authority, and if we were going to do anything on civil rights, we should do it in that field where we had the authority.... I felt strongly that this was where the most good could be accomplished." He went on to describe what it could do for the African Americans and the nation: "From the vote, from participation in the elections, flow all other rights far, far more easily. A great deal could be accomplished internally within a state if the Negroes participated in elections and voted."[2]

The right to vote was at the heart of the Kennedy initiatives. Kennedy was looking at the matter pragmatically. "Here you had almost 50 percent of the population in the state of Mississippi who were Negro, 40 percent of the state of Alabama, and a large percentage in Georgia." Kennedy argued that if half or a third of that population were able to vote "they could have a major influence." Kennedy acknowledged that many civil rights groups wanted to approach the problem differently: "Martin Luther King and I didn't see eye to eye on some of these matters, nor did I with a good number of these other groups."[3] But Kennedy believed that this approach was good on several levels. First, "This was an area where we had the authority. We didn't have the authority to give protection or to move in some of these other fields, but we did have authority in voting, and we could do something about it."[4] In many ways Kennedy was correct and it was the right way for the Justice Department to proceed. The Justice Department was charged with upholding the law, and the Fifteenth Amendment guaranteed the right to vote so people could have a voice in government. Kennedy had a record of using the system to foster change, expose corruption and seek out justice.

Kennedy also saw this approach at fostering change for the future: "I thought it could make a major difference and far, be far more held than anything else that they could do, if they just focused attention and registered a hundred people a day.... And that was the key to opening the door to all of what they wanted to accomplish in education, in housing, in jobs, and public accommodations — all rested in having the vote and being able to change the situation internally."[5] Kennedy went even further to set up the Voter Education Project to help raise money for this cause. Some in the civil rights cause took hold of this effort, but there was still some resistance from some of the leaders.

Robert Kennedy had a great deal of autonomy on this venture. Once again, John Kennedy was more interested in foreign policy and wanted to focus his efforts on that front. While he was a willing to extend himself for the cause, he relied on Bobby to distinguish the proper way to assert himself politically. "I never would have to call him," Bobby remembered. He said that he wasn't just the president's brother, "but somebody that was as close and that we knew each other well." With that, Kennedy didn't have to call President Kennedy with every concern in the realm of civil rights.[6] This was why John and Robert Kennedy made such a formidable political team. Since the McClellan committee, these two brothers had used their influence to help each other. In fact, Kennedy said that he "could look at it much better than [JFK] could, and I'd know that if, once I looked at it, it was clear, that it was the thing that should be done." He did acknowledge that it became more difficult when the circumstances could have resulted in harm for the president. Then they would talk.[7]

Another reason why Robert Kennedy wanted to pursue this avenue for change in civil rights was that "it would be less internal struggle and strife within the country as a whole by the Department of Justice or the federal government coming down into the southern states and telling them what they should do; they could do it themselves." Finally, Kennedy believed that there would be "less opposition to it."[8] While civil rights groups looked to bring the issues to the forefront through protest, this approach could have lasting effects on the governments in the South. Further, it would empower younger generations to make a difference through legislation. Finally, this was the first time that an administration had offered help in this endeavor. In that respect, Kennedy was forward thinking and did a great deal for the movement, despite the fact that it had not been acknowledged by civil rights leaders and was even met with resistance.

"Every effort to make the local people take care of the situation was right."

Nicholas deB. Katzenbach was a lawyer who served under Robert Kennedy and was an integral part of the team that would promote civil rights. Katzenbach started as assistant attorney general and would eventually hold the post of attorney general under Johnson. He was intimately involved in these civil rights cases. Katzenbach met Robert Kennedy in between the election and the inaugural. He was recommended by Byron White to serve in the Justice Department. At their first meeting Bobby kept referring to Katzenbach as professor. Katzenbach remembered that first meeting where Kennedy had "a little bit of an edge. He asked me a little bit about myself— not very much — and said Byron had spoken highly of me, that I was being considered for the job of Assistant Attorney General in charge of the Office of Legal Counsel but there were other people being considered. It really wasn't much of an interview. It didn't last very long."[9]

In any event, Katzenbach had already formed a favorable opinion of Robert Kennedy. This impression fed into the "Band of Brothers" mantra later in their relationship, which led to a strong bond between the two men, making Katzenbach all the more determined not to fail.

I rather liked the picture that he was painted — not always favorably — by the American news media about Bobby as being the fellow who wasn't going to be beaten or licked or put down by anything.

And I thought the concept of efficiency, which is the major way in which the news media painted his running of the campaign, as one with walkie-talkies and this and that and the other thing — simply getting it done and getting it done well — was a picture that the United States needed very much abroad, needed more than it did idealism and so forth.[10]

Indeed, Bobby was very tenacious and unwilling to give up. When presented with obstacles he did what was necessary to overcome them. This was an important element of how he handled crises as well as the Justice Department. That said, it was not to the extreme portrayed in the media from the time. However, as time progressed and Katzenbach got to know Kennedy, he remembered, "In fact, I felt more that way about him before I knew him than I did afterwards."[11] The first time Katzenbach met President John F. Kennedy was after an event at the White House: "And I went through the receiving line, and I recall the President saying to me, 'Oh, you're with Bobby. I'm very happy that you are with Bobby,' which I thought was a remarkable feat of memory, that he would remember who was with Bobby."[12]

Katzenbach was involved in the Freedom Rider episode. He remembered being in Byron White's office during the crisis, debating whether the Justice Department should get involved:

> The thing I remember most vividly about that was the issue one night as to whether we ought to send all these people down there and finally Bobby saying, "No, not yet." And Byron White was terribly upset about this because he felt the timing on it was wrong and that we should have sent people down before we actually did. And he had presented quite objectively both sides of the issue to Bobby, and Bobby had talked with his brother and then said, "Let's let it go." And Byron had felt that he was very wrong, to let it go any further.[13]

While he did not have as big a role as others in the crisis, Katzenbach was involved mostly on the legal questions and served Kennedy behind the scenes at the start. It was the beginning of a larger responsibility that he would take with him to the University of Mississippi crisis and beyond.

For Katzenbach, the Freedom Riders were a preview, or so he thought, of how the administration would address civil rights issues. "I don't think there was any doubt as to the sense of justice about it, but there was some doubt as to the implementation of it, and understandably, I guess. But there was an awful lot of caution involved in the Freedom Riders initially, and I suppose also some lack of caution."[14] Katzenbach went on to say,

> And then when there was an unwillingness initially to send marshals, I think I was fairly gung ho, about sending marshals down. I think Bobby was more cautious, and I think the president was more cautious about this. I think, in retrospect, they were probably right about this, but then I wondered whether real guts were behind us. I wondered that for probably about twenty-four hours. Then I was convinced that there were.[15]

For Katzenbach to consider where the administration was going shows that there was very little direction in the early months of the administration. Further, it is evidence of how important the Freedom Rides were to Robert Kennedy's growth as attorney general. Instead of handling these issues in crisis mode, he started to become proactive with the issues, first with the ICC and then with voting rights.

As the crisis went on Katzenbach had a sense of where the Kennedys were trying to lead the federal government. "I think the basis for attempting to deal with this as a problem in which you made every effort to make the local people take care of the situation was right," he said.[16] Katzenbach recalled how the Kennedy brothers felt about civil rights: "From the outset, I never had any question about the attorney general or the president in terms of the objectives in this regard. I think the objectives were hopefully put in terms of voting and doing something about voting and doing it in that way."[17] Voting remained important because it was within the realm of the law to enforce. The Justice Department could act and propose legislation. Sending troops was always something that President Kennedy wanted to avoid.

The Kennedy brothers' strategy to have state and local government handle the race issue was a primary part of their thinking. Katzenbach remembered,

> The psychological block that both of them had come out of the campaign, which was understandable enough, which was that they weren't going to use troops in the South. Of course, this [was] an issue in the campaign, and President Kennedy had fairly well undertaken not to use troops in a good deal of criticism of Little Rock and the way it was handled.... And I think the strategy was never to use troops, which was why I felt so badly at Ole Miss [University of Mississippi] when troops were used because this was the one thing they had rather determined never to do.[18]

It was never the intention of the Kennedy brothers to send troops into the South. Such an act would have been a great divergence from their plan and a revolutionary act. They were both very keen on the political and Constitutional ramifications of their actions. Their reluctance to commit troops was a part of that awareness. Not only would it derail their Congressional agenda, it would also embolden the South to stand even stronger, resisting any efforts to integrate. Both Kennedys were aware of this, and while they wanted to change the country's attitude toward race, they also recognized that it would take time.

Over time there was a change in how the Kennedy brothers saw civil rights. Katzenbach says, "I think they grew during the period. I think it would be hard to put a time on them. I would think that it probably came after the University of Mississippi episode. I think up until then there had been the sort of an effort which ought to have been successful and might have been successful if it had been started earlier." Katzenbach argued that voting rights played a big role in these incidents that led the Kennedys to see the broader picture. He said, "If Negroes had been voting ten or twelve years before this, this kind of an incident would not have occurred."[19] That political power was something that the Kennedy brothers saw at the start as an important element of success in the South. The growth that Katzenbach refers to is more of an awareness of civil rights issues. While the Freedom Rides may have opened their eyes to the inequality in the South, the episode at Ole Miss was the catalyst that changed the direction that the Kennedys were headed.

"We will continue to make progress. That is what is important."

After the Freedom Riders, Kennedy embraced the notion of registering voters in the South. For years since the passage of the 15th Amendment, African Americans had been denied the right to vote through Jim Crow laws that dated back to the 19th century. Robert Kennedy believed that empowering African Americans with the vote would be a surefire way to bring change in the South. In fact, Kennedy set up the Voter Education Project (VEP), with tax exempt status to spearhead the operation.[20] Voting was key to get the issues out there for the country to debate and propose legislation. Katzenbach remembered: "I think initially the attorney general had an idea that, let's concentrate on voting, let's get people voting, and maybe if we can get them voting fast enough we will not have these other problems." Their philosophy was that the use of troops was a detriment to such efforts. "This was a sort of a little bit of a loss of virginity in a way because after that it became easier to use troops if that's what had to be used."[21]

In June 1961, Burke Marshall attended a conference in Mississippi where he gave lectures to students on the merits of a voter registration effort. It was not uncommon for the Justice Department to stump these efforts.[22] While it did not have the immediate effect that the Freedom Rides did, nor was it something that the media would embrace, voter registration signified that Robert Kennedy was willing to foster change in the South. Southern leaders would not like to have an electorate that could remove them from office and usher in genuine reform to the laws at the state and local level.

On June 16, Robert Kennedy met with Freedom Riders at his office. As usual the attorney general was casual, walking around in his socks. Among the delegation were Wyatt Walker, Diane Nash, Charles Sherrod and others. They were looking for federal support for the Freedom Riders to continue their work in the South, exposing Jim Crow. Kennedy was not interested in extending federal aid to further Freedom Rides, telling the group that they were counterproductive. Instead, Kennedy wanted the group to spend time registering voters in the South. If the movement put resources into that effort then the Justice Department would aid them in their endeavor.[23] This offer was sincere, and Kennedy had already started moving government resources into this venture. This meeting was as much a means for him to gain political support from highly placed people in the movement as it was to accommodate the Freedom Riders.

Many in the room were not happy with what Kennedy was suggesting. In fact, Charles Sherrod had to be held by the pockets in his pants as he said, "You are a public official, sir. It's not your responsibility to, before God or under the law, to tell us how to honor our constitutional rights. It's your job to protect us when we do." This outburst didn't phase Kennedy at all as he continued with his position that registering African American voters might not be as grand as the Freedom Rides, but it could have everlasting effects on Southern culture.[24] Kennedy was not only using the law as a means to support the movement; he was also trying to control the movement by defining the issues that the movement confronted. It rightfully irked these people who risked their lives to assert those rights. That said, to Robert Kennedy's credit, he went to great lengths to protect the Freedom Riders in Alabama and Mississippi. Kennedy must have felt emboldened to try and enter the movement as someone who controls the discourse. He was successful in keeping the riders safe, petitioning the ICC and working for voter registration. Many civil rights leaders appreciated the efforts. In fact, Fred Shuttlesworth told his church, "We thank Jack, Bob, and God."[25]

The voting registration movement was seen by many as not enough and too gradual. Arthur Schlesinger writes that the "voting rights thesis was not universally accepted." However, the administration was committed to the strategy and felt that while it might not have an immediate impact, the vote was the very best way for future change. While many leaders in the black community believed that this was an effort to stop protests, Schlesinger contended that the "Kennedys were determined on peaceful change."[26] Eventually the civil rights leaders embraced the vote. James Forman of the SNCC believed that registration efforts could make people more aware of the issues. James Farmer and CORE took a leadership role in this endeavor in September, and Martin Luther King finally embraced the notion, writing, "The central front, however, we feel is that of suffrage." He believed that the vote would give the movement a "concrete tool" that could "correct injustices," changing Southern culture and the "nation as a whole." The Voter Education Project lasted for fifteen years with John Lewis at its head as executive director.[27] The lasting presence of the organization that Kennedy help build demonstrates how significant this effort was to the civil rights movement. Further, it substantiates the Kennedy brothers' influence on the movement. While many saw them as politicians, unwilling to make a stand, there was more to their leadership. Further, it seems that the question of whether or not the movement should focus on voter registration was moot. Schlesinger wrote, "Voter registration in a hostile setting was direct action." In fact, the movement went into small communities and instilled, as one CORE worker said, "black residents there with enormous hope and pride."[28]

As Robert Kennedy believed, many in the South were not happy with his complicity with the civil rights movement. They blamed Bobby for all the troubles, not the president. One Mississippi housewife said, "Kennedy has too many brothers."[29] Bobby was more than happy to take the blame for his efforts with civil rights leaders.

The Justice Department issued a memorandum toward the end of 1961 that outlined any civil rights progress for the year. Ironically, it started by quoting the famous line from the Inaugural Address, "Let the word go forth, from this time and place, to friend and foe alike, that the torch has been passed to a new generation of Americans," and continued to mention the piece on human rights "to which this nation has always been committed, and to which we are committed today at home and around the world."[30] While the inaugural was criticized by many as ignoring civil rights, including this passage in a memorandum that discussed the progress of such initiatives suggests that the Kennedys believed that they did, in fact, mention the issue in the speech. On the other hand, it could have been an effort to link the speech to civil rights initiatives in the hopes of silencing critics. Nevertheless, it's clear that this report believed there was a connection. It stated after the quote: "That philosophy is being carried out. Progress is being made in every area of civil rights."[31]

First the report pointed to the sub-cabinet group on civil rights. This group, according to the memo, met monthly to "coordinate federal programs." In addition a special assistant was appointed to work closely with the president and representatives from the Civil Rights Division of the Department of Justice, the President's Committee on Equal Employment Opportunity and the Civil Rights Commission. While this was an important facet of civil rights progress, its influence was minimal and many of the most important decisions that propelled civil rights to a new level happened at the ground level or within the Department of Justice itself—not a sub-cabinet group. The second item that the report addressed was voting: "It has been the policy of Attorney General Robert F. Kennedy to seek effective guarantees and action from local officials and civic leaders voluntarily and without court action."[32] It went to state that the department had tried to work with local governments, but that in the cases where the local officials would not work it out, they went to court. The Department of Justice, according to the report, was very busy in this area. They wrote that while the previous administration had filed voting discrimination cases in six southern counties, which the Kennedy administration was prosecuting "vigorously—and successfully," Kennedy had "active investigations" in sixty other counties.[33]

The third item dealt with employment, saying, "The Administration took steps early to end discrimination in employment, both within the federal service and in connection with government contracts." It went on to point out that JFK had established the Committee on Equal Employment opportunity, "giving it far greater enforcement powers than any predecessor agency." It said that under the leadership of Vice President Lyndon Johnson and others "the committee has persuaded 25 of the largest government contractors to take specific action to recruit, train, hire, and upgrade Negro employees."[34] The Kennedys clearly saw the Equal Employment Opportunity act as a feather in their cap, saying that they acted "early" to create better circumstances for African Americans. They saw it as a step to integrate the nation and bring greater equality. The Kennedy administration was doing what it had said it would during the campaign. With the exception of their grand pronouncement that they would work on housing with a "stroke of the pen," they attacked voting and employment, which were two very important facets of the civil rights movement. In addition, they went further than previous administrations on transportation and school desegregation.

The Freedom Riders thrust the issue of interstate transportation into the national spotlight. In the fourth section of the memo the Justice Department said that it had made "substantial" progress in desegregating "public transportation — bus, air and rail." They addressed the Freedom Rides, saying that when they challenged the segregated system in the South, "the Administration moved vigorously and effectively to restore order in a highly explosive situation and prevented major bloodshed." They continued to make their case for the power of the federal government, saying that they "had clear responsibility to protect interstate travelers and to restore order when local officials could not or would not do so."[35] While the Freedom Rides had annoyed and frustrated the weary Bobby Kennedy, they had become another success for the administration in its fight for justice. For them to use this episode as "progress" for the year demonstrated that the administration needed to be challenged by the civil rights leaders. It was important, however, how they cited this success. At this point in the administration civil rights was still a hot topic that could cost Kennedy votes in Congress. Moreover, it could cost him seats in the mid-term elections. They chose to emphasize that this was not about civil rights. Instead it was about maintaining "domestic tranquility," which according to the Constitution was within the powers of the executive branch, furthering the emphasis on the notion of federalism.

The memo went on to say, "Because of the Government's stand in Alabama, it was unnecessary to take further action a few days later when a similarly tense situation developed in Mississippi." Further, it also stated that the Department of Justice ordered the "immediate investigation" of the bus burning in Anniston, resulting in the indictment of nine men (which resulted in a hung jury). It also explained how Robert Kennedy "petitioned the Interstate Commerce Commission for regulations requiring desegregated facilities in terminals used in interstate bus travel."[36] It finished by saying that this move had had effects in both the railroad and air travel industry. Of all the work that the Justice Department did, this clearly had the largest impact, reaching into several aspects of American culture to foster change in the status quo. However, the Kennedys needed to be pushed into it. If not for the Freedom Riders, the desegregation of interstate transportation would have come later. What those civil rights leaders did was demand that the government protect their rights under the Constitution, and it made a difference for subsequent movements for such rights. However, they needed a strong response from the federal government if they were going to be successful. The Kennedys used this as an example of progress for their administration, but it did not acknowledge that without the Freedom Rides they probably would not have initiated this stand.

Perhaps the greatest indictment of the previous administration came with the section on schools. The memo stated the following: "In school integration there has been a basic change in policy — in implementing the U.S. Supreme Court's desegregation decision from abstention by the Federal Government, except during crisis or disaster — to affirmative and anticipatory action." It emphasized, "The Administration has moved with vigor to protect the integrity of the court orders, to preserve the due administration of justice and to encourage and assist local officials and community leaders who are effective in promoting peaceful desegregation of the schools."[37] The memo discussed the various instances where the Kennedy Justice Department intervened in school desegregation. It mentioned the four cases in Louisiana that the department had confronted. In addition it discussed Prince Edward

County in Virginia. It stated that the administration had gone into Atlanta, New Orleans, Little Rock, Memphis and Dallas and desegregated the systems without "violence or disrespect for the law." The memo said that many children in the South were now attending desegregated school under peaceful and safe conditions. This was due to the "responsible affirmative action taken by an increasing number of officials and civic leaders." It finished by quoting President Kennedy congratulating these communities for their hard work to desegregate the system. These instances had "given the world a convincing demonstration of the American people's respect for the law which is fundamental in the maintenance of our rights as free men and women."[38]

While this memo pointed to the success stories within the administration, there was still much work to be done and the Kennedys were only starting to evoke change. That said, they had done more in the eleven months than the last administration had done in the six years it was in office after the *Brown* decision. In fact, Eisenhower himself disagreed with the decision, believing that it took rights and powers away from the states, which was a definition contrary to the Kennedys. The Kennedys had a Lincolnesque problem wherein they had to politically determine when to hold the line and when to compromise. Lincoln's great problem was to keep hold of the border states and stop any further hemorrhaging of the nation. John and Robert Kennedy had a different issue: they lived in an age when everyone was equal under the law and they did not have to wait for those rights — they already had them, but they were not being enforced. In that sense the Kennedys were moving into new ground and needed to tread lightly but also acknowledge that these men and women were entitled the same rights as all other Americans, which was exactly what they did in 1961. The following year, however, would present major problems for the nation not only in domestic unrest, but also foreign policy, threatening the very fabric of the nation.

"We are making progress in this country."

On December 3, 1961, Robert Kennedy addressed the National Conference of Christians and Jews Dinner. During a speech about religious issues in the nation he alluded to the issue of race in the United States, linking it to religious injustice in the nation. "There are sections of the United States," he said, "where citizens are denied the right to vote because of their race; Negroes still have not been accorded equal employment opportunities in many of our states.... In some areas American Negroes as well as African diplomats and students are denied decent housing and service facilities in public places."[39] Despite the fact that he was addressing a delegation that combated religious intolerance and helped get people, like his brother, elected to high office, Bobby Kennedy chose to highlight the race issue in America. This demonstrated that he saw this issue as one of the most important that he had to deal with. It also implied that he saw this as something that the audience could relate to, as he had vocalized before.

Robert Kennedy went on to say that President Kennedy "named two Negroes to District Judgeships and appointed Thurgood Marshall to the United States Court of Appeals." Kennedy was touting the administration's success stories in civil rights for the group. "When I came to the Department of Justice," Kennedy went on, "there were only ten Negroes employed as lawyers; not a single Negro served as a United States Attorney — or ever had in the history of the country. That has changed."[40] Kennedy emphasized with the audience that these men were a part of the government not because of their "race or the color of their skin," but because they had outstanding qualifications and were the right people for the job. The speech quickly turned from one that considered the religious undertones in America to how the Cold War and civil rights movement were linked.

Bobby Kennedy used this opportunity to stress that while America was not perfect, it was still better than the communism that the nation struggled against. Referring to the race issues, he said, "We are making progress in this country. The President and the Federal Government are working diligently toward that end." He knew then, as many learned in the months ahead, that the path to change would take time. "Obviously, we are going to face difficulties in this area for a long time to come. The problems will not disappear overnight. But this country will continue to move ahead in this field." He went on to say, "We will not accept the status quo. We will continue to make progress. That is what is important."[41]

Kennedy said, "Yes, we have our problems in Alabama, but to be blunt, we are not shooting old women and young children in the back as the Communists are doing in Berlin." From that point on the speech diverged into Cold War rhetoric, where Kennedy minimized the race issues in America compared to the violence in other countries. He said, "This is a free society. Our faults are discussed. Our mistakes make a rich grist for the Communist propaganda machine. This we accept."[42] While the speech was heavy in Cold War banter, there was still real mention of the race issue in America and that Kennedy was unwilling to back down. He planned to challenge the status quo. Indeed, up to that point in history his Justice Department had been willing to reach out and make a difference in the race issues that plagued America. Kennedy finished the speech by saying, "Upon you and I, and our fellow countrymen, falls the challenge of protecting, not only our country, but the free people of the world in the hour of maximum need—of greatest danger." Kennedy saw his role in this story as something of a calling, a responsibility to the people of the world and the United States as leaders of the free world. "With confidence born and nurtured by knowledge and truth, and with the courage of free men, we shall prevail." Robert Kennedy was coming of age.

"Walk together, children. Don't ya get weary."

Just off the Freedom Rides, the SNCC hoped to make a difference in Albany, Georgia, and use the ruling from the ICC as a test case for the integration of the city's facilities. Charles Sherrod and Cordell Reagan went to Albany to open a field office and make connections in the community. Both had been active in previous protests ranging from the Freedom Rides to the sit-in movement, bringing experience to the venture.[43] Sherrod and Reagan slowly ingratiated themselves with the locals, setting up a situation where they could challenge the segregation laws and the ICC ruling from the Freedom Rides. On November 1, 1961, when the ICC ruling went into effect, they led a student sit-in at a bus station. The group left before anyone was arrested, but it was clear that they could test the boundaries further. After that, the SNCC, NAACP and other groups formed a coalition known as the Albany Movement.[44]

The movement started in earnest when Chief Laurie Pritchett arrested three members as they attempted to eat in a Trailways bus station. In addition, Bertha Gober and Blanton Hall of the SNCC, who were also students at Albany State College, were arrested that same day for entering the waiting room of the bus station.[45] These students were trying to keep the momentum that the Freedom Rides had started earlier in the year. They wanted to challenge the segregated system, but also to test the strength of Kennedy's actions in the wake of those rides. After the arrest of the five students the movement took on a new form that involved protests and boycotts. The trial of the five students led to mass demonstrations. As a result of their conviction Gober and Hall were expelled from Albany State College, which ignited a march of four hundred people, culminating in a signed petition demanding their reinstatement.[46]

The demonstrations were led by other civil rights leaders who came from out of state. These leaders brought a new level of organization, resulting in demonstrations that led to the arrest of 267 high school and college students.[47] The next day more than 200 demonstrators were arrested. Pritchett told the media, "We can't tolerate the NAACP or the SNCC or any other nigger organization to take over this town with mass demonstrations."[48] Pritchett arrested demonstrators in an orderly and nonviolent fashion.[49] The arrests eventually exceeded 500, resulting in the governor sending in the national guard.[50] At this point in the crisis Burke Marshall telephoned Asa Kelley, the Albany mayor, for a resolution to the crisis.[51] The Kennedy administration did not want to take a large role in this movement. The local police and state were handling it, which was in line with their philosophy on dealing with race matters. They may not have liked the racist rhetoric of Pritchett, but he did maintain law and order.

The arrests mounted and leaders of the movement considered bringing in Roy Wilkins of the NAACP or Martin Luther King and the SCLC. Taylor Branch writes that as the leaders met in the wake of those arrests, "the strain showed beneath their excitement as they discussed what to do next."[52] After news of beatings in the prisons, the group decided on Martin Luther King.[53] The build-up of this movement led to Martin Luther King addressing a rally on Friday, December 15, at Shiloh Baptist Church. The parishioners were in song, and as King made his way to the pulpit they started singing, "Martin King says freedom, Martin King says freedom." King started slow and referred to movements that were taking shape in Africa. He argued that they could not sit back and wait for the march of progress. King continued, making a distinction between love and justice, expressing how Christianity was inexorably linked to nonviolence. King finished that part of the sermon and started to talk about the issues in Albany.[54]

From the pulpit at Shiloh Baptist, King ingratiated himself with the crowd, gaining solidarity with the men and women who literally were throwing themselves in jail. King said, "They can put you in a dungeon and transform you to glory.... If they try to kill you develop a willingness to die." King talked about going to jail "without hating the white folks." The crowd applauded, listened intently as King kept speaking. "Say to the white man, 'We will win you with the power of our capacity to endure.'" King had the crowd involved in the sermon. He started saying, "But we shall overcome." He urged them to fight on. "Don't stop now. Keep moving. Walk together, children. Don't ya get weary. There's a great camp meeting coming." King moved away from the podium and the crowd took over singing, "We shall overcome."[55] King's presence made a difference for the movement, and it gave them a new level of commitment from the people while at the same time it was an attempt to catapult the Albany Movement into the national spotlight.

The day after his speech at Shiloh Baptist, King led a march with 250 demonstrators to city hall, where he was arrested.[56] When a reporter asked about his role, King said, "I had just intended to give an address, but seeing that negotiations were broken between Negro and white, I felt I had to join the pilgrimage."[57] King vowed that he would stay in jail. He announced through the jail cell bars, "I will not accept bond. If convicted, I will refuse to pay the fine. I expect to spend Christmas in jail. I hope thousands will join me."[58] King, however, went back on that pledge when the city agreed to comply with the ICC decision and release other demonstrators.[59] Meanwhile, Robert Kennedy gave the Albany Movement moral support, but chose to embrace a "hands off" policy. He believed that as long as law and order were maintained there was no real reason for the federal government to intervene. He told the press that the only way there could be progress was if "local leaders talk it out."[60]

After King's release and an agreement with the city, the Albany protests stopped. Robert Kennedy called the mayor and congratulated him, but he did not call the SNCC, the NAACP or the SCLC. King praised the city officials on the agreement as well as Pritchett's nonviolent mass arrests.[61] The solution in Albany was in line with Robert Kennedy's philosophy on government's role in these situations. He always wanted to support local and state authorities, but stop short of federal intervention. Pritchett was clever enough not to let the situation get out of hand. In addition, the governor's decision to send in the guard demonstrated that the state could deal with the problem by itself.

With the city officials dragging their feet to comply with the ICC decision, the SNCC tried to revive the movement in April 1962. SNCC protesters were arrested trying to desegregate a lunch counter. However, it wasn't until July that the movement gained momentum once again. King and Abernathy returned for sentencing from the December protests. The two civil rights leaders opted for the forty-five day jail sentence rather than pay the $178 fine.[62] The city's people reacted with both violent and nonviolent protests. President Kennedy inquired about the situation to his brother, who responded that he was in touch with the city officials. Burke Marshall called Coretta Scott King and said he was trying to arrange King's release.[63] Thirty-two people were arrested when they marched on city hall to protest King's incarceration.[64]

King and Abernathy were released from prison after an unidentified black man paid their bail. Much to the dismay of King and Abernathy the continuing protests resulted in violence; King called for a "day of penance" to keep in line with the nonviolent philosophy. Despite this the National Guard was called back to Albany. King and Abernathy marched again on city hall and were arrested. The jails were filled and Pritchett started to use other jails in nearby towns.[65] James Giglio writes that King looked to the Kennedy administration for assistance. However, the Albany Movement put the Kennedys in a difficult position. They wanted to support a moderate for governor in Georgia, so they encouraged both sides to work together.[66] President Kennedy finally responded at an August 1 press conference.

In response to civil rights leaders criticizing Kennedy's "moral leadership," President Kennedy commented on the Albany Movement. At four o'clock on that Wednesday afternoon, in the State Department auditorium, Kennedy said:

> I have been in constant touch with the Attorney General and have received more or less daily reports, and he's been in daily touch with the authorities in Albany in an attempt to provide a solution. There is — what is involved here is partly local laws and partly those laws which involve the National Government, particularly as they might involve public facilities, and some of these matters are in the court.... Let me say that I find it wholly inexplicable why the City Council of Albany will not sit down with the citizens of Albany, who may be Negroes, and attempt to secure them, in a peaceful way, their rights.... The United States Government is involved in sitting down at Geneva with the Soviet Union. I can't understand why the government of Albany, City Council of Albany, cannot do the same for American citizens.... We are going to attempt, as we have in the past, to try to provide a satisfactory solution and protection of the constitutional rights of the people of Albany, and will continue to do so. And the situation today is completely unsatisfactory from that point of view.[67]

King and Abernathy were convicted but given a suspended sentence. The movement weakened and started to falter. They were not receiving the press that they hoped they would get. Bill Hansen of SNCC commented, "We were naive enough to think we could fill up the jails.... We ran out of people before [Chief Pritchett] ran out of jails."[68] Clayborne Carson argues, "In a purely instrumental sense, the Albany protests could be viewed as a serious set back for the civil rights movement." He went on: "The initial objective of desegregation in the bus and train terminals involved no more than compliance with federal rulings, and the broader civil rights goals of the movement ... remained in contention."[69] Howard Zinn wrote that the SNCC "were educating in the ultimate sense of the word, bringing out from deep inside the Negro people of that area the muffled cries, the dreams so long kept to themselves."[70] Despite the fact that the Albany protests did not produce what the SNCC, SCLC or NAACP had hoped, it did inspire more soldiers for the movement and served as a lesson that King would not forget when he went into Birmingham the following year. McWhorter argues, "The real lesson of Albany was that nonviolence could not succeed without violence — segregationist violence." She went on to write that Laurie Pritchett had said that you could kill "the Movement with kindness." In fact, Pritchett had considered the violence during the Freedom Rides in 1961. He "concluded that the police had harmed their own segregationist cause, provoking the federal government as well as the public conscience in a way that the integrationists' actions alone were not able to do." He studied Gandhian methods and planned to "fill the jails."[71]

In a larger sense the Albany Movement proved that it was necessary for the federal government to take a role in any civil rights effort for it to produce a lasting result. While Robert Kennedy and the Department of Justice wanted the state and local officials to take a lead, the Freedom Rides, integration of schools and voting rights demanded that the Kennedy administration be involved if there was to be a larger impact on the movement. King and other civil rights leaders also learned that they needed the federal government involved.

10. Martin and Bobby

"This legislation is needed. It is constitutional. I urge its enactment."

In the middle of the Albany Movement and just before the issues at Ole Miss, Martin Luther King and Robert Kennedy had a few things to say about civil rights. King and Kennedy had different ways to approach civil rights, yet they were committed to similar outcomes. They were both moralists and passionate about their work. Moreover, they believed that their plights were just and righteous. In a March 3, 1962, article in the *Nation*, King expressed his dissatisfaction with the administration:

> The Kennedy Administration in 1961 waged an essentially cautious and defensive struggle for civil rights against an unyielding adversary. As the year unfolded, Executive initiative became increasingly feeble, and the chilling prospect emerged of a general Administration retreat.

King continued by saying that Kennedy had backed away from an executive order to end discrimination in housing. However, he did show some optimism for the future: "He has begun 1962 with a show of renewed aggressiveness; one can only hope that it will be sustained."[1] King expected a lot from the administration. Indeed, his dealings with Robert Kennedy during the Freedom Rides had left a mark on this young civil rights leader.

King went even further in the article about how Kennedy showed confidence and had done more than previous administrations: "Undaunted by Southern backwardness and customs, they conceived and launched some imaginative and bold forays. It is also clear that this Administration has reached out more creatively than its predecessors to blaze some new trails, notably in the sensitive areas of voting and registration." King also said, "President Kennedy has appointed more Negroes to key government posts than has any previous administration. One Executive Order has been issued which, if vigorously enforced, will go a long, long way toward eliminating employment discrimination in federal agencies and in industries where government contracts are involved. So it is obvious that the Kennedy Administration has to its credit some constructive and praiseworthy achievements."[2] This praise was not easy to come by from King. In fact, he was very careful not to endorse Kennedy despite the fact that he had been so instrumental in getting King released from jail in 1960.

Martin Luther King had high hopes and wanted more from the Kennedys. When he wrote this article he had not endured the humility and failure at Albany. King went on to say:

> With regard to civil rights, then, it would be profoundly wrong to take an extreme position either way when viewing the Administration. While the President has not yet earned unqualified confi-

dence and support, neither has he earned rejection and withdrawal of support. Perhaps his earnestness of attitude, fed with the vitamins of mass action, may yet grow into passionate purpose. The civil-rights movement must remain critical and flexible, watchful and active.[3]

King was careful not to admonish the Kennedy administration, because he knew that there were other initiatives in the future where he would need Robert Kennedy's support. That said, King did not completely endorse John Kennedy's initiatives. Despite the success he pointed to earlier in the piece, King wrote, "The year 1961 was characterized by inadequacy and incompleteness in the civil-rights field." He went on, "It is not only that the Administration too often retreated in haste from a battlefield which it has proclaimed a field of honor, but — more significantly — its basic strategic goals have been narrowed. Its efforts have been directed toward limited accomplishments in a number of areas, affecting few individuals and altering old patterns only superficially." King wanted more. He continued, "It is clear that to date no Administration has grasped the problem in this total sense and committed the varieties of weaponry required for constructive action on so broad a scale."[4]

King wanted genuine leadership from the government, not token gestures. Moreover, he expected civil rights to be in the forefront of possible legislation. He said that the government was quick to spend billions of dollars on defense, but nothing on behalf of twenty million African Americans. There were things happening in the South to change this inadequacy. "City after city was swept by boycotts, sit-ins, freedom rides and registration campaigns. A new spirit was manifest in the Negro's willingness to demonstrate in the streets of communities in which, by tradition, he was supposed to step aside when a white man strode toward him." There was a new spirit taking over the black communities in the South, despite the inaction of the government. "Thus 1961," King wrote, "saw the Negro moving relentlessly forward against an opposition that was occasionally reasonable, but unfortunately more often vicious."

King acknowledged that this was the year when nonviolence was victorious, leading many African Americans to success in their plights for justice. King commented on the new movement and how it was going to change the nation, making it a better place for all Americans. It was indeed a time when a person's voice could make a difference and often did. The 1960s served as a rebirth for America; many would remember where they were when certain things happened. It was time when African Americans were using their voices and the government listened. Not since the American Revolution had it been possible to have such an impact on a person's place in society. America was changing, and the Kennedys and King were in a position to affect that change.[5]

King argued that if Kennedy showed leadership, the people would follow, ushering in a new era for America. After all, he wrote, "The Negro in 1962 — almost one hundred years after slavery's demise — justifiably looks to government for comprehensive, vital programs which will change the totality of his life." If Kennedy took the initiative, according to King, he would go down in history. "The development of a plan for the nation-wide and complete realization of civil rights would accomplish several purposes. It would affirm that the nation is committed to solve the problem within a stated period of time; it would establish that the full resources of government would be available to that end, whatever the cost.... Finally, a plan would enable the nation to assess progress from time to time, and would declare to those who dream that segregation and discrimination can still be preserved that they must begin to live with the realities of the twentieth century."[6] King wanted leadership. John Kennedy was not giving that leadership to the African American community. Robert Kennedy, however, would continue to bring his message to Congress and the people of the

United States. The end of 1962 would prove to be a watershed moment for the administration and the movement.

In March 1962 Robert Kennedy went before the Judiciary Committee in the House of Representatives to testify on eliminating literacy tests and the poll tax, which had plagued African American voters in the South since the end of the Civil War. "With the adoption of the fifteenth Amendment in 1870, it became illegal to practice racial discrimination in the voting process. Yet it is necessary today, almost one hundred years later, to file lawsuit upon lawsuit to make the reality of this constitutional command."[7] Carefully choosing his words, Kennedy's argument was that this was a Constitutional right that has been denied to United States citizens. Further, the United States had an obligation, under the law, to secure that right.

Kennedy used statistics with the committee saying that in 1959, "in sixteen counties in which Negroes of voting age were the majority, not one Negro was registered to vote. In forty-nine other such counties fewer than five percent of the eligible Negro citizens were registered."[8] Kennedy was not one who shied away from a fight, but he would only fight the ones that he believed in. Kennedy's politics held him back somewhat, yet his actions after the Freedom Rides were not of a politician looking to do what the party wanted. Instead, he started to embrace a slow, progressive movement to change the racial situation in the country. He may not have had the full support of his brother's administration yet, but he was finding his own way, crafting his own voice.

Kennedy gave several examples where African Americans struggled with the literacy tests and were denied the right to vote, while other white citizens were given help, passing the tests. While Kennedy was able to bring litigation against these acts, more needed to be done. "The Federal Government must deal with this problem. The issue is not whether to act, but how." He continued, "Let me emphasize that we ask for nothing more than new remedies for old wrongs." He said, "The problem is deep-rooted and of long standing. It demands a solution which cannot be provided by lengthy litigation on a piecemeal, county-by-county basis."[9] Kennedy wanted the government to act, and he was willing to risk political capital to bring the vote to African Americans. The passion with which he approached this bill is evidence that he truly believed that the vote was the right way to attack the abuses in the South. He was not trying to placate civil rights leaders, nor was he trying to satisfy Southern Democrats with less hostile legislation; he was getting to the heart of what he believed was the problem.

Kennedy brought up the Constitutional basis for such legislation, saying, "The Fourteenth and Fifteenth Amendments are the affirmative grant of power to congress to enact legislation to guarantee the rights protected by those Amendments, including principally the right to vote." He went on, "Congressional action adapted to correcting this evil is not a questionable innovation. It is overdue." He finished on the literacy tests, saying, "This legislation is needed. It is constitutional. I urge its enactment." Kennedy was a civil rights advocate in this speech not only for African Americans but also for Puerto Rican citizens, saying, "Denying the franchise to literate persons of Puerto Rican origin is not reasonable," and that they were protected under the 1898 Treaty of Paris and given full citizenship, which entitled them to all the rights and privileges of any citizen as protected under the Fourteenth Amendment.[10]

Kennedy moved on to the poll tax, saying frankly, "After the Civil War, poll tax legislation was adopted in some states ... to limit the Negro franchise." He also said, "The poll tax is mainly objectionable, however, because it clogs voter registration, and limits participation in the processes of government. Our American belief in government by all the people makes it imperative that such obstacles finally be removed."[11] His testimony was a clear example that he was committed to real change in government. Kennedy wanted African Americans to believe that the system would help them in time. Kennedy cited Article I, sections 4 and 8, as well as Article IV, section 4, of the Constitution as reason to create a law to abolish the poll tax. "My basic reason for my belief is this: in America, the right to vote is the rule and restrictions on that right are the exception." He went on, "The poll tax is an arbitrary, meaningless requirement, having no reasonable relationship to the rights and privileges of citizenship, and it may therefore be forbidden under the provisions I mentioned."[12] Indeed, the poll tax kept those who could not afford to pay a fee from exercising a right that was a guaranteed under the Constitution.

Kennedy was very passionate about the vote. Prior to his speech before Congress, there was talk of how they would handle the issue of literacy tests in the South. Burke Marshall remembers

> I was frustrated at the time of the voting suits, I think, so we decided that we should have the bill in there and so he created this bill down here in the Civil Rights Division, the attorney general. Senator Mansfield thought it was a good bill, so it was introduced as an administration measure. And I would say that the president's view of it, I would say it was tolerant, that he was tolerant of letting the attorney general try this. And I don't think he ever had too much confidence that it would work, but he was just tolerant of it. In fact, as I remember, the president called me up the day after it was introduced and said, "What's this bill of yours and Bobby's?" something like that.[13]

John Kennedy supported his brother, but it was clear the this was Bobby's bill and he would do whoever possible to make the vote available to every eligible person in the country.

After the cloture failed on Bobby's bill, Marshall went to Senator Mansfield and asked if there was any chance at getting cloture. "He said no, and I asked him what we should tell people that were interested in civil rights legislation, and he said, 'Tell them the truth.' And I said, 'What is the truth?' And he said, 'That you'll never get a civil rights bill with a Democratic president.'" Marshall remembered that Mansfield's

> view of it was I think that he needed somewhere around twenty-five Republican votes in order to get cloture and that a Democratic president could never claim or never persuade that many Republican senators to vote for cloture.... There was no public pressure for that bill. We couldn't create any. We could hardly create any interest in it."[14]

There was no support for the bill and no way to generate public interest in the bill. However, years later it would be possible to do exactly what Mansfield said was not possible. The political climate had changed and it was largely because people like John and Robert Kennedy and others pushed the status quo and challenged Jim Crow in a variety of ways.

"Much remains to be done."

On June 22, 1962, three months after his speech before Congress, Kennedy addressed the National Newspaper Publishers Association at Morgan State College in Baltimore, Maryland. He called civil rights "the biggest domestic news story of our time." He also said that the "story broke almost a hundred years ago. Negroes were emancipated and shortly thereafter the Constitution was amended to guarantee them the full rights of citizenship." Kennedy said that it was an "unhappy thing" that African Americans had not been able to enjoy the benefits of the Thirteenth, Fourteenth and Fifteenth amendments. It was time to do something about that, he said. Kennedy was especially vocal to this group, as they were the people who would write about the movement.[15] Indeed, most of the literature about the civil rights movement has been from news reporters.

Robert Kennedy said, "First, we are moving to make sure that every American is free to exercise his right to register and vote." He said that the government was working on many fronts to make sure that these rights were secured for every American. "This progress doesn't come about with the wave of a magic wand. It takes work." Kennedy believed that the vote would make a difference. "The ramifications of their vote are just beginning to be felt. When they are joined at the polls by Negroes over all the state, the South and the country, I think the civil rights of all our citizens will be better protected."[16] To some degree, it was naive for Robert Kennedy to believe that the vote would make such a difference, since it had been denied for so many years. That said, it is evidence that he was an idealist and believed in the American democratic system.

Kennedy went on to talk about how African Americans were serving the government in different capacities. He also said that President Kennedy had talked to several businesses, and they were adopting measures to ensure employment on the basis of equality. Kennedy also talked about education, saying, "The federal government is taking an active role assisting local officials to expedite school integration." Kennedy mentioned interstate travel and that the administration was working hard to integrate all forms of travel in the United States.

> This progress does not mean that all is well. As you know, there is much more to be done.... There has been far too much hypocrisy in the field of civil rights. It is easy enough to give rousing speeches or call for legislation which has no possibility of passage. But the President is anxious to accomplish things, not merely talk about them.[17]

Kennedy wanted to take the movement to the next step. He looked to the newspaper people in the room to help spread that message, saying, "Newspapers can generate action in this country. They not only record current history, they help determine what course it will take." From that point on, Kennedy spoke about the responsibility that all the reporters had in this movement.[18]

This was a new way to combat racism for Kennedy. He looked to others in this fight, because it was clear that such a complicated problem needed assistance on all levels to be successful. Newspapers could be particularly helpful, Kennedy argued, at the community level. "Where there is an aggressive, vigilant, honest newspaper there is likely to be a progressive, clean community." Conversely, he said, "Where the newspapers are fat and lazy, the community is in danger of becoming a backwater festering corruption, vice and indifference." Once again, Kennedy pointed to the freedom of the press, a fundamental democratic American right under the Constitution. He believed in that system and used every aspect to push this agenda. Kennedy saw newspapers as another way to fight racism and injustice. "Your coverage of this big story of our time, the civil rights story, will determine, in large measure, the attitude of the Negro community." He implored the reporters to tell the stories of hatred and discrimination, but also when a government acted to right injustice. Kennedy said that when the news reported a race issue, the Soviets used it as propaganda. It was the responsibility of newspapers to tell the whole story. He stressed the word "responsibility."[19]

Kennedy stressed, "Our newspapers must be free to report every facet of American life for this is not a freedom guaranteed to them but a guarantee of freedom for all Americans. With liberty for the press, as with all liberties, comes responsibility. Newspapers occupy a position of trust to the public to report to them all the news — not just that which they wish to read or that which an editor thinks they should read." Kennedy asked the newspaper reporters to keep up the fight, saying, "So I urge you to continue to banner across your front pages any discrimination in schools, voting, or employment. But I also urge you to banner across the same pages the news that the 'For Whites Only' signs are coming down; that Negroes are registering and voting as never before; and that new employment opportunities are opening up every day." Kennedy concluded, saying, "No American will be denied his human rights or his Constitutional rights because of his race, creed, religion."[20] Kennedy's speech demonstrated his passion and belief in the American system. He trumped John Kennedy's success in civil rights, but also recruited others to spread the word of injustice and what the government was doing to secure the rights of all Americans.

At the Statler-Hilton Hotel in Los Angeles, California, on July 26, 1962, Robert Kennedy outlined four areas of civil rights that the federal government had moved on with "heartening success." He was making a speech to the National Insurance Association. The first of the four areas was voting. Robert Kennedy argued, "A much greater effort is being made to win the franchise for Negroes in the South. This is basic to all the rights of citizenship and from it all other rights flow." He pointed to the civil rights acts of 1957 and 1960 as giving him the authority to assure that the ballot was "not denied to qualified voters because of race, creed, or color."[21] This was similar to Kennedy's earlier speeches of 1962. Kennedy was clearly trying to stay on message, which was that the best way to affect civil rights was through the vote. He went on to say that African Americans who were teachers, ministers and scientists were being denied the right to vote on the ground that they were illiterate.

Kennedy said that the second area where there had been progress was in employment. "More and more Americans are being hired on merit and not being denied a chance to work because of the color of their skin." He went on, "This has long been the policy of the federal government, but we are taking action to see that equal employment opportunity is not just a pious declaration but a reality."[22] The lofty rhetoric was typical of the New Frontier, always leaving a grand message, using ideas and notions that were somewhat unattainable. However, it was that very rhetoric that led people to believe that it was in fact possible and it would happen under his watch.

The third area in which Kennedy told the crowd he was going to make a difference was in school desegregation. This policy would be especially helpful in the months ahead. While Kennedy was making this speech, James Meredith was working to challenge school desegregation at the University of Mississippi. "We are not waiting until violence occurs when the meeting of force with force is the only alternative." Clearly the Freedom Rides had left a mark on Kennedy, and he was determined to make a difference in the movement without further bloodshed. Kennedy said that the federal government was "protecting the integrity of court orders and working with local citizens and officials to bring about desegregation peacefully and with respect to the law."[23] Robert Kennedy's mantra was that all change could happen within the confines of the justice system. This was naive in some respects, as change in the United States has come from both within and outside of government.

The fourth and final area was interstate travel. Kennedy said, "Segregation has virtually disappeared from interstate transportation." He went on to say that the "For White Only" signs were being taken down at railroad, bus and airline terminals. "This has been done without the passage of new legislation." Kennedy proudly stated that the Justice Department tested existing laws and used the Interstate Commerce Commission to intervene.[24]

Kennedy acknowledged, "Much remains to be done and this administration understands its responsibility to continue working hard to remove racial discrimination in other areas. The job will not be completed until every American has full access to all rights of citizenship in every corner of the land." Speaking his belief that popular ideas would someday reign, he said, "I am firmly convinced that this day is coming because the majority of American people in the South, as well as in the North, East and West, want to make progress and they are not satisfied to accept the status quo." Kennedy wanted to invoke the memory of another politician who had made a difference in civil rights. "On Washington's birthday in 1861, President-elect Abraham Lincoln spoke in Independence Hall on his way to Washington. He spoke of the men who wrote and fought for the Declaration of Independence." Kennedy quoted Lincoln's summing-up of the essence of the document: that its promise was "not only of liberty to the people of this country, but hope of the world ... that in due time the weights should be lifted from the shoulders of all men and that all should have equal chance."[25]

Linking success in the civil rights movement to U.S. prestige abroad was a common way Kennedy demonstrated the urgency of his plight. Indeed people in the nation identified with the Cold War and its dire circumstances. Kennedy hoped those feelings would help his effort. He said that he had recently taken a trip around the world, and many people were asking about the civil rights issues that the nation was dealing with. He asserted to the crowd, "We are not going to be able to convince people in other lands that we mean what we say in the Declaration of Independence and in our Constitution if a large number of our citizens are denied their full rights." Kennedy told the crowd that it was their shared responsibility, as business people, to make a difference in this disparity that confronted so many Americans. He quoted President Kennedy, saying, "Our youth are our greatest resource and the social and economic implications of protracted unemployment among the one million job seekers today, the many millions who will enter the labor force in the next few years, demand immediate attention and action." Robert Kennedy urged the people in that room to "interest" themselves in this problem, linking the economic stability to the civil rights issues he was trying to change.[26] Kennedy was very skillful in this speech in particular. After laying out all the issues that African Americans faced, he cleverly brought the speech back to what the people in the room could do to help the cause. In addition, he told them that he would work with them in their endeavors to provide new opportunities for Americans.

Kennedy said that he would work for "better schools and job training." He also wanted to "encourage high school students to stay in school" and even bring back many who had left. In addition, he wanted to provide loans for students, give guidance to students who wanted to pursue a trade, provide high school and college students career advice, and help graduates find work. "We want to make sure that every American has the chance to develop his talent. Education is basic but the federal government cannot do this job. It must be done at the local level by men and women like yourselves." RFK was rallying the troops to push his civil rights agenda. Moreover, he linked it not only to the success of African Americans but all Americans. He finished by saying, "Our youths have long lives ahead of them. Today an America of equal opportunity for all its citizens is just around the corner and we have no time to lose. Let's plant our trees this evening."[27]

Martin Luther King and Bobby Kennedy had a vision for America. Both were idealists, looking to foster change in different ways. They needed each other for this change to take place. King's article in the *Nation* points to the growing frustration that he and others were feeling toward the Kennedy administration. Robert Kennedy's speeches demonstrate his passion to contribute to the cause and lay a foundation for future endeavors that would change the movement. They were both visionaries so committed to their cause that they could not see the similarities in each other. They were both idealists. Robert Kennedy's biggest challenge, however, was just ahead of him.

11. "Hello, Governor"

"I have always felt that I must do my best."

When Robert Kennedy was asked in May 1962 by Ed Spivak what he saw as the biggest problem that lay ahead for him, the attorney general responded, "Civil rights."[1] The Freedom Riders, the Albany Movement and problems registering black voters awakened Robert Kennedy to problems of race in America. Nothing, however, would prepare him for what was in his immediate future. The world would come to the brink of destruction that October, and the nation looked as if it would be torn in half as Kennedy confronted issues in Oxford, Mississippi. Arthur Schlesinger argued, "The Kennedy civil rights strategy, however appropriate to the congressional mood of 1961, miscalculated the dynamism of a revolutionary movement."[2]

James Meredith, a veteran of the air force, wanted to attend the University of Mississippi. He felt that under the *Brown* decision, he had a right guaranteed by the court order and the Constitution. Meredith learned as much as he could about the Kennedy campaign in 1960. William Doyle writes, "Meredith carefully scrutinized Kennedy's speeches as well as the strong Democratic party platform on civil rights, and when Kennedy narrowly won the election, Meredith decided the time was now right to put his plan in action."[3] Many African Americans were aligned with the Republican party. It was the Republicans who had freed the slaves and fought a war against oppression and slavery in the nineteenth century. However, when Franklin Roosevelt made an effort to extend New Deal legislation to African Americans, many started to move toward the Democrats. It was not until the Kennedy administration that African Americans moved in force. Kennedy's rhetoric was a driving force in this political shift. Meredith said later, "The objective was to put pressure on John Kennedy and the Kennedy administration to live up to the civil rights plank in the Democratic platform." He went on to say, "It was an effort to force Kennedy's administration to either live up to it or suffer the public relations consequences of not doing what he was pledging."[4]

On February 7, 1961, Meredith sent a letter to the newly appointed Kennedy Justice Department. He wanted to involve the federal government in his plight to gain an equal education under the law, which was guaranteed by the Supreme Court in the *Brown v. Board of Education* decision in 1954. He wrote, "Whenever I attempt to reason logically about this matter, it grieves me deeply to realize that an individual, especially an American, the citizen of a free democratic nation, has to clamor with such procedures, there still seems little hope of success." Meredith went on to explain that he had applied for admission to the University of Mississippi and had not been rejected or accepted. He said that "delaying tactics" were being used by the state in an effort to eliminate his application over time. Meredith said that he had "no great desire to protect my hide, but I do hope to see the day when the million Negroes that live in the state of Mississippi will have cause not to fear as they fear today."[5]

Meredith had wonderful things to say about America, writing that it was a great nation. American values had done a lot to help the world move in new directions in the realm of rights. "It has led the world in freedom for a long time." He wrote, "I feel that we can and we must continue to lead in this respect." Perhaps the most compelling part of Meredith's letter was when he told the Justice Department about his background. Despite the fact that he had to walk four miles to school every day for eleven years while the white school bus passed him, he considered himself lucky to have had the opportunity. He recalled, "Each day I passed by one of the largest farms in the county, and there I saw boys my own age and younger that fed cows all day." He also wrote that he was never taught by someone with a college degree. "I have never known that I could help solve this situation, but I have always felt that I must do my best."[6] Meredith valued education and wanted to pursue it at a higher level. It took determination, spirit and passion to overcome those obstacles and stay in school. Robert Kennedy should have known that this man would not back down until he saw equality under the law. Kennedy himself shared such zeal and could relate.

Early in his career one of RFK's faults was his inability to empathize with others. He got so involved in his tasks that he could not see beyond them. Meredith was among these special individuals who Howard Zinn argued were young and came from the southern parts of the country that were the most segregated, taking away opportunities for African Americans. Meredith shared a kinship to John Lewis. They both were exposed to the rural parts of the South and wanted more than that life. This drove them to embrace a new America. Meredith saw that new America in the Kennedy brothers. That perception is something that is undervalued and should be acknowledged when considering the Kennedy brother's legacy in civil rights. Symbols hold a great deal of power in history. It was that symbolism that drove the Freedom Riders and Meredith. The Kennedys responded when it mattered and could pave the way for future changes in American freedom and society.

Meredith believed in American ideals and even wrote about it. In his last year of high school he participated in an essay contest, which he won. His topic was, "Why I am Proud to Be an American." "My theme," he wrote, "was that I was not proud because I was born with as many or more desirable things in life as the next man, but because in my country an individual has the opportunity to grow and develop according to his ability and ingenuity, and is not restricted from progress solely on the basis of race. Basically, I still believe in this possibility." Meredith also wrote about his nine years in the Air Force, saying that based on that experience, "I can safely say that there is no logical reasons to justify denying a law abiding citizen the rights of full citizenship solely on the basis of race."

Meredith wanted more from the American experience. He expected that the Kennedys would come forward to defend this idea that America was founded on. Meredith continued asking, "What do I want from you?" He wrote, "I feel that the power and influence of the federal government should be used where necessary to insure compliance with the laws as interpreted by the proper authority. I feel that the federal government can do more in this area if they choose and I feel that they should choose." He finished saying that in view of the information he gave the Justice Department, "I simply ask that the federal agencies use the power and prestige of their positions to insure full rights of citizenship for our people."[7] Meredith's February 1961 letter came on the heels of the inaugural and prior to the Bay of

Pigs and Freedom Rides. It serves as evidence that many believed in what Kennedy said about a New Frontier. Meredith could have challenged the system earlier, but he waited for the Kennedys to make his stand, thus putting faith in them not only to integrate school, but also for his very survival.

James Meredith had contemplated when the right time would be to force the issue of his admission at Ole Miss. He wrote in 1966 that the election of John F. Kennedy "provided the proper atmosphere for the development of such a situation." He went on, "The strongest point in our favor was the civil rights platform which Kennedy insisted upon at the Democratic convention." He figured that the since the black vote had such an impact on the election, this was the time to act.[8]

"You are also citizens of the United States."

Burke Marshall was frustrated with the way that civil rights was acknowledged in 1962. He said in an interview, "Even after the Freedom Rides with all the sit-ins and other kinds of protests going on, the Negro and the problem of the Negro was still invisible to the country at large until the spring of 1963, and the president's moral crisis speech at that time and the results of the president's meetings in June, early July, 1963. There were some repercussions from those meetings which brought this to the attention of the country and the country responded to it. But at that time it wasn't."[9] Marshall remembered when the issue of Meredith's enrollment came to his attention. "There was a case filed by Meredith. I don't know exactly when. But among other things, shortly after I came into the government I went over all the matters that were pending in court that might cause problems for us, and one of the matters was the fact that there was an application and litigation involving the University of Mississippi." He goes on to recall: "Meredith, I think, applied in January 1961, and as a matter of coincidence he applied just before or just after inauguration. There was a rumor that was widely believed in Mississippi in 1962 that President Kennedy or the attorney general had something to do with stimulating Meredith's application, but the fact is the president didn't know anything about him, I'm sure, until September of 1962, and I doubt that the attorney general knew anything about him until about that time too."[10]

The Supreme Court directed that Meredith be admitted in the fall of 1962. Justice Hugo Black set aside a stay petition and Meredith was allowed to enroll at Ole Miss if he wanted. Marshall remembered, "Governor [Ross] Barnett made a television speech in which he invoked the doctrine of interposition, and it was perfectly clear from that time on, if it hadn't been clear before, that we were going to have a very difficult time. It was a question from that moment ... of trying to turn the state of Mississippi away from the course of actual insurrection."[11] Marshall remembered that John Kennedy was not involved until later. The president believed that Robert Kennedy and the Justice Department would be able to handle the issue. Barnett's replies gave them an idea that there was going to be trouble. Marshall remembered, "The Attorney General's effort was to persuade Governor Barnett to give up the course of action he was taking, which, as I say, led to insurrection. And everything that we did was with that purpose in mind — everything that was done by the Department of Justice during the week that proceeded the riots at Oxford."[12]

There were several conversations leading up to James Meredith challenging the segregation laws at the University of Mississippi. Ross Barnett, the governor of Mississippi, challenged the Kennedy administration with the notion of interposition, wherein the state would have the right to not acknowledge a law or ruling of the federal government if it felt that the item violated its constitution. Of course, the supremacy clause of the United States Constitution says differently: all federal law supersedes any state law. Robert Kennedy engaged in phone callas with the governor and others from Mississippi to move the process along. On September 15, 1962, Kennedy called Barnett in the first of his many attempts to find a peaceful, legal solution to Meredith enrolling in the university.

Barnett opened the conversation by asking how Robert Kennedy was doing and said that he was returning the attorney general's call. "Yes, I tried to get in touch with you," Kennedy said. "I thought we should discuss some of the details how to work this thing out with this fellow coming on Thursday." Of course, the "fellow" was Meredith, and Kennedy was trying to work with the Southern governments to make sure not only that there was no violence, but also that federalism was upheld and the states took care of these issues, without the help of the federal government. Barnett responded, "I will cooperate in any way I can."[13] While Barnett was saying that he would cooperate, he was really trying to stand fast on the segregation issue. Kennedy emphasized, "I think the first extremely important point that we are both interested in is that there be no violence, no disturbance, that he is protected." Barnett said in response, "I promise you, sir, that there will be no violence. The people do wanted [sic] to get involved in violence, strife and I have urged them not to do so and I do not anticipate any trouble."[14]

While Barnett pledged that the people of Mississippi would cooperate, Kennedy responded that the Justice Department had "heard reports from various sources that the people of Mississippi are aroused—that there might be violence when he comes in or in one or two days after." Barnett reassured him again, "Mr. Kennedy, I do not anticipate violence. You know, I am opposed to violence." Barnett was naive to think that his citizenry would not resort to violence. In fact, there was a long history of violence in his state when it came to race relations. The governor was culpable for the violence more than any other official involved in the Ole Miss affair. His determination to stop Meredith did not quell violence. Indeed it made the people even more obstinate.[15] The efforts on the parts of Southern governors to uphold segregation only aggravated the situation, encouraging many to act violently against a challenge to that system. Barnett, more than any other official to that point was wrong and contributed to that atmosphere.

Kennedy made it clear to Barnett that Meredith would be coming with marshals. Barnett responded, "If you let me know when, there will be no violence. If there would [sic] be trouble it would be a great shock to me, you know." Kennedy reemphasized on that phone call that marshals would be the only ones accompanying Meredith. "We will not have any others." They left the conversation saying that they would talk again the following Monday. It was difficult to know then that the situation would be much larger than the two of them had anticipated. While Kennedy was ready for violence, he would have to utilize more than a "couple of marshals" to integrate Ole Miss. Barnett's statement that it would be a "great shock" to him if there were violence is even more evidence that he was not considering the situation as it was in his state. It is possible that Barnett, being so against this and challenging the Kennedy administration publicly, emboldened the people, which changed the atmosphere from September 15 to September 30, when they finally brought in Meredith.[16]

On September 17 at 7:00 P.M. Robert Kennedy called Barnett to follow up on their conversation of September 15. While there is no transcript, Kennedy wrote a memo of the conversation. In that conversation Barnett "made the point that he felt that Meredith should register at Jackson at the State House at 3 o'clock on Thursday. He said that this would be a most convenient hour and place for them." Kennedy asked if this was unusual, and the governor responded that while the vast majority of students registered at Oxford some of them registered in Jackson. Kennedy said that he would cooperate, however, "Meredith would have to be consulted and that I thought it was very possible that he would want to register at Oxford rather than Jackson." Kennedy said that he would look into this and get back to the governor. Thus began a cat-and-mouse game that Barnett played with the Kennedys in an effort to avoid registering Meredith. Barnett was looking for any way that he could stymie or block the integration of Ole Miss.[17]

Kennedy returned Barnett's phone call on September 17 at 12:30 P.M. He had spoken to Meredith's lawyer and had an answer for the governor about registering in Jackson. Kennedy said that Meredith "feels strongly that he would like to register at Oxford and it's our judgement that it is the best judgement." Barnett responded, "General, I think you're making a mistake there." Kennedy shot back, "Well, I think it's up to the boy." Kennedy went on, "The vast majority of the students are registering in Oxford and he doesn't feel he should do anything unusual. But I think you can provide for his safety, can you not?" Kennedy made it clear, in his own way, that if the state could not guarantee his safety then the federal government would intervene, and Barnett did not want that. Despite the fact that Kennedy preferred to keep federal forces out of the South, he understood the reality that he might have to do something. Kennedy told Barnett that Meredith wanted to register on Thursday. Barnett asked if they could do it Monday. He claimed that he was trying to "figure this thing out." He went on, "From a psychological standpoint the atmosphere will be better, that's what I'm thinking about." This was just another tactic to delay the registration, which also contributed to an atmosphere in which Barnett was not fully cooperating with the Kennedys, despite his assurance that he was.[18]

After Kennedy asked if Barnett wanted him to go back to Meredith with this proposal, the governor moved from thinking about the situation to making demands about where Meredith would register. Barnett went back to the original issue of registering in Jackson, saying, "I don't understand why he won't come here." Kennedy shot back, "The students are registering at Oxford and he wants to register at Oxford." In addition to changing the day, Barnett tried to get Meredith to come to Jackson instead of Oxford, saying, "They're going to have such a gang up there at Ole Miss and a lot of them might resent it." Kennedy grew impatient, saying that Meredith had considered it. "Let me go over this again." Kennedy asserted, "We approached his lawyer and his lawyer said 'we want to go to Oxford.'" Kennedy ended to conversation, saying that they would consider another day and get back to him.[19]

On September 18 at 6:05 P.M. Burke Marshall called Ross Barnett about the Meredith issue. Marshall was calling instead of Bobby, and Barnett said that he wanted a message sent to the attorney general: "That the Board of Trustees for the institution of higher learning convened yesterday afternoon and entered an order to the effect that Meredith, the Negro man, will come here to register, here in Jackson, Mississippi, at the State Office Building."[20] He went on to say that the trustees were the ones with the authority to control registrations. Barnett thought that he was holding all the cards. Past administrations may have bowed to the South, but the Kennedys were doing all that they could to integrate on the terms of those who were making the sacrifice.

Marshall said that Meredith wanted to register in Oxford and that Barnett had made this suggestion to Kennedy already. Marshall asked if the registrar, Ellis, was not going to be in Oxford for some reason. Barnett said that he did not have any control over the board and that this was their decision, despite the registrar's location. Marshall thanked him for the phone call but reminded him, "there is a court order which is against some officials of the University and I don't know what action the court might take on this order." Barnett thought he could use the fact that Meredith asked the board in a telegram what time and what place that he should "offer himself" and that this decision was in response to the telegram. Barnett said, "They have answered it by entering an order that he register in Jackson." When asked if the board was going to register him, the governor responded, "They have not taken a vote on it yet."[21]

The next day after the conversation with Marshall, Kennedy called Barnett and asked him point blank, "If he comes to Jackson will he be registered?" Barnett responded similarly to Kennedy as he did to Marshall. "They have the right to control and direct all of the activities of the university. It may be the majority will not permit him to register," Barnett said. He was adamant that Meredith register in Jackson. "They are going to make a mistake if they go to Oxford. The Board of Trustees has decided they want him to present himself in Jackson. If he doesn't do what the board says, it won't be our fault." Kennedy shot back, "If he goes to Oxford, you won't take responsibility for his safety?" Barnett said that the board were "very peaceful" and that this thing had the whole nation upset.[22]

Later in the day on September 19, Marshall and Attorney General Patterson of Mississippi spoke on the phone regarding the Meredith situation. Louis Oberdorfer, Katzenbach, McShane and Guthman were all present. The call was done on speaker phone so everyone could hear what Patterson had to say. They were trying to work out the details of when Meredith would register. Meredith was scheduled to register at 3:00 P.M. the next day at Oxford. Despite Barnett's pleading they were planning to take Meredith to Oxford for his registration. The Kennedys were adamant about getting this done on their terms. More importantly, Robert Kennedy, who was put in charge of the whole operation, wanted the law upheld. If there was an order from the court to register Meredith, then it would be upheld by his Justice Department. RFK also did not want to let his brother down. This episode had the potential to harm JFK's presidency. McShane planned to accompany Meredith with a couple of other Marshals. Burke Marshall assured Patterson, "He is very familiar with this sort of thing." Patterson said that Colonel Birdsong of Mississippi would "accompany him to Oxford and when the business has been completed there, they will accompany him to where he wants to go." They were coming from Memphis and most likely planned to go back there. Birdsong was with Patterson and everything seemed all set for Meredith to come the next day. They had arrangements to call each other and a plan on what roads to take. However, there was still other issues to resolve before Meredith could register at Ole Miss.[23]

Patterson called Marshall on the morning of September 20, saying, "I will not be able to assure you of the things I thought I could yesterday when I spoke with you. I regret it with all my heart, and I want you know that it is a thing over which I had no control at all." Patterson was referring to a warrant that had been issued for Meredith's arrest; he said that there might be an attempt to arrest him as he registered for classes.[24] This is another example of the governor putting as many roadblocks in the way of integration as possible. While there may have been a warrant for his arrest, there was certainly something that the governor of a sovereign state could do to assist the federal government. The warrant had the potential to throw off the whole plan, making it virtually impossible to get Meredith into the school. The Justice Department went to work to fix this problem.

Robert Kennedy called Patterson at 12:30 P.M. as a follow-up to Marshall's phone calls. Marshall was in the room, and Patterson was again on speaker phone for everyone to chat about this latest development. They were disconnected at first, but once back on the phone

Patterson asked Marshall how he was. Marshall shot back, "I am quite busy, General." Marshall told Patterson that Judges Mize and Cox had issued a restraining order that prohibited Meredith's arrest and that they intended to bring Meredith to register. Patterson said that he was there with Tom Watkins, a close friend of the governor, and that the governor's office directed that there would be no arrest. Despite those assurances, Patterson said, "I don't want to make any commitments to you or the attorney general of the U.S. that I can't follow through 100 percent." He went on, saying that he wanted to look into this from a standpoint of "mechanics." Patterson wanted to speak with Watson and the governor, who was away at his sister's funeral, before he committed anything to the Justice Department.[25] This was yet another obstacle thrown in Meredith's path. It was not over yet.

Burke Marshall wrote in a memo that after his 9:50 am call to Patterson he had discussed the Meredith situation with the attorney general. Later that morning he called Tom Watkins and told him, "We understood the governor intended to have Meredith arrested." Marshall pointed out that there was, in fact, a court order that prohibited such an action. Later that afternoon, Marshall wrote, "Watkins called back and said that he had discussed the matter with the governor and that Meredith would not be arrested." Despite that assurance, Marshall heard from Al Rosen of the FBI that an agent reported that a sheriff was going to arrest Meredith. Kennedy followed up with a call to Barnett at 4:50 P.M.[26] The fact that Kennedy had to make deals to assure that the law was upheld is an example of both the times that he lived in and the politics of the day. It also is proof that Kennedy was not aloof when it came to civil rights. Actually he and his team were creative in their approach and hoped to carve a path where other leaders could forge ahead, making a clear impact in civil rights legislation.

Before Kennedy talked to Barnett about the Meredith situation, he looked to Patterson for some assurance that Meredith would not be arrested. Before Robert Kennedy knew that there was a sheriff who planned to arrest Meredith he called Patterson at 3:15 to arrange Meredith's registration. Kennedy said that Meredith, planned to connect with Birdsong. Patterson made it sound as if Meredith would have no issues. "Whatever the registrar does — if he denies admission and denies registration, I assume they will have accomplished their mission." Kennedy responded, "That's correct." Patterson was very helpful and Kennedy even said, "I really appreciate your help. It will make a helluva difference."[27] While the goal was to enroll Meredith, it was also to demonstrate that the system needed to be challenged and that the law would eventually be upheld by a higher court. Kennedy knew that, but he wanted to fulfill his obligation to Meredith and give him the proper protection under the law. Kennedy's demeanor changed a little over an hour later.

The Justice Department received word contrary to what Patterson had said earlier in the day, so Robert Kennedy decided to call him back. Kennedy started the conversation, saying, "General, how are you? We just got word from the Bureau down there that they talked to the sheriff of Oxford and he said that he had orders to arrest Meredith." Patterson replied, "Oh my gosh." Kennedy went on to say that Barnett had given the sheriff these orders. Kennedy went on, "The best thing for both of us to recognize ... if the court has said he can't be arrested and then could be arrested — arrest him in the company of a couple of Marshals — put handcuffs on him and take him to jail — that's a direct problem for all of us."[28] Kennedy was upset and felt betrayed by Patterson and Barnett. At this point it seemed that Meredith was not going to be able to register, and this issue has dragged on too long. In fact, Barnett's tactic to hold off registering Meredith did as much to exacerbate the situation as did his boldness in the face of federal power.

Kennedy called Barnett after his conversation with Patterson. Kennedy told Barnett that he had "spent the good part of the day working on this problem of the possibility of the arrest of Meredith." He stressed that Judges Mize and Cox had prohibited this arrest and that this matter had been worked out the day before. Barnett assured Kennedy that he planned to "abide by that." He said, "I understand he is coming here to the University and not to Jackson and present himself here." RFK responded, "That's correct," as if this was no longer up for discussion, which it was not. The fact that Barnett kept pestering Kennedy over where Meredith would register is even more evidence that he was trying to control the situation and stop the integration of the university. Barnett said, "I told the sheriff here that that's the understanding not to arrest him and they agreed not to do it. They will go away without any arrest. Everything will be peaceful. There won't be any violence here." Kennedy told him that he had information to the contrary, but Barnett assured him that it was not true. RFK thanked him and then called Patterson to thank him as well.[29]

On Monday, September 24 at 9:50, Robert Kennedy called Barnett about the Board of Trustees decision to register Meredith. "Did they agree to that?" Barnett asked. "Unanimously," Kennedy shot back. "All of them? That's really shocking to me," Barnett said in disbelief. When asked if the trustees had signed anything, Kennedy said, "They all got up in Court and agreed." Barnett again was baffled by this turn of events, saying, "I'm surprised at that, really. They were so firm about it two days ago. They changed their minds might quick." Barnett asked if the court threatened them in any way and RFK responded, "No, they asked the court what they wanted them to do and the court told them and they said they would do it. They met and agreed unanimously they would take this step." Barnett said again, "I am surprised. I thought they were going to stand steadfast."[30]

Kennedy responded to this turn of events, saying, "I think there's a great problem here. If we don't follow the order of the federal court, we don't have anything in the United States. I understand how you feel and the feeling of the people down there. You are citizens of the State of Mississippi but you are also citizens of the United States." Barnett reached for something to sway Kennedy, saying, "I expect we got more than 1,000 letters this morning." Kennedy was not affected by what Barnett had to say. "That's not the problem," Kennedy started. "Whether the 1,000 people think so or whether I think so or whether you think so. The court has acted and there is nothing we can do. If you are working to avoid anarchy and disorder and tremendous distress, there is really not much choice on it. He is coming back again now." Kennedy followed up with his typical righteous attitude that the law should prevail and any other consideration should not be counted. While he was right, it was not a practical, realistic solution to the situation. Arguably, this naiveté also contributed to the violence on the Ole Miss campus.[31] Also, he had said that he understood Barnett's problem and the feeling of "the people down there," but that was rarely a concern. He was focused on the law.

Barnett again asked if Meredith was going to Jackson or the university. Kennedy was only interested in whether the Governor could arrange for Meredith's safety. Barnett, in a desperate effort to keep Meredith out of Ole Miss, replied, "He's under two court injunctions." Kennedy shot back, "The federal court has also taken that under consideration and it going to issue an order that anyone who arrests him is violating the federal law." Barnett, always the states' rights advocate, said, "They don't pay attention to the Mississippi courts. That's pretty rough, Mr. Kennedy. That's pretty low down." Barnett went on to say, "They're not paying no attention to what the chancery courts have to say. Without any hearing—strike it down. General, that won't work. It won't work in any court."[32] Barnett was backed into a corner, and he finally started losing his cool with Kennedy. It was probably the first time that he realized that Meredith was going to be admitted to the university. Every avenue that he had tried to stave off the inevitable was now closed to him. The only thing left was for him to violate the court order and stand in front of Meredith as he tried to enroll at the university. Barnett was a true segregationist. While some of his objection was political, deep down he truly believed in separation of the races.

Kennedy was not gracious in his victory. He was plain spoken and wanted to get protection to Meredith. "The court has taken action and I don't want to get into a major conflict down there." This turn of events really shook up Barnett. He replied to Kennedy, "I tell you I won't tell you what I am going to do. I don't know yet." Kennedy shot back, "I've got to see that he's protected," which was a veiled threat that he would send troops if necessary. In addition, his reference to a "major conflict down there" was a reference to such action.[33] Barnett was more concerned at the precedence this set, which further weakened the state's position. "I can't tell you what I'm going to do." He also said, "I don't appreciate such doings you know. I've got no respect for it.... They can't strike down orders without hearings. The lawyers here are very disturbed and lawyers all over the nation." Barnett pleaded with the attorney general, saying, "Kennedy, you ought to rescind this order. Really and truly, you ought to do something about this thing, General. I am frank." Barnett's plea would not be heard. At this point, Kennedy was committed to civil rights and planned to uphold the law. He was not looking to supersede law, because it gave him the power to act on his moral beliefs that Meredith should be able to attend Ole Miss.[34] Kennedy could have ignored the order, as others had in the past. His resistance to disregarding it was evidence that he morally agreed with it and wanted to see integration happen.

Instead of Kennedy responding to Barnett's rant about the courts, Kennedy said, "I think what's going to happen — he is going to arrive in the state tomorrow and make an effort to register. I think the registrar is going to register him and the trustees have made this decision. The only problem is whether he is going to be protected by the state of Mississippi or left to us." Kennedy concluded, "That's what I want to decide with you this evening." Kennedy was at his best here, when he really pressed Barnett. When Barnett tried to make excuses, saying, "I don't know what steps we will take. I will have to discuss it with several people," Kennedy simply said, "Will you call me, Governor?" Barnett tried to get another word in, saying, "General," and Kennedy interrupted, repeating, "Would you call me?" Barnett was on the ropes and said that he needed more time to consider what he was going to say. Kennedy again asked, "Will you call me then?"[35]

Barnett was noncommittal and needed to work out with his advisors what his next step was to interfere with Meredith's registration. Kennedy wanted assurances that Meredith would be protected and wanted to avoid the federal government getting too involved in what was essentially a state matter. Kennedy said, "I have the responsibility for his protection. I don't want to send in a lot of extra people with him. Do you think I should plan to do that?" Barnett said, "I frankly don't know what to tell you. I am shocked. I really am." Kennedy said quickly, "I will have to make plans to send people in to protect —" Kennedy was cut off by the "shocked" Barnett. "To send people in to protect him. I certainly haven't heard of anything —" Kennedy returned the favor by jumping on Barnett, saying, "If you can guarantee his protection — you have always kept your word — I am certainly happy to put that in your hands." Kennedy was trying to control the conversation but also play to the Southerner's penchant for honor and keeping their word. When Barnett asked how he could assure Kennedy, the attorney general responded, "The same way you assured us the last time."[36]

Kennedy said that he wanted local authorities, not the federal government, to assure Meredith's protection. "I would much rather have it on your hands. If I can get assurances we will stay out of it but we have to have assurances from you." Kennedy not only wanted to maintain the axiom of federalism, he also wanted to avoid issues in the South, where they abhorred federal intervention. That said, he also needed to point out to Barnett that this was no longer a state concern and the federal government had spoken. "Can I run through this situation with you briefly," he said to Barnett. "First the court ordered — then we have had the dispute over the period of the last week. Now it has gone before the court of appeals and they declared unanimously with one absentee that Meredith should be registered that the University of Mississippi." Kennedy continued, "The federal courts have acted. This is a union with Mississippi as a member as is Massachusetts. As I said before, as well as being a citizen of the State of Mississippi you are also a citizen of the United States." Kennedy declared, "The federal courts now have issued a ruling and to prolong this any further, we are all on the brink of a dangerous situation."[37] Barnett ended the phone call saying he would get back to Kennedy the following day. This was Kennedy's best phone call with Barnett yet. He asserted federal authority as well as putting Barnett on the defensive. Prior to this conversation, Barnett had been overconfident that he could control the situation. Whether it was trying to get the registration moved to Jackson or subverting the registration with a possible arrest of Meredith, Barnett might have believed that he was going to win.

These phone calls represented Kennedy's willingness to both work with the South and maintain the position of the federal government to act in the face of Barnett's defiance. These types of conversations were important in maintaining the integrity of the union, but they were also important in bringing the Southern leadership into the mainstream. Without that element the South would continue to defy federal law, maintaining the segregation laws of the South. Barnett was about to make the situation much worse than it already was and embolden those in the South who saw this as against their way of life.

12. Leading to Confrontation

"It is such a major step for us."

Robert Kennedy and Ross Barnett continued their discussions behind the scenes while the civil rights movement raged on in the South. The next day, September 25 at 12:20 P.M., Barnett called Robert Kennedy back. He seemed in better spirits. He told Kennedy that he was "fixing" to call him and that they were "exercising every diligence to prevent violence." Barnett also said that he had been in session. The two of them started to talk about logistics as to when Meredith would be down there to register. Kennedy came out and said, "He will go to campus or Jackson. Whatever we arrange with you. Will there be anything done by state officials or the city officials to interfere physically?" Barnett was noncommittal.[1] Part of the reason that Barnett was in a better mood was that he had had time to think about a way to circumvent this situation. Much the dismay of Kennedy, Barnett refused to say specifically what he was planning.

Kennedy had to find new ways to ask Barnett what was going to happen when Meredith came down to register. Each time, Barnett stayed away from saying what he was planning. He even shot back to Kennedy, when asked again if anyone is going to make "any effort to interfere with him," that "We're going through the same thing as before." Nonetheless Kennedy was persistent. He asked Barnett if anyone was going to arrest Meredith, and Barnett said no. Kennedy was getting frustrated with the game and posed to Barnett, "You are not going to keep him out physically? He gets there and says 'I want to go in.' Will someone stop him?" Barnett had to concede, "He may be faced with that."[2] Barnett was playing a game with Kennedy. In fact, he most likely thought that the young attorney general was not up to the task of getting the better of him. Kennedy was ready to jump through the phone line.

Despite the man hours and court order, Barnett flew in the face of the federal government and was going to make it even more difficult for Meredith to register. Kennedy said, "That's quite different now. Is someone going to try to physically stop him?" Barnett said, "He'll probably be told." Kennedy asked "Who will tell him that?" Defiantly, Barnett said, "I am going to tell him that." Kennedy wanted details and Barnett refused to give him anything. Barnett said, "If he breaks through the line I don't know what will happen then. If he is confronted with a line." Kennedy said, "He is going through it." Barnett replied, "I won't tell you what is going to happen. He is going to have to listen to what we have to say."[3]

Kennedy was not giving up. This is, perhaps, one of the qualities that made him so vital to the civil rights cause. When he believed that he was right, he never quit. Kennedy said, "I understand he has a court order permitting him to register." Barnett shot back, "We have an injunction saying that he can't register. Mississippi ought to be recognized like any other courts." Kennedy assured him, "We recognize them," but Barnett was not swayed, saying, "I don't believe you do." Barnett went on to say that he considered that Mississippi had the highest court and even one with more "integrity and honesty" than the federal courts. Kennedy was starting to lose his famous temper, saying, "This discussion won't get us very far." Kennedy went on to ask if someone planned to physically keep him from going in, and Barnett said, "If it brings on a breach of peace." Kennedy wanted this to succeed. His persistence at figuring out Barnett's plan coupled with this tenacious approach to the problem of getting Meredith shows that he was committed and ready to change the climate of the nation. "That's what is going to be the problem," he said to Barnett. Then he added, "It is such a major step for us."[4] He didn't refer to the African American cause, nor did he refer to Meredith. He used the word "us," meaning the nation and his brother's administration. Robert Kennedy needed someone in the South who shared his vision of America.

Barnett challenged the attorney general, asking if the courts in New Orleans had a right to control Mississippi. "That's the issue," he said, "and I won't test it out." Kennedy responded, "I think you have had the test and I think it is quite clear in the United States that the federal courts have the last say. You might not like it." Kennedy continued, "These matters have been resolved many years ago in the course of our history." RFK emphasized, "I said last night that you are not only a citizen of the state of Mississippi but also a citizen of the United States." The situation was getting worse. The previous phone calls had dealt with logistics and stall tactics. This phone call challenged history and the law. It challenged ideas that had been an issue since the Kentucky and Virginia resolutions. "I am going to obey the laws of Mississippi," Barnett said. "Are you going to obey the laws of the United States?" Kennedy asked. Barnett stood firm: "I have taken an oath of the State of Mississippi and I can't violate —." Before Barnett could finish his sentence Kennedy asked, "Haven't you taken the oath of the United States?"[5] The conversation took a turn into debating the role of the federal government. Barnett said to Kennedy, "Yes sir, and that is what we are trying to preserve and it's being whittled away."

RFK: "The courts have acted on it, Governor."
BARNETT: "Yes, they are whittling it away piecemeal by piecemeal."
RFK: "What about the Constitution?"
BARNETT: "The Constitution is the law of the land but not what some court says."

They were at an impasse that was as old as Jackson's nullification crisis and the Civil War. Kennedy had history on his side, but Barnett had the people of Mississippi, who were willing to hang Meredith from a tree if he tried to cross the sacred threshold of Ole Miss. Kennedy finally said, "Governor, I think we have to resolve this point between us."[6]

Kennedy was finally seeing the depth that he was in. He said, "I will have to reconsider how many people we send in. I suppose then I will have to send more people in to get him on campus? As I say I thought this was resolved. Do you want to have a pitched battle?" Barnett said in response, "That what it's going to boil down to — whether Mississippi can run its institutions or the federal government is going to run things." Barnett suggested that they bring Meredith and let him say no. Then they could go back to court on the matter. Bobby was in disbelief, saying, "I don't understand, Governor. Where do you think this is going to take your own state?" Barnett said defiantly, "A lot of states haven't had the guts to take a stand. We are going to fight this thing." Barnett said that he wanted to fight

it in the courts. He blasted Kennedy, saying, "This is like a dictatorship. Forcing him physically into Ole Miss. General, that might bring on a lot of trouble. You don't want to do
that." He finished, saying, "You don't want to physically force him in." Kennedy quickly
responded, "You don't want to physically keep him out."[7] Kennedy tried to take a stand
with Barnett, but the old-school governor was taking a stand and finally starting to show
his hand in this game with the Kennedy brothers.

Barnett stressed that if Meredith entered, it violated Mississippi law. RFK stressed that
the federal courts had acted and that Mississippi was a part of the United States. Barnett
said, "We have been a part of the United States but I don't know whether we are or not."
RFK asked, "Are you getting out of the Union?" Barnett was agitated and said, "It looks
like we're being kicked around — like we don't belong to it. General, this thing is serious."
Kennedy snapped back, "It's serious here." Barnett was trying everything possible to delay
a standoff between the federal government and the State of Mississippi. "Must it be over
one little boy — backed by a communist front — backed by the NAACP which is a communist
front?" Kennedy said, "I don't think it is." To which Barnett replied, "We know it is down
here."[8] Kennedy and Barnett's reference to them being in two different places and to Mississippi getting "kicked around" and not being a part of the Union are evidence that there
were still major differences between the North and the South. The American people were
not sold on the civil rights issue yet. The South resisted and the North did not fully comprehend. However, the Kennedys did support these movements. It took the Kennedy brothers to take a stand, illuminating the racist ideology in the South and bringing these issues
to the people, leading to greater equality under the law.

Barnett finished the conversation, saying, "I am going to treat you with every courtesy
but I won't agree to let that boy to get to Ole Miss. I will never agree to that. I would rather
spend the rest of my life in a penitentiary than do that." Kennedy said, "I have a responsibility
to enforce the laws of the United States." Barnett responded, linking RFK with the NAACP,
saying, "I appreciate that. You have a responsibility. Why don't you let the NAACP run
their own affairs and quit cooperating with that crowd. We would appreciate that a lot."
Barnett lumped Kennedy in with the civil rights group. He also said "we," implying that
Southerners on the whole despised this interference. RFK responded, "Governor, I am only
in it because there is an order of the court. I believe in the federal courts, in the Constitution
of the United States, I believe in this Union. That is why I took an oath of office and I
intend to fulfill it. The orders of the court are going to be upheld. As I told you, you are a
citizen not only of the State of Mississippi but also the United States."[9] With that they
ended the phone call, not any closer to a decision on how Meredith would enroll at Ole
Miss. Kennedy was not trying to show the might of the United States. It was clear that
Kennedy had more resources at his disposal. He did however, want Barnett to know that
he would go as far as possible to maintain law and order and uphold the decision of the
courts. However, while at first this was a charge of his office, it was slowly becoming personal.
Kennedy did not want to involve his brother.

"But he likes Ole Miss."

Burke Marshall writes, "Between the attorney general's conversation with the Governor
at 12:20 P.M., and the conversation at 3:25, I discussed this matter with the attorneys for
the Board of Trustees." They had agreed that Meredith would come to the Federal Building
and be registered. "At the time of the attorney general's conversation at 3:25 with the governor, that was the understanding."[10] At 3:25 P.M. on September 25, Robert Kennedy called

Barnett again to secure Meredith's registration. The two leaders discussed the fact that Meredith would be coming to Jackson. When asked where Meredith was going to register Kennedy, responded, "I am not sure. I am going to work that out." Barnett brought back the same issue that he tried to move not days before, saying, "The court order orders him to register here." Kennedy coolly said, "I will study that and I will be in touch with you afterwards."[11]

Kennedy's efforts in negotiation were like no other attorney general. He clearly wanted this to work out not only for Meredith, but for other students who tried to integrate the schools. He was coming to a realization that civil rights was more than a political or legal issue that needed to be dealt with. Kennedy's determination is evidence that he planned to change the country, leaving a new legacy and different landscape than when he inherited the office. Kennedy pressed Barnett, asking, "There will be no interference and he will be protected there?" Barnett said, "There will be no violence at all." Kennedy asked again, "And no interference with him?"[12] He had learned that he had to be specific with Barnett, because he could not be trusted and would twist words or use the fact that Kennedy did not specifically ask him a question, which in turn meant that he had been truthful all along, despite his omissions of actions he had planned.

Marshall wrote, "Following the telephone conversation at 3:25 I was informed ... that Ellis [the registrar] was physically prevented from leaving the State House to go to the Federal Building." According to Charles Clark, attorney for the Board of Trustees, "Mr. Ellis was under subpoena to a legislative investigating committee, and ... they would use police if necessary to prevent him from leaving the room where he was to be questioned." The president of the Board of Trustees said that they were going to follow the order in that Meredith was to be registered by 2:00 P.M. Otherwise, he would have to appear at the Oxford campus to be registered. Meredith received an extension from Judge Tuttle. Marshall and others decided that Meredith would go to the State House to register. Kennedy spoke with Barnett at 6:00 after this decision.[13] The Justice Department was not surrendering its position. It was determined to get Meredith registered, which would set a precedent for future issues. Barnett and his people were doing everything they could not only to stop Meredith, but to stifle any sort of federal intervention in the South. Furthermore, by stopping his registration they set up a situation in Oxford that would cause damage. This cause was larger than one person going to college. It would have reverberations throughout the nation. The country, however, had not yet caught on to this thinking yet. It almost seemed that the country needed a crisis such as this to realize that there were problems in the South that needed attention.

Kennedy called Barnett with the intention to bring Meredith to the State House. He wanted to secure a place for him at the building that was safe. "Can you clear the crowds so we don't make a big circus?" Kennedy asked. Barnett said that the people would not bother him. "It will make it difficult. Just make sure the way is clear," Kennedy shot back, ignoring Barnett's assurance that people wouldn't bother Meredith. Kennedy persisted with Barnett, asking him about the people that were already there. Barnett said there were about 15 or 18 people. "You will have that under control?" Kennedy asked. "Oh, absolutely," said Barnett.[14] Fifteen minutes later at 6:25 P.M. Kennedy called Barnett telling him that Meredith was on his way and was accompanied by three men.[15]

James McShane and John Doar picked up Meredith at Dillard University in New Orleans. Doar had with him the orders from the Fifth Circuit Court, which told Barnett that he could not be evasive or obstructive with Meredith's registration. Doar, McShane and Meredith met Barnett at Jackson, where he proclaimed interposition, denying Meredith admission to the university. State legislators chanted, "Get going! Get going!" Another said, "Three cheers for the governor!"[16] Barnett's belligerence contributed to an atmosphere of hate and racism, which was already pervasive in Mississippi. That cultivation of such feelings was derelict, caused suffering and cost many lives.

Kennedy spoke with Barnett at 7:25 and started the conversation, asking, "Everything all right down there?" Barnett said smoothly, "Why certainly," as if there was no doubt that he would maintain law and order. "Nobody even made any overt acts whatsoever. Just as smooth — they did a lot of cheering and booing." Barnett said that Meredith did not get registered. "I told Meredith and the others, the marshals, that when I took the oath of office as governor I swore that I would uphold the laws of the State of Mississippi and our own Constitution and the Constitution of the United States." Kennedy responded quickly, "He is going to show up to classes tomorrow." Barnett was in shock, again. "At Ole Miss? How can he do that without registering?" Kennedy said coolly, "If there is any problem — I don't think they will raise any problem about it. He made his effort to register — but he is going to show up for classes. I think they arranged it." Kennedy said further, "It is all understood." Barnett said, "I don't see how they can. They're going to give them special treatment? They can't do that, General." Kennedy said again, "He is going to classes. He is going to be there."[17] Kennedy had enough of the games and was looking beyond the courts and trying to negotiate a deal with the school itself.

Barnett was unsure what to do next. He said, "Well, I don't know what will happen now. I don't know what we will do. I didn't dream of a thing like that." Kennedy was visibly agitated when Barnett said, "I am glad we didn't have any violence, you know. That always looks bad. There was no bloodshed today — tomorrow or any other day I can't guarantee it. I can't stay up at Ole Miss."[18] First, the mere fact that Barnett was concerned with appearances rather than actual lives or lost or violence speaks to the heart of the issues and how he handled them. He would say something similar to Kennedy on another phone call. This concern that it might "look bad" was not a priority for Robert Kennedy. They wanted everyone safe and the law upheld. Perhaps that was biggest difference between the Kennedys and others in civil rights. While they may have had that approach during the campaign, they were seeing civil rights as a matter of right and wrong, not what was politically expedient. Kennedy's response shows a level of frustration.

"We will send someone to protect him," Kennedy declared. Barnett tried to speak, saying, "I don't think —" but Bobby interrupted, saying, "You can't control the bloodshed, why do you do it?" Barnett said that he couldn't stay there all day, but Kennedy assured him that all he needed was to "keep somebody up there to keep him safe." Barnett was trying to stop integration at any cost. He started to rant again: "If you knew the feeling of 99½ percent of the people in this thing you would have this boy withdraw and go somewhere else." Bitterly, Barnett went on, "I am sure though you don't appreciate, you don't understand the situation down here." Barnett suggested that he send Kennedy a committee to help him look into the issue. Kennedy snidely remarked, "How about while the committee is here, letting him get in that university? Let's try it for six months and see how it goes."[19] Kennedy didn't like Barnett's condescending attitude and gave it back to him.

The back and forth continued. Barnett said that it was best that Meredith did not go to Ole Miss. "But he likes Ole Miss," Kennedy replied. Barnett tried one last time to get Kennedy to back down, saying that Meredith was "being paid by some left wing organization to do all of this" and that the NAACP was a "front organization for the Communists." Kennedy ignored Barnett, saying, "I understand, Governor. He will be there sometime early tomorrow morning."[20] With that they ended the conversation. Kennedy was finally seeing the hypocrisy that had plagued the South since the civil war. Moreover, Barnett's condescension emboldened Robert Kennedy to make sure that the law was upheld and Barnett ate his words. The condescending attitude may have sparked the famous Kennedy competitiveness. Kennedy followed up with another conversation later that day.

Just after that phone call, at 7:35 P.M., the governor and Kennedy talked again about Meredith's arrival at the college. Kennedy was unsure what exact time Meredith was going to arrive. Barnett still tried to avoid the situation, saying to Kennedy "General, why don't you keep that boy away?" Kennedy responded with what was truly the heart of the issue and the basis for his intervention. "Governor, this isn't a question of the boy going to the University of Mississippi. It's the federal government. If you were here as attorney general you would have to do the same thing. I never knew the name up until a week ago and have no interest." Kennedy disassociated himself with Meredith purposely because it served him politically. Also, it emphasized to Barnett that this was about upholding a court order, not supporting the NAACP or Meredith. Kennedy continued, "Hell, it's my job and my responsibility to see the laws are upheld. I would not be here if I were not prepared to do that." Kennedy went on, saying that the people who were making these decision were not Northerners. "You have lots of judges on the court from Southern states and they were all unanimous, they were not weak-kneed…. I am just making sure the laws of the United States are being maintained." Exasperated, Kennedy said, "I can't understand that you cannot understand this principle. You and I don't want to get into an argument about that."[21]

Barnett, always up to a challenge, responded, "We would argue all night about that. You can never convince me that white and Negro should go together." Barnett was never willing to help the Kennedys. At the heart of his defiance was racism. He was doing everything in his power to diminish the work of the NAACP and the Kennedy Justice Department. Kennedy, however, was a good sparring partner and willing to argue a point, especially when it was the right point. "That doesn't have anything to do with you or me," Kennedy shot back. "One of the questions here is moral turpitude," Barnett said. Kennedy flat out asked him, "Are you against him because he is a Negro?" "Oh, No —" Barnett said. Kennedy pounced on him, asking, "Would you let another Negro into the University of Mississippi?" Barnett was losing his edge: "It depends on a lot of things — qualifications — I would have to uphold the law." Kennedy was finally seeing what this was all about. "What you said a little earlier," Kennedy continued, "that you never could see the two races going to school together — this has nothing to do with moral turpitude." He finished, saying, "You just don't want a Negro going to the University of Mississippi."[22] Kennedy always wanted to be on the right side of history. He felt that way when he was with McCarthy, which was why he left, and he was starting to see this issue as something similar. The movement was changing. This was a moment where true change was happening, because a leader in the government was seeing the racist ways of the South for what they were, not what they could offer politically.

Barnett tried to retort, saying that if a "white boy should be convicted of a crime he would never get to the University." Kennedy shot back, "You can't tell me this was stirred up because he was convicted of a crime — it's because he is a Negro." Barnett said, "That's one of the reasons." Kennedy never shied away from a fight. It was a part of the famous Kennedy competitive nature. "That's one of the reasons. We're talking man to man. That's the reason — you don't want a Negro going to the university." Kennedy pushed his agenda further, saying, "The problem is it has nothing to do with my personal feelings — this is the law. Wouldn't you be enforcing the laws if you were here?" Barnett was also incensed, saying, "Not the laws you're trying to enforce. That's not the law." He went further, saying, "I think you owe it to the American people to tell the Supreme Court that the *Brown vs. Topeka* decision is not the law of the land."[23] Barnett's comment here might have something to do with the fact that Eisenhower went on record saying that the *Brown* decision was wrong and he did not agree with it.

The phone call was getting nowhere. Kennedy asked what were they supposed to do about the circuit judges who made this decision: "Are they crazy?" Barnett said that the judges were not following the "law of the land" and he did not feel he needed to oblige. They agreed that Meredith would be there at 10:00. Barnett asked, "You are not anticipating any violence?" "I am not anticipating any violence," Kennedy said. Barnett concluded, "No sir, we don't want any violence on that campus."[24]

Burke Marshall wrote to Bobby Kennedy about his conversations with Tom Watkins on the morning of September 26. Marshall said that when he called Watkins he said that he "thought he should make another effort to change the direction of the governor." Marshall went on, saying, "The physical prevention of Meredith's entry into the university amounted simply to a question whether the governor or the federal government had the most men, and that we obviously had the most men." Marshall also wrote that he was sure that the court would want Barnett to appear before it and if necessary would issue a bench warrant.[25] Marshall was doing his best to find a compromise on the situation before it got out of hand. Despite his efforts, Watkins proposed a solution that had the potential to make it even worse.

According to Marshall, Watkins suggested that in the next "effort to escort Meredith into the university we should 'gently' push the governor aside physically, and that we should use 'the mildest kind of force.'" Watkins claimed that this would make Barnett's point and give him an out because "the federal government would have forcibly brought about desegregation."[26] This suggestion, which was most likely at the behest of Barnett, is another example where Barnett hoped to gain politically on the situation. Perhaps he believed that there was no way to win and he needed to do what ever necessary to save face in this situation. If they went through with this, it would only embolden the people, making it even more dangerous for the marshals and Meredith. In fact, in the midst of the riots, Bobby Kennedy commented how this idea would have made the situation worse.

Given that the situation was getting out of control, Marshall said that they administration would consider this, which made them just as complicit in such a charade for the Mississippi and American people. Jim McShane and John Doar did, in fact, use force the next time they approached the campus, but were met with greater resistance and wanted to stay away from any escalation. Marshall called Watkins in the afternoon, telling him of the situation. Watkins said that they had not used enough force. Watkins wanted "25 marshals with sidearms." Marshall, in a desperate attempt to stop this game, agreed, but made it clear that this amount of force was "token." Watkins ran it by the governor, who agreed, but wanted the marshals to come with guns drawn. Further, he told Marshall that there was to be "token resistance," but the governor would be there to call it off. Marshall wrote that Barnett stated three times that he wanted the guns drawn. If the Justice Department agreed to this, they would be responsible for the safety of the situation, which was contrary to what they had been arguing from the start. Barnett said that the "people of Mississippi were peaceful," and there would be no problem. Bobby Kennedy disagreed, and Marshall told Watkins that the Justice Department had changed its mind. The situation was building momentum and eventually something was going to give.[27]

The next morning McShane, Doar and Meredith tried again. This time they went to Oxford only to be met by Lt. Governor Paul Johnson. McShane tried to physically move into the building. "Governor, I think it's my duty to try to go through and get Mr. Meredith in there." Johnson stood firm, saying, "You're not going in." McShane tried again, saying, "I'm sorry, Governor, that I have to do this, but I'm going in." Despite McShane's determination, the group was not admitted to the building.[28] They turned around and retreated for the second time in two days.

On September 27 Meredith questioned Kennedy's commitment to the cause. He remembered in 1989, "In order to prevail I had to get the federal government on my side, and that was the whole reason for making the maneuver to put the Kennedy administration under the gun with their promises. I was well aware of the contact between Ross Barnett and the Kennedys." Meredith continued, "My greatest fear was a deal between Barnett and Kennedy. I had no trust of either of them, and less trust for Kennedy than for Barnett, because the law barred Barnett from reelection, but I knew John Kennedy wanted to be reelected."[29] In fact Meredith believed that the federal government should have gone in with more force and even commented to a justice official, "I question your sincerity."[30] Meredith was tired of waiting, but the Kennedys were working night and say to secure his place at Ole Miss. This was not something that could happen with a "stroke of the pen." This was a very complicated political situation and needed to be handled carefully. Kennedy, like many other presidents prior, was not only considering the immediate concerns, but also the issues that would remain when he left the office. He was setting precedent in race relations, like Lincoln before him, and he wanted to do it in a way that would leave a legacy.

Robert Kennedy remembered that Tom Watkins called the next day, saying that if the marshals "came down and drew their guns that Barnett would step aside and let them in the campus." Kennedy asked if Watkins had talked to the governor and had his approval, which he did. Kennedy also wanted Watkins to talk to Barnett and be sure that they would register Meredith and "preserve law and order thereafter." At this point Kennedy considered this situation where the marshals would pull their guns to get by the governor, but he wanted to have only one of the marshals do that. Watkins was non committal and wanted RFK to discuss that with Barnett. There was a sense that Kennedy was doing whatever it took to get Meredith registered, but still had limits on the "show" on the charade that Barnett was proposing. His chief concern was carrying out the order of the court and maintaining law and order after the registration. RFK talked to Barnett, who insisted that all the marshals draw their sidearms.[31] On the night of September 26 after his call to Barnett, Robert Kennedy called Meredith and said, "It's going to be a long, hard road and difficult struggle, but in the end we're going to be successful." Meredith responded, "I hope so."[32]

On September 27 at 2:50 P.M., Kennedy and Barnett squared off again. When RFK asked Barnett how he was, he replied, "I need a little sleep." This was draining on every person involved and Barnett was starting to lose the edge he believed that he had at the start of the crisis. When Kennedy described the new situation where one of the marshals would pull his gun, Barnett was confused, saying that he "was under the impression that they were all going to pull their guns." He went on to say, "This could be very embarrassing."[33] Barnett wanted to look like he was holding the line for the Mississippi cause and not compromising. In fact, he referred to many people thinking that he was compromising already, but he told his supporters and the people of Mississippi that he would stand firm and not let Meredith in the school.

While Bobby wanted to get this done, he was reluctant to have all the marshals draw their guns, thinking that it would create "harsh feelings." Barnett was insistent: "They must all draw their guns. Then they should point their guns at us and then we could step aside. This could be very embarrassing down here for us. It is necessary." Barnett assured Kennedy that everyone would cooperate and that there would not be any violence. In this conversation Barnett put on Lt. Governor Johnson, who said to Kennedy, "We are telling them to lay their clubs aside and to leave their guns in their automobiles. But it is necessary to have all your people draw their guns, not just one."[34] Indeed, the Mississippi leadership was not making this easy for the young attorney general. Bobby was a little out of his element. He was always straight with people, the constant moralist. These old-school politicians were trying to pull the wool over the eyes of the Mississippi people instead of saying that the federal government had every right to follow up on the order. It is further evidence that their lack of leadership contributed to the situation that would subsequently result in a riot, killing and hurting people.

Robert Kennedy was realistic and afraid of the how the Mississippi people would respond to the drawing of guns, that such a show would understandably "disturb your people." After Kennedy said this he wanted Johnson to affirm that law and order would be preserved. In fact, Bobby kept at this, asking to speak to the governor again. He made it clear that he wanted protection secured "at the local level."[35] Kennedy was cognizant that the issue rising between the federal and state governments was something that he wanted to preserve. The true nature of the Constitution made this clear. State and local authorities would handle their own issues, not the federal government. Kennedy was trying to uphold the constitutional principles while also enforcing a court order, which was directed by the same constitution. It was an interesting position to be in for the attorney general and he was careful not to cross that line. However, the situation was getting worse and he needed other options.

One hour after the first phone call on September 27, Barnett called Kennedy back. Barnett wanted to wait until Saturday morning. "We want the people to subside a little bit." The big issue was that there was a court case on the following day with the Fifth Circuit Court in New Orleans, to determine if Barnett should be held in contempt for blocking Meredith's registration on September 25. Kennedy said that if they waited until Saturday that could cause problems for the governor not only with the larger crowds but also with the courts. Barnett brought up the fact that some in the South claimed he was compromising. Kennedy assured him, "You are not compromising — you are standing right up there.... We're not going to make any statement on this." Kennedy was referring to the arrangement for Barnett to step aside and let Meredith through. "I am happy it gets resolved," Kennedy said. Kennedy even agreed to have all the marshals pull their guns as long as the governor took over and preserved law and order in the wake of the confrontation. Barnett and Johnson wavered on saying that they could protect Meredith and the marshals.[36] "They are going to point their guns —" Barnett said. Kennedy shot back, "I'm asking from you law and order be preserved in Mississippi and you have no choice then." Johnson got on the line with the same message: "We got a few intense citizens here.... We cannot assure anybody that those people or someone may be hotheaded and start shooting." Kennedy responded that if this was in contradiction to what they had promised half an hour before, he would hold back the marshals.[37]

While Johnson and Barnett wanted more time, Kennedy was reluctant to back down. He wanted an assurance from Barnett that he would control the situation. On the phone with Kennedy, Barnett said, "One man had a gun and I said, 'how many times does it shoot?' and he said '6 times and if that doesn't get the job done I got a little one here for number 7.' That's what we want to control." At this point, Kennedy questioned sending in Meredith with the marshals. He was concerned about his safety and did not want any violence. In addition, Barnett wanted Kennedy to put off the court's deciding if he was in contempt. "They said I should show force against you," Kennedy said to Barnett about the court. "They're [mad] at me and mad at you." Barnett said he was willing to sit in jail. "I'm trying to uphold the laws —" Kennedy responded, "If you can get this fellow in the university this evening a lot of our problems would be resolved." Kennedy suggested that they try to get him in another way, where people would not see him.[38]

Barnett was noncommittal and tried stall tactics, hoping that Kennedy would not force Meredith into Ole Miss. He was wrong. Kennedy was even more determined now that Barnett was so belligerent to the courts and the authority of the president of the United States. Kennedy moved from not sending them to making preparations for Meredith and the Justice Department officials to be there at 5:30 P.M., Mississippi time. The phone call ended with Meredith going to register. Barnett was not done trying to stall Ole Miss's integration. The two talked again at 4:20 P.M. Washington, D.C., time.[39]

During the 4:20 phone call Barnett said to Kennedy, "We are going to put forth every effort and I don't think there will be any violence." Kennedy asked, "Do you think we should take the chance? I don't think we should take the chance if there are any questions about it." Kennedy asked Barnett to announce to the group that there would be no violence. "Can I rely on you that there won't be any violence?" Kennedy asked. "Yes, sir," Barnett replied. "I am taking a helluva chance. I am relying on you," Kennedy stressed to the governor. Barnett finished the phone call, saying, "I am just telling — Everyone thinks we're compromising." Kennedy retorted, "I am just telling you that we are arriving and we are arriving with force."[40] The brief phone call would not be their last of the day.

While Meredith was on his way, Barnett and Robert Kennedy spoke again at 5:35 P.M. Washington, D.C., time. Meredith was supposed to register around 5:30 Mississippi time. It seemed that it was not going to be as easy as the leaders thought, and Barnett was rethinking this arrangement. Kennedy too was concerned about the arrangement. He had received a report from the FBI saying that once Meredith got into the university "it would be the responsibility of the marshals to preserve law and order." Kennedy said, "I didn't want a misunderstanding." Barnett said that he did not plan to "guard him all the time."[41] This was at the heart of the issue with Barnett and Kennedy. Bobby wanted, indeed expected, Barnett to secure the safety of Meredith. It was the responsibility of the state to maintain law and order. In addition, John Kennedy had spoken out against Eisenhower when he sent troops to Little Rock. Kennedy almost had to send troops during the Freedom Rides and did not want to do that here. Robert Kennedy, in his quest for justice, was also looking after his brother's legacy as well as the safety of everyone involved. It was a tough burden to carry, but he was used to it.

Barnett gave Kennedy a hard time. Either he was trying to stall, yet again, or he truly could not guarantee Meredith's safety. Kennedy emphasized that his agreement to maintain order was not with the local officials, it was with the governor and lt. governor. While Barnett was saying that he always maintains law and order, Kennedy was afraid that he was not being straight with him. "This is a difficult situation and you understand you have to watch it more carefully," Kennedy said. He went on to emphasize, "But you have given me now your word as an individual and as governor of the State of Mississippi as far as humanly possible — not superhuman — that law and order will be preserved." Barnett replied, "Yes, sir. This thing here — I don't propose to do anything out of the ordinary." Kennedy said, "If it looks like you are going to have some difficulty there you are going to take some steps." Barnett said, "We always do that." Exasperated and losing his patience, Kennedy said, "Governor, I don't know whether you are trying to tell me something without saying it. I am relying a good deal on your word and I don't want to be misled." Barnett assured Kennedy that if the situation got out of hand the state would intervene. With that, they parted, but there was still one last time that they would speak that night.[42]

Barnett was very concerned about the registration and started having second thoughts. At 6:35 he told Kennedy, "I'm worried — I'm nervous, I tell you. You don't know what's going on." Barnett went on, "There are several thousand people here in cars, trucks. Several hundred are lined up on the streets where they are supposed to land." Kennedy responded, "I had better send them back." Barnett was losing it, saying, "There is liable to be a hundred people killed here. It would ruin all of us. Please believe me. Talk to the Lt. Governor, he'll tell you." Clearly annoyed, Kennedy said, "I just have to hear from you, Governor." Kennedy was hoping that this would be the end of the crisis. Much to his dismay, the governor did not plan to let Meredith enter the school. "There are dozens and dozens of trucks loaded with people. We can't control people like that. A lot of people are going to get killed. It would be embarrassing to me." Kennedy responded to the Barnett's selfish remarks, saying, "I don't know if it would be embarrassing — that would not be the feeling."[43] Kennedy's annoyance illuminated even further the fact that Barnett was concerned about the loss of human life as much as the political fallout. In addition, it was evidence that the two men operated from different perspectives. Robert Kennedy wanted to do what was right. Barnett wanted to do whatever would keep him in office. Kennedy reluctantly sent Meredith and others back. They were back at square one. In preparation for the possible confrontation at Ole Miss, on September 28 the Joint Chiefs of Staff and Robert Kennedy presented JFK with a Mississippi invasion plan. There were two task forces, Alpha and Bravo. They planned a force of "riot fighters" to enter Mississippi. The Pentagon was ready with an even larger plan that involved both the 82nd and 101st Airborne in case things got out of control.[44]

Kennedy was being pushed by Barnett, but he wanted to try and control the situation. He remembered in 1964, "What I was trying to avoid, basically, was having to send troops, and trying to avoid having a federal presence in Mississippi. In my judgment, what he was trying to accomplish was the avoidance of integration of the University of Mississippi, number one, and if he couldn't do that, to be forced to do it by our heavy hand and by — and his preference was with troops." Kennedy remembered that Barnett was trying to work with Kennedy so there were no troops or, even better, was no Meredith to register. "And while he was doing that he got sort of more and more involved himself in rather foolish ways."[45] While Kennedy wanted to avoid a federal presence, he also did not want to give Barnett a reason to blast the administration. Troops were something that the people of Mississippi would hate, and they would stand behind the governor.

13. Enter JFK

"Under the Constitution ... I have to carry out the orders."

The bottom fell out for Barnett on Friday, September 28. The Fifth Circuit Court of Appeals ruled regarding the contempt charge. Barnett was found guilty, which made him even more dangerous to the Kennedy brothers. Marshall presented the case for the Justice Department. The court gave Barnett until the following Tuesday to retract his action and let Meredith register with the university.[1] On the day following this ruling, President Kennedy called Barnett to discuss the situation. This was a new level of involvement on the part of the Kennedy administration, and events from this point on were elevated to include the president. Robert Kennedy tried one last time to get the governor on board without his brother.

Bobby Kennedy was on the cusp of finally getting Meredith on campus. Over the next twenty-four hours Bobby Kennedy got the president to call Barnett and take a stand on getting Meredith registered. That stand sent reverberations throughout the movement and brought the State of Mississippi to chaos, but, in its wake, ushered in a time when the government, with the direction of the Kennedy brothers and later Johnson, could make a difference in the lives of Americans. On September 28, Robert Kennedy spoke with Barnett about getting Meredith on campus after the debacle the previous day.

Barnett started the conversation by thanking Robert Kennedy for the assistance and for letting him know when Meredith was coming. He asked, "I wonder if we could keep that good relation going?" Kennedy interrupted the governor, clearly frustrated, saying, "It seems to me just notifying you stirs up rather than help the situation." Barnett said that the situation was larger than he expected and said, "Some of them are pretty rough and rugged, you know."[2] Kennedy made a statement that proved he knew what was coming and wanted the governor to be ready. Kennedy suggested, "What if you make a statement coming out for law and order, that you put the situation in Oxford in the hands of the state police ... give [them] the responsibility for law and order and see, because of the near disorder yesterday, that no more than 3 or 5 people could get together." Kennedy advocated taking law enforcement out of the hands of the locals and concentrating it in the state police system. "I think if something like that was done and you made it clear to the student — it doesn't have a thing to do with Meredith — you made it clear to the state and the students not to get together in any one place and your state police will have the responsibility for law and order," Kennedy concluded, "then you would have the situation in such control that at an appropriate time we could then work out when this fellow could come in."[3]

Kennedy's suggestion was in line with his philosophy on the movement. It gave the burden of maintaining law and order to the state. He wanted to avoid federal intervention, but was ready to use it if necessary. Barnett's comment in response was, "General, it wouldn't amount to a hill of beans. Those people down there would not pay attention." If Barnett claimed that it wouldn't make a difference it is pretty clear that he never intended to fully enforce what he promised to Robert Kennedy. Barnett tried to find another alternative to delay Meredith from coming down. Kennedy finally said, "Governor, he's going to the University of Mississippi." Barnett responded, "It looks to me, General, like such a foolish thing for him to keep his mind on that."[4] Barnett was never fully committed to cooperating with Kennedy. That was where the riots started — not with the Kennedy brothers. Barnett was on the wrong side of history.

Kennedy was ready to do battle with Barnett. He clearly had JFK's support. He reminded Barnett that the court had already decided that Meredith would go to Ole Miss. When Barnett suggested another school Kennedy said, "They have already given their orders and it will be carried out."[5] This was not the same attorney general who managed JFK's campaign. This was a man who wanted what was right. This was a man who was awakened to the problems in American society. This was a man who wanted to change the climate of the nation and indeed played a role making this cause commonplace, ushering in new waves of protest. Mostly, this was a man who wanted to see the Constitution upheld and courts respected. Kennedy told Barnett, "If you can't maintain [law and order] in your state, obviously it would be taken by us."[6] One of the last things that Barnett said to Robert Kennedy was, "If you send troops, marshals, don't send Negro marshals. They won't do." Kennedy said that he wouldn't do that and there were probably no "Negro" marshals. Barnett reemphasized, "It just wouldn't do to send Negroes."[7] The two leaders left the phone call only to chat again at four o'clock. Kennedy and Barnett were not any closer to an agreement. At this point, Kennedy had already consulted his brother and was ready to enter the next phase.

The same tape system that had been used in the Cuban Missile Crisis was at work in this crisis. In the wake of the issues from 1961, John Kennedy installed a tape system the following year to keep a record of all the deliberations that his administration had over these issues. It was at work during the Ole Miss crisis. From this tape, the Kennedys and their advisors were engaged in how to handle this domestic crisis.

In the midst of the crisis JFK looked to his advisors to find a solution that was appropriate. On September 29, between 1:20 P.M. and 1:40 P.M., one advisor considered various options. Before Barnett backed out of the deal late that day, they were already considering sending in the national guard. In fact, one advisor said that Sunday would be a good time to get the guard on the ground. "Sunday is the psychologically quiet time.... Sunday always looks like everybody was going to church.... The *Life* magazine pictures will look like the very devil." The advisor went on, "On the other hand it's the easiest time to mobilize, when there's nobody around." The speaker went on to say that Barnett might call out the guard on his own and argue that there would be no disturbance if JFK called off Meredith. "I can't call off Meredith for that," President Kennedy said. In fact he acknowledged, "I don't have the power to call off Meredith." One person said that if President Kennedy did not call off Meredith than Barnett would say that he was inciting all this trouble. "Already said that," JFK responded coolly. The Kennedy brothers were willing to let Barnett call out the guard. "Well, let him do it. Let him do it," said JFK. "I don't mind that," Robert Kennedy said.[8]

John Kennedy's acknowledgment that they had no control over Meredith is evidence that they had very little to say about the Meredith's direction or commitment to the cause. They could not tell him to not register. That said, there is nothing in the record that implies that they wanted Meredith to stop, or wait, as Barnett wanted. In fact, the record only shows that Bobby Kennedy supported Meredith and wanted to see him registered at Ole Miss. What is clear is that the Kennedy brothers wanted Barnett to take the lead in maintaining law and order, not because it was politically expedient, but because under the Constitution it was the right thing to do.

Calling the national guard was forefront in JFK's thinking. That was evident when he contemplated with the group when the appropriate time would be to call up the guard. First, Kennedy wanted to give Barnett a chance to respond to any issues. President Kennedy said, "The question still will remain with us today as to whether we will call out the guard today, federalize the guard today, put it on alert, start an immediate step in the guard, or whether we wait till Monday and do it." Kennedy wanted to wait to see what Barnett's reaction was before he committed. The brothers contemplated what Barnett would do and how he would react to any move from them. President Kennedy believed that "he won't ... say he's gonna keep order." Bobby tried to say, "No, I think he's...," but he was interrupted by his brother, who said, "He'll give me an answer saying, 'If you will just call it off, uh, then we can keep order.' So it won't be a clean answer to it. So we still have to..." RFK chimed in, saying, "Yeah, but you can, of course, you can phrase the telegram in such a way that's going to make it very difficult." Robert Kennedy's advice was exactly what JFK wanted to hear. "All right," the president said, "let's get this wire written." That was how decisions were made in the Kennedy White House. The back and forth was a testament to how much the brothers relied on each other. It's also evidence that President Kennedy trusted his brother's advice and needed to look no further for a solution than the people in the room, especially Bobby. It's that relationship that makes these brothers distinct in American history. Moreover, it became their signature way of dealing with issues and was an effective way to come to conclusions.

The group continued to consider both political and military options for the crisis. They moved toward a conversation with Barnett, followed by a telegram asserting their position. One advisor suggested moving elements of the 100th Cavalry Regiment into position around Mississippi. It was as though they were preparing for an invasion. JFK even asked, "What about a map of the town and so on?" There was talk of consulting Brigadier General Charles Billingslea and Secretary of the Army Cyrus Vance, who would eventually play a role in the crisis. President Kennedy asked if Billingslea would give an "analysis of what we would do with the various forces." One person said that Billingslea had "already been working on [it]." Militarily the administration prepared for the worst case scenario and wanted everyone on board in case they had to move forces into Mississippi. These were not the actions of a leader who planned to do only what was necessary. Indeed it was the equivalent of sending troops into battle. There were plans, maps, contingencies and troop movements. In addition to the military, President Kennedy wanted to speak with Senator John Stennis of Mississippi after he spoke with Barnett and sent the telegram.

The Kennedy brothers were in tune with each other and ready to make decisions. They were constantly looking for options, both military and political, to find a solution so that in the end Meredith would be registered. Never once did they comment that Meredith should not registered. They practiced a realpolitik normally reserved for international politics. In many ways this episode was like an international conflict. Southern society was not caught up with Northern society when it came to race relations. The Democratic party had struggled with the issue since the end of the Civil War. The Kennedy brothers were breaking new ground and needed to tread lightly. Their actions, however, helped others maintain this movement toward racial equality. They were realistic and wanted Barnett to maintain law and order, not because of politics, though it did play a role, but because it was the proper way to address such issues according to the Constitution. Barnett's belligerence was contrary to the principles of federalism and violated the supremacy clause. The Kennedys did not need to go any further than the law. It was on their side and they used it well. Barnett, more than the Kennedys, made decisions based on political expedience. In addition, the Kennedys were moving toward embracing the civil rights movement, hence, making it a part of their legacy.

Since Robert Kennedy and Ross Barnett were at an impasse, it was time to involve President Kennedy. Clearly frustrated and ready for a resolution to the crisis, Robert Kennedy was ready for his brother to be involved in the crisis that had plagued him for the days preceding the final confrontation with Barnett. Before President Kennedy spoke to Barnett he jokingly announced to those in the room, "Governor, this is the President of the United States — not Bobby, not Teddy."[9] Before President Kennedy reached for the phone to talk to Barnett, Robert Kennedy said, "Go get him, Johnny boy."[10] On Saturday September 29 at 2:30 P.M., President Kennedy made a phone call to Barnett. Kennedy started the conversation, saying, "Well, I'm glad to talk to you, Governor. I am concerned about, this, uh, situation, uh, down there, as I know, uh..." Barnett called it a "horrible situation." Kennedy went on to state that he had a larger problem. "This, uh, listen, I didn't, uh, put him in the university, but on the other hand, under the Constitution.... I have to carry out the orders of the, carry that order out and I don't, I get, uh, I don't want to do it in any way that causes, uh, difficulty to you or to anyone else."[11] Kennedy was trying one last go at handling this diplomatically, so to speak, in an effort to save face for Barnett and help his agenda with Southern politicians. The difference between Bobby and Jack was that the president took a political approach with Barnett, appealing to their roles as executives. The attorney general saw this as a moral and legal issue, in that Barnett had no right to deny him entrance into the university. President Kennedy emphasized that he had an obligation to uphold the court order, "But I've got to do it. Now, I'd like to get your help in doing that."[12]

Barnett asked if Kennedy had spoken with Tom Watkins, an advisor to the governor who tried to mediate the issue. After consulting Bobby in the adjoining room President Kennedy said, "The problem is as to whether we can get, uh, the, we can get some help in getting this fellow in, uh, this week." He went on to say, "Now, evidently we couldn't, the attorney general didn't feel that, uh, he and Mr. Watkins had reached any final agreement on that." Kennedy went on about the court order, asking what Barnett's feeling was on the matter. "You know what I am up against, Mr. President. I took an oath, you know, to abide by the laws of this state and our constitution here and the Constitution of the United States. I'm, I'm on the spot here, you know." Barnett went on about state statutes, but Kennedy made it clear that he was committed to the cause, saying, "Well, of course the problem is, Governor, that, uh, I got my responsibility, just like you have yours."[13] This was the first time that a president had taken such a stand against a Southern governor. The Freedom Rides were the first step to prepare Kennedy for this type a domestic issue. This was a grand test, similar to the Cuban Missile Crisis, which was just on the horizon. His leadership was in perfect form and he sounded presidential in dealing with Barnett on the phone.

Barnett said, "Mr. President, let me say this. They're calling, calling me and others from all over the state, wanting to bring a thousand, wanting to bring five hundred, and two hundred, and all such as that, you know." Kennedy responded, "I know. Well, we don't want to have a, we don't want to have a lot of people getting hurt or killed down there." That was chief on both his and Bobby's minds at the height of this conflict. The two leaders agreed to let Tom Watkins visit Robert Kennedy and decide what the next step was going to be. As Barnett was leaving the phone Barnett uncharacteristically thanked the president for his "interest in our poultry program and all those things."[14] Kennedy laughed softly on the other end of the line. They would not be laughing together in the next few days. After the conversation President Kennedy remarked to Bobby, "You've been fighting a pillow all week."[15] However, John Kennedy was still not done with Barnett. The next day would prove to be a pivotal point in the crisis. Contrary to President Kennedy's statement that they would wait a few days, the attorney general called back and said differently.

"Governor, this is the president speaking."

On September 29 at 3:16 John Kennedy and Barnett spoke again. This time the president handed the phone to the attorney general. Barnett and Robert Kennedy talked about Tom Watkins. Barnett still wanted the marshals to force him aside, but Kennedy did not think that was a good idea. Robert Kennedy said, "Under our understanding for Thursday that, uh, the marshals would show up and that, uh, you and the others would step aside and Mr. Meredith would come into the university." Kennedy went on to say, "Well, he felt, uh, when he mentioned, uh, he talked to me today, he said that he thought that, uh, would create some problems, uh, which they could not overcome. And, uh, he suggested at that time, uh, some alternatives which were, uh, not, uh, very satisfactory."[16] Barnett's use of Tom Watkins is a clear indicator that he was trying to stall this integration as long as possible. Kennedy, on the other hand, was not willing to negotiate and put anyone in harm's way.

Barnett stressed that he wanted Watkins to make a trip to see Bobby. Kennedy went on to say, "I'd be glad to see him, but I thought that unless we had some real basis, uh, for, uh, some understanding and working out this very, very difficult problem that the, really he was wasting his time; and that, uh, that one of the basic requirements, in my judgment, was the maintenance of, uh, law and order, and, and that would require, uh, some, uh, very, uh, strong and, uh, uh, vocal action by, uh, you yourself."[17] This was where Robert Kennedy had Barnett in his crosshairs. Barnett said that he would maintain "law and order ... the very best way that I can." Robert Kennedy was not convinced when Barnett said, "I talked to the student body the other day and told 'em to really, to have control of the physical and mental faculties. But it didn't do much good, it seemed like." He also said, "They cheered and carried on; but then they just started raving and carrying on, you know."[18] Kennedy wanted more. Barnett was noncommittal because he believed that it was against Mississippi law, but also that it would hurt him politically. Bobby did not let him off the hook. In fact, he challenged him.

Kennedy wanted Barnett to take a larger role in maintaining order. If Barnett had done that, there might not have been such a violent end to this standoff. Robert Kennedy requested at the "very minimum and as a start, uh, an order by you and the state, that, uh, that, uh, people could not congregate, uh, in Oxford now in groups of three or five, larger than groups of three or five; uh, the second; to get the school, uh, authorities to issue instructions to the, uh, students that that if they congregate in groups that, uh, they are liable for expulsion." Any engagement would help Kennedy maintain order. Ultimately the court had made its decision and it was up to him to see it through. "If that was done this afternoon, I think that would be, uh, a big step forward. And that anybody carrying an arm or a, arms or a club, or anything like that would be liable to punishment."[19]

Kennedy emphasized that those kinds of steps from the governor would make a difference. Barnett said, "General, I certainly, I'll tell the chancellor to announce to all the students to keep law and order and to, uh, keep cool heads. But, the trouble is not only the students, but it's so many thousands of outsiders will be there."[20] He was not willing to say anything for the Meredith case. In his own hypocritical way, he believed that he was being truthful and honorable by not lying to Kennedy. Instead his actions caused major damage to the integrity of the process. Further, if Kennedy did not press him, then Meredith would not have been able to register at Ole Miss. He needed the might of the federal government.

At this point it seemed that Robert Kennedy lost his patience with Barnett. It had been a long couple of weeks and he wanted this done. He restated the suggestion about congregating, and when Barnett was noncommittal he said that JFK had a few questions for him. Barnett was trying to get Tom Watkins to speak with Kennedy again, clearly in an effort to stall Kennedy's efforts. Kennedy shot back, "Well, he doesn't have any suggestions." Kennedy went on to say that Watkins "said something about sending the, Meredith, uh, sneaking him into Jackson and getting him registered while all of you were up at Oxford. But that doesn't make much sense, does it?" Barnett countered Kennedy, saying, "Why doesn't it? That's where they'd ordered him to go at first, you know."[21] This was all part of the game that Barnett believed he could keep up with the Kennedys. Barnett went on about going to Oxford when Robert Kennedy said that the president had some questions and "wanted answers to make his own determination." Barnett then launched into a tirade, saying, "I've taken an oath to abide by the laws of this state and our state constitution and the Constitution of the United States." Barnett dramatically cleared his throat and continued, "And, General, how can I violate my oath of office? How can I do that and live with the people of Mississippi? You know, they are expecting me to keep my word. That's what I'm up against, and I don't—" Barnett was interrupted, not by Robert Kennedy, who he believed that he was still talking to, but by president Kennedy. Bobby was done talking to him, and the president dramatically stated, "Governor, this is the president speaking."[22]

President Kennedy started in on Barnett. It was important that JFK demonstrate to Barnett that he was as willing as Robert Kennedy to uphold the court order. This was why they were such a good team. Without JFK's support, Bobby did not have the power to make Barnett listen. Bobby was a tool for the president to use in this circumstance. "I know that your feeling about the, uh, law of Mississippi and the fact that ... you don't want to carry out that court order. What we really want to, uh, have from you, though, is some understanding about whether the state police will maintain law and order. We understand your feeling about the court order and your disagreement with it." Kennedy wanted Barnett's rhetoric to end. He had other concerns. The events of the previous day concerned him enough to take the initiative on security. "But what we're concerned about is, uh, how much violence is going to be and what kind of, uh, action we'll have to take to prevent it. And I'd like to get assurances from you about, that the state police down there will take positive action to maintain law and order."[23] At the heart of the Ole Miss crisis was what role the federal government should play in state affairs. Barnett was unwilling to commit his resources to such a task, because it violated Mississippi law and would upset the Mississippi people. Kennedy knew all this, but wanted to talk about the real issue—not rhetoric.

Barnett continued to lose power as the crisis continued. It was only a matter of time before Kennedy took full control of the situation. The federal government had the upper hand. He knew that Kennedy was going to send the marshals and Meredith was going to enroll. He was trying to assess how much political damage this would inflict upon his administration. "They'll, they'll take positive action, Mr. President, to maintain law and order as best we can," Barnett assured Kennedy. Barnett said that he would protect Meredith, but still wavered on how much protection he would provide.[24] Barnett stressed to Kennedy that the situation had gotten out of hand. He wasn't sure that he could maintain order. He said that the last time they tried to bring Meredith in, "there was such a mob there it would have been impossible. There were men in trucks and shot guns and all such as that." He went on to say that they "were just enraged." He emphasized to JFK, "You just don't understand the situation down here."[25] Perhaps Kennedy was not clear about the Southern climate. However, he understood his role in this crisis as president of the United States.

At this point in the conversation Kennedy emphasized his position to Barnett. "This is not my order, I just have to carry it out." Kennedy made it clear that this was job and despite his feelings he had to carry it out and would do it. "So I want to get together and try to do it with you in a way which is the most satisfactory and causes the least chance of, uh, damage to, uh, people in, uh, Mississippi. That's my interest."[26] Barnett tried to get Kennedy to wait. Kennedy made it clear that if they did not have Barnett's support then they would be right back at the start again. Barnett stressed to Kennedy that he planned to cooperate with the administration. At that point, Barnett said that he would talk to Watkins, and JFK consulted his most trusted advisor, his brother.

"You know that's General Grant's table."

Nicholas Katzenbach remembered that he had little communication with the president and really went through Robert Kennedy, which demonstrates the power that Robert Kennedy had in crafting the civil rights message: "I don't recall any time being physically present over in the White House with the president before going down there to Oxford. At night I talked with him on the phone at some considerable length from time to time and then subsequently." Katzenbach remembered, "There was a tremendous account of concern on the part of the president and on the part of the attorney general in terms of avoiding troops." They were concerned about being criticized in a similar manner as Eisenhower was for Little Rock and "the promise that President Kennedy had made in the campaign that troops would never be used in the South."[27] Kennedy was one of the many people in Congress who had criticized President Eisenhower for Little Rock, which was why had he made it a part of his campaign rhetoric.

Later that night, Bobby Kennedy negotiated a deal with Barnett to sneak Meredith into campus and get him registered while students were away for the weekend. Barnett agreed, saying that he would tell the people of Mississippi that he did not know about it. It seemed like the best deal for both sides, with the potential to avoid the violent standoff that seemed inevitable. Hours later, Barnett backed out of the deal. Faced with the dilemma of upholding the court order and seeing no other alternative, President Kennedy issued a proclamation to stop Barnett and then he federalized the Mississippi National Guard.[28] Barnett's double nature left an impression on Burke Marshall, who remembered, "On Saturday evening about 9:00 or 10:00, Governor Barnett called the attorney general at his home and said he couldn't do this. At that time it was decided that the president would have to issue a proclamation, and we had to make preparations to use military forces if necessary to get Meredith registered. So he did issue a proclamation on Saturday night, very early Sunday morning."[29] Indeed this was a climactic part of the crisis. The governor had it within his power to let Meredith register without bloodshed. It was his actions that led to the riot and the violence. Had Barnett worked with the Kennedy administration Meredith would have been registered and the issue would have been resolved. The court had ruled in the case, and if the nation was going to be governed by laws then the leaders had to uphold those laws, despite their disagreements with them. It also demonstrated that the Kennedys were done playing games with Barnett.

John Kennedy consulted Norbert Schlei of the Office of Legal Counsel, who brought the proclamation to the White House that night. Kennedy took Schlei into a small study, where he read the documents, commenting, "Is this pretty much what Ike signed in 1957 with the Little Rock thing?" After Schlei pointed out a few items, Kennedy signed and gave it back to Schlei. He motioned to the table where he signed the documents and said, "You know that's General Grant's table." The two parted. Schlei went to tell reporters about the proclamation. Almost immediately after the meeting Kennedy called down to Schlei from the top of the stairs, "Don't tell them about General Grant's table."[30] Kennedy knew that this was a historical standoff. The vestiges of the Civil War were visible not only in the states' rights rhetoric, but also in the actions of the people in Mississippi. Confederate flags and frenzied crowds were not willing to accept Meredith.

On that same night, at the Ole Miss football game in Jackson, Barnett was greeted by 46,000 Mississippians ready to go to war. The crowd at the stadium were chanting, "We want Ross! We want Ross!" and a very large Confederate flag was carried across the field. They went crazy and stayed on their feet, applauding as the governor made his way to the center of the field.[31] With his arm defiantly raised in the air he addressed the crowd at half-time, saying, "I love Mississippi. I love our people. I love our customs."[32] Never once did he tell them to be responsible or avoid violence. Instead of helping the situation, Barnett contributed to the growing furor in the South. It was after that game that Barnett commented to one of this advisers who wanted him to let Meredith register, "I can't do it. Did you see that crowd?"[33] He, more than any other leader in the crisis, is to blame for the ensuing riot. Instead Barnett asserted Mississippi "customs," which implied that he was not going to back down and remain steadfast in the face of the federal government. There was a stark difference in how these two leaders handled this crisis. John Kennedy issued a proclamation for force, while Barnett incited people to take the same stand that he was taking. The ghosts of the Civil War were circling.

As the situation grew more serious Marshall and Kennedy debated getting the military involved. "Then on Sunday we made — I say we, the attorney general and I — made a final effort on it on Sunday to persuade Barnett to stop this, because it was perfectly clear that what he was intending to do would involve an armed conflict between United States troops and citizens of Mississippi." In an effort to get Barnett to protect Meredith and uphold the order, Bobby called Barnett. Marshall recalled that Robert Kennedy "told Governor Barnett that the president was going on the television that night to explain to the country what he would have to do, which was to use military forces to enforce a court order, and that in the course of his explanation to the country he was going to have to tell how the governor had made this agreement for the secret registration of Meredith and then had backed down on it. And that was the only thing at any time that made an impression on the governor. And he pleaded in a childish, whining sort of way [for] the president not do that."[34]

Robert Kennedy did indeed call Barnett on Sunday at 12:45 P.M. Barnett started the conversation by saying that they should postpone Meredith's registration. Robert Kennedy responded curtly, "We can't do that." Barnett said, "Then you had better have enough troops to be dead sure that peace and order will be preserved at the university." He said, "I am going to do everything in my power to preserve peace." Barnett wanted to read a proclamation saying Meredith should not be admitted and should be forced aside by the marshals. Kennedy said, "I don't think that will be very pleasant, Governor. I think you are making a mistake handling it in that fashion." He went on saying frankly, "I suppose that if you feel it is helpful to you politically. It is not helping the people of Mississippi or the people of the United States." Kennedy said that it was "silly" to put on a "facade" where his people stepped aside and the marshals drew their guns. "This is a real disservice," Kennedy concluded.[35]

Barnett was taken back and defended his actions, saying that he was not trying to benefit politically. He said that he was against integration. "I just can't walk back." The two tried to make another arrangement for Meredith, but Barnett balked again. Finally Kennedy revealed that the president was planning a televised speech. "He is going through the statement [he] had with you last night. He will have to say why he called up the National Guard; that you had an agreement to permit Meredith to go to Jackson to register and your lawyer, Mr. Watkins, said this was satisfactory." Barnett responded, "That won't do at all." Kennedy replied, referencing the deal to bring in Meredith the night before: "You broke your word to him."

> BARNETT: "You don't mean the president is going to say that tonight?"
>
> RFK: "Of course he is; you broke your word; now you suggest we send in troops fighting their way through a barricade. You gave your word. Mr. Watkins gave him his word. You didn't keep it."[36]

Kennedy saw this refusal to keep the bargain as a slap in the face. Perhaps he finally realized that Barnett was not negotiating in good faith, which was very common among the southern politicians in the civil rights movement.

Despite Barnett's assurances that he was not making decisions for political reasons, he pleaded with Kennedy, "Don't say that. Please don't mention it." Moments later in the conversation Barnett apologized: "I didn't mean to break my word." He implored Kennedy to speak with Watkins again. Kennedy had him on the ropes and he knew it. Watkins was on the phone. "No sense in talking," Kennedy said. "You made an agreement with the president of the United States and I was on the phone, and the agreement, within an hour and a half, was broken by the governor." He continued, saying that he had had an agreement with Barnett on Thursday and it was broken as well. "You are putting the president in an impossible situation. He is going on TV as announced and will tell how all of this came about. He has been out in an extremely untenable position."[37] Kennedy was furious.

Watkins tried to be the voice of reason with Kennedy, saying that would be "a serious mistake." Kennedy kept at him, saying, "Now he says bring out the troops; have his army there so he will be the great political hero. We are sick and tired of playing that down." Kennedy put Marshall on the phone, who reiterated the administration's message to Barnett and Watkins:

> Last night you were talking to the president of the United States about a national problem of great dimensions. He was willing to suffer criticism, I am sure, to do everything he could to permit the governor to get out of a situation he got himself and the State of Mississippi into, without violence. That's why he reached the agreement with the governor that he did. That's why it is absurd to think you can reach an agreement with the president of the United States and then call it off.

Marshall was tired of these games as well. He went on to say to Watkins, "You and the governor should realize that the president of the United States can't be played with in this sort of fashion."[38] Ultimately Kennedy and Marshall said they would hold off on telling the country about the deal, but they had to get Meredith into Ole Miss. In addition, the governor needed to assure the administration that law and order would be maintained.

The Kennedy administration did not want to use the army, but realized that if they did not have Barnett's support that it was a very strong possibility. An agreement was made between Burke Marshall and Tom Watkins "that Meredith could be taken down to the university that night, that afternoon, Sunday afternoon, and be registered and that the state police would cooperate and maintain law and order and there would be no resistance. And that was the way that the arrangement was made for what was done on Sunday evening." As a result of those decisions, President Kennedy postponed his televised address so he could say that Meredith was enrolling at the college while he was making the address.

Marshall remembered that there were reasons why President Kennedy wanted to address the nation: "He wanted to make a television address in order to explain to the country what he was doing, which was a terribly serious effort." The fact was that this was not as serious as Little Rock, at that point, but there were circumstances that could be cause for larger issues, which did in fact present themselves over time. "But this was different and much more dangerous and much more disastrous because Barnett was intending, as of Saturday night and Sunday morning, to have lines of state police and sheriffs and deputy sheriffs and then a citizen's army surrounding the campus. And it appeared on Sunday morning that Meredith would have to be taken through this business by military and that thereafter probably Governor Barnett would have to be arrested."[39] There was a great deal of uncertainty in this crisis. Robert Kennedy wanted to have greater control over the events, which was why he sent Nicholas Katzenbach to Oxford. Marshall remembered, "When we made this arrangement with Barnett on, in the middle of Sunday, it was certainly the best thing to do because it avoided a direct conflict between the state officials and federal officials, military, shooting. But [President Kennedy] couldn't know how it would come out or anything so he had the problem of postponing the speech, which I think he did twice, until he saw how it happened."[40]

Robert Kennedy wanted someone that he trusted on the ground in Mississippi. Katzenbach remembered that fateful day when the attorney general came by his office: "I went down there, was in the office on that Sunday, up in the attorney general's office. There was a television program that morning, which one of the networks wanted to put on, on what the legal issues were. The attorney general asked me to go out and appear on that program. I went out there, appeared on that, came back to the office. And he said, 'Do you have any plans for this afternoon?' I said no. He said, 'Well, I'd like you to go down there and follow through on this plan, and be in charge of things, and get some people to go with you.'"[41] From that point, Katzenbach was tied to the outcome at Ole Miss. In a similar fashion as he did with Seigenthaler, Kennedy wanted eyes and ears at the site. This was another example of how these Justice Department attorneys became soldiers for freedom, working for justice in the segregated South.

The Kennedys wanted closure on this crisis. Moreover, Barnett's duplicitous nature had finally forced Kennedy's hand so that he insisted that Meredith was registered. To some extent, the Kennedys were not entirely prepared for what was coming. Even though they federalized the National Guard, they thought in the end reason would prevail and Barnett would comply.

14. Inside the White House;
Riot at Ole Miss

"Bob, I'm very sorry to report..."

Nicholas Katzenbach was a Rhodes Scholar and former professor at the University of Chicago. He had fought in World War II, having his plane shot down into the Mediterranean and then spending twenty-seven months in a prison camp. He escaped twice and was captured twice. He was no stranger to hard times and was ready to do what was necessary to secure Meredith's registration. He was Robert Kennedy's point-man in Mississippi.[1] RFK joked with Katzenbach in a similar way as he did with Seigenthaler and King during the Freedom Rides: "Hey Nick. Don't worry if you get shot, because the president needs a moral issue."[2]

Katzenbach got on a plane and went to Mississippi to set up a command post. He had others with him, but he was the leader. Katzenbach remembered arriving at the airport. "It was a tremendous crowd of about a thousand people all milling around the place and nobody knowing quite what was going on, a lot of marshals there and army trucks. The first thing I did was to put ten cents in the phone and call up the attorney general and find out whether or not there was any change in the plans. He said no. So, I decided to take half the marshals down with me and leave half at the airport, because Meredith would be arriving later. So I worked that out through Jim McShane. As we started to go down there we were met by the commander of the State Highway Patrol."[3] Immediately Katzenbach's leadership skills took over, and he acted to create some order in the chaos that had already taken root in this situation.

Once at Oxford, Katzenbach heard that Burke Marshall had been talked out of registering Meredith that night since it was a Sunday. It was a religious decision, and he wanted to avoid the sabbath. Katzenbach now had the problem of what to do with the marshals who were on campus. The marshals, with their white helmets and yellow arm bands, were out of place on campus. Students saw them and started chanting, "Go to hell JFK!" among other things.[4] The marshals' presence infuriated the students and led to a larger altercation as people started to come and view the group. Katzenbach started to craft a command center at the Lyceum building. The issue however, was that the position he chose, though strategically thought out, was also a sacred symbol for the University. He remembered:

> We arrive down there with two hundred marshals or so, and so they dispersed around the Lyceum building. Meredith was still not there, and the idea was to make the place secure and then bring Meredith in. That was the reason I'd left half the marshals at the airport. We arrived down there, and the marshals surrounded the building. Then some students began to gather around and jeered

and catcalled and called nasty names and so forth and so on, flipped cigarettes at these army trucks which we had used to transport things, threw bottles — it gradually accelerated — threw some rocks. On the outside it was mostly just jeering. I went inside the Lyceum building, arranged for the key to Meredith's room and for his registration the next morning.[5]

Katzenbach recalled that the governor had a representative at the scene in State Senator George Yarbrough, who was with State Senator John McLaurin. Colonel Birdsong, commander of the Mississippi State Highway Patrol, also met Katzenbach. "The marshals were there. There was a line of marshals around the Lyceum Building and there were sort of State Highway Patrols sort of outside the marshals, between the marshals and the crowd."[6] Birdsong and others said that since the marshals were there, they could leave with the State Highway Patrol. The Southerners wanted to extricate themselves from any possible trouble.

The riot had not begun yet, so Katzenbach saw to it that Meredith was escorted to his room in Baxter Hall through a back entrance. This part of the plan worked perfectly. He was secured by two marshals, who were the only two of all the marshals with orders to shoot if Meredith was threatened by anyone. The other marshals who were slowly getting surrounded at the Lyceum building were not allowed to shoot. Katzenbach informed Robert Kennedy that Meredith was on campus. The attorney general phoned Barnett to tell him the news. Barnett prepared to give a speech to the nation, directed at Mississippi, saying that he had been overpowered by the federal government. There were over a thousand students outside the Lyceum when Katzenbach returned. Poised for what seemed like war, they were yelling and throwing things at the marshals.[7] Students continued to gather and the situation grew worse.

As the crowd moved in, the marshals asked for help from the Mississippi State Highway Patrol, who led the marshals to the campus and were commanded by Colonel Birdsong. Barnett promised that they would help maintain law and order. Some of the highway patrol helped, while others contributed to the chaos, ultimately contributing to the violence that followed. One highway patrol officer laughed, while another quipped, "Let the mob go ahead."[8] Emboldened by Barnett, these Mississippians only contributed to the danger and the crowd's belligerence. In fact one officer commented to a marshal, "To hell with you, you son-of-a-bitch, I didn't invite you down here," while another directed a student on the proper method to slash tires: "Cut right into the sidewall — by the valve stem."[9] The crowd was just gaining momentum, and it seemed that no authority would be able to stop it.

The crowd turned into a mob, which in turn started to attack anyone not related to Ole Miss. In one case a student took a fire extinguisher and shot it into the face of a black U.S. Army truck driver, while another student threw a pile of burning newspapers onto the canvas in the back of the truck and proclaimed to the mob, "Let it burn!"[10] The students also attacked reporters who were there to show the country what was happening in Oxford. Gordon Yodor, a cameraman for Hearst Movietone, and his wife were surrounded by students while they were still in their station wagon. In an attempt to push back the crowd, Yodor threw a camera at them. His efforts were not successful, and the mob broke the windshields and started rocking the station wagon back and forth while the couple was still inside.[11]

Yodor's wife, a Jackson, Mississippi, native, pleaded with the crowd to leave her husband alone as they pulled him from the car. "You nigger-loving bitch, you Yankee bastard," they yelled at her. A student watching asked her boyfriend what they were going to with Mrs. Yodor. "Kill her, I guess," he said "She's a nigger-lover, ain't she?" Two highway patrolmen got to the Yodors, bringing them to safety, just in time as the station wagon was flipped over by the mob. The mayhem continued as Dan McCloy, a photographer from *Newsweek*, was also attacked. He was finally brought to the Lyceum building for protection.[12] Some members of the highway patrol contributed to the chaos. For example, when the marshals apprehended three men from the mob, they were subsequently released by one patrolman who said, "Let them kill the nigger."[13]

Amidst the chaos and violence Senator Yarbrough told Katzenbach, "You have occupied this university and now you can have it. What happens from now on is the responsibility of the federal government. We are withdrawing the highway patrol."[14] This was an unexpected twist for Katzenbach, who was continually dealing with new developments in this operation. "No, you can't do that! That would be a horrible mistake," Katzenbach said to Yarbrough. Despite Katzenbach's pleading, Yarbrough seemed resolute, saying that he wanted to avoid bloodshed and that was only possible if they withdrew. Katzenbach demanded that all officers must maintain law and order. "I want to be very clear about the fact that I think the withdrawal of state troopers will not avoid violence, but will be the one decisive thing that will lead to violence. He asked Yarbrough to call Barnett, but the senator, much like his governor, remained obstinate, and said that the patrol was going to pull out.[15]

Barnett promised that the State Highway Patrol would play a role in maintaining law and order. As the main contact on the ground, Katzenbach asked Joseph Dolan if he could get an open line to the White House. Dolan found a pay phone in the Lyceum Building hallway and spoke to the White House operator, saying, "We want to keep this line open all night. No matter what happens, don't cut it off."[16] Katzenbach remembered, "The gist of my argument was, if he removed the State Highway Patrol, that would lead to violence. I was confident that if that happened, something would occur that would be disastrous." He went on in that interview:

> The argument proceeded along those terms, both of us wanting to preserve order and each of us taking diametrically opposed methods of doing it. I appealed to Colonel Birdsong in this respect. I said, "Well, this was not something that Senator Yarbrough or I could judge, that I wanted the views of a professional police officer as to which would be more likely to lead to violence and which would be more likely to avoid it." Colonel Birdsong responded, "For God's sakes don't put me in the middle."[17]

Katzenbach asked either Ed Guthman or Joseph Dolan to let Robert Kennedy know that the State Highway Patrol was beginning to withdraw and that the situation would eventually get worse if that happened.

At 7:30 P.M., while the students were at war with federal marshals, Barnett went on the air and said that he had been told by the attorney general that Meredith had been placed on campus and was "accompanied by federal officers." The announcement would have an impact on the mob. Barnett went further, bordering on melodrama:

> Surrounded on all sides by the armed forces and oppressive power of the United States of America, my courage and my convictions do not waver. My heart still says "never," but my calm judgment abhors the bloodshed that would follow. I love Mississippi. I love her people.

He closed the speech, speaking to the marshals and the Kennedys: "You are trampling on the sovereignty of this great state and depriving it of every honor and respect as a member of the United States. You are destroying the Constitution of this great nation. May God have mercy on your souls."[18]

The crowd was getting worse and there was a possibility that the marshals, who were under the control of Katzenbach, would have to use tear gas. The State Highway Patrol did not have gas masks, and Birdsong was worried that they would be affected. Katzenbach remembered, "I said the situation was getting very difficult, but I would make every effort not to gas his state troopers. I just wanted his state troopers to move the crowd back. Well, they would, they moved the crowd back a foot or two feet, but the rocks and everything else would come in. It was getting dark, and things were getting kind of worse."[19]

By 7:40 P.M. RFK told Katzenbach to relay to Yarbrough that JFK was still prepared to tell the world about the secret negotiations that he and the governor had engaged in during the crisis. Yarbrough did not know what Kennedy meant. RFK called Barnett, who had just finished his speech, who called Yarbrough and told him to bring back the highway patrol. Very begrudgingly, Yarbrough called back the men that he had let go.[20] Students approached the Lyceum building, despite pleas from Yarbrough, who launched himself into the crowd. The president was minutes away from his speech and the situation got out of control very quickly. Bricks, rocks and other debris showered the marshals. When a lead pipe hit a marshal, McShane ordered tear gas canisters fired into the crowd. Some of the gas hit the unsuspecting highway patrolmen. Some were leaving and some were coming back.[21] The situation grew worse, and Katzenbach used his resources as effectively as possible. While Katzenbach worked to maintain law and order, the Kennedy brothers were at the White House monitoring the situation.

In the middle of the chaos, Bobby Kennedy was getting an update from Colonel Birdsong. Upon hearing of the report that tear gas had been fired at the crowd, Guthman grabbed the phone and said, "Bob, I'm very sorry to report we've had to fire tear gas. We had no choice."[22] Katzenbach remembered,

> The whole evening, while it was tragic in ways, was amusing in other ways. We had some reporters trapped in the Lyceum building, and from time to time, because of the shortage of all of us and without really any very good command post, from time to time I or somebody else — Dean Markham was on the phone most of the evening — would hand it to a newspaper reporter and say, "Here, hold this phone.'" And the newspaper reporter would not know whether he was going to have the attorney general or Burke Marshall or the president on the other end of the phone, and he was doing his reporting there, and a number of them were talking with the president that evening as well as us. And that conversation went on as we just reported.[23]

While the riot gained momentum President Kennedy prepared to speak to the American people. Robert Kennedy told Katzenbach, "I'll do something to try to stop the president."[24] Despite Bobby Kennedy's best efforts, the president was already in front of the cameras for the world to see. He did not know that Oxford had become a war zone.

"I accept it."

John Kennedy started his speech by saying that a decision had been made in the Meredith case: "Mr. James Meredith is now in residence on the campus of the University of Mississippi." While Kennedy had federalized the National Guard the night prior, he emphasized, "This has been accomplished thus far without the use of National Guard or other troops. And it is to be hoped that the law enforcement officers of the State of Mississippi and the federal marshals will continue to be sufficient in the future." He hoped that the students and citizens would return to normal operations the next day. Kennedy emphasized, "Our Nation is founded on the principle that observance of the law is the eternal safeguard of liberty and defiance of the law is the surest road to tyranny. The law which we obey includes the final rulings of the courts, as well as the enactments of our legislative bodies. Even among law-abiding men few laws are universally loved, but they are uniformly respected and not resisted."[25] Kennedy believed any action against this decision was contrary to the principles that the United States was founded on. This was an important distinction. Kennedy's acknowledgment of such ideals brought out a political face of the movement, making it more mainstream, acceptable. This had larger implications beyond the crisis, impacting the movement on several levels.

Kennedy continued to acknowledge the law and the role that it would play not only in that episode, but in future, similar circumstances. "Americans are free, in short, to disagree with the law but not to disobey it. For in a government of laws and not of men, no man, however prominent or powerful, and no mob, however unruly or boisterous, is entitled to defy a court of law." This was always how RFK planned to address these issues, and his brother's address made his resolve even stronger. Kennedy went on to tell the country that there had been a series of court cases leading up to this moment. The final decision said that Meredith had the right to enroll at the University of Mississippi and that it was the responsibility of the federal government to see that order through. He said, "Even though this government had not originally been a party to the case, my responsibility as president was therefore inescapable. I accept it. My obligation under the Constitution and the statutes of the United States was and is to implement the orders of the court with whatever means are necessary, and with as little force and civil disorder as the circumstances permit."[26] Kennedy's leadership in this instance was very vocal, for the nation to see. The fact that he took a stand on a civil rights issue, and did not hide from a technicality or politics is a testament to his forbearance as a leader. Robert Kennedy was behind the scenes, urging his brother that this was the right thing to do. Bobby was at the heart of this struggle and he, more than any other, was the force that put President Kennedy in front of the nation giving a major address on civil rights.

Kennedy went on to justify federalizing the Mississippi National Guard. He also said that they had tried to work with the officials of Mississippi and that other options, "including persuasion and conciliation, had been tried and exhausted." Kennedy also wanted it known that this instance was not easy and, indeed, had a long history to consider. "Neither Mississippi nor any other Southern state deserves to be charged with all the accumulated wrongs of the last 100 years of race relations. To the extent that there has been failure, the responsibility for that failure must be shared by us all, by every State, by every citizen." He thanked the Southern universities who had integrated the state system and applauded the Mississippi people "who have placed the national good ahead of sectional interest." Then he spoke to the students of the university, saying, "It is you. It lies in your courage to accept those laws with which you disagree as well as those with which you agree." Very powerfully, and emphasizing the stakes at hand, Kennedy said, "The eyes of the Nation and of all the world are upon you and upon all of us, and the honor of your university and state are in the balance. I am certain that the great majority of the students will uphold that honor." He finished by saying that it was time to move on and "close" the book of this case: "Let us preserve both the law and the peace and then healing those wounds that are within, we can turn to the greater crises that are without and stand united as one people in our pledge to man's freedom."[27]

Kennedy left the Oval Office and moved into the Cabinet Room. While he made his speech, the battle of Oxford had been raging, and the students did not hear the speech given so eloquently by their president. Burke Marshall remembered, "When he finished his speech, it was still a student riot was all it was." Marshall recalled, "Tear gas had been fired, but it was still just a student riot. It was unpleasant, but you couldn't tell how it would go." Marshall and Kennedy had an open line with Katzenbach, keeping watch on the situation. "And at the time he finished his speech it wasn't too bad, and they advised us they thought they could keep it under control. But then of course as the evening went on and people started arriving with guns and shooting at the marshals and the state troopers left, it got much worse."[28] Marshall continued,

> Now the president, as I say, he accepted what was happening, and what he thought about was the army and the reaction of the army to this. By a certain amount, I guess within a fairly short time after the riots started, we concluded, based upon what Nick particularly told us and other people told us from Oxford, we concluded that we had to send the army in. And so that order was given. The proclamation of the president had already been issued the night before and an executive order was prepared. And it was just a matter of a minute to sign it.[29]

The proclamation became the basis of federal action, and the military was now involved in the riot, which was some thing that Kennedy had wanted to avoid. Secretary of Defense Robert McNamara called out the National Guard from Memphis, Tennessee. The administration wanted them on the ground in ninety minutes, but after the president's speech, in which it seemed that things were under control, the men had relaxed and left the air strip. In the meantime the riot was getting worse and there were people getting seriously hurt.

The president's speech had some reverberations for the rest of the crisis, causing confusion and a slow response from the military. Katzenbach recalled, "That had all kinds of repercussions throughout the evening, because when the troops were on ready at Memphis, heard the president's speech and that everything was fine, they all relaxed, and we had trouble renewing that."[30] Katzenbach wanted to avoid using the troops if it was possible:

> The riot started at 8. I just didn't want troops, but at the same time it was obvious we had a number of people wounded by gun fire, by buck shot, and by shot guns, and many of the marshals were saying we needed troops and pressing on needing troops. I wasn't totally sure that we needed that at that point, and so I told the president he ought to start the troops on the way, but I was hopeful that he had control over them so he could call them off in case we could get the riot under control. I think I was probably over conservative on this, although it didn't make much difference because they kept saying they would be here in fifty minutes, and I was saying maybe we would have it under control by then, and actually they didn't arrive for three or four hours.[31]

The president was also hesitant to send troops. It took some time, however, to get the troops into Oxford. Katzenbach remembers, "One, I think the army had just simply underestimated the time that it would take. Secondly, the president's speech had hurt. They had gone off alert at that point. Then we had needed more gas, and we had desperately said we needed more gas, so they had sent us more gas from Memphis."[32]

"I don't think it's worth screwing around."

Throughout the crisis Robert Kennedy, John Kennedy and others were in the Cabinet Room communicating with the justice officials on the ground. They were engaged and ready to make decisions. Robert Kennedy had been working for weeks for this moment. With his brother watching over, he took the lead. "Have you got all the marshals there now?" Robert Kennedy asked Ed Guthman, who was on the phone. JFK commented, "State police or —" Bobby went on, "How many've you got? ... How are the state police? ... Is the crowd getting bigger?" These men attempted to anticipate any major issue before it got out of control. Robert Kennedy got off the phone and said, "I think they have it in pretty good shape." They commented that one marshal had broken his arm.[33]

Robert Kennedy wanted first-hand information to make his decisions. Ed Guthman was among Katzenbach's men on the ground. Robert Kennedy asked him, "Is it under control? ... Would you bring in the guard?" He continued to ask Guthman questions about the crowd. "Are they mad at the marshals?" John Kennedy, who was clearly listening to his brother's conversation with Guthman, commented that if people came in from "Alabama, things were liable to become worse." It's almost as if Bobby Kennedy was one step ahead of his brother's thinking, saying to Guthman, in anticipation of things getting worse, "Okay, well, I'm going to see if I can get these, yeah, troops started anyway." He continued, "I think it's, uh, better that we can, can control the situation." RFK said clearly, "I don't think it's worth screwing around." Bobby Kennedy wanted to control the outcome and was willing to do anything in his power to make that happen. He was already thinking that troops would be needed and wanted them on alert. While JFK would be the person to make the order, it seemed clear that Bobby had a say in those matters. The tacit, off-the-cuff comment is evidence that he had license to make decisions in this crisis that would be supported by his brother. JFK commented, "It's going to be a long fall in Oxford, I think."[34]

When Robert Kennedy got off the phone, they started to move in the direction of using the military. To the group he said, "Well, he thinks the situation's under control now, but, uh, you know..." His last comment demonstrated his uncertainty, and it was important for JFK to say before Bobby finished his thought, "I think we ought to get the guard, you know, within shouting distance." Robert Kennedy said, "Yeah." Robert Kennedy commented that if they "had control over the air.... If you have, uh, gas, you got a pretty good, uh, operation going. They got five hundred marshals."[35]

The group looked at logistics ranging from gas to other operational aspects. Robert Kennedy briefed the president, telling him, "You see, they're sitting there, and they're throwing iron spikes, and they're throwing coke bottles, and they're throwing rocks." They considered getting someone from Ole Miss to address the crowd. The group discussed the prospect of John Vaught, the Ole Miss Rebels football coach, speaking to the students. Bobby liked the idea saying, "Let's see if we can get him." Marshall immediately got on the phone to see if they could. John Kennedy asked, "What's Barnett doing?" Robert Kennedy replied with his wry sense of humor, "I suppose laughing at us."[36] There was some laughter to his comment. They were trying to stave off calamity, working together for solutions to each problem as it presented itself to the group.

The situation rang somewhat reminiscent of other types of crises in the Kennedy White House. It seems fitting that Kenny O'Donnell commented, "This reminds me a little bit of the Bay of Pigs." To that Bobby replied, "Yech!" At one point in the discussions the group considered air support for troops. In fact it was Bobby who mentioned it. Sorensen agreed with O'Donnell, saying, "Well, especially when Bobby said we'd provide air cover!" To that comment there was laughter. "My guess is, Bobby," Sorensen commented, "That we'll have ... control of outsiders down pretty good." This was an element that Robert Kennedy had already considered. Robert Kennedy responded to Sorensen, "Yeah, we haven't had any trouble from outsiders yet. I suppose you'll always have the difficulty of, uh, of, uh people storming into the campus." Kennedy continued, "They've got a lot of gates. It's a hell of a big campus, you know." RFK suggested putting marshals and others at the gates. The other option acknowledged was, "We can always, uh, storm in there at, uh, eight o'clock tomorrow morning, or ten o'clock tomorrow morning."[37] Kennedy was worried that the whole plan was going to fall apart. Events were not shaping up the way that he wanted them to and he was willing to consider other options.

Robert Kennedy had particular disdain for Ross Barnett. He had spent a great deal of time working with the governor to get Meredith registered. The cat-and-mouse game had taken its toll on the young attorney general. "The problem is, you see, when you don't have the, anybody there that's really interested in maintaining law and order, and where their primary interest is to get us to bring troops in." Sorensen agreed. Bobby was clearly referring to Barnett. He went on to ruminate, "If you can imagine what would've happened if we'd gone through with what he wanted to do tomorrow morning..." Kennedy went on:

> Walk in there with, uh, and trying to get through, and he's there with all his.... That's what this plan was that he'd be there with his state police and sheriffs, and the assistant sheriffs and the volunteers behind them, four lanes. And then we would push our way through them?

Sorensen commented that they wouldn't fire, but then Bobby said, "Nobody else knowing the plot but him and me."[38] Robert Kennedy had considered accepting this deal earlier in the crisis, but then again it had been a much different climate and he had more control over the outcome of the situation.

The group continued to consider other options. Marshall was coming up short with Vaught so Robert Kennedy said, "Why don't I try." His wife had said he was out, but Marshall suggested that she might have been lying to Dean Markham, who had made the call to the house. Sorensen asked Robert Kennedy, "What do you think the chances are that Barnett is being honest with you?" Robert Kennedy responded, "I don't think he is telling 'em to lay off, and I don't think they're enjoying this. You know it's one thing to get in for the wrong reason and not have a problem and then, then might have a sense of greater, greater problems." Sorensen replied, "He said he didn't want to get anyone killed though, or does he mind that?" Robert Kennedy referenced something that Barnett said to him on the phone: "The only thing ... he said the other day to me, 'If fifty people get down here, you've got, get killed down here, it might be embarrassing for the two of us'"[39] This comment clearly left a mark on Bobby and was evidence that Barnett could not get beyond the political ramifications that the crisis could have on his time in office.

The administration started to move into combat mode as they made arrangements for the National Guard to play a role in the crisis. The Kennedy brothers commented about a company in the armory at Oxford. Robert and John Kennedy were concerned about the time lapse, but Bobby said, "I mean, if you can tell, from what they say, they're going to be alright for an hour." Bobby Kennedy briefed his brother, saying that there would be about eight or nine hundred National Guard within four hours. They would arrive at the armory. When pressed on time and logistics, Robert Kennedy, who seemed to be running the operation, said they would have a company there in an hour and eight hundred within four hours.[40]

Robert Kennedy was at the helm of this operation, and his brother clearly had complete faith in him. Bobby commented, "Well, I think, what we, we at least show that the marshals, couldn't do it by themselves, so?" To that John Kennedy responded, "We, are we showing him? Or are they showing us?" The whole room started laughing. Meanwhile, Robert Kennedy was on the phone with Katzenbach assuring him that there were reinforcements on the way and that Billingslea would be in touch. JFK asked, "Need any more marshals or equipment?" The group stayed in touch with the Justice Department "soldiers" on the ground. Robert Kennedy stayed on the phone with Katzenbach, commenting, "And they should be home, and they should be home and watching the president on television." He went on to ask if Katzenbach had enough tear gas.[41]

Robert Kennedy was in communication with his brother from the start of this crisis. Kennedy remembered in 1964 that when he spoke with his brother about what to do in Mississippi "there was never a, sort of any doubt or question about what had to be accomplished." He went on, "I kept him advised, then, as it got to a critical point, of what we were doing. And then we thought it had been accomplished that Sunday night when I went over there, and then, it hadn't." Kennedy remembered that he had received a telephone call from Katzenbach. "I mean, that was a terrible evening because then the people were being shot, and it was, and then of course, it was right on me because I had been responsible for it." Kennedy blamed himself for using the marshals and for the fact that the troops did not arrive on time. "It was really my responsibility."[42] The fact that Kennedy looked to himself for blame is evidence that John Kennedy saw him as the person who would direct this aspect of the government. Robert Kennedy was the head person on civil rights in the nation from 1961 to 1964, a period that had some of the most critical crises in the nation up to that point. His leadership was important.

The riot was gaining momentum, which prompted Bobby Kennedy, in the Cabinet Room, to ask the person on the phone, "Does it look under control?" Bobby continued the conversation and asked, "Well, would you favor that I had troops coming in there?" He remarked, "Well, they're on their way." He continued to ask if Katzenbach knew about the tear gas that was coming in to keep the riot back. Later in the conversation JFK said, "We have riots like this at Harvard just because some guy yells." The room laughed again. Bobby wanted to talk to Katzenbach, who was not on the phone yet. He asked, "Where is, uh Nick? Is he up in the attic?" to more laughter. Sorensen commented, "He's in the pill box."[43] This atmosphere was not because the Kennedys saw this as something to disregard. On the contrary, the Kennedys, Robert especially, used humor in these moments because it was so tense. It was their way of making sure that everyone was not constantly on edge. It gave people an assurance that they knew where to go next and was a tactic that left the impression that they could handle any situation. It was also a comment that Robert Kennedy was not going to be upstaged by his brother. The famous Kennedy competitiveness came out, even in these situations.

There was some debate about whether the Kennedys should have used troops sooner or should not have listened to Barnett and his assurances that he would maintain order. Robert Kennedy said, "What we did was right and the procedure that we followed was right; the execution was wrong, and the person who had been responsible for that execution was me." Kennedy continued, "I was the attorney general, and the fact that I said troops would arrive and they didn't arrive was my fault ... and, therefore, made it particularly difficult for President Kennedy because I had worked it all out, and this was my area of responsibility."[44] Again, Robert Kennedy was concerned with his brother's administration and what ramifications this crisis would have on it.

In the Cabinet Room Bobby stayed on the phone and tried to assess what else could be done. He finally got Katzenbach on the phone. Bobby asked if he was in touch with the military and if the gas was on its way. "Do you want these troops in there?" Robert Kennedy asked. Bobby expected that Katzenbach would be able to assess the situation. Then there was an exchange in which Bobby said, "He got hit by what? ... Is he gonna live? ... The state police have left?" The injuries were starting to pile up, people were getting hurt and Meredith still wasn't registered. This was where it seemed things started to unravel. Marshall got in touch with Watkins and Barnett. He assured Kennedy, and others, that the governor, according to Watkins, "spoke to the highway patrol and that, uh, everything was under control."[45] In reality, however, the riot was getting worse. In fact a retired general was trying to lead a group against integration.

Major General Edwin Walker, retired, was a staunch segregationist, yet he led troops to integrate Little Rock, on President Eisenhower's orders, in 1957. No longer under orders, Walker looked to rally a new generation of troops against Kennedy and integration. Bobby told the room, "Walker's been out there, downtown getting them, uh, people stirred up." Bobby wanted to consider arresting Walker. In fact, some of Bobby's sources came from the FBI, who had agents on the scene. Robert Kennedy wanted the FBI to get a warrant. JFK asked, "By the way, what's his crime?" They decided on inciting a riot. President Kennedy recognized that the situation had the potential to escalate. He started asking his brother questions:

> How many agents to you have down there? I think you ought to get those MPs [Military Police] into there and over on the way to the airport. I don't see what you've got to lose, if they're at the airport. You can always send them back.

The two brothers started talking about getting more tear gas in to control the riot. President Kennedy clearly expected this to get worse. He went on to say that's what "happens with all these wonderful operations. War." The president continued ruminating over the situation. "General Walker.... Imagine that son-of-a-bitch having been commander of a division up till last year and the army promoting him."[46] Walker continued to stir up the crowd and there were going to be casualties. This was a war, as John Kennedy stated in the midst of planning. It was built on the long struggle to realize the founders,' then Lincoln's, vision of what the Declaration meant to *all* Americans.

The situation kept throwing new variables at the group, making each hour more difficult than the last. They needed marshals on Meredith and logistically had to get more tear gas on campus. There was clearly tension in the Cabinet Room, which many tried to lighten with levity. John Kennedy remarked, "I haven't had such an interesting time since the Bay of Pigs." Robert Kennedy, always in competition with his brother's wit, said, "The attorney general announced [today], he's joining Allen Dulles at Princeton [University]." The room broke out in laughter.[47] Robert Kennedy felt culpable for the riot and the events that brought JFK into this crisis. He was charged, by his family and others, to vanguard the Kennedy legacy, and he took it seriously. Robert Kennedy remembered that the president was torn between "an attorney general who had botched things up, and the fact the attorney general was his brother." In the heat of the riot Katzenbach called RFK and asked if the marshals could open fire. President Kennedy heard the conversation between Bobby and Katzenbach and responded, "They were not to fire under any conditions."[48] The exception to the rule was to protect James Meredith. Kennedy did acknowledge that if the situation had gotten worse then that order might have changed.

John and Robert Kennedy decided to go beyond the National Guard and use the United States Army to control the riot and integrate the school. However, getting the army there proved to be difficult for the Kennedys and added to their frustrations. Robert Kennedy was upset on a larger level that the military did not respond in the time that they said. Marshall remembered:

> The president's concern was the fact that the army wasn't living up the schedule. They'd said ninety minutes or whatever it was and they weren't there. So he kept calling up [Secretary of the Army]

Cy Vance and talking to him about this, and he told Cy what if this, you know, were real, we were having an invasion or something, getting in a war, it wasn't just a question of sending troops in to quell a riot but that you had to use troops for some international crisis.[49]

Not only was the crisis hurting United States prestige, it also exposed an inadequacy in our military, which could lead to larger consequences and further disaster. That night in the Cabinet Room, Bobby made it clear that it was up to Katzenbach what level of military response they needed in this situation. President Kennedy, again, saw that this was going to need more than marshals on the ground. "I wouldn't hesitate to put 'em in there," JFK said. He went on to say that Robert Kennedy could be "looking like you're not doing enough rather than too much right now." The president finished, saying, "Better get 'em over there." President Kennedy saw this becoming bigger and more difficult to deal with. "You see, once some one fellow starts firing, everybody starts firing." He said that concerned him the most.[50]

While the Kennedys wanted to avoid the military it seemed that once they decided to get them in motion, they were too slow to commit. Bobby Kennedy said to another person on the phone, "I don't want it to, uh, make it appear that, well, we didn't do enough." In the midst of the riot a state trooper was hurt, shot by one of the rioters. JFK said, "That's too bad." Bobby wanted to get better control of the situation. He constantly assessed what his people would need on the ground. He asked questions over the line they had open to the crisis:

> Well, do you think that they're gonna move in there with some guns, though, from out of town? ... How do the marshals feel? ... I mean if anything, is there anything you can do to send, you can't send anybody in and arrest Walker, can we?

Before making a decision, Kennedy commented on the phone to Katzenbach, "Well, Nick, I think we just, uh, we should, uh, if, it's gotta be up to you, uh, being on the scene as to whether you need these fellows, but I think it's gone beyond the stage..." While Bobby wanted Katzenbach's take on the situation, his brother wanted a presence on the ground, and it seemed appropriate to get that moving.

At this point in the crisis Robert Kennedy started to get upset with the reaction by the military, which would come up again in the crisis. Kennedy said to Katzenbach, clearly exasperated, "They keep telling me that you're in touch with the military.... So are you in touch with them?" Kennedy impatiently asked, "Well, can you ask them what the, what the hell they're doing?" John Kennedy came in the room sometime later and asked, "What's the problem now?" Robert Kennedy responded, "Well, it's not a problem, it's just, uh, nothing. It's the same problem of getting people in there. He thinks that they may have it under control." President Kennedy asked, "I mean, are you questioning whether to bring the guard in?" Bobby's main concern wasn't whether to bring them in, rather "when they're gonna get there." Robert Kennedy alluded to "all the rest of it" that he'd been "thinking about" and said they were dealing with "unknowns."

RFK worked tirelessly to get information and make certain that the marshals were supplied until further assistance could make its way to Oxford. He recognized that the National Guard needed to be on the scene as quickly as possible. In addition, the decision to use the army was pivotal, but they were not on the scene yet. The Kennedy administration witnessed firsthand how all of this was playing out. Robert Kennedy had complete faith in his staff. When JFK asked about McShane, Bobby said that the marshals liked him. "He's pretty tough," said JFK. Bobby responded, "He knows what he's doing. I don't think anybody's gonna push him around much." With the decision to bring in the military made, John and

Robert Kennedy turned their attention to Cy Vance, secretary of the army, and how they could get forces on the ground faster. Meanwhile, JFK went to call Barnett.

While Bobby Kennedy looked at logistics and supplying the men at war with the students and other elements in Oxford, John Kennedy made a call to Ross Barnett, hoping for the governor to take a larger role in this debacle as it played out on the Ole Miss campus. Barnett started the conversation by saying that he had ordered the "commissioner of highway patrol to order every man he's got." Barnett wanted Meredith moved off campus. President Kennedy said, "We couldn't consider moving Meredith ... if we haven't been able to restore order outside. That's the problem, Governor." Barnett wanted to go up to Oxford and talk to the crowd using a microphone. Kennedy clearly didn't trust him and said, "I'll tell you what..., if you want to go up there and then you call me from up there. Then we'll decide what we're gonna do before you make any speeches about it." Barnett told Kennedy that the state trooper who was hit had died. President Kennedy was upset earlier according to the conversation in the cabinet room. He said, "You see, we gotta get order up there, and that's what we thought we were going to have." Barnett pleaded with Kennedy to give "an order to remove Meredith." Exasperated and clearly irritated, Kennedy shot back, "How can I remove him, Governor, when there's a riot in the street, and he may step out of that building and something happen to him. I can't remove him under these conditions." Barnett, who didn't know what to say, responded "Uh, but, uh." Kennedy, in clear control of the conversation, said, "Let's get order up there, then we can do something about Meredith." Barnett wanted to surround the building, but Kennedy made it clear: he wanted "order," then they would talk further about Meredith. "They gotta protect Meredith."[51]

As the riot gained steam, Robert Kennedy asked Ed Guthman. who was on the ground to help the justice department officials entrenched at Ole Miss: "Well, how long can you hold there?" Kennedy asked. President Kennedy rejoined the group after his phone conversation with Barnett. Bobby told the room, "They're storming where Meredith is." President Kennedy said, "You better try to stick and hold the line and then I suppose get in the car and start to see if they can, may not be able to move him out, I suppose." Ken O'Donnell remarked, "You don't want to have a lynching." Robert Kennedy took the line and said to Dean Markham, "Well, I think they have to protect Meredith now.... They better fire, I suppose ... they gotta protect Meredith." Robert Kennedy wanted assurances from Markham that Meredith would be protected. Robert Kennedy gave the green light to fire on people who would hurt Meredith. In this instance he put more value on Meredith's life than any other person there. In fact, the marshals were not permitted to fire on the crowd to defend themselves. Kennedy realized that Meredith represented something larger and that if anything happened to him it could have calamitous effects on the movement.

The Kennedy brothers discussed Barnett's phone conversation with JFK. "He wants us to move him," John Kennedy said. JFK assured his brother that he told the governor they could not move Meredith under the current situation. Bobby said, "I can't get him out. How am I gonna get him out?" President Kennedy reiterated, "That's what I said to him. Now the problem is, if we can get law and order restored.... Okay, we'll move him out of there if he can get order restored." Robert Kennedy was on the phone trying to understand the situation, which was getting more serious. "They're shooting it up," Bobby said at one point. He emphasized, "'I think we just have to protect him no matter what it is." President Kennedy inquired again about moving Meredith, but Bobby told the group, "They're firing at the marshals." Ed Guthman was "so scared he can't talk," said Ken O'Donnell. While Robert Kennedy wanted to maintain order, he was determined to protect Meredith at all costs.

Robert Kennedy made it clear to Nick Katzenbach that while the marshals could not fire on the crowd, "I think that they can fire to save him." Katzenbach briefed Kennedy on how the situation was deteriorating. Kennedy asked, "Is there much firing? ... Is there anyway you can figure out a way to scare 'em off?" At this point, it's clear that the army had to get involved. Kennedy just wanted to control the situation. They tried to find out why the army was taking so long. They were trying to contact Cy Vance. Robert Kennedy's frustration was apparent: "Damn army! They can't even tell if ... the MPs have left yet." He went on to say, "Who knows what the reason is? Cy Vance doesn't know yet." O'Donnell agreed with his old Harvard roommate: "The president of the United States calls up and says, 'get your ass down there.' 'yeah, yeah.' I don't think they'd be in the fucking plane in five minutes."[52] Since the Bay of Pigs the military had been an issue with the Kennedys. They did not trust them. Some in the military, most notably Curtis Lemay, felt the same about the Kennedys. It seemed that this relationship not only plagued foreign policy matters, but also domestic concerns.

Bobby's disdain toward Barnett continued: "It's not about the policemen, about other people being shot. Did you get Barnett, to get, uh, Meredith off the campus." He went on, "Just to get Meredith off the campus. That's what he wants." Robert Kennedy believed that he and Barnett were still playing the game that they had been at for weeks. He was tired of the cat-and-mouse game. From Bobby's perspective Barnett disregarded the bloodshed and destruction and only wanted to keep Meredith off the campus. John Kennedy saw it differently: "Well, he wants to be able to say that he asked me to get him off and I, uh, refused." Kennedy emphasized that the main problem was that Barnett had to "get law and order, and then you can discuss what to do about Meredith. But he can't do anything.... He doesn't even get a hold of the state police."[53] The Kennedy brothers were dealing with this crisis differently. While they were working together, they both brought different talents to the table. JFK saw the politician in Barnett and even related with it. He understood that Barnett had to do and say certain things. Bobby, on the other hand, believed that the right thing to do was register Meredith. Anything contrary to that was not only wrong, but against the law. Together they brought different approaches to domestic issues that had not been seen in the White House.

Robert Kennedy continued to work the phone. Word came in that Paul Guilford, a reporter for Agency France Presse, had been shot and killed during the riot. Katzenbach told Bobby the latest information, which Bobby told the people in the room: "He says the fellow from the London paper died." To that JFK commented, "We ought to get some more troops." He also commented on the length of time that it was taking to get troops on the campus. Robert Kennedy continued talking to Katzenbach:

> I think you want to get somebody that, uh, up there that ... knows how important it is to keep Meredith alive.... It should be somebody that you know.... Stay right by Meredith and, and shoot anybody that puts a hand on him.

O'Donnell lamented about the military and commented, "I have a hunch that Khrushchev would get those troops in fast enough. That's what worries me about this whole thing."[54] Robert Kennedy's insistence to Katzenbach to protect Meredith was significant. He maintained his position throughout the crisis and almost seemed as if he was not only upholding Meredith's right under the law, but also refused to give in to Barnett. O'Donnell's speaks to the point that this was not only a domestic issue, but also had implications in the world at large. Khrushchev and others would use it against Kennedy in typical Cold War fashion.

The group received word that the National Guard had arrived, led by Captain Murry

Faulkner, cousin of the writer William Faulkner. One of the guards had been injured. As the guard tried to control the scene, the group assessed what was next. They were still waiting for the army to make a move on the university. Bobby was talking to Ed Guthman, his communications advisor, on the phone, asking, "What are we going to do about all this?" He went on to comment, "We're gonna have a helluva problem about why we didn't, uh, handle the situation better.... I think we're gonna have to figure out what we're going to say." Bobby left the phone and came back, saying, "The point that we want to get over, you know, is that, uh, the governor ... made this arrangement. We didn't sneak him in. I think that's gonna be the cry, that we snuck him in unprepared." Robert Kennedy went on to emphasize the issue with the State police and how they were trying to maintain law and order.[55]

A lot of things were going on at the White House as the Kennedys and their staff tried to deal with the problems. For example, Robert Kennedy called Cy Vance to discuss the fact that the army still was not on the scene. Vance explained, "The problem is one of ... getting in there, and they're just going to get in wherever they can on campus." Robert Kennedy said, "We could use at least a couple hundred right there." Bobby questioned transportation, to which Vance said, "They will land on the campus. These are their instructions. Wherever they can get in, Bob." Vance was noncommittal about when the army would arrive, saying, "Bob, I don't want to guess at the thing because I don't know precisely."[56] The riot only gained momentum as the night moved into early morning. In the midst of this episode John Kennedy called Barnett a second time.

Even with the riot raging John Kennedy was still battling Barnett on getting Meredith off campus. President Kennedy said that Katzenbach, Guthman and others had told him that the situation was not good. "They wouldn't, uh, feel that, uh, they could, uh, take a chance on taking him outside that building." Kennedy went on, "Now if we can get these fellows? I hear they got some high powered rifles up there that have been shooting sporadically." The president peppered Barnett with questions: "Can we get that stopped? How many people have you got there? We hear you only got fifty." Barnett took some exception to that comment, stating that they had approximately two hundred, saying, "I'm doing everything in the world I can." Kennedy responded, "Well, we've got to get this situation under control. That's much more important than anything else." Kennedy was concerned about the rifle fire and made it clear he did not want to risk Meredith.[57]

Barnett brought it back to his own issue, saying that people were "wiring me and calling me saying, 'Well you've given up.' I had to say, 'No, I'm not giving up any fight.'" Kennedy tried to interrupt, saying, "Yeah, but we don't want to —" Barnett kept going, disregarding the president: "'I'll never give up. I, I have courage and faith, and, and, we'll win this fight.' You understand. That's just to Mississippi people." Despite the chaos and bloodshed confronting Barnett, he was still trying to play politics. Kennedy, the consummate politician, responded, "I understand." That said, Kennedy was not all politics. There were clearly other issues that needed to be addressed and Barnett was too concerned about how he looked to his constituents. Kennedy continued, "But I don't think anybody, either in Mississippi or any place else, wants a lot of people killed." Barnett said he would issue "any statement, anytime about peace and violence." To that end, Kennedy told Barnett to get his state police under control and then they could proceed to the next step.[58] The problem was that Barnett was unable to control the situation and the Kennedys would have to step in to help not only Meredith, but also the people of Mississippi, who Barnett claimed to protect.

Barnett's defiance early in the crisis emboldened the Mississippi people to push back on any federal intervention. Indeed, it was a part of Mississippi's heritage to advocate for states' rights. When Kennedy and Barnett spoke again it was clear that the governor had lost control of the situation and the army was the only way to gain any semblance of order in Oxford. After speaking with Birdsong, Barnett reported to JFK that he had approximately one hundred and fifty patrolmen on the scene. JFK countered him, saying, "We got a report that they're in their cars two or three blocks away." Barnett assured Kennedy, "I told 'em, just like you asked me, to get moving." Kennedy wanted an update on the rifle shooting, to which Barnett said it was "strangers." Kennedy had enough. He told Barnett he did not want a lot of people killed and guardsmen, marshals and state troopers had already been shot.[59]

As the crisis went into the next day, Robert Kennedy spoke directly to General Creighton W. Abrams, Assistant Deputy Army Chief of Staff for Military Operations. Robert Kennedy asked about troop size and deployment. Kennedy was direct and blunt with Abrams, asking, "What was the delay in getting them out of Memphis?" Abrams responded that this was the "best response they could make, apparently, under the circumstances." Kennedy inquired about the leadership and said he thought that the military would have been quicker with its response. Abrams agreed, saying that they "expected a much more rapid response than has occurred. I know General Billingslea did." Kennedy was not in the mood for any other setbacks. He sounded flat as he asked the questions and was clearly tired from all the stress and tension that night. He continued to push the general, wanting better answers and hoping that there would be some action.

KENNEDY: "What happened then?"
ABRAMS: "I don't know."
KENNEDY: "Is somebody gonna find out?"
ABRAMS: "Yes, sir."

Interestingly enough, Abrams didn't take orders from the attorney general, yet he treated Robert Kennedy's orders as if they came from the president. Deliberately sighing into the phone from exhaustion and frustration, he asked Abrams about another battle group that would provide relief to Katzenbach. Abrams said that they had been able to get ahold of them and they were diverting them to the scene. Again, however, the military did not have an exact estimate as to when they would arrive on the scene and needed to get back to Kennedy with the definite time.[60]

Into the early hours of the morning John Kennedy spoke with Abrams while the attorney general had General Billingslea on the line. Abrams informed President Kennedy that the MP company had arrived on campus at 2:15 am, local time. Abrams told the president that the 503rd would arrive at 4:30 am, local time, which was two hours from when they were speaking on the phone. Kennedy asked more questions of the general regarding the rest of the troop movements. According to Abrams, the whole group would be on the ground by 6:00 am, local time. Kennedy especially wanted the general to consider setting up communications at the airport for the incoming soldiers.[61] The military was on the scene, but Kennedy wanted to be certain that Barnett did not waver.

Barnett and President Kennedy spoke again during the crisis. Barnett complimented Kennedy on his speech the night before, saying, "I think you said it mighty well last night." Kennedy was more interested in getting Barnett to agree to help the situation now that the military was on the scene. The president did not want to have the federal government in the face of the Mississippi people. "I want your help in, uh, getting these state police to continue to help during the day, because they're their own people," President Kennedy said. The president was concerned that there was going to be a lot of "strange troops in there" and the state police should "be the key." Kennedy emphasized that Barnett needed to control the roads and make sure that they stopped a lot of outsiders from coming in. Barnett finally agreed with the president.[62]

The army was slow to respond to the riot at Ole Miss. At 3:33 am they still had not left Oxford Airport. President Kennedy commented, "They always give you their bullshit about their instant reaction and split-second timing, but it never works out. No wonder it's so hard to win a war."[63] The first of the army reached the campus after 4:00 am. By the morning there were 16,000 soldiers in Oxford. The town had a population of 10,000. By the morning the casualties had finally been tallied. Two men were dead, and 166 marshals and 40 soldiers had been injured. In addition, 200 people had been arrested, which included General Walker. Kennedy was seriously thinking about arresting Barnett. The president went to bed at 5:30 am and said that he wanted "to be called if anything happens." By the time Meredith took his first class, which was in Colonial American History, there were 23,000 soldiers in Oxford.[64]

The Ole Miss episode showed a committed group in the White House using all available resources to integrate a Southern university, fulfilling a court order. The White House tape system illuminated the determination, desire and frustrations of the Kennedy brothers. While it was extremely difficult and wrought with danger, on many levels, this was a necessary step for the nation to take to embrace integration. It was important that a president, instead of a civil rights leader, stand up for Meredith. Without the Kennedys, Meredith would have failed.

James Giglio argues that the Ole Miss episode proved to be a "learning experience" for both Kennedys. Barnett would not keep his word, reneging on deals and playing a cat-and-mouse game with the administration.[65] Giglio writes, "For the Kennedys the University of Mississippi fight represented yet another successful example of crisis management — one that had approval of the American majority." Giglio went on to argue that the crisis left "an enduring intellectual impact on Kennedy, causing him to recast beliefs about Reconstruction following the Civil War — and hence race relations during the 1960s."[66] Bobby Kennedy continued to bring his brother further along in embracing a new policy on race relations by bringing scholars such as David Herbert Donald to the White House, who would expose the president to new interpretations of Reconstruction.[67] Indeed, this was a turning point for both Kennedys, but more for Robert Kennedy. After this episode it was plain that integration and challenging the social mores of the South would be difficult. He needed to confront this injustice as forcibly as he would Khrushchev only a couple of weeks later.

15. The Kennedy Brothers

"The progress has been made and is significant because it is right."

In October 1962, just after the Ole Miss crisis, U2 spy planes found medium range ballistic missiles in Cuba. These missiles had the ability to carry nuclear warheads into the United States, giving the Soviet Union, and Cuba, first-strike capability against the United States. For thirteen long days Kennedy and his team of advisors considered that a nuclear exchange with the Soviet Union was inevitable. However, Kennedy's Executive Committee (EXCOMM) of advisors were able to find a way to keep the United States out of war, staving off calamity. That episode, more than most, in the twentieth century showed how the leadership of one person could make a difference. President Kennedy considered all alternatives and instead of following the military, he had the forbearance, in the wake of the Bay of Pigs, to consider other options that kept America away from that nuclear exchange. By that time, Kennedy was a seasoned veteran in brinkmanship and finally came into his own.

The Kennedy brothers were confronted with another civil rights crisis in 1963. The Ole Miss crisis had made it plain that civil rights needed to be addressed, and Robert Kennedy was willing to take his commitment further. The path to a major shift in the movement began in Birmingham, Alabama.

In the wake of Ole Miss, the Kennedys shifted their outlook on the civil rights. Arthur Schlesinger argued, "After Oxford, the Kennedys began to understand how profoundly the republic had been trapped in history." He went on, "Nothing tested the nation more severely than the challenge of racial justice."[1] Prior to the travails at Birmingham, the Kennedys started to publicly state their position on civil rights. Robert Kennedy articulated in several speeches this evolution in his thinking on civil rights.

On October 6, 1962, Robert Kennedy addressed a group in Milwaukee, Wisconsin. In his speech he praised James Meredith as heroic, lending "his name to another chapter in the mightiest internal struggle of our time." He also said that the marshals who intervened in Mississippi "remained true to their orders and instructions and stood with great bravery to prevent interference with federal court orders."[2] The speech was about making a difference in the nation. It stressed people like John Adams in the Boston Massacre trial and Clarence Darrow's defense of Eugene Debs as making a difference by defending a belief, which was linked to American ideals. Linking Meredith to such a group demonstrates Kennedy's respect for him and his commitment to change at the risk of great sacrifice.

After the Milwaukee speech Robert Kennedy accepted the Stephen S. Wise Award for advancing human freedom. Kennedy said, "Persisting passion and prejudice do not surrender to efforts of the past; continuing and unremitting effort is required." He went on to say, "Such effort has been the policy of this government for many years and of this administration since its start." Kennedy discussed the various achievements of the administration in the realm of civil rights, from the order for equal opportunity in the workplace to appointing judges and members of the Justice Department with a keen sense of the civil rights issue. Kennedy exclaimed, "All this activity is bringing results."[3] Robert Kennedy believed that his actions were making a difference in civil rights. He cited several desegregation cases and talked about voter registration. He also said that the federal government would not allow hospitals receiving federal aid to discriminate racially. He stressed that all of this had been done "within the framework of the law." Kennedy made his case that the administration was making a difference and that people around the nation wanted the "status quo" to change. He said, "The progress has been made and is significant because it is right."[4]

This speech is one of the first times that Robert Kennedy said that a civil rights decision was made because it was "right." Instead of stressing that it was made within the law, he emphasized this notion instead. This marked a shift in Kennedy's thinking as early as October 1962. Taking it a step further, Kennedy also intimated that there were people around the nation who believed the same thing — that the nation was moving in a new direction. He did follow up, saying that this change was "dictated not only by our consciences and our ideals, but also by our laws." It is equally important to mention that Kennedy saw these aspects of challenging civil rights as joined, wherein the righteous spirit was also the legal one and should be embraced universally. That in itself was a unique and clever way to justify a righteous tone in his speeches.

Kennedy also discussed the Ole Miss affair, saying, "In recent weeks, the nation and the world have seen a great tragedy visited on one of our states because state officials refused to obey court orders and accept their responsibilities of leadership." He said that President Kennedy had been "obliged" to take action in Oxford. "It was not to enforce the law for the benefit of a single student, but to enforce the law on behalf of every American citizen, and to make it clear that this is a country which lives by the law." He affirmed, "Thus we must accelerate our efforts to banish religious prejudice, racial discrimination and any intolerance which denies to any Americans the rights guaranteed them by the Declaration of Independence and the Constitution."[5] He saw this fight as being as important as that with the Soviets; he stressed to the audience that those ideals were the reason that Americans put themselves in harm's way throughout the world.

In another speech on January 4, 1963, Robert Kennedy was present when the Emancipation Proclamation was out on display at the National Archives. In his remarks to commemorate the Emancipation Proclamation he said, "No single deed has done more than Lincoln's signing of the Emancipation Proclamation to redeem the pledge upon which this republic was founded — the pledge that all men are created equal." Kennedy said that it was proper that they all gather together to observe this event and see themselves as the "heirs of Lincoln." He said further, "It is also a time to consider both our common responsibility toward achieving the promise of American life for all our citizens, and the implications of this document for an entire world."[6] Again, Kennedy changed his rhetoric to include loftier, grander notions. He implied that there were responsibilities that had been ignored by the whole nation.

Kennedy spoke about the responsibility that his generation had to protect the world the document proposed. "In this generation," he said, "we have seen extraordinary change in America — a new surge of idealism in our life — a new profound reality in our democratic order." Alluding to the civil rights successes of the past two years, he said, "Much has been done." However, he acknowledged, "More must be done, first because it is right, and because in making equal opportunity a reality for all Americans, we make it a certainty for each American." In this speech he explicitly stated again, "because it is right." Kennedy went even further, saying that the world was looking to America's leadership. He said that America was "on duty" around the world because the "freedoms which Lincoln lived and died for belong to all men." He finished by quoting a passage from JFK's inaugural and said that they met there to honor JFK's commitment and the Emancipation Proclamation, which "gave [JFK's] commitment both shelter and force."[7]

In his State of the Union Address on January 14, 1963, President Kennedy demonstrated that he was embracing a new approach to civil rights, laying the groundwork for his February 28 message to Congress on civil rights. He emphasized "We need to strengthen our nation by protecting the basic rights of its citizens." He went on to say,

> The most precious and powerful right in the world, the right to vote in a free American election, must not be denied to any citizen on grounds of his race or color. I wish that all qualified Americans permitted to vote were willing to vote, but surely in this centennial year of Emancipation all those who are willing to vote should always be permitted.

While Kennedy's speech was a mixture of all the issues that America faced in the year ahead, he said, "We shall be judged more by what we do at home than by what we preach abroad."[8] Kennedy's comments complemented Robert Kennedy's speeches, which signified the change in the movement. The Kennedy brothers were working together to realize their vision of America. John Kennedy put his brother out there to test the message on a small stage while he followed on a larger one. In another sense he was giving Bobby independence to follow his own agenda and test the waters at the same time.

In a speech on January 22, 1963, to the Center for the Study of Democratic Institutions in New York City, Robert Kennedy touted his civil rights record. He said that historians would someday acknowledge the "unflinching commitment of the federal government to civil rights" and the "voluntary compliance of Southern officials and citizens in this." Kennedy went on to say that there were major accomplishments in transportation and education. Further, he emphasized President Kennedy's commitment to equal employment as well as his order to prohibit discrimination in federally assisted housing, which some civil rights leaders saw as belated. He said, "The trail is long — we've crossed rough terrain; and there's more ahead — much more to do for the American Negro, the American Indian, the migrant worker — minorities yes, as the American people are themselves a minority in this world." He also said, "If freedom is to thrive in any corner of the world, there must be communication and a sense of law. There can be no meaningful discussion of civil rights until these concepts have been examined."[9] The speech was more about the Cold War and how the Soviet Union had ignored the rights of the people in the communist system. However, it serves as evidence that Robert Kennedy's plea for equality in the nation was also his way of fighting the Cold War; in essence, an extension of his brother's foreign policy.

"Above all it is wrong."

On February 28, 1963, John Kennedy sent a message to Congress on voting rights, which was a precursor to a bill that would be introduced a couple of months later. While many saw it as a token gesture and pointless in some ways, it was a monumental decision for the president to address voting issues and civil rights in such a forthright way. He accompanied this legislation with a message for Congress on civil rights, which outlined the bill as well as highlighted the issues that leaders needed to consider with its passage. Kennedy started the message by quoting Justice Harlan, who said, "Our Constitution is color blind and neither knows nor tolerates classes among citizens." He emphasized, "But the practices of the country do not always conform to the principles of the Constitution. And this message is intended to examine how far we have come in achieving first-class citizenship for all citizens regardless of color."[10]

Kennedy wrote, "One hundred years ago the Emancipation Proclamation was signed by a president who believed in the equal worth and opportunity of every human being. That proclamation was only a first step — a step which its author unhappily did not live to follow up, a step which some of its critics dismissed as an action which 'frees the slave but ignores the Negro.'" Kennedy stressed in his opening, "The harmful, wasteful and wrongful results of racial discrimination and segregation still appear in virtually every aspect of national life, in virtually every part of the nation." He brought in statistics:

> The Negro baby born in America today-regardless of the section or state in which he is born — has about one-half as much chance of completing high school as a white baby born in the same place on the same day — one-third as much chance of completing college — one-third as much chance of becoming a professional man — twice as much chance of becoming unemployed — about one-seventh as much chance of earning $10,000 per year — a life expectancy which is seven years less — and the prospect of earning only half as much.[11]

These truths hurt not only the African American, but also the nation as a whole. Kennedy wanted the members of Congress to see that this issue was as dire as any that they would face in the wake of the Second World War. This new generation of Americans, as Kennedy pointed in the inaugural, needed to confront this issue.

Kennedy attacked the issue of race like no other president since Lincoln. He was realistic and made it clear that it was bad for the nation. Kennedy said,

> Race discrimination hampers our economic growth by preventing the maximum development and utilization of our manpower. It hampers our world leadership by contradicting at home the message we preach abroad. It mars the atmosphere of a united and classless society in which this nation rose to greatness. It increases the costs of public welfare, crime, delinquency and disorder.

He finished by saying, "Above all, it is wrong." President Kennedy was almost at the same point intellectually on this issue as his brother, but he was not fully committed yet. However, he made it clear where he intended to move his administration on this issue. "Therefore, let it be clear, in our own hearts and minds, that it is not merely because of the Cold War, and not merely because of the economic waste of discrimination, that we are committed to achieving true equality of opportunity. The basic reason is because it is right."[12] There was a combined effort by John and Robert Kennedy to get this message on the righteousness of possible civil rights legislation out to the public. They were setting up the moral argument for voters and Southern politicians. After Ole Miss they orchestrated this series of speeches that changed the rhetoric on civil rights from focusing on a violation of laws to one of morals. They were finally feeling that they could do more with this issue, and Bobby went to great lengths to persuade his brother of the importance of such legislation.

Kennedy affirmed that this legislation had more reasoning than political expedience. By making the civil rights initiative righteous, President Kennedy was embracing his brother's tenets on this topic, which was evidence that Bobby was having an impact on his brother's politics. President Kennedy was still noncommittal in taking a position on civil rights. However, the administration's actions in the previous two years made a difference in the climate, and it was more likely that a president of the United States could, in fact, stake a stand on this issue with very little ridicule from the people. That had not been the case in 1960, which speaks to the power of Kennedy's actions coupled with the civil rights leaders who pushed the administration to respond. Unlike the Southern governors who emboldened the South to defend segregation, the Kennedys hoped to inspire others to see the issues their way in the hopes of creating a new atmosphere.

Kennedy first addressed the right to vote: "The right to vote in a free American election is the most powerful and precious right in the world — and it must not be denied on the grounds of race or color. It is a potent key to achieving other rights of citizenship." He added that the 1957 and 1960 civil rights acts gave the administration the power to enforce that right, "and this Administration has not hesitated to use those tools." He went on to say that while these acts were useful they were hampered by long delays in between the lawsuit and outcome. "The legal maxim 'Justice delayed is Justice denied' is dramatically applicable in these cases."[13] This new legislation was designed to attack the voting issues in the South. This was Bobby Kennedy's cornerstone for attacking racism, and he hoped to foster a foundation where African Americans had a larger say in government, which would in turn changed the legislation in these states. It was a very democratic way to approach the problem.

Kennedy proposed five initiatives to secure the right to vote in the South. Voting referees would make sure that there were qualified voters. Any voting civil rights suits should take precedent over other suits. He said there should not be tests for federal elections; anyone who had completed the sixth grade should be eligible to vote, and that accomplishment should "constitute a presumption that the applicant is literate." Finally he urged that every state legislature consider an amendment to the state constitution that banned poll taxes. Kennedy's proposals for the vote would all be adopted eventually. His message on this topic demonstrates his forward thinking and that he pushed for the vote to be front and center in any civil rights initiative. After the vote Kennedy moved into education.

President Kennedy started his piece on education by affirming the *Brown* decision: "That decision represented both good law and good judgment — it was both legally and morally right." By stating that the decision was "morally right," he reiterated that he was moving the discourse surrounding civil rights in a new direction. Many schools in the nation had followed suit. He added, "The shameful violence which accompanied but did not prevent the end of segregation at the University of Mississippi was an exception." Kennedy said that the administration had already addressed many concerns in the nation regarding desegregation. "Despite these efforts, however, progress toward primary and secondary school desegregation has still been too slow, often painfully so. Those children who are being denied their constitutional rights are suffering a loss which can never be regained, and which will leave scars which can never be fully healed." Kennedy recommended that the government create a program of "technical and financial assistance to aid school districts in the process of desegregation in compliance with the Constitution."[14]

Kennedy finished by saying, "Finally, it is obvious that the unconstitutional and outmoded concept of 'separate but equal' does not belong in the federal statute books. This is particularly true with respect to higher education, where peaceful desegregation has been underway in practically every state for some time. I repeat, therefore, this administration's recommendation of last year that this phrase be eliminated from the Morrill Land Grant College Act."[15] Kennedy not only wanted to strike at segregation and its inequality, he wanted the term associated with it stricken from the books. This is an interesting comment given that there were other issues in legislation that had not been taken out regarding slavery and other racist acts by the government. To be sure, Kennedy was trying to rewrite the law.

Kennedy went on to propose an "extension and expansion of the commission on civil rights," saying, "I recommend, therefore, that the Congress authorize the Civil Rights Commission to serve as a national civil rights clearing house providing information, advice, and technical assistance to any requesting agency, private or public." He went on to attack employment, saying, "Racial discrimination in employment is especially injurious both to its victims and to the national economy. It results in a great waste of human resources and creates serious community problems. It is, moreover, inconsistent with the democratic principle that no man should be denied employment commensurate with his abilities because of his race or creed or ancestry." Kennedy said that the Committee on Equal Employment Opportunity has attempted to attack these inequalities. He also said that the federal government was working hard to integrate the workplace and that he would instruct the Department of Justice, through the National Labor Relations Board, to address discrimination among unions and other private sector jobs.

Kennedy moved on to public accommodations, saying, "No act is more contrary to the spirit of our democracy and Constitution — or more rightfully resented by a Negro citizen who seeks only equal treatment — than the barring of that citizen from restaurants, hotels, theaters, recreational areas and other public accommodations and facilities." This was the most visible sign of segregation in the South and had been tested by many civil rights leaders through nonviolent protest. Kennedy said that the federal government would deal with this type of discrimination, as it related to federal law, when necessary. He emphasized federal facilities, conceding, "In these and other ways, the federal government will continue to encourage and support action by state and local communities, and by private entrepreneurs, to assure all members of the public equal access to all public accommodations. A country with a 'color blind' Constitution, and with no castes or classes among its citizens, cannot afford to do less."[16] This did not solve the issue in local establishments and seemed token. He had no legislation tied to this issue, which had bothered so many civil rights leaders. However, the Kennedys believed, and rightfully so, that the federal government's power had limits. To that end, they were careful where and how they asserted federal power. When it was plain that they could intervene, they did on numerous occasions.

President Kennedy suggested other uses of federal money to prevent discrimination, from housing to the Coast Guard Academy to other types of employment. "In short, the executive branch of the federal government, under this administration and in all of its activities, now stands squarely behind the principle of equal opportunity, without segregation or discrimination, in the employment of federal funds, facilities and personnel." Kennedy said that the steps proposed in the message "do not constitute a final answer to the problems of race discrimination in this country." Instead, they were a "list of priorities" that he would act on if given legislation to sign. He also hoped that this message encouraged those in the same plight for equality. "This is an effort in which every individual who asks what he can do for his country should be able and willing to take part."

Invoking Lincoln and the issues of the Civil War he finished by saying, "The centennial of the issuance of the Emancipation Proclamation is an occasion for celebration, for a sober assessment of our failures, and for rededication to the goals of freedom. Surely there could be no more meaningful observance of the centennial than the enactment of effective civil rights legislation and the continuation of effective executive action."[17] While this message accompanied legislation for voting, Kennedy's overall comments addressed issues that prior presidents had avoided. This was his version of an emancipation proclamation. Like Lincoln, he had hopes for the document that went beyond its message. Lincoln's proclamation was radical and actually had very little impact on some states that still had slavery and were in the Union. In fact, like civil rights leaders of the 1960s, abolitionists wanted more in the 1860s.

Kennedy's decision to send this legislation to Congress was unexpected, and his staff stayed up all night preparing the language for the bill, despite the fact that many saw it as a "limited afterthought."[18] While some civil rights leaders dismissed the measure, Kennedy's message was significant as it was evidence of his evolution to embrace civil rights as a moral, not political, issue. The administration's bill was something that looked for a solution to the injustice in voting rights. To be sure, Robert Kennedy played a role in convincing his brother of the importance of such legislation. It certainly laid the groundwork for future civil rights acts. Robert Kennedy defended the legislation and hoped that it was the start of the future for race relations for the nation. With the Cuban Missile Crisis behind them and the administration trying to establish a peaceful world, the Kennedys were getting ready to make good on their promise to a new generation of Americans.

"I don't think that that is very satisfactory."

On March 3, Robert Kennedy appeared on *Washington Report* to discuss President Kennedy's civil rights message to Congress on February 28. Robert Kennedy said there would be legislation in education and in the field of voting. "We have done a great deal of work over the period of the last two years in many parts of the United States to insure that everyone has the right to register and vote in an election." Kennedy went on to reminisce about what he had thought when he took the position as attorney general. "I think if there was anything that shocked me when I became attorney general it was the fact that there are large numbers of our population, hundreds of thousands of individuals, who cannot vote because of the fact that they are Negroes."[19] Kennedy went on to say that he believed that everyone should have the right to vote in the United States and that this legislation would hopefully make a difference if it were passed. While many civil rights leaders, including King, saw this as a futile attempt by the administration to bring about civil rights legislation, Kennedy saw it as a step in the same direction that the administration had been following for the last two years.

Kennedy condemned the literacy tests from the South, saying that there were professors who could not pass this test and were deemed illiterate according to these laws. He said that these tests were the major obstacle in the way of many Americans and that they had "no objective standard." He went on, "It is our feeling that participating in an election, registering and voting in elections, is basic to all rights. And if that can be accomplished in this important field of civil rights, many of these other problems will come along naturally." Indeed Kennedy believed that this, above all, was the "silver bullet" that could cure the ills of racism. This belief was naive and, to some extent, hurt his credibility with the black community. He followed up that statement with a comment on why things needed to be addressed immediately despite the misgivings of some in the Democratic party, who vowed to "stiffen resistance" if he labored on.[20]

Kennedy said that he believed that much had been done but there was still much to do. "And I don't think you can look at a situation, not just in the South, but all over the United States, where there is discrimination in this country, where we hold to believe in certain principles, where we go around the world and tell everybody what a fine democracy we are — and yet we have these practices where in many areas of the country we treat a portion of population as inferiors — it doesn't seem to me it makes any sense." Kennedy went on, "And we talk about the progress we make — considering that it has been one hundred years since the Civil War, and still these practices are taking place, where an individual cannot even register and vote in an election for the president of the United States because he happens to be a Negro.... I don't think that that is very satisfactory." Kennedy's comments paved the way for others to think in those terms. Kennedy invoked the Fourteenth Amendment to explain why there was a legal obligation for the federal government to get involved.[21]

Six days after his *Washington Report* interview it seemed that Robert Kennedy was moving even closer to embracing a moral position on civil rights. "I suppose it's inevitable that most of us are near-sighted about national problems," he said to the Civil Rights Committee of the New York City General Labor Council on March 9, 1963. He also said that there were many things that the nation tended to focus on as far as issues that "apply close to home." When it came to civil rights, however, Kennedy said, "we very quickly become far-sighted." Kennedy said that the nation was quick to "point accusing fingers at the South." He mentioned Little Rock, the Freedom Riders and Ole Miss. "Yet we respond to discrimination right around us with blank and uncomprehending stares. The attitude is 'the other fellow is wrong' and the more wrong he is, the more that he automatically put us on the side of angels." Kennedy acknowledged in this speech that there was a right and wrong response to the civil rights issue in the nation. He even said, "There is no question that segregation in the South is socially, politically and morally wrong." Kennedy would never have made that statement in 1960. The Freedom Rides and the issues at Ole Miss coupled with his dealings with civil rights groups had changed his attitude. He even went so far as to condemn the Northern attitude to race, saying, "There is a deep-seated segregation in the North, also, and it is just as wrong. Racial discrimination is a national, not a regional problem, and it cannot be solved simply by individual instances of federal action on behalf of Freedom Riders or a single college student."[22]

Robert Kennedy wanted to bring his passion for justice into the civil rights discourse. He admonished the North and the South, exclaiming that it would take the nation to confront this problem. He said that the "solution required the hearts, the voices, the mind and the muscle of individuals and organizations all over the country, public and private." He went on in the speech to quote President Kennedy's message to Congress, applauding the members of the labor community for their commitment to "social justice and social action." He touted the progress of the Equal Opportunity Employment Committee and pushed the passage of the voting bill before Congress. RFK finished, saying, "It took courage and effort for the labor movement to achieve the economic standards it enjoys today. It will take the same kind of effort to achieve the social ideals we profess in the field of civil rights.... We stand not only for labor or the Negro or minority groups, but for the ideal of freedom and dignity which underlies our society."[23]

Kennedy wanted broad support for this civil rights agenda. His speech and the *Washington Report* interview were attempts to reach larger audiences. On both occasions he quoted the president's message, which points to the fact that they saw it as a means to describe their position on the movement. It was their equivalent of a proclamation, despite the misgivings of the Martin Luther King and other civil rights leaders. Robert Kennedy followed up those comments with a speech in Louisville, Kentucky, commemorating the Emancipation Proclamation.

Robert Kennedy started his March 18 speech at Freedom Hall in Louisiana by paying tribute to Abraham Lincoln's vision. "We join today, on the Centennial of that proclamation to rededicate ourselves to the parallel doctrine that all Americans, of whatever race or creed, shall also be equal." Kennedy proclaimed that Lincoln's proclamation was an "act of great courage and great clarity." He quoted Lincoln's famously saying, "If my name goes down in history, it will be for this act. My whole soul is in it. If my hand trembles when I sign this proclamation, all who examine this document hereafter will say: 'He hesitated.'" Robert Kennedy said that Lincoln's hand "did not tremble. He did not hesitate. As always, he saw with greater vision than those around him what issues were at stake in the war."[24]

Kennedy's homage to Lincoln was more than just a memorializing of the occasion; it was also a way for him to show the nation what was at stake in the civil rights movement. He also wanted to demonstrate that strong leadership was necessary to change the way that people thought. He went on to quote Lincoln again, who said on another occasion, "In giving freedom to the slave, we assure freedom to the free." Kennedy said that the signing of the document "started the clock of progress ticking toward the day when all Americans could live, in practice, according to the national ideal that all men are born free, with equal opportunity." Despite Lincoln's vision, Kennedy argued that the clock of progress had stopped and the "separate but equal" doctrine "lay like a dead hand on the springs of progress. The nation had not retained nor understood the clarity of Lincoln's purpose."[25]

Kennedy talked about how the Supreme Court had made segregation legal, but the nation has changed since then. He mentioned how Justice Harlan wrote in dissent against the segregation ruling. "In our generation, that view is no longer expressed in dissent. It represents the view of the majority of our nation." He continued, "We can see now, with the vision and clarity of Lincoln and Harlan, the toll exacted by discrimination — whether overt segregation or covert bigotry." Kennedy acknowledged that Lincoln had seen the proclamation as a "central act" of his administration and "the great event of the nineteenth century." In solidarity with Lincoln, while celebrating the meaning of the proclamation, he said, "Today we maintain that America's present accelerating effort toward the fulfillment of Lincoln's central act is the great event of our century." These are not the words of someone who is trying to shy away from confronting segregation.

Kennedy's speech did a lot to define his position on segregation and make it clear that this was no longer a political issue. He emphasized that voting was the key to full equality and that equal education was something that he was committed to. He also said, "We must move ahead throughout the country in achieving, for all our citizens, access to public places and the freedom to live where they choose." Robert Kennedy quoted his brother's February 1963 message to Congress and emphasized that he was going to follow up on all those initiatives. He proclaimed, "The results of racial discrimination carry on for generation after generation. To face this openly, and to try to meet it squarely, is the challenge of this decade of change."

Robert Kennedy finished the speech with an allusion to his brother and Lincoln. "The act we celebrate today must not be considered a purely American experience. It is the torch that men will pass from hand to hand into every dark place in the world where slavery, of one kind or another, exists." His constant referral to that generation is important, as it points out that he saw his generation as the one that would be the light for equality. He ended the speech by saying, "This work will go forward firmly, without malice and with charity not merely because of the Cold War but, as the president has said, 'because it is right.'" In a direct reference to Lincoln's second inaugural, when he famously said, "With malice toward none, with charity for all," Kennedy wanted to make a clear link between his brother's presidency and Lincoln's. This speech, more than any other, made it clear that segregation was something that Kennedy would fight. He planned to use the power of his brother's administration to make a difference. Indeed, it was clear that not only did he see his work as being as noble as Lincoln's, but also that this was something that would no longer be tolerated. From Bobby's point of view, segregation was wrong. This was a clear divergence from the campaign and set the tone for future acts by the Justice Department. Of course, Robert Kennedy would not have made the speech without his brother's consent.

On April 1, Robert Kennedy sent the Voting Rights Bill to the Capitol for its passage. In his message to the Speaker of the House, Robert Kennedy outlined that the bill was meant to remedy "defects" within the Civil Rights Acts of 1957 and 1960. "While those acts have proven a useful tool in the protection of voting rights, a considerable period of time measurable in terms of years, frequently elapses between the filing of the lawsuit and its ultimate conclusion. The result is that with respect to specific elections occurring during that time, the right to vote is lost forever." In addition to securing the right to vote, the bill addressed the "application of arbitrary and discriminatory standards in determining the qualifications of persons seeking to register and to vote in federal elections."[26] This was the first step for Robert Kennedy, paving the way for a larger commitment on civil rights. It is significant that he referred to John Kennedy's message to Congress. While this was not the sweeping reform that African Americans had hoped for, it was a move in the right direction and signaled a shift in their thinking.

On April 25, Robert Kennedy addressed the University of South Carolina chapter of the American Association of University Professors. At this speech he spoke a great deal about foreign policy and how the Justice Department fought crime and followed through on several initiatives. He concluded his speech with the voting rights act that he had sent to Congress earlier in the month, calling civil rights "the toughest and gravest internal challenge which the United States faces today." Kennedy continued, "I speak of this as a need, not a choice, for that is what it is. We as a nation have no choice but to make progress towards full equality of opportunity." He quoted President Kennedy's message, emphasizing that he saw it as "right." Kennedy also said, "We are still a people moved by moral force. We believe that all men are created free and are equal before the law. One of our overriding moral drives now is to make that true for Negroes as well as others." He said that the national government was going "to do everything possible to eliminate racial discrimination. We are committed in the world to the cause of freedom."[27]

Robert Kennedy said that it had been 100 years since the slaves were freed. "During that time in many places little progress has been made to give full liberty to the descendants of slaves. Now time is running out fast for this country." Kennedy went on to say, "We must recognize, as responsible citizens and as responsible government officials, that the Negroes in this country cannot be expected indefinitely to tolerate the injustices which flow from official and private racial discrimination in the United States." Kennedy saw this as a matter of crisis that had to be addressed. "The troubles we see now," he went on, "agitation and even bloodshed, will not compare to what we will see a decade from now unless real progress is made." He laid out the issues for the audience saying,

> So despite the changes that are required, and sometimes resisted, we are fortunate as a nation that these three great needs of our time — the moral drive for equality, the necessities caused by our position before the world, and the surge for equality by Negroes throughout the country — are met in the United States, as has been true of other needs in the past, by recognition in the law.

He finished strongly, saying he was obligated to uphold the law and that he believed "that in this case the law accurately reflects the needs of the country and its people." He even quoted a passage from Thomas Paine, written in 1776: "In America law is king."[28]

In the wake of Ole Miss, Robert Kennedy's awareness of the racial issue in the country was palpable. In his ten speeches from October 6, 1962, to April 25, 1963, Robert Kennedy made his argument for equal rights for African Americans under the law. While this was largely a push for voting rights legislation, it was rooted in civil rights as a moral, not a political, issue. Indeed, part of President Kennedy's State of the Union and his February 28, 1963, message to Congress had the same tone. To be sure, it was Robert Kennedy who had a passion to take on this fight. Despite his criticism from civil rights leaders, Robert Kennedy did more to bring the issues to the public than any public official to that date. His efforts paved the way for larger initiatives at the federal level. His speeches in this period signify the shift in policy as well as the effect that Ole Miss had had on the need for such reform. Kennedy was the driving force for change. Not only was Robert Kennedy working on his brother to make a stand in civil rights, these speeches point to the fact that he was attempting to gather more support. Robert Kennedy was ready to make a larger commitment to this cause. The Kennedy brothers made it clear that in 1963 civil rights would be the cornerstone of their domestic agenda. The Ole Miss crisis was the final act that illuminated the need for leadership. Martin Luther King and the SCLC stood ready to press the Kennedy brothers and see just how sincere those speeches were.

16. King and Birmingham

"But I have to make a faith act."

Birmingham, Alabama, was the stage for violence during the Freedom Rides in 1961. Nearly two years later, the issues with the local government set in motion events that would join Martin Luther King and Robert Kennedy once again. In November 1962, President Kennedy had signed an executive order banning racial discrimination in housing. Finally, he followed through on his "stroke of the pen" promise from the campaign. Martin Luther King, Jr., said that the order "carries the whole nation forward to the realization of the American dream."[1] While Kennedy's effort was seen as late to some civil rights leaders, it was significant in that he was taking measures in civil rights that he previously stayed away from. The Albany movement and Ole Miss crisis led up to his decision to sign this order and together served as a symbolic prelude to 1963, which would lead to two confrontations in Alabama, a civil rights act and a march on Washington, D.C., that would inspire future generations of Americans.

As 1963 approached, Martin Luther King looked to Birmingham for his next chapter in the civil rights movement. Meredith's case with the University of Mississippi was proof that when confronted with the reality and ugliness of segregation, the Kennedy administration would act on behalf of the movement. King wanted a second Emancipation Proclamation from Kennedy and when he was denied, he turned all his energies to a campaign in Birmingham, which was viewed by many as the greatest symbol of the segregated South. In December 1962 King sent Wyatt Walker and Andrew Young to Birmingham to get a plan together.[2] This planning involved very distinct phases. First they would have small-scale sit-ins, drawing attention to the movement. The second phase would involve a boycott of downtown businesses, leading to a third phase of mass marches and finally a call to others to come to the city. It was called Project-C for "confrontation."[3] The group was ready for this confrontation to challenge Bull Connor's pernicious, racist government. Their one hesitation was how to get support from the local leadership. To that Fred Shuttlesworth said, "Don't worry Martin, I can handle the preachers." King replied, "You better be right."[4]

Martin Luther King believed that Birmingham was going to be his largest test to date. He was committed to nonviolence, but knew that Bull Connor's tactics had the potential of hurting, even killing, someone. Taylor Branch writes that King "became a brooding, pensive man as he contemplated the leap ahead. King spoke about some of the basic, formative beliefs that propelled him into the movement in many of the speeches leading up to Birmingham."[5] The evidence suggests that he anticipated a standoff— one that would irrevocably change the movement. In fact, King disappeared from public view to "purify" himself for the struggle that he believed he was going to endure in Birmingham.[6]

King struggled in the early days of the protest to get the attention of the media. Despite the fact that one demonstrator was attacked by Bull Connor's dogs and a hundred people were in jail, the media ran other stories instead.[7] Mayor-elect Albert Boutwell declared, "I urge everyone, white and Negro, calmly to ignore what is now being attempted in Birmingham."[8] Bobby Kennedy asked Burke Marshall to contact King and tell him that the demonstrations were "ill timed." He cited the recent vote in which the Birmingham voters approved a charter reform that ousted racist mayor Arthur Haws as well as Bull Connor.

In addition to there being almost no media attention, African American business owners discouraged King from taking on this demonstration. Also, Governor Wallace and other officials set out to stop King once and for all. They consulted Laurie Pritchett in the hopes of duplicating how he had handled the Albany Movement. Connor was able to secure an injunction similar to the one that Pritchett had used to contain King.[9] King, Abernathy and Shuttlesworth pledged to violate the injunction in the hopes of springboarding the movement to the next level. They argued, like Thoreau did in the nineteenth century, that such an injunction violated their rights and was not a just law, and that they could not "in good conscience" obey the order.[10] King struggled to get volunteers to accompany him to jail. Seeing that this was not the popular attitude among people he trusted, including his father, King took time and thoroughly deliberated whether he was going to violate the injunction. He finally decided to take a stand on April 12, Good Friday. King asked Ralph Abernathy to accompany him on this protest. "I don't know what will happen.... But I have to make a faith act." Wearing a work shirt, blue jeans and walking shoes, King endeavored to inspire the movement.[11]

King's actions signified a last effort to gain national attention and regain a place of leadership among the black community. While many saw him as the movement's leader, his misstep at Albany coupled with the scrutiny of many prominent African Americans threatened that leadership. He needed something big and significant to recapture African American support and push the Kennedys to respond. King was under a great deal of pressure to do well in this demonstration.

King and Abernathy left the Sixteenth Street Baptist Church and led forty protestors who were willing to go to jail with them. As the group walked down the street people came out to see. Upon seeing King many cheered, showing their support. The police followed the group and then they pounced, arresting many. King was arrested by a detective who apprehended him by the back of the belt and pushed him into the paddy wagon. In total, fifty-two people were arrested. Some were not even part of the protest.[12] The *New York Times* reported the next day, "The march was the most spectacular of the many demonstrations held since the direct action assault on Birmingham." The *Times* also reported, "There has been much opposition in the Negro community here of more than 100,000 to pressing the campaign."[13] King had the media attention that he longed for. He was put into solitary confinement after his arrest and not allowed to call anyone or speak with his lawyers.[14]

Coretta Scott King called John Kennedy hoping for some help. Robert Kennedy returned the call, saying that the president was with their father, who was sick, and could not return the call. Kennedy said that they were having "a difficult problem with local officials." He assured Coretta that he would "look into the situation." The next day, the president called Coretta from Palm Beach to voice his concern, saying that her husband would call soon. Within fifteen minutes King was talking with his wife. When Coretta told him about the Kennedy calls he responded, "So that's why everyone is being so polite."[15] Bobby told Harry Belafonte, who was calling on King's behalf, to "tell Reverend King we're doing all we can." In his characteristic humor during these tense moments Kennedy said, "I'm not sure we can get into prison reform at the moment."[16]

Robert Kennedy wanted to get involved in Birmingham. Diane McWhorter writes that Kennedy's "renowned 'ruthless' side had begun to chafe against his carefully cultivated passivity toward SCLC's mission in Birmingham." He kept asking Marshall why they could not get involved in the situation. To that Marshall responded, "Well, who do you want to lead the army — me or you? One step leads to another, and if you don't understand where you're going you've got to resist starting."[17] Kennedy's insistence on getting into the Birmingham affair is further evidence that this was the final stage in his transition to a civil rights warrior. He was no longer concerned with the issues of federalism as he had been in 1961 and 1962. Instead he wanted to right a clear wrong.

King did not have the full support of the black community in Birmingham, nor did he have the blessing of the Justice Department. In addition, news reports from several media outlets, including *Time* magazine, criticized him for the demonstrations, arguing that King needed to let the new government take over and bring in new reforms. However, the piece that stood out for him, as he sat in jail looking at newspapers that were smuggled in by his lawyer Clarence Jones, was an article with the headline "White Clergymen Urge Local Negroes to Withdraw from Demonstrations." It was on page two of the April 13 *Birmingham News*.[18] This article became the focus of what would become a poetic defense of King's involvement in Birmingham and demonstrated to the world at large the injustice of the South and the justification of nonviolent action as a viable remedy to the race issues that had plagued the nation. King also took great exception to John and Robert Kennedy. He started writing the letter in the margins of the article as he remained in solitary confinement.[19]

King's eloquent letter started by addressing the "Fellow Clergymen" who criticized him in the press. He wrote, "I came across your recent statement calling my present activities 'unwise and untimely.' Seldom do I pause to answer criticism of my work and ideas." Indeed, this was something King saw as a necessary response. He was against a wall and needed inspiration. Not only for himself, but also the movement. He wrote, "But since I feel that you are men of genuine goodwill and that your criticisms are sincerely set forth, I want to try to answer your statements in what I hope will be patient and reasonable terms."[20] He proclaimed, "I am in Birmingham because injustice is here." In response to so many who believed that King should stay out of the affairs of other states, he said the following:

> I am cognizant of the interrelatedness of all communities and states. I cannot sit idly by in Atlanta and not be concerned about what happens in Birmingham. Injustice anywhere is a threat to justice everywhere. We are caught in an inescapable network of mutuality, tied in a single garment of destiny. Whatever affects one directly, affects all indirectly. Never again can we afford to live with the narrow, provincial "outside agitator" idea. Anyone who lives inside the United States can never be considered an outsider anywhere within its bounds.[21]

This philosophy is one that King used in several speeches. This notion that Americans need to act in the face of injustice was not only his philosophy, but also Robert Kennedy's. To be sure, Kennedy wanted to see justice throughout America. His speeches are a testament to his commitment to that goal.

King argued that he had done his due diligence to do what is right. "In any nonviolent campaign there are four basic steps: collection of the facts to determine whether injustices exist; negotiation; self-purification; and direct action. We have gone through all of these steps in Birmingham." He concluded, "We had no alternative except to prepare for direct action, whereby we would present our very bodies as a means of laying our case before the conscience of the local and the national community."[22] King went on to say that he had waited as long as he could. Birmingham was a place that needed action. He said, "Nonviolent direct action seeks to create such a crisis and foster such a tension that a community which has constantly refused to negotiate is forced to confront the issue." He went on, "But I must confess that I am not afraid of the word 'tension.' I have earnestly opposed violent tension, but there is a type of constructive, nonviolent tension which is necessary for growth."[23] King was not only defending why he forced the issue at Birmingham; he was also defending his philosophy throughout the movement. He hoped that the national community would respond and wanted to see recognition of the issues in the South.

King also commented that the concept of freedom was something that was not easily won. "We know through painful experience that freedom is never voluntarily given by the oppressor; it must be demanded by the oppressed." In a direct response to Robert Kennedy he wrote, "Frankly, I have yet to engage in a direct-action campaign that was 'well timed' in the view of those who have not suffered unduly from the disease of segregation." He wrote, "For years now I have heard the word 'Wait!' It rings in the ear of every Negro with piercing familiarity. This 'Wait' has almost always meant 'Never.' We must come to see, with one of our distinguished jurists, that 'justice too long delayed is justice denied.'" King went on with the notion that his actions were "ill timed." He wrote, in one long sentence,

> But when you have seen vicious mobs lynch your mothers and fathers at will and drown your sisters and brothers at whim; when you have seen hate-filled policemen curse, kick and even kill your black brothers and sisters; when you see the vast majority of your twenty million Negro brothers smothering in an airtight cage of poverty in the midst of an affluent society; when you suddenly find your tongue twisted and your speech stammering as you seek to explain to your six-year-old daughter why she can't go to the public amusement park that has just been advertised on television, and see tears welling up in her eyes when she is told that Funtown is closed to colored children, and see ominous clouds of inferiority beginning to form in her little mental sky, and see her beginning to distort her personality by developing an unconscious bitterness toward white people; when you have to concoct an answer for a five-year-old son who is asking: "Daddy, why do white people treat colored people so mean?"; when you take a cross-country drive and find it necessary to sleep night after night in the uncomfortable corners of your automobile because no motel will accept you; when you are humiliated day in and day out by nagging signs reading "white" and "colored"; when your first name becomes "nigger," your middle name becomes "boy" (however old you are) and your last name becomes "John," and your wife and mother are never given the respected title "Mrs."; when you are harried by day and haunted by night by the fact that you are a Negro, living constantly at tiptoe stance, never quite knowing what to expect next, and are plagued with inner fears and outer resentments; when you go forever fighting a degenerating sense of "nobodiness"–then you will understand why we find it difficult to wait.[24]

This epitomized the movement's reasoning and served to define the cause for future generations. Despite the fact that it was published after the movement, it served as an explanation of why King was pushing for change.

King goes on in the letter about white moderates, saying that at times they were more of an impediment than a help to the cause. He wrote:

> I must confess that over the past few years I have been gravely disappointed with the white moderate. I have almost reached the regrettable conclusion that the Negro's great stumbling block in his stride toward freedom is not the White Citizen's Councilor or the Ku Klux Klanner, but the white moderate, who is more devoted to "order" than to justice; who prefers a negative peace which is

the absence of tension to a positive peace which is the presence of justice; who constantly says: "I agree with you in the goal you seek, but I cannot agree with your methods of direct action"; who paternalistically believes he can set the timetable for another man's freedom; who lives by a mythical concept of time and who constantly advises the Negro to wait for a "more convenient season." Shallow understanding from people of good will is more frustrating than absolute misunderstanding from people of ill will. Lukewarm acceptance is much more bewildering than outright rejection.

His points can be seen as a direct criticism of the Kennedys. Often times they told King that they were on his side, but that their hands were tied. Indeed, this must have been frustrating for King as he tried to lead his movement. His point on "order" is most definitely something that the Kennedys were publicly mentioning in both the Freedom Ride case and the Ole Miss crisis. To be sure, Robert Kennedy's insistence that the movement in Birmingham was "ill timed" is directly challenged. To further his point he wrote, "I had hoped that the white moderate would understand that law and order exist for the purpose of establishing justice and that when they fail in this purpose they become the dangerously structured dams that block the flow of social progress."

Besides defending his actions in Birmingham and admonishing the "white moderate," King also started to distinguish the differences in the black civil rights movement that were developing in the nation. He wrote, "You speak of our activity in Birmingham as extreme. At first I was rather disappointed that fellow clergymen would see my nonviolent efforts as those of an extremist. I began thinking about the fact that I stand in the middle of two opposing forces in the Negro community." He said that the first part of the movement was "a force of complacency, made up in part of Negroes who, as a result of long years of oppression, are so drained of self-respect and a sense of 'somebodiness' that they have adjusted to segregation." The second part of those forces was "one of bitterness and hatred, and it comes perilously close to advocating violence. It is expressed in the various black nationalist groups that are springing up across the nation, the largest and best-known being Elijah Muhammad's Muslim movement." He went on, "Nourished by the Negro's frustration over the continued existence of racial discrimination, this movement is made up of people who have lost faith in America, who have absolutely repudiated Christianity, and who have concluded that the white man is an incorrigible 'devil.'"[25] King said that he was in between these two movements and was convinced that if he had not fostered nonviolence in the South, there would have been bloodshed.

King went on to discuss the issues that he saw with the Birmingham Police department, saying that they were "ugly" and "inhumane." The article in the *Birmingham News* commended the police for being nonviolent. King wanted the article to commend the people who were putting their lives on the line instead. "I wish you had commended the Negro sit-inners and demonstrators of Birmingham for their sublime courage, their willingness to suffer and their amazing discipline in the midst of great provocation." He went on, saying that one day the South would recognize the real heroes like James Meredith and the elder citizens who stood up for justice.

King ended the letter by stressing the importance of these issues and that he believed that it was the right time to bring them to the forefront. "If I have said anything in this letter that overstates the truth and indicates an unreasonable impatience, I beg you to forgive me. If I have said anything that understates the truth and indicates my having a patience that allows me to settle for anything less than brotherhood, I beg God to forgive me." King's letter was seen by many as a direct justification of the Birmingham protest. In a larger sense, it was a justification for the whole movement and why African Americans were fighting for their rights. It explained why they chose nonviolence as a tactic and ridiculed those who were not with them in this fight for equal rights under the law. The letter played a role in the movement as the beginning of King's final ascent to the leadership. His "I Have a Dream" speech was the final piece that pointed to his leadership as well as an example of his philosophy and where he saw the nation moving.

The famous letter was not published right away, so many in the movement did not read King's eloquent justification of his methods. His prestige was at stake and he contemplated a new direction for the Birmingham situation. King was found guilty of violating an injunction on April 26. He appealed the decision and continued his protest.[26] On May 2, King recognized that he needed something new in the protest so people would stand up and notice the issues in the South. He responded by sending nearly one thousand children to challenge Bull Connor's segregated system. King believed that this would give young African American children pride in their race and reinforce the idea that they could make a difference in the movement. Robert Kennedy believed that the children would be hurt.[27] It is yet another example where the two leaders differed on tactics, yet both wanted the same outcome. Connor responded with force, arresting nearly a thousand. He gave King what he needed to awaken the nation and the world to the oppression in the South. This action catapulted the movement to a new level, lending a new voice and imagery to the tragic realities that many African Americans had to endure every day. Images of German Shepherds biting into these children, coupled with fire hoses that pushed little girls down the street, tore the bark off nearby trees and loosened bricks from buildings with their force captured the awareness of the nation.[28] One reporter heard Bull Connor say, "I want to see the dogs work. Look at those niggers run."[29]

Despite the fact that John Kennedy said he was "sickened" by the pictures of dogs biting into children, the administration still held firm on their insistence to have the local authorities handle the issue.[30] Bobby Kennedy issued a statement regarding the use of children and "timing" of the protests. He also asked Marshall to call King and ask for a suspension of the demonstrations, then followed up by sending Marshall and Joe Dolan to Birmingham to mediate the government dispute.[31] James Hilty writes, "The Kennedys ... saw themselves as problem solvers and facilitators laboring to bring order out of chaos, to make sense of Martin Luther King's confused demands, and, in the process, to assert their superiority without exercising raw authority."[32]

Marshall secured an agreement with the Birmingham government. Marshall emphasized to the white leadership that King was did not want a revolution, only what was right and fair. In addition, he tried to work with the African American community to accept that there would be progress in the near future.[33] He remembered in 1964 the situation in Birmingham as he made his way to get involved: "They were in the streets, there were pictures throughout the nation, throughout the world, police dogs and fire hoses and one thing or another. So it was a matter of great concern to the president, to President Kennedy at that time because it was sort of a hopeless situation in terms of any lawful resolution of it."[34] Marshall went on discussing the situation and what his intentions were: "The purpose of going, in a sense, was to do something. It was very difficult, I found out that day, really, to some extent — I talked to King and I asked him what he was after. He really didn't know."[35] Marshall's goal was to get control of the situation and acknowledge the rights of African Americans in Birmingham.

King went back to his group and they discussed what they wanted. The main issue was that there was not a city government that could respond to their demands. Marshall recalled what King said to him: "Well, they came up with some demands, requests, they came up with a program at least, it was directed mainly at the large downtown stores, principally on the fact that the lunch counters were closed to Negroes and that there were no Negroes employed in other than the janitorial capacities." Marshall met with business leaders in downtown Birmingham and asked for biracial talks. The merchants concluded that with the prospect of further demonstrations they needed to move forward with some agreement.[36]

King's group came back with a document called "Points for Progress." It had four points. The first wanted "immediate desegregation of all store facilities," the second point argued for the an "upgrade" for store employees and "non-discriminatory" hiring. The merchants did not promise that they could help with the third and fourth points. King's group expected the merchants to pressure the government to drop all charges on the demonstrators and also exert similar pressure "to establish a biracial committee to deal with future problems and to develop specific programs" for hiring African Americans, voter registration, school desegregation and other aspects of integration throughout the city. The merchants said that they could not interfere with the courts and that they still did not know which government would be in charge.[37]

Marshall recalled, "Well, of course, you know, they hadn't been thinking about it and they were — just anything that Martin Luther King wanted was poison to them. But the initial report was that that was hopeless."[38] Marshall went on to say,

> There was no legal remedy. That was clear from the start, and I know that we discussed that with the president, President Kennedy, so then he understood it, but most of the country didn't. You know, they wanted him to send in troops, they wanted him to do this, that, or the other thing. But in fact the complaint was over service in the lunch counters. That was the principal complaint, and it was not a complaint that could be solved under law in any way at that time.[39]

The negotiations stalled and the demonstrations continued. With little room left in the jails and violence on both sides of the demonstrations, the situation was getting worse and there was pressure from Marshall to find a solution. The merchants could not guarantee a settlement, but they were able to get the Senior Citizens' Committee involved, who had played a role in the change of government eight months earlier.[40]

"Where are we with Birmingham?"

With Burke Marshall in Birmingham, Robert Kennedy participated in a four-hour cabinet meeting on the Birmingham situation. Also present was Nick Katzenbach. Kennedy recalled being in touch with Marshall, who wanted to get the leaders in Birmingham to consider not only the government stand-off, but also the racial issues. Although Marshall wasn't present he contacted members of the group after the meeting. According to him,

> They thought what to do for four or five hours, and they ended up with nothing. I mean there was nothing to do. They went through the possibilities. I talked to Nick about it, I think, afterwards, or Ted or one of them on the telephone, and they'd been all through this and they couldn't think of anything to do other than what I was doing, which was to try to explain the Negro situation to the white people and the white people's situations to the Negroes when they wouldn't talk to each other.

Marshall also said that for President Kennedy "it was a matter of national and international concern at the time because of the mass of demonstrations."[41] In an effort to help Marshall in Birmingham, Robert Kennedy tried to make things happen behind the scenes. He said, "I got hold of Douglas Dillon to make some phone calls to bankers and steel companies. And we had meetings with some of the department store owners, officials, to see if they'd do something about desegregating some of the department stores, making them available to Negroes."[42] Robert Kennedy was committed to finding a solution in Birmingham.

He talked to Coretta King, contacted business leaders and sent Marshall to get involved in Birmingham.

Marshall worked with the different groups, and in the evening on Tuesday May 7, a white group of four and members of the movement met to discuss an agreement. Marshall and an aid to the Boutwell administration were present. They took a few hours and sketched out a settlement that included desegregation of downtown stores, upgrading the status of employees and creating a biracial committee. While they could not make the agreement official, they left that meeting knowing that they would meet again the next day. After meeting with the leadership on Wednesday, King decided that due to the increasing hostilities in the demonstrations and the fact that they were close to an agreement, there should be a one-day moratorium on the demonstrations. The main issue was the release of those arrested at the demonstrations. Fred Shuttlesworth, however, did not agree, and there was a period on that Wednesday when the situation slowly unraveled. Marshall was in the thick of it. King wanted to explore these options and hold off on demonstrations, while Shuttlesworth felt he was being left out of negotiations and wanted to keep going. Marshall said, "We made promises to these people." Shuttlesworth said "What promises did you make to what people?" He said that any promises that were made without his approval were not good.[43]

Despite the setback and an effort by Connor to stop the negotiations by arresting King and Abernathy again, the Birmingham Truce Agreement was finalized on Thursday night and announced on Friday, May 10. In substance the document called for desegregation of facilities incrementally over sixty days with the incoming Boutwell administration, a "program of upgrading Negro employment," and a biracial committee.[44]

The Kennedy brothers worked together to find a solution in Birmingham. Robert Kennedy recalled that JFK wanted to see "if we could have some solution to it. I think he understood that there wasn't anything very much legally that we could do, but he wanted to find out, so that a lot turned on the success of Burke's efforts." Kennedy remembered, "I kept telling [President Kennedy] that I didn't see that we could do anything more legally. So we were involved in it just trying to find some solution through mediation."[45] However, in the wake of the agreement, the racist elements in Birmingham went to work. On Saturday night, they bombed Martin Luther King's brother A.D.'s home. They also bombed the hotel where Martin Luther King had been staying while he was in Birmingham. As a result of this new turn of events there were riots in the streets of Birmingham once again.[46] The administration was worried that the situation was going to get worse and the agreement would fall apart.

In a May 12 meeting Robert Kennedy, John Kennedy, Burke Marshall, Robert McNamara and others discussed the Birmingham situation and their response. President Kennedy started asking, "Where are we with Birmingham?" Robert Kennedy briefed his brother on the bombs at Birmingham and reported that the governor had moved in to assist. RFK also said that there were buildings on fire and riots as a result of the bombs. He said that Martin Luther King was going back to hold a rally. He said that both sides had weapons and the situation could get out of hand, despite what Connor said. "As far as sending troops," he said, "we discussed this for a long period of time. Of course there are obvious drawbacks." Bobby Kennedy said, "We don't have a clear cut situation that we had in the other situations." Kennedy went on saying that it was not like Montgomery with the Freedom Rides. He implied that they needed a clear, legal reason to send in troops, which points to the fact that they wanted to help the movement. In fact, Robert Kennedy sounded disappointed when he said that the governor would maintain law and order.[47]

Robert Kennedy acknowledged that the group that had been causing some of the problems was the African American community, and they did not want to send troops against them. "The argument for sending troops in and taking some forceful action is what's going to happen in the future." He went on, "You're going to have these kinds of incidents. The governors virtually taking over the city." John Kennedy liked it and explored it with the group. The troops would be on standby, outside the city limits. The group looked for a middle ground, something to stave off calamity. The president also believed that the arrangement, which was negotiated by the administration, would have to be honored by all the parties. Bobby Kennedy suggested nationalizing the guard. President Kennedy said, "First we have to have law and order and for the Negroes not to be running around the city." The second thing he wanted was to have the arrangement working. The interesting part of this exchange is that the administration was trying to involve itself in a local affair, despite what the Constitution said. They were at a point in the movement where federalism did not trump what was right. Robert Kennedy's first impulse was to get involved. He would not have been so fast to suggest that in 1961 or 1962. Both Kennedys wanted to influence this movement.

John Kennedy alluded to legislation as a means to alter the state of things in Birmingham, indeed in the rest of the United States. "The other remedy we have," President Kennedy said, "is legislation through the Congress this week." To be sure, civil rights legislation was something that Kennedy had been priming the people for since his message to the Congress in February. This might be the incident that Kennedy needed to propel that legislation to another level. John Kennedy was afraid that if they sent in troops the government would withdraw from the agreement. Burke Marshall spoke up, saying that in fact the government was doing everything it could to honor the agreement. They went on in this conversation about sending in the troops and the possible reaction to any such movement by the white businessmen in Birmingham. Marshall said that the businessmen wanted to look more like Atlanta and be able to take care of their own issues. Troops symbolized that they needed to help to maintain order. He did say, however, "They might rather have that than have a racial war down there."[48]

President Kennedy wanted the agreement carried out and they explored options that would create an atmosphere in which that could happen. They debated landing troops or keeping them at the airport. Marshall said, "I think the knowledge that the troops are available ... might have a calming effect. President Kennedy made it clear that they'd issue a statement to send in troops if the local authorities could not handle the riots. The administration was concerned with the agreement, keeping the African American community from rioting and what message the troops would send to the people in Birmingham and even the nation. Robert Kennedy was worried that this was going to get worse."[49]

Robert Kennedy voiced his opinion that African Americans could bring this situation to another level with rallies and a call for presidential action. They were at an impasse, because there was no real action that the administration could take in this situation. Bobby believed that eventually people will start asking what President Kennedy was doing about this. "That's the real problem, whether we have an excuse for doing something today." Again, Robert Kennedy was looking for an "excuse" to get involved. He was not afraid to commit federal forces, but he needed to have a legal reason for sending in troops or any kind of force. Bobby said, "Perhaps we indicate our interest. Putting out a strong statement by you. Putting troops in there [and sending Marshall back down]. One, two, three, we've done something."[50] This was why President Kennedy had Bobby so close to this situation.

He trusted his younger brother and always considered his advice. Bobby looked out for the president and would always put JFK's interest over his own.

President Kennedy liked the idea of sending in troops as a precaution and started to ask questions after Bobby made his case. "Where do we put the troops?" President Kennedy asked. They started to debate logistics on where to put them and how long it would take. They also considered using the Airborne and wanted certain options at the ready for JFK's order. President Kennedy said he would send troops to the airport and issue a statement. He also said that Marshall would go to Birmingham in an effort to negotiate with all the parties. JFK even inquired how long it would take if they wanted to send troops that instant. In an effort to avoid the same deadly outcome as Ole Miss, Kennedy wanted to know the quickest response time for all the troops. He anticipated something big happening and wanted to be prepared. One of the largest issues in Oxford the previous fall had been the length of time it took for the troops to get to the scene of the riot. President Kennedy asked many questions of the group. He wanted details of troops and possible strategies. To make sure they had accurate information, Robert McNamara was a part of the discussion, which brought a new level to this meeting and also demonstrated that Kennedy took this seriously enough to involve the secretary of defense.

Burke Marshall and Robert Kennedy spoke to the possibility of further issues with the African American community. Marshall reported on his phone conversation with Martin Luther King, saying that he did not condone the violence. He went to say that King was going to try and "organize the Negroes" and go around the communities. Robert Kennedy spoke about a possible riot, saying, "It would be damn tough." He believed that the troops were a "psychological move" and had the potential to stave off possible issues. Despite what their critics said, the Kennedy brothers had a decent track record of involving themselves in these events. To be sure, if there were troops in waiting, it demonstrated that they were responding to the crisis and were ready in case it got out of hand. President Kennedy was almost ready to commit. He did say, "Law and order isn't any good unless we can get this agreement implemented."

The psychological advantage of having troops in the waiting seemed to carry the discussion. These men were getting ready to send more troops into the South. They discussed the 82nd Airborne. This was a not a knee-jerk reaction. It was a well thought out, reasonable response to a difficult situation where the federal government had very little jurisdiction, especially since the governor had pledged to maintain law and order. It certainly spoke to the fact the Kennedys did not trust the local authorities or the segregationist governor. The administration had the Freedom Rides and the Ole Miss episode as their guide. In addition, they had more exposure to this issue and were even veterans in how to handle these problems. President Kennedy was quick with questions and in tune with his advisors. He was involved and committed to act. They discussed putting six or seven hundred troops in that night. "Well, that might be necessary," JFK said. He continued, "The fact that they're federal troops might have a calming effect." He was looking to restore order and maintain the agreement.

In addition to committing the troops John Kennedy wanted to avoid the communication problems he had in Oxford. He wanted to be involved and make decisions with the right information. He wanted success. JFK saws troops as a way to control the riots. That was the major advantage to this move. He also wanted to make a statement and "call on people" to maintain law and order. There was some debate on what the statement would say and who would write it. In the end, the Kennedys were making a move on Birmingham.

The fact is that they had very little legal basis for sending troops to the South, nor did they want to challenge a situation where the governor of the state, despite his segregationist position, was addressing the situation. Therefore, the Kennedy brothers' discussion and actions in this case are especially important. It signified a change in their strategy. They were no longer concerned with the legal right or even with the fact that federalism would be violated. They were acting because it was the right thing to do.

President Kennedy made a statement about what he intended to do in Birmingham. From the Oval Office at nine o'clock P.M., Kennedy said, "I am deeply concerned about the events which occurred in Birmingham, Alabama, last night." President Kennedy went on to say:

> This government will do whatever must be done to preserve order, to protect the lives of its citizens, and to uphold the law of the land. I am certain that the vast majority of the citizens of Birmingham, both white and Negro, particularly those who labored so hard to achieve the peaceful, constructive settlement of last week, can feel nothing but dismay at the efforts of those who would replace conciliation and good will with violence and hate.

Kennedy applauded Marshall's efforts and was concerned that the agreement would unravel. He said that the agreement was important. "It recognized the fundamental right of all citizens to be accorded equal treatment and opportunity." In this sense he was following up with his earlier February message that civil rights was a moral, not political, issue. It certainly paved the way for the future legislation that they were discussing. Kennedy said to the people of Birmingham, "Violence only breeds more violence." He outlined the measures he was taking to secure the agreement. First, he said that he was sending Marshall back to Birmingham. Second, he said, "I have instructed Secretary of Defense McNamara to alert units of the Armed Forces trained in riot control and to dispatch selected units to military bases in the vicinity of Birmingham." Finally Kennedy announced that he had federalized the Alabama National Guard so Governor Wallace would not interfere with his efforts.[51]

Kennedy's involvement had an effect on the Birmingham situation. While there were still issues of strong personalities and power struggles within the movement as well as some problems in the press with the white leadership, Boutwell took control of the city after the Fifth Circuit Court of Appeals ruled in his favor.[52] Connor was out and the city would move forward on the desegregation policy. A combination of efforts from King, Shuttlesworth, Marshall and the Kennedys had forced a decision. It was a monumental victory and paved the way to future legislation. In fact, Burke Marshall remembered, "I think without having a meeting or discussion about it, everyone concluded that the president had to act and, as I said, not only face this himself, but somehow bring the country to face this problem and resolve it. So it was a question of how to do that, and it involved, at least among other things, legislation."[53] After Birmingham the Kennedy brothers started to look at legislation that would allow the federal government to get involved in this type of situation. This was an unprecedented turn of events and demonstrated that they were willing to sacrifice political capital and make decisions based on the justice and righteousness of the situation.

17. Crimson Tide: George Wallace and Robert Kennedy

"You have done more for civil rights than anyone else."

On May 24, Robert Kennedy met with a group of African American writers and artists. James Baldwin, who wrote a piece for the *New Yorker* about African American despair, had met Robert Kennedy at the White House the previous year. They had another meeting and decided that Baldwin would arrange a larger meeting, which would take place at the Kennedy apartment in New York.[1] There were many people there who wanted to talk to the attorney general about several issues. Harry Belafonte, Lena Horne and many other highly affluent African Americans were in attendance. One of the attendees was Jerome Smith, a Freedom Rider and CORE member. Baldwin remembered later that Smith "set the tone of the meeting because he stammers when he's upset and he stammered when he talked to Bobby and said that he was nauseated by the necessity of being in that room." Baldwin went on to say, "I knew what he meant. It was not personal at all.... Bobby took it personal."[2] Robert Kennedy thought that Smith meant that by being in the same room with him he felt nauseous, which was not what he meant. As a result of what Bobby saw as a clear insult, he turned away from Smith and focused on the other people in the room. That was a mistake and brought ridicule from the other attendees. Lorraine Hansberry said that there were a lot of "accomplished" people in the room, "But the only man who should be listened to is that man over there," referring to Smith. Kennedy directed his attention back to Smith, who went on about how he could never fight for his country because of the treatment he had endured, which incensed Robert Kennedy, who was extremely patriotic.[3]

The meeting continued, but Smith did indeed set the tone. Lena Horne said that Smith "just put it like it was." She exclaimed that he was articulating "the plain, basic suffering of being a Negro." It seemed that Kennedy was not relating to Smith, which prompted Hansberry to say, "Look, if you can't understand what this young man is saying, then we are without any hope at all, because you and your brother are representatives of the best that a White America can offer." She finished by saying that if Kennedy was insensitive to Smith, then there was "no alternative except our going in the streets."[4] Kennedy tried to ingratiate himself to the group by talking about his Irish heritage, which was a mistake, as they reminded him that their ancestry went back even further, yet the Kennedys were on top and they were still trying to find their place in society. Kennedy defended the actions of his Justice Department, to whom he referred as "special men." Baldwin said that there was a disconnect and Robert Kennedy did not "understand our urgency." Kenneth Clark, another attendee, remembered, "Bobby became more silent and tense, and he sat immobile on the chair. He no longer continued to defend himself. He just sat and you could see the tension and the pressure building in him."[5]

The meeting continued for three hours, and Robert Kennedy was taken to task by the people in the room for his civil rights policy. Kennedy remembered, "They seemed possessed. They reacted as a unit. It was impossible to make contact with any of them." Afterward Clarence Jones, Martin Luther King's lawyer, approached Kennedy and told him that King appreciated the way that he had handled the Birmingham affair. Kennedy responded, "You watched these people attack me over Birmingham for forty minutes, and you didn't say a word. There is no point in saying this to me now." Belafonte tried as well to make it easier for Kennedy, saying, "You have done more for civil rights than any one else." To which Kennedy responded, "Why do you say this to me? Why didn't you say this to the others?" Belafonte said that it would diminish his standing with the others.[6] It certainly demonstrated that politics permeated both sides of the movement.

The Baldwin meeting was a turning point for Kennedy in many ways. He said to Arthur Schlesinger when he retuned to Washington, "They don't know what the laws are — they don't know what the facts are — they don't know what we've been doing or what we're trying to do." Kennedy contended, "It was all emotion, hysteria."[7] Schlesinger contended that Kennedy began "to grasp as from the inside the nature of black anguish. He resented the experience, but it pierced him all the same. His tormentors made no sense; but in a way they made all sense. It was another stage in education."[8] James Hilty writes, "The meeting at least forced him to reconsider the notion that the experience of the Irish Americans or any white ethnic group could compare to that of African Americans." In addition, he experienced the "deeper, rawer emotions of racism." As a result of such an experience he "gained insight into the larger meaning of the civil rights movement itself."[9] This new revelation was important to the movement, because it brought Robert Kennedy closer to the ideals embodied within the movement. This is significant because he could influence his brother to make a greater commitment to the movement. Robert Kennedy came away from this episode similarly to the way he did during the campaign when his brother called Coretta. First he was enraged. However, upon further reflection, he acted on his morals and sense of justice. In fact, just a few days after the meeting, he told Edwin Guthman that if he had grown up black he would have felt the same as Baldwin and the others in the group.[10]

Robert Kennedy acknowledged that the Birmingham crisis was a pivotal point in the movement. "What Bull Connor did down there, and the dogs and hoses and the pictures with the Negroes, is what created in the United States that more needed to be done." Kennedy said in 1964 that very few people had been concerned about civil rights until this crisis. Kennedy also talked about this conversations with the president. He said, "Perhaps because of brothers, or whatever it might be, we didn't make speeches to each other or even discuss the fact which was obvious — I mean, reach the conclusion that legislation was necessary." Kennedy said that sending Marshall down there to work with the leaders was the first step and the most that they could do constitutionally.[11] After sending Marshall there was a discussion of what kind of civil rights legislation they could get through Congress. Robert Kennedy recalled that they asked themselves, "What kind of legislation could we get by? What kind of legislation would deal with this kind of problem? What kind of legislation could we associate with this difficulty? That's the basis of the legislation that we sent up."[12]

Soon after Birmingham and the meeting in New York with the Baldwin group, Robert Kennedy started discussing with Burke Marshall what sort of legislation would address these civil rights concerns. The settled on one that would address public accommodations to start and be rooted in the commerce clause of the Constitution.[13] Robert Kennedy acted independently from President Kennedy. "I think that what we wanted to do was to deal with the problem," he remembered. RFK argued that there were two ways to deal with it: "either to protect people, which is what had been generally suggested, or deal with the substantive problem that caused these difficulties." Under the Constitution, it was very difficult for the federal government to intervene where the local officials were supposed to act. "Therefore," Kennedy said, "what was acceptable was to try to get to the heart of the problem." Kennedy reasoned that in the wake of Birmingham, "people were enough concerned about it, and there was enough demand about it, that we could get to the heart of the problem and have some chance of success."[14]

At this point in the presidency the Kennedy brothers were invested in finding some solution to the civil rights dilemma. The president had already claimed in his February 28 message to Congress that there was, indeed, a right side of this argument. That message coupled with the situation in Birmingham created a climate where they could at least test the waters for a larger commitment to civil rights. However, like Lincoln waiting for the right moment, Kennedy still needed an Antietam-like victory before he could issue any sort of legislation.

When the brothers discussed the legislation they wanted to do it without Martin Luther King. If King were involved it would seem as though he had forced Kennedy's hand. In fact, John Kennedy commented that they needed to meet with King after the legislation went to the hill, "Otherwise, it will look like he got me into it." Kennedy said further, "The trouble with King is that everybody thinks he's our boy, anyway. So everything he does, everybody says we stuck him in there." Kennedy concluded, "We ought to have him well surrounded.... King is so hot these days it's like having Marx coming to the White House."[15] John Kennedy was always the politician while Robert Kennedy genuinely looked to make strides in the racial divide that plagued the nation. Robert Kennedy said, "We were looking for solutions, and we abandoned the solution, really, of trying to give people protection."[16] The Kennedy brothers saw that strategy as reactionary and not laying the necessary foundation for the future to which they were committed. In the wake of the Cuban Missile Crisis and Ole Miss, the Kennedy brothers were hitting their stride, planning to set precedent, leaving a lasting legacy.

Robert Kennedy remembered that during the years he was in office many people believed that they should be doing more for the people in the movement. Critics believed that they needed to bring in more troops and marshals to some of these civil rights initiatives. "And we were resisting that all of the time, except when we had some legal basis for it ... and the situation warranted it." The climate after Birmingham was different. RFK recalled, "Well, now we had to do something to deal with this kind of problem, and the country wanted something done and would support action being taken. So that's why we moved in the direction that we did."[17]

The Kennedy brothers were like Lincoln in that they needed a victory to push the agenda they talked about in Georgetown on that snowy day. Birmingham had not been a clear victory. When Lincoln asked his cabinet in the summer of 1862 about the Emancipation Proclamation, there was a slight pause in the room. William Seward, his secretary of state, was the first to speak. "Mr. President I approve of the proclamation, but I question the expediency of its issue at this juncture." Seward said that he feared "it may be viewed as the last measure of an exhausted government." He said that they should wait "until the Eagle of victory takes his flight."[18] Lincoln used the bloodiest day in the war as his victory. On September 22, 1862, approximately 22,000 Union and Confederate troops fell at Antietam. Despite the heavy casualties, the Union held the field. Lincoln issued his Emancipation Proclamation. Birmingham set the stage for the nation to accept a civil rights bill. The Kennedy brothers would get their victory at the University of Alabama.

"I don't want another Oxford, Mississippi."

In the midst of dealing with Bull Connor and the demonstrations in Birmingham, Robert Kennedy was trying to avoid another standoff at an American university. George Wallace, the Alabama governor, had vowed not to let any African Americans into the University of Alabama in Tuscaloosa. It was a part of his campaign pledge to the people of Alabama. He made clear his position on segregation when he said, "I draw the line in the dust and toss the gauntlet before the feet of tyranny. And I say segregation now! Segregation tomorrow! Segregation forever!"[19] Robert Kennedy knew that there was a movement to send two students, Vivian Malone and James Hood, to the summer session at the university, and he wanted to meet with Wallace, in person, to avoid another situation like the one that took place in Oxford, Mississippi.

On April 25, 1963, Robert Kennedy, Burke Marshall and Ed Guthman went to Montgomery, Alabama. There was an army presence there that day, with state troopers surrounding the Capitol building. Robert Kennedy remembered in 1964 that the troopers were "unfriendly. And that was completely unnecessary, but the point was to try to show that my life was in danger coming to Alabama because people hated me so much."[20] Marshall remembered, "The meeting with the governor was bound to be unproductive because the first thing that he said when Bob came into the room was, that 'I'm going to tape this whole proceeding,' and he switched on the tape recorder. And it was all speeches."[21] Robert Kennedy said, "I don't think that the Union or the country means anything unless the orders of the land are enforced." Kennedy started with this lofty ideal and what the country represented. He asked Wallace, "Do you think it is so horrifying to have a Negro attend the University of Alabama?" Wallace responded, "I think it is horrifying for the federal courts and the central government to rewrite all the law and force upon people that which they don't want." He went further, saying, "I will never submit myself voluntarily to any integration in a school system in Alabama." The conversation went on with Kennedy emphasizing that he had a duty to uphold the Constitution. Kennedy wanted the matter handled in the courts. "I just don't want it to get to the streets. I don't want another Oxford, Mississippi." To that Wallace replied, "You folks are the ones that will control that matter, because you have control of the troops."[22]

The two men went back and forth on the issue of troops and federal authority. "We have a responsibility, Governor, to insure that the integrity of the courts is maintained," Kennedy said, ... "and all the force behind the federal government will be used to that end." In his characteristic way, Robert Kennedy wanted to prove to Wallace that he had the upper hand and would eventually use as much force as necessary to uphold the ideal that he felt was right. Wallace jumped at an opportunity to expose a possible plan by Kennedy to bring troops into Alabama, saying, "That is what you are telling me today, if it is necessary you are going to bring troops into Alabama."

KENNEDY: No, I didn't say that, Governor.

WALLACE: Well you said all the force of the federal government.

KENNEDY: To make sure that the orders of the court are obeyed.

WALLACE: I know, but all the force includes the troops, doesn't it?

KENNEDY: Well I would hope ... that we should be able to litigate a settlement.

Wallace kept pressing Kennedy, saying, "But it does involve troops if the law is disobeyed." At this point it is clear that Kennedy knew what Wallace was up to. From the start, Wallace wanted to record the conversation so he could release to the people of the state that there was a plan by Bobby Kennedy to send troops to the South. Instead of playing into his plan, Bobby turned the table on the governor, saying, "Well, I am planning and hoping that the law will be obeyed.... Maybe somebody wants us to use troops, but we are not anxious to."[23]

Wallace realized that this was a turn in events and made it clear what he wanted. "I can assure you of this: that I do not want you to use troops, and I can assure you that there is not any effort on my part to make a show of resistance and to be overcome." Kennedy replied, "I am glad to hear that." The meeting continued with Wallace pushing Kennedy to commit to either using or not using troops. Kennedy did not confirm either way. His main argument was one of the supremacy clause of the Constitution and the need to uphold any court order.[24] This was the foundation of his civil rights strategy from the start of the administration and he had not diverted from it yet. He planned to use the tools that the Constitution and the courts gave him to bring equal rights to all. Those tools were the "force" that Bobby was referring to. Kennedy remembered in 1964 that the meeting was difficult because there was no way for them to come to an agreement with the tape recording the whole conversation. Kennedy said, "It was necessary, then, for both of us to say things to each other that, on the basis that it was going to be played on the local ... radio station." He concluded, "At least for me, I couldn't let anything he'd say go by, sort of, as if it had been unanswered. It made it difficult."[25]

On May 17, 1963, Robert Kennedy made a speech at the Cold War Seminar in Asheville, North Carolina. The speech itself focused on the initiatives that the administration was taking to combat the Soviet Union. "The enormous global struggle which we call the Cold War is bring fought at every level," he said. Kennedy used the civil rights issues as a way to illustrate how America can be better. He said the democracy rests on rights and freedom of the individuals. "The aims of any governmental system can be described in idealistic terms. But what is their significance if such a system cannot correct injustice?" Kennedy used the racial issues in America as an example, quoting President Kennedy's message to Congress and the statistics about chances for African American citizens and success. He went on to say, "The most important fact is that our system *can* correct injustice because freedom of action in America carries with it civic responsibility. And the truth is that we must correct injustice, not because it is bad press around the world, but because it is injustice." He did concede, however, "The damage done to the United States in the eyes of the world press by incidents like Birmingham is great, [but] it is superficial. What really counts is how citizens of the communities of America respond to such problems." Here Robert Kennedy was using the racial issues as a point of strength. While our system may have been oppressive in some parts of the nation, there were people who were standing up for their rights, which was a very American thing to do, and it was applauded by the attorney general.

Robert Kennedy took this evidence further in his speech, saying that every person could be a soldier in the Cold War "by fighting to improve the soul and not just the face of America." He went on, saying, "For example, we must recognize, as responsible citizens and as responsible government officials, that the Negroes in this country — in the North as well as the South — will not tolerate indefinitely the injustices which flow from racial discrimination." Kennedy believed that there was larger responsibility that went beyond the demonstrations. Every American needed to make the civil rights movement their cause. Not only did he link this to justice for the African Americans, but he also considered that if people supported the movement, it would help the Cold War. "The American Negro is only beginning to raise his voice in protest. His protest is justified, and our responsibility is clear."[26] Kennedy's solidarity with the movement in the wake of the Birmingham riots was something that no other attorney general had demonstrated. It meant that Robert Kennedy had finally moved to a new phase in his development as a civil rights warrior. He felt that the movement was just and righteous. Not only did he want to support it as attorney general, he wanted to directly contribute to its success. He was in a unique position to do just that.

On May 18, 1963, President Kennedy made a speech at Vanderbilt University. The occasion marked the ninetieth anniversary of the university. Speaking about the role that the students would play in the future, President Kennedy said, "This nation is now engaged in a continuing debate about the rights of a portion of its citizens. That will go on, and those rights will expand until the standard first forged by the nation's founders has been reached, and all Americans enjoy equal opportunity and liberty under law." To be sure, Kennedy was speaking of the same issues that his brother had been the day before. In fact, he reiterated the theme of responsibility in the next section of the speech, saying, "But this nation was not founded solely on the principle of citizens' rights. Equally important, though too often not discussed, is the citizen's responsibility." This was a theme in the inaugural that had carried over into the administration. "The protection of our rights can endure no longer than the performance of our responsibilities. Each can be neglected only at the peril of the other. I speak to you today, therefore, not of your rights as Americans, but of your responsibilities." He went on to say that people in society have different responsibilities depending on their roles. Then he said, "Increased responsibility goes with increased ability, for 'of those to whom much is given, much is required.'"

Kennedy took this point further later in the speech when he said, "The educated citizen has an obligation to uphold the law." This was his way to complement his brother and maintain the axiom that law and order was the only way that American society could operate. With that came acknowledging the court and its decisions:

> Certain other societies may respect the rule of force — we respect the rule of law. The nation, indeed the whole world, has watched recent events in the United States with alarm and dismay. No one can deny the complexity of the problems involved in assuring to all of our citizens their full rights as Americans. But no one can gainsay the fact that the determination to secure these rights is in the highest traditions of American freedom.[27]

President Kennedy was working with his brother to get the message out that they supported the movement. Linking its success to victory in the Cold War and telling the future leaders of the nation that they had a responsibility to consider these rights is evidence that these leaders wanted to influence the movement and leave a legacy in civil rights. Moreover, they believed in this issue now and made it a part of their administration as well as a platform topic for the 1964 election. President Kennedy's insistence that the rule of law be adhered to as well as his solidarity with the movement by stating its actions were within the "highest traditions of American freedom" were unprecedented. The Kennedy brothers were finally making their case for the nation, indeed the world, about where civil rights and the racial issues that plagued America were headed. They wanted to be in the lead and on the right side of history.

"But we are committed to making that progress."

On June 3, 1963, Robert Kennedy went on the *Voice of America* program. After Kennedy spoke about all the progress the administration had made in the field of civil rights, he was asked in his interview why he thought African Americans were suddenly "demonstrating so vigorously and for their rights?" Kennedy responded, "Well, because I think they have lived for several hundreds of years in the United States and in many sections of the country they are treated as second class citizens, and the progress that should have been made has not been made." Kennedy was finally at a stage in his development where he was no longer concerned about Southern politicians or the ramifications to the domestic agenda for the Kennedys. This was the domestic agenda. By June 1963 the Kennedy were getting ready to make a big push on civil rights. "I think in the last couple of years real and major progress has been made," he said. He continued, admonishing others, "But I think frequently white people here in the United States have talked about this, have given lip service to the problem, and we haven't really done what we should have done. We haven't accomplished what we should have accomplished."[28] He concluded, "I think the record is bad." Perhaps Kennedy took what the Baldwin group said to him and saw that this movement had not been met by the government with the necessary, indeed just, support.

Kennedy believed that this was a big issue for the administration and pledged that he intended to keep moving in the right direction. "But now I think we are paying in the United States for the sins of the past. But we are committed to progress, as I say. It is going to require a great understanding by all races and by others who live in other countries." He went on, "No country is free of problems or difficulties or internal upheavals. We realize this is our greatest one. And we realize we haven't done what we should have done, and we are going to try and make up for it." This last comment is evidence that Kennedy had recognized what the Baldwin group had said to him and he would act on their behalf. This is a similar realization to the one that he had when the campaign called Coretta Scott King and he was furious at first, only to call the judge on Martin Luther King's behalf. He concluded, "But we are committed to making that progress. The government is, and the vast majority of people are."[29]

Kennedy made it clear to one interviewer that the Birmingham episode, with its graphic representation in the news, was something that was very difficult to fight. "I think that in those pictures are pictures of what actually has taken place in the United States, and we have had them in the past and in my judgment will have them in the future." He went on to say that there were many aspects of American life where African Americans had made progress: voting, education, and employment. "A lot has been done, but it is not glamorous, it is not attention making, because it just is statistics, so it doesn't receive the attention that the dog attacking a Negro or the policeman standing over a Negro woman [does]." Kennedy defended his record, but when it came to this type of publicity, he said, "We can't crush that. We can obtain more legislation which will be of some help, but I would mislead you if I said that is all going to disappear because what you have to do — it is not going to be done by governmental edict or the president of the United States saying we are going to stop this." Kennedy understood and presented the enormity of the problem. It went beyond mere legislation, the country needed to grow. "[President Kennedy] can't order people in a local area, local police, to take orders, who take orders and instructions of the local authorities, he has no control over them."

The civil rights issue was one in which the executive branch had been trying to define its role since Lincoln's assassination. Kennedy said that his brother could do something that might have an effect. "So what he has done, and has attempted to do, and will continue to do, is to give the leadership to the American people to show that we have to make progress in this field and that the United States Government and the United States people are committed to it." Kennedy continued by saying that it was unfortunate that those pictures went abroad and affected the United States' position in the world. "But that is only a secondary reason for doing what we have to do. The first reason is because it is the right thing to do, and as President Kennedy said, we are going to do this because it is the right thing to do."[30] Kennedy stumped the new message to the people of the nation and the world with this interview. He reiterated what his brother had said in the February address to Congress, which set up the larger address, which was only days away, on civil rights.

Kennedy made it even clearer that the policy of the administration was going in a different direction, when asked about the court's role in this process. He acknowledged that in the cases of the University of Mississippi and the University of Alabama, the court orders were important. "But in the last analysis, in my judgement, what is needed in these various districts and the various districts of the United States is people to accept their moral responsibility." He said that the federal government should not have to come in and force the people to accept integration. The people had to do this "because it is morally the right thing to do, and that we are all brothers and that we have to live as brothers. I think that as long as you have that, and understanding of that, and the acceptance of that in the United States, that is where real progress is going to be." Kennedy acknowledged that federal laws were important and necessary. "But in the last analysis, to make this thing work, men have to accept each other as brothers and realize this is the moral and right thing to do." This different way of looking at civil rights paved the way for politicians who were struggling themselves with how they should embrace the movement. Robert Kennedy crafted a message that was difficult for segregationists to beat. To be sure, he was talking to Wallace as much as he was the American people and the world. He wanted to bring the racial issues to a critical mass — forcing the nation to accept this as a moral issue. By doing this there was only one side that the people could choose — the right one.

In this interview Robert Kennedy also made it clear that President Kennedy was behind this move toward a moral approach. "I think he has come in personally," he said. While Kennedy did not reference the talk that JFK and he had when he was asked to be attorney general, he did acknowledge that he had a unique place in this administration. He said that as attorney general, and being in charge of the Civil Rights Division, "[President Kennedy] is in that extremely personally, the fact that his brother is the one that is involved in all these day-to-day details in connection with this matter. Obviously I wouldn't be doing anything in this field without his approval and his concurrence." He went on to say that all the major decisions from the marshals in the Freedom Rides to troops in Mississippi were made by his brother. In addition, he said that President Kennedy had spoken out on several occasions, referring to his Vanderbilt speech and the February message to Congress. "The stress now is on the problems that we have, and we do have problems. Tremendous things have been accomplished over the past two years."[31]

The Kennedy administration was ready for the confrontation with Wallace. In fact, they were in better shape than when they had confronted Ross Barnett. In addition, Ole

Miss gave them a precedent to cite as a successful integration. While Wallace pledged to stand in the front of the building blocking the student's entrance, Bobby Kennedy, Nick Katzenbach and Burke Marshall expected that and strategized a way to avoid another riot like there had been at Ole Miss. One way that the administration intended to stave off conflict was through a relationship that Robert Kennedy had fostered.

Kennedy knew the president of the University of Alabama. Dr. Frank A. Rose was a young, up and coming leader. Robert Kennedy had known him for the last ten years. The two leaders had received the Ten Most Outstanding Young Men Award in 1954 and had "corresponded and talked." In addition, Kennedy had worked with Rose's assistant and discussed the issues about the University of Alabama. Kennedy also had fostered a relationship with some on the Board of Trustees.[32] These were all tactics that he had not had at his disposal for the University of Mississippi. He also had not had the experience of Ole Miss as a learning curve. Kennedy was careful and deliberate with each move he made in this integration episode.

George Wallace was determined to defy the federal government in this instance. Dr. Rose had told Kennedy and Marshall that Wallace was going to be difficult, but that he would probably be able to get support from the board. In addition, Rose wanted to stay in touch with Kennedy. He was afraid that Wallace might "destroy the university."[33] Kennedy remembered in 1964, "[Rose] was on our side. He wanted to keep the university open, and he was anxious to make arrangements for ... these Negro students to be permitted to go to the university, and he was anxious to cooperate with us." However, Rose did not want his complicity known to the state of Alabama or the governor. "He wouldn't talk to us on the phone," Kennedy remembered, "but he'd come out of the state or come up and talk, meet..."[34] Robert Kennedy said that Rose was under "tremendous pressure" and had offers from other universities, "but he stayed at the University of Alabama because he didn't want to see [it] destroyed." That said, he did contribute to the "show" that the governor and other officials put on for the people of Alabama. For example, he put chalk lines down to help the governor get the best angle in the doorway for the camera crew. He also interfered with a plan to register the students at two different campuses by changing the times of registration so that Wallace could make both. Kennedy said, "I didn't mind the show so much. The problem really was what the show was going to consist of, what it was going to lead to. And that was the great problem for us, because the governor of Alabama, I guess, learning from what had happened to the governor of Mississippi, wouldn't talk to me, or talk to us."[35]

Kennedy was concerned about Wallace. He did not want to arrest him, but he kept receiving reports that he was "crazy" and "scared." Kennedy said, "What we were doing [was] playing, really ... a very difficult operation with him." Kennedy did acknowledge that at some level he helped him by calling up the National Guard. When President Kennedy nationalized the guard, they were already in position, which saved time. Marshals were never considered in this situation because Rose made it clear that Wallace would not step aside for the marshals.[36]

Nicholas Katzenbach was sent down to take the lead in the integration. President Kennedy was "consulted continuously," according to Robert Kennedy. One of the biggest issues was whether the administration would have to call out the army, and in fact Kennedy said, "Battle plans were made with the army and General Abrams, who was on the scene down there." In addition to that, the Justice Department had obtained an order against the governor that had the potential of at least six months in prison. Burke Marshall recalled, "I imagine that affected his actions somewhat." The Justice Department was not after Wallace. This was a way to get the governor to register the students. Kennedy said, "We wanted to get the students in. We didn't want to have to charge him [with] contempt, and we certainly didn't want to arrest him." He said that if they arrested him, they would "have to occupy Alabama."[37]

Robert Kennedy tried any possible alternative to creating a standoff at the University of Alabama. On June 8, 1963, he attempted to call Wallace and got an aide instead. The aide would not help RFK. To that, Kennedy said, "I thought we were going to handle it as civilized people?" He then informed the aide that there was nothing to negotiate and that two black students would be attending the University of Alabama.[38] Robert Kennedy was ready for a confrontation. He had the court order and the National Guard was already in position, ironically ordered there by Wallace himself. Kennedy and his Justice Department officials prepared for the standoff, which would take place three days after Kennedy's call to Wallace on June 11, 1963.

Robert Drew made a documentary of the events that took place leading to the confrontation between Wallace and Kennedy. The film was titled *Crisis: Behind a Presidential Commitment.* It opened with Bobby in his Hickory Hill home, at the breakfast table with his children. He left the breakfast table to take a call, presumably about Wallace and what he planned to do to stop Malone and Hood. The film went back and forth from Hickory Hill to the governor's mansion in Alabama. Bobby kissed his children goodbye and left for the White House. Drew filmed Wallace saying, "This is a moral issue.... I believe that separation is good." Bobby moved into his large office where papers were strewn all over the desk. He rolled up his shirtsleeves and put on his glasses. Burke Marshall walked behind the desk and the two men looked at their strategy. Wallace was in a similar situation with his advisors, preparing for the standoff at the University of Alabama.[39]

With Katzenbach and Doar in Tuscaloosa managing the crisis on the ground, Robert Kennedy and Burke Marshall met with President Kennedy. Drew filmed the president in his rocking chair, listening to the possible solutions to the crisis and what his advisors believed that Wallace was planning to do. In addition, they spoke about a possible speech on civil rights. He didn't want to commit yet, and depended on Bobby to gauge when the appropriate time was to send such a message to the nation. Robert Kennedy did not want to have the same outcome that they had had at Oxford a year earlier, and looked at every possible scenario. President Kennedy was in constant motion as Marshall and his brother briefed him. They were debating whether they should federalize the National Guard. JFK moved around a lot and seemed impatient. He wanted to make a decision, but knew that he needed to wait for the right moment.

Katzenbach insisted that Wallace had every intention to stop them at the door. He led the group in Tuscaloosa. Kennedy and Marshall stayed in Washington, but they were in constant communication. At one point in the documentary, Bobby Kennedy was talking to Katzenbach and he got on the phone with Bobby's daughter Kerry. Bobby had his feet on his desk and sleeves rolled up again. When Kerry was finished the two men talked about the strategy to bring in the students. In the end, they decided that if they were turned back, they would not leave campus, but instead would escort the students to their dormitories. Meanwhile, President Kennedy would federalize the National Guard. Once in place, Katzenbach would use the Guard as protection and bring the students into the school for registration.[40] There were many factors that Kennedy, Marshall and Katzenbach had to figure out as the day approached. Robert Kennedy remembered, "We came up with the idea of ...

having Nick go in and, without the students, and ask [Wallace] to step aside. That permitted the governor to refuse entrance, but it also permitted us not to charge him with contempt because the students weren't there." Kennedy believed that it was important not charge Wallace. Equally important, however, "was keeping the students on campus."[41]

Kennedy commented on the complexity of this situation as "damned difficult." He believed that there were a lot of aspects to consider. First, they did not know how Wallace was going to respond. Also, they did not know "whether these Alabamians, who were members of the National Guard, would perform their duty," Kennedy said. Marshall remembered that they used any means to keep Kennedy and himself informed. The FBI "was instructed to watch the roads for people coming in from the outside."[42] This had been a factor at Oxford and they wanted to make sure that it was not a problem in Tuscaloosa.

Nick Katzenbach made his way to the entrance and read a statement to Wallace asking for Hood and Malone to be admitted. In front of cameras, Wallace also read a statement saying that he would not permit them to enter the school. He claimed that this was an "illegal usurpation of power by the central government."[43] Wallace refused to move. As planned, Katzenbach turned and went back to the car. He brought the students to the dormitories. In Washington, President Kennedy signed an order federalizing the National Guard. A few hours later, led by General Abrams, who would become a four star general and a member of the Joint Chiefs, the guard had Wallace step aside, and they escorted the students into the building. Robert Kennedy was listening to the events in his office, and once the students made their way to register, he lit a cigar.[44]

Kennedy and Marshall had worked hard, behind the scenes, to keep this integration peaceful and successful. Kennedy said that all the work they did in the three months prior to June 11 "had a big effect." They got in touch not only with politicians but also with businessmen. "We called, we broke down to a book the names of every company that had ... more than a hundred employees, a hundred and fifty employees in the whole state of Alabama." This was similar to their tactic in Birmingham, where Marshall talked to the local businesses, looking to integrate downtown. "Then all those names were distributed at a cabinet meeting to all members of the cabinet." Additionally, Kennedy got in touch with all members of the department and agencies in the government and they called everyone on the list, "just so they would understand the importance, ... what we were trying to do, understand their own responsibility."[45] This resulted in a great deal of pressure from businesses throughout the state on Wallace, to which he was not sure how to respond. The success of this integration led President Kennedy to make a historic statement about civil rights.

18. Marching Orders

"He urged it, he felt it, he understood it."

By the end of the University of Alabama crisis Robert Kennedy had made the full transition to embracing an agenda that focused on civil rights. He wanted his brother to speak out on the issue and provide leadership like no other president. Kennedy remembered in 1964, "After the problems in Birmingham, there was a feeling by some of us that the president should go on television and discuss this problem." It was not an easy proposition. He recalled that timing was an issue and, of course, what would be said to the people. In addition, the University of Alabama crisis was something of an enigma; "We didn't know that, whether, [it would be] like the University of Mississippi, the president would have to go on and announce the use of troops, or explain the fact that there had been violence." With all that in mind, Kennedy believed that they should wait. Indeed, like Lincoln had needed Antietam, the Kennedys needed a victory before they could announce any major legislation.[1] Prior to the success at the University of Alabama it was unclear how they would handle a speech on civil rights.

The success at the University of Alabama gave Kennedy the victory he needed to announce a civil rights bill. However, very few advisors wanted President Kennedy to put himself out there. Burke Marshall said, "Every single person who spoke about it in the White House — every single one of them — was against President Kennedy sending up that bill." Robert Kennedy, however, wanted his brother to make the address and send up the legislation. Marshall went on to say, "He urged it, he felt it, he understood it. And he prevailed. I don't think there was anybody in the Cabinet — except the president himself— who felt that way on these issues, and the president got it from his brother."[2] In fact while Ted Sorensen and other advisors were also supportive, Bobby Kennedy was the main person who persuaded his brother that this was the right thing to do. That said, it was President Kennedy who phoned Bobby just after the integration of the University of Alabama to say he was going on television at eight o'clock that night. Robert Kennedy, Burke Marshall and Ted Sorensen went to the White House to work on the speech.

President Kennedy already had an idea of what he wanted to say in the speech. Robert Kennedy had been in touch with the president all during the integration of the University of Alabama. "I called him about the fact that the governor stepped aside and let Nick come in ... if you look back over that period of time — it was really a pleasant moment after working so hard." The anxiety and tension over what Wallace would do was something that had haunted Kennedy. He said, "Nobody was certain until the time that [Wallace] did [step aside]. And I think it was then, really [that President Kennedy] finally decided to go on television."[3] Robert Kennedy, Burke Marshall and Ted Sorensen were charged with drafting what the president would say on television.

The civil rights speech was not planned out in the same Kennedy fashion as the inaugural or even the American University speech, which had been the day before. The American University speech was a divergence in Cold War thinking and looked toward peace and detente in the battle with the Soviets. It was possible that Kennedy saw a similar opportunity to lay out his domestic agenda with a speech on civil rights the same way he did with the American University speech for foreign policy. Sorensen was not ready for another major address. He took what Robert Kennedy and Burke Marshall gave him and started writing a draft for the president.[4]

The Kennedy brothers, Sorensen and Marshall met in the Cabinet Room to flesh out the speech further. Sorensen took notes and went back to his office to draft a speech. John and Robert Kennedy stayed in the room for about twenty minutes. Bobby remembered that JFK "thought he was going to have to do it extemporaneously, so the two of us talked about what he'd say in the speech. And he made notes ... on the back of an envelope or something." They worked literally up the to eight o'clock deadline. Sorensen worked on the speech until about five minutes to eight. After looking at it President Kennedy said he had "what he wanted." Robert Kennedy suggested that he still do some of the speech "extemporaneously."[5] With that President Kennedy faced the cameras and gave one of the most powerful civil rights speeches in the history of the presidency.

President Kennedy was happy to report to the American people that the University of Alabama had been integrated successfully and peacefully. He went on, however, to discuss the issue of rights further. From the start, Kennedy laid the foundation for a new way to see this rights revolution that was unfolding in America. "I hope that every American, regardless of where he lives, will stop and examine his conscience about this and other related incidents." Speaking with a notion of conscience, he made this an issue of right versus wrong. He continued, "This nation was founded by men of many nations and backgrounds. It was founded on the principle that all men are created equal, and that the rights of every man are diminished when the rights of one man are threatened." Kennedy's message was clear from the start: the rights of all individuals would be protected under the law. Kennedy went on, "When Americans are sent to Viet-Nam or West Berlin, we do not ask for whites only. It ought to be possible, therefore, for American students of any color to attend any public institution they select without having to be backed up by troops."

This was a paramount speech for the civil rights movement and paved the way for future legislation. Indeed this speech was something that Johnson needed when he took over the presidency and passed the Civil Rights Act in 1964. Touching on the two issues that had confounded the administration, Kennedy went on,

> It ought to be possible for American consumers of any color to receive equal service in places of public accommodation, such as hotels and restaurants and theaters and retail stores, without being forced to resort to demonstrations in the street, and it ought to be possible for American citizens of any color to register and to vote in a free election without interference or fear of reprisal.

These two aspects were the bedrock principles of the legislation that Kennedy sent to Congress and became the core of the act that was passed in 1964.

Kennedy went on to cite the same statistics from his February message to Congress. More importantly, however, told the America people that this issue was not regional, nor was it partisan. He also said that is was not a legal or legislative issue. He contended that the law could not make people see what it was right. "We are confronted primarily with a moral issue. It is as old as the scriptures and is as clear as the American Constitution." With this line, John Kennedy changed the nature of the racial discourse in the country. He led up to it brilliantly, defining the rights and freedoms held by citizens of the United States. Then he made this issue a moral, rather than a political decision, hence resting the responsibility on the shoulders of the people to change the environment that had been oppressive to many people in the nation. "The heart of the question is whether all Americans are to be afforded equal rights and equal opportunities, whether we are going to treat our fellow Americans as we want to be treated." Kennedy responded to the criticism that King and many other civil rights leaders had expressed. He asked, if an African American could not eat at the same counter as whites or send his children to the best schools, "if, in short, he cannot enjoy the full and free life which all of us want, then who among us would be content to have the color of his skin changed and stand in his place? Who among us would then be content with the counsels of patience and delay?" It was a show of solidarity that no American president had ever endeavored to demonstrate in public. He was the first, and his brother was a big influence on the decision to make such a speech.

The way John Kennedy dealt with this issue was similar to how Lincoln had dealt with the slavery issue during the Civil War. Both presidents needed to worry about the political implications their actions would have on the nation. While Lincoln was concerned about the border states and the integrity of the Union, Kennedy worried that his actions would cost him key support in the South, which would stymie his other domestic policies. Both presidents experienced a sort of evolution while in office. Lincoln was not an abolitionist, but embraced the concept of freeing the slaves because it was right. Kennedy was not a strong civil rights advocate, but at the behest of his brother and seeing the injustice in the nation, he eventually embraced his role as a civil rights advocate, committing his presidency to the task. In a direct allusion to Lincoln he said,

> One hundred years of delay have passed since President Lincoln freed the slaves, yet their heirs, their grandsons, are not fully free. They are not yet freed from the bonds of injustice. They are not yet freed from social and economic oppression. And this nation, for all its hopes and all its boasts, will not be fully free until all its citizens are free.

John Kennedy laid out his goals for 1964 in those two days in June. At American University he advocated for peace and understanding. In the Oval Office the next day he envisioned an American with civil rights for all.

Kennedy made his message even clearer by comparing the U.S. to other nations around the world. The Kennedy brothers were strong nationalists and believed in American ideals. Kennedy said,

> We preach freedom around the world, and we mean it, and we cherish our freedom here at home, but are we to say to the world, and much more importantly, to each other that this is a land of the free except for the Negroes; that we have no second-class citizens except Negroes; that we have no class or cast system, no ghettoes, no master race except with respect to Negroes?

Americans had a responsibility to the world to be leaders for freedom. From John Kennedy's perspective, they could not achieve that role if American citizens were not equal in the eyes of the law.

Kennedy went further, pointing to Birmingham and the fact that the United States government had made promises to African Americans in the wake of Lincoln's death.

Now the time has come for this nation to fulfill its promise. The events in Birmingham and elsewhere have so increased the cries for equality that no city or State or legislative body can prudently choose to ignore them. The fires of frustration and discord are burning in every city, North and South, where legal remedies are not at hand. Redress is sought in the streets, in demonstrations, parades, and protests which create tensions and threaten violence and threaten lives.

Kennedy pointed to these elements as a way to show the American people that the government had a responsibility to all of its citizens, not just the white ones. Kennedy's reference to the "fires of frustration and discord" are evidence that he was worried about violence overwhelming the movement and people getting hurt. He needed to act.

The Kennedy brothers wanted to contribute to the movement through legislation and by ensuring that the people obeyed the law. This was essential for there to be any real change in the nation. John Kennedy said, "A great change is at hand, and our task, our obligation, is to make that revolution, that change, peaceful and constructive for all." Kennedy made it clear his intentions: "I am, therefore, asking the Congress to enact legislation giving all Americans the right to be served in facilities which are open to the public — hotels, restaurants, theaters, retail stores, and similar establishments." Kennedy went on to say that he was looking for legislation that would empower the government to intervene in cases that involved desegregation and voting issues. He commended the many people who had devoted time to the cause and acted accordingly during these protests. "Like our soldiers and sailors in all parts of the world," he said, "they are meeting freedom's challenge on the firing line, and I salute them for their honor and their courage."

Kennedy finished, pushing for solidarity with the movement and the American people. "My fellow Americans, this is a problem which faces us all — in every city of the North as well as the South." He went on to say, "This is one country. It has become one country because all of us and all the people who came here had an equal chance to develop their talents." Kennedy hoped to make a connection with the many people in the nation who, as he said in the American University speech, "cherished" their children's future.

We cannot say to 10 percent of the population that you can't have that right; that your children can't have the chance to develop whatever talents they have; that the only way that they are going to get their rights is to go into the streets and demonstrate. I think we owe them and we owe ourselves a better country than that.

He asked for "help in making it easier for us to move ahead." He also alluded to Justice Harland, once again, saying that the Constitution should be "color blind." He finished by saying, "This is what we are talking about and this is a matter which concerns this country and what it stands for, and in meeting it I ask the support of all our citizens."[6]

Watching in Atlanta, Martin Luther King immediately drafted a response to Kennedy, saying, "I have just listened to your speech to the nation. It was one of the most eloquent[,] profound and unequiv[oc]al pleas for justice and the freedom of all men ever made by any president. You spoke passionately to the moral issues involved in the integration struggle."[7] The *New York Times* reported King saying that the address was "a hallmark in the annals of history." He reiterated what he drafted the night of the speech and added, "I am sure that your encouraging words will bring a new sense of hope to the millions of disinherited people of our community." Roy Wilkins, the executive secretary of the NAACP, said that Kennedy had done a fine job explaining the moral issue, but fell short in addressing discrimination in the workplace.[8] While there was jubilation in other parts of the nation, tragedy struck Jackson, Mississippi, as Medgar Evers was gunned down outside his home. His children pleaded with him, "Please, Daddy, please get up." As the neighbors moved Evers onto a mattress and into a station wagon he said, "Sit me up! Turn me loose." Those were his last words. The civil rights leader died an hour later.[9] Evers's death is another example how violent and out of hand the movement had gotten.

"...until full equality is achieved."

There was a great deal of political fallout that the president endured in the wake of the speech. The violence in the South, for example, was a problem abroad, and he had Dean Rusk, his secretary of state, counter these issues diplomatically. He lost a few points in the polls and suffered some setbacks in Congress. He stepped back, making room for the attorney general to take over the message for this fight. President Kennedy said that civil rights "has become everything."[10] Bobby Kennedy was confronted with demonstrators outside the Justice Department on June 14, 1963. Three thousand demonstrators said the Justice Department needed to hire more African Americans. Robert Kennedy did not appreciate the criticism given the fact that his brother's presidency was suffering and that it was at his behest that the president had made such a stand on civil rights. Jack Newfield remembered, "The hostility radiating from his blue eyes became even more intense," as Kennedy addressed the crowd, using a bullhorn. He said, "Individuals would be hired according to their ability, not their color." He reiterated those remarks on *Meet the Press* ten days later.[11] Robert Kennedy wanted to protect his brother's presidency, but he also wanted to do what was right. He went out and continued pushing the message that his brother had set out in his speech to the nation. There was finally some momentum in this field and he was willing to take a stand, outlining a method to rid the nation of Jim Crow.

In a June 16, 1963, editorial entitled "Civil Rights: 'The Fiery Trial,'" the *New York Times* said, "The country is now faced with a crisis of civil rights and a crisis of conscience." Alluding to Kennedy's speech it went on to say, "If we face this crisis as Americans instead of sectionalists, if we regard this as a national rather than a racial problem, the United States as a country and we as individual citizens will emerge stronger." The editorial did admonish Kennedy, saying that until that speech it had "moved too slowly and with little evidence of deep moral commitment." However, it went on to say that Kennedy "now demonstrates a genuine sense of urgency about eradicating racial discrimination from our national life." The editorial made it clear that it was Kennedy's job alone and that the nation needed to contribute to this movement. "For this is a national crisis," it argued. Making an allusion the racial problems of the nineteenth century that were still pervasive in American society, the *Times* wrote:

> The subject of President Kennedy's program is no less than President Lincoln's when he said, in his second annual message to Congress 100 years ago: "Fellow-citizens, we cannot escape history. We of this Congress and this Administration will be remembered in spite of ourselves. No personal significance, or insignificance, can spare one or another of us. The fiery trial for which we pass will light us down, in honor or dishonor to the latest generation."[12]

This issue had permeated both Lincoln's and Kennedy's administrations largely because there was very little leadership to make headway in race relations in the United States. Kennedy was the first president in one hundred years to make such a stand for equal rights under the law.

On June 19, 1963, President Kennedy sent the Civil Rights Act of 1963 to Congress with a message reiterating his speech to the nation from June 11. In addition to that speech, Kennedy alluded to the issues that he had addressed in his February 28, 1963, message to

Congress, in which he had outlined voting legislation, a Civil Rights Commission to enhance the government's authority, and an effort toward school desegregation. "Although these recommendations were transmitted to the Congress some time ago," he wrote, "neither house has yet had an opportunity to vote on any of these essential measures. The Negro's drive for justice, however, has not stood still — nor will it, it is now clear, until full equality is achieved." Kennedy was referring to the continued demonstrations throughout the nation. He wrote to Congress,

> The growing and understandable dissatisfaction of Negro citizens with the present pace of desegregation, and their increased determination to secure for themselves the equality of opportunity and treatment to which they are rightfully entitled, have underscored what should already have been clear: the necessity of the Congress enacting this year — not only the measures already proposed — but also additional legislation providing legal remedies for the denial of certain individual rights.[13]

Kennedy went on to outline the legislation for Congress, sending identical letters to the House and the Senate for their consideration.

President Kennedy started his message by stressing equal accommodations in public facilities. "Events of recent weeks have again underlined how deeply our Negro citizens resent the injustice of being arbitrarily denied equal access to those facilities and accommodations which are otherwise open to the general public." He went further, calling this injustice a "daily insult." Next, the president outlined efforts to confront school desegregation: "Many Negro children entering segregated grade schools at the time of the Supreme Court decision in 1954 will enter segregated high schools this year, having suffered a loss which can never be regained." He pointed to the socioeconomic ramifications: "Discrimination in education is one basic cause of the other inequities and hardships inflicted upon our Negro citizens." JFK also pointed to fair and equal employment, arguing, "Unemployment falls with special cruelty on minority groups." President Kennedy also called for biracial human relations committees in every city, which was an allusion to the effort in Birmingham, and the use of public funds for African Americans. "Simple justice requires that public funds, to which all taxpayers of all races contribute, not be spent in any fashion which encourages, entrenches, subsidizes or results in racial discrimination." These were the main aspects of the Civil Rights Act of 1963, which he hoped to push through Congress.

JFK finished his message with the same tone that he had used when ending his speech on June 11. He said that this bill would not solve all the problems of racial unrest in the nation. The country needed more than legislation, and it needed citizens to support such an endeavor. He said that the act was "imperative." He continued, "It will go far toward providing reasonable men with the reasonable means of meeting these problems; and it will thus help end the kind of racial strife which this nation can hardly afford. Rancor, violence, disunity and national shame can only hamper our national standing and security." He alluded to another president who had dealt with racial issues. "To paraphrase the words of Lincoln: 'In giving freedom to the Negro, we assure freedom to the free — honorable alike in what we give and what we preserve.'" Kennedy finished, emphasizing to Congress that it was not because of international issues, "economic efficiency" or "domestic tranquility" that they should enact this legislation, "but, above all, because it is right."[14] His message was communicated not only by him, but by the person who advised him to take stand on this issue — the attorney general. Robert Kennedy had his marching orders from President Kennedy.

When Robert Kennedy spoke in Philadelphia on June 21, 1963, to commemorate the document, he said that it was fitting "that we should pause to examine the meaning and the spirit of our Constitution now, at an hour in our domestic history that can only be described as a time of profound national unrest." His allusion to the civil rights issues within the nation was not lost as he followed up, after mentioning some of the great presidents and quotes about the Constitution, by asking, "What about the America we know now, at a time when the inadequate phrase 'civil rights' has come to reflect an urgent nationwide struggle for equality by the ten-and-a-half percent of our people whose skin is not white?" Kennedy argued that the Constitution set up the "basic particulars" of civil rights with the Thirteenth and Fifteenth amendments. "The time is long past when any sensible American could tolerate the denial of free voting rights to all races, or the existence of 'White Only' signs on public facilities — even by the narrowest interpretation, these things are unconstitutional."[15] Robert Kennedy finally had the support of the people and President Kennedy to publicly support the movement and to use the law to make a difference.

Kennedy pointed to the *Brown* decision, as he did in the May 1961 speech on Law Day, as an important decision that set the precedent to end segregation. He asked the audience, "But must we now wait, as intelligent modern Americans in a changing society, must we now wait for the Supreme Court to spell out each new particularity of civil rights for us?" He answered, "Whatever color we are, let us hope not." Kennedy said that the Constitution was not meant to be interpreted "word-for-word." He told the audience, as his brother did only ten days prior to this speech, "These are moral issues, not legal ones, and their constitutionality is a matter of common sense ... not in its words alone but in what those words imply, in the underlying truths it teaches." These are the basic tenets that Kennedy believed that the Constitution inspired. He said, "Racial discrimination is not worthy of us.... The shameful scenes of riot and bloodshed in Oxford last fall and Birmingham this spring, were only [symptoms] — outward manifestations of an inner disease. And the infection is by no means localized."

Robert Kennedy made it clear that the American people needed to take a stand together. "This is a national crisis, and it is immediate." He said that the federal government had done its part and planned on following up with further measures. However, when it came to morality, the federal government could not completely take the lead. "In an era of great social flux and upheaval, it would be idle for anyone to suppose that real enlightenment can be brought about by governmental edict." Kennedy finished by pointing to the "spirit" of the Constitution and saying that it would drive the age. This speech is an example of how the Kennedy brothers were working with each other not only to get this legislation passed, but also to take a leadership role in the revolution that President Kennedy had alluded to in his speech on June 11. It is a much different approach to civil rights legislation than the brothers had taken at the start of the administration, or even during the campaign. The Kennedy brothers were responding to the people's desire to see civil rights legislation. They contributed to a shift in popular opinion. Their rhetoric, combined with federal support for civil rights, was the final piece to make the movement valid in the eyes of the people. With that, they used that realization to bring true change to the nation.

"We can, we must and we will."

On June 26, 1963, Robert Kennedy continued his support of the Civil Rights Bill. He spoke before the House Committee on the Judiciary regarding the bill. To illustrate the volatility of the debate, there was a "total embargo" on the contents of the statement until 10:30 am that day. No person could even paraphrase, allude to or hint of its contents.

Kennedy started his statement by saying that this bill would "go a long way toward redeeming the pledges which this republic was founded — pledges that all men are created equal." He continued, "In this generation, we have seen an extraordinary change in America — a new surge of idealism in our life — a new profound insistence on reality in our democratic order." He started with a righteous tone, defending his position on the bill. "Much has been done. But quite obviously much more must be done — both because the American people are clearly demanding it and because, by any moral standard, it is right." The Kennedy brothers set forth a message that there was, in fact, a right and wrong position on this issue. They no longer advocated for an approach that would placate the Southern vote; neither did they express that federalism was an obstacle to support these efforts.

Kennedy once again pointed to the meaning of the Constitution and how it played a role in American society. "Nothing is more contrary to the spirit of the Constitution — and even to the spirit of common sense — than to deny the full rights and privileges of citizenship to people who are obligated." He said that the Constitution provides the means for redressing this inequity. "If we do not use those means, we compound the wrong."[16] He went on to say that the bill "embodies" President Kennedy's commitment for action on this issue. He referred to the three statements that President Kennedy had made on civil rights in 1963. In addition, he talked about how there had been demonstrations since the president's June 11 speech. "The demonstrations show not only that an ever increasing number of our Negro citizens will no longer accept an inferior status. They have drawn sharp attention to the handicaps which so many Negro citizens experience simply because they are not white."[17] Robert Kennedy went on to advocate for each part of the bill, as President Kennedy outlined it in his message to Congress that accompanied the bill.

Robert Kennedy argued that the provisions in this bill would offer rights to African Americans and bring better stability to the nation. With regard to public accommodations the attorney general said, "Many of the demonstrations I have mentioned earlier, and the violence which has sometimes accompanied them, stem from attempts by Negro citizens to gain access to such facilities." The attorney general went on to describe how the bill would rectify these matters. He also pointed to the Commerce Clause of the Constitution and the Fourteenth Amendment as giving Congress the authority to legislate on these matters, taking away the right for state and local governments to enforce Jim Crow laws. In addition, he cited the Supreme Court's rulings in favor of civil rights, which had never been overruled. Kennedy stressed that Congress had the authority to make laws regarding this, despite the claim by many that these facilities in question were privately owned, saying, "It is well established that a privately owned business is not exempt from government regulation where it is engaged in interstate commerce." Again, he pointed to the Commerce Clause as a legal means to make such law. He made it clear that federal intervention was necessary: "Discrimination in stores, restaurants and hotels is a daily insult to a large number of American citizens."[18] Kennedy then moved to school desegregation.

Robert Kennedy stressed the *Brown v. Board of Education* decision in 1954 and the subsequent decision that stated all schools must be desegregated with all "deliberate speed." The bill would give great authority to the attorney general to investigate and prosecute instances where these decisions were not being upheld. He argued that many involved in these cases were "prevented from instituting litigation by lack of financial resources, by the unavailability of adequate counsel, or by intimidation," and said this bill would help the Justice Department pursue these cases. He concluded by saying that the bill would "smooth the path upon which the nation was set by the *Brown* decision."[19] While he spent more time with public accommodations it was clear that Kennedy was still concerned about desegregating public schools, despite the Supreme Court ruling and his success at Ole Miss and the University of Alabama as well as other local schools in the South. Of course the previous issue was something that the administration was addressing for the first time, and there was no precedent for him to legally point to, which explains why he spent so much time on it.

Robert Kennedy turned to voting rights as his next point, saying, "We can, we must, and we will make strong and continuing efforts to guarantee all our citizens the right to vote without discrimination. In a democratic system such as ours the right to vote, and thus participation in the processes of self government, is in the long run the most fundamental right of all." He concluded, "Obviously, if Negroes could participate fully in the electoral process in areas where racial discrimination is most prevalent, their grievances would secure attention and legitimate demands would be speedily met." This had been Kennedy's position on voting rights since he took over in the Justice Department. The main reason why Kennedy pointed to this aspect of the civil rights movement early in the administration was that there were clear, legal means for the Justice Department to intervene. The passage of this act would give him even more power in this area and pave the way for more change.

A commission on civil rights, the use of federal funds, equal employment, and a community relations service were all discussed by Robert Kennedy. He concluded, "With respect to the bill in its entirety, it must be emphasized that racial discrimination is far too complex a problem to be solved overnight. It has been with us since before the United States became a nation, and we can not expect it to vanish through the enactment of laws alone." He stressed that the nation was in turmoil and that "this country can no longer abide the moral outrage of racial discrimination." The nation was at a critical crossroads. "If we fail to act promptly and wisely at this crucial point in our history, grave doubts will be thrown on the very premise of American democracy." Linking the bill to the success of American ideals was as important as starting his statement with the spirit of the Constitution. He finished by saying that this plea came not only from the courts or even President Kennedy. "This bill springs from the people's desire to correct a wrong that has been allowed to exist too long in our society. It comes from the basic sense of justice in the hearts of all Americans."[20]

Kennedy's statement was not only an endorsement of the Civil Rights Act, but also a statement on where his efforts at attorney general were directed. Moreover, it served as a springboard to tell the nation that these were his beliefs. In the past, once Robert Kennedy found his cause, he fought for it with gusto. Like the McCarthy or McClellan committees, he believed in this act and believed it was important that he play a role in bringing justice to Americans. While it may have taken him some time to openly discuss these notions, they were now a part of his charge as attorney general, forever linking his period in office with strong civil rights initiatives.

"I may lose the next election because of this. I don't care."

As Robert Kennedy pushed his bill through Congress, civil rights leaders rallied to make sure that this bill became law. In an effort to support this bill, these leaders decided that they would make a march on Washington, D.C. In an effort to head off this massive protest Robert Kennedy convinced President Kennedy to hold a series of meetings with African American leaders in the hopes of taking the heat off the president as a target for these protests.[21] On Saturday, June 22, Martin Luther King and other civil rights leaders met at the White House. At first, King was bombarded by Burke Marshall and Robert Kennedy, who told him that there were communists in his organization. J. Edgar Hoover, the FBI Director, had evidence that some of King's closest confidants, especially Stanley Levison, were communists, hurting King's prestige. According to Taylor Branch, Kennedy used this information "in order to gain a measure of control over King."[22] When Robert Kennedy's interviewer, Anthony Lewis, asked in 1964 if there had been any concern over King's affiliations with communists, Kennedy said "no." Commenting on the notion of communists infiltrating the civil rights movement, Kennedy said, "I think that there was a lot of feeling that the Negroes didn't know exactly what they wanted and that they were not very well led in certain cases, and then there were a lot of responsible ones, and then there were some irresponsible ones."[23]

The issue of Martin Luther King being tied to communists was something that plagued his relationship with the Kennedys. The principal people who were charged with being communists were Stanley Levison, a close advisor to King, and Jack O'Dell, a member of the SCLC. Robert Kennedy consulted the FBI on the evidence regarding these two individuals and even advised Burke Marshall to warn King about his affiliations with the men.[24] When the Kennedys looked to send the civil rights bill to Congress, Robert Kennedy increased the flow of reports about Levison and O'Dell. He wanted to have a full understanding of the situation before King came to the White House on June 22.[25]

President Kennedy also spoke with King about the issues with Levison and O'Dell. The president took King into the Rose Garden and made a similar warning to King about communists, saying, "I assume you know you're under very close surveillance." While King said little in response, the president also warned King about Levison. Kennedy was more concerned about his bill. He told King that the conservatives were against the march, and getting the bill through Congress was going to be difficult. "If they shoot you down, they'll shoot us down too. So we're asking you to be careful," President Kennedy said.[26] The fact that Kennedy linked King's success to his own is evidence that he saw this movement in broad terms and felt solidarity with the civil rights leader. It was also uncommon for a president to warn any citizen about surveillance. Kennedy had respect for King and saw his leadership as important to the passage of the bill.

The meeting moved to the Cabinet Room, where there were several civil rights leaders waiting for the president. President Kennedy went around the table, shaking hands and saying "hello" to each person. In the corner the attorney general sat with one of his daughters on his lap.[27] John Lewis remembered the meeting: "It was mind blowing for me to be there." He had just been elected as chairman of the SNCC. "Here I was, at the White House, meeting with John F. Kennedy, meeting with Bobby Kennedy."[28] The president made welcoming remarks, spoke about the historic nature of this meeting, and said that they had to get the civil rights bill through Congress. JFK pointed to low polling numbers since he had made the statement on civil rights. "I may lose the next election because of this. I don't care," President Kennedy said.[29] There was some other discussion on other matters, but ultimately Kennedy made it clear that he was committed to seeing this bill succeed in Congress. Kennedy was concerned about the march, saying that it might give those in Congress who were against the bill ammunition against the cause. "I don't want to give any of them a chance to say 'Yes, I am for the bill, but I am damned if I will vote for it at the point of a gun.'" He went on in response to a question asking if he supported the march, saying, "We want success in Congress, not a big show in the Capitol." King responded, "Frankly, I have never engaged in any direct action movement which did not seem ill-timed. Some people thought Birmingham was ill-timed." President Kennedy added with a smile, "Including the attorney general."[30]

Robert Kennedy was still worried about the communist aspect of the movement. Jack O'Dell originally resigned in 1962, but then after King's meeting with the Kennedys made it permanent. Levison also broke ties with King, saying, "The movement needed the Kennedys too much. I said it would not be in the interests of the movement to hold on to me if the Kennedys had doubts." However, he and King decided to stay in touch through Clarence B. Jones, a New York Lawyer.[31] Jones did not try to conceal this relationship, and King himself had told others of his conversation with Kennedy in the Rose Garden. In light of this Robert Kennedy met with Courtney Evans, liaison for the FBI, on July 16 and said that he was considering wiretaps on Martin Luther King and Clarence B. Jones.[32] However, when Evans gathered the evidence and requested the wiretap order to Kennedy, the attorney general had a change of heart. Evans wrote a memo to his superiors that Robert Kennedy "was now of the opinion that this would be ill-advised." Kennedy had reasoned that King was constantly on the move and that if the act was found out it could lead to embarrassment. There was not enough evidence to risk the tap. With that in mind Evans wrote in a memo that the Bureau would not take any action on King, either at home or office, "in the absence of a further request from the attorney general."[33] However, to make sure that King kept his promise to stay away from the communist element, Kennedy did approve the tap on Jones.[34]

Robert Kennedy did not believe that Martin Luther King was a communist. In an effort to stop those rumors in Congress he prepared a letter to Senator Michael Monroney of Oklahoma saying, "Based on all available information from the FBI and other sources, we have no evidence that any of the top leaders of the major civil rights groups are Communists or Communist controlled."[35] The Kennedys wanted to help King and the movement by keeping his affiliation with any communists away from the public. President Kennedy's warning is evidence that he saw the movement tied to his bill. He wanted to see success and believed that King was an important element to consider. Furthermore, Robert Kennedy's reluctance to put a tap on King's phone lines is another example where he wanted to trust the leader and was willing to publicly stake his reputation on the line with the letter to Senator Monroney.

On July 17, President Kennedy held a press conference about a variety of issues. One reporter said, "Mr. President, it's pretty generally acknowledged that your administration has done more for civil rights fundamental advances than any in many years. Do you find that the demonstrations which are taking place are a handicap to you, specifically the Washington march in August? Do you think that this will —" Kennedy stopped the reporter and gave his answer, saying, "No. I think that the way that the Washington march is now developed, which is a peaceful assembly calling for a redress of grievances, the cooperation with the police, every evidence that it is going to be peaceful, they are going to the Washington Monument, they are going to express their strong views." He continued, saying that it was in a "great tradition ... I look forward to being here." Kennedy made it clear that this demonstration was going to be peaceful. "We want citizens to come to Washington if they feel that they are not having their rights expressed. But, of course, arrangements have been made to make this responsible and peaceful." The arrangements were being organized through the Justice Department. Kennedy referred to other demonstrations where the National Guard had to get involved, so he stressed, "But I do feel also — so I have warned against demonstrations which could lead to riots, demonstrations which could lead to bloodshed, and I warn now against it."

In the same response, President Kennedy sent a message to Congress regarding his civil rights bill. There were many in Congress who did not want to see this march on Washington, because they thought that it would lead to violence. "Some of the people, however, who keep talking about demonstrations never talk about the problem of redressing grievances. I would hope that along with a secession of the kind of demonstrations that would lead to rioting, people would also do something about the grievances." Kennedy went on, "You just can't tell people, 'Don't protest,' but on the other hand, 'We are not going to let you come into a store or a restaurant.' It seems to me it is a two-way street." Kennedy pressed this issue not only as a show of support of the march, but also as a way to tell Congress that they had to act, because it could stop the violence. Kennedy implored Congress to act and said that his administration had been addressing these issues since the violence in Birmingham. He also said that since the White House had been involved there had been gains. He stressed, "So something can be done." He finished by saying, "So I would suggest that we exercise great care in protesting so that it doesn't become riots, and, number two, that those people who have responsible positions in government and in business and in labor do something about the problem which leads to the demonstration."[36]

In addition to endorsing the March Kennedy commented on the existence of communists in the movement. "We have no evidence that any of the leaders of the civil rights movements in the United States are Communists. We have no evidence that the demonstrations are Communist-inspired. There may be occasions when a Communist takes part in a demonstration. We can't prevent that." He went on to say, "But I think it is a convenient scapegoat to suggest that all the difficulties are Communist and if the Communist movement would only disappear that we would end this." He went on to stress his earlier point that neither he nor the attorney general could make the racial strife go away if they ignored it and stopped talking about it. "The way to make the problem go away, in my opinion, is to provide for a redress of grievances."[37]

President Kennedy's statement demonstrated solidarity with the civil rights leaders. His endorsement was important. Of course, Robert Kennedy and Burke Marshall had anticipated such a question. Robert Kennedy remembered, "We discussed it before, and we discussed it afterwards."[38] Burke Marshall believed, "It made a great deal of difference. I meant the fact that he took that attitude rather than the attitude that almost everyone in the Senate and in the Congress were taking and most of the government officials — most white people." Marshall went further, saying that it was important that President Kennedy take this approach to this March: "If he had publicly ... taken the attitude that ... was very widespread — that you can't possibly have several thousand or hundred thousand Negroes without having a riot, if he's viewed it that way, talked about these people that way, I would think the character of it would have been terribly different." Marshall concluded, "There would have been hostility towards him and towards the government." Robert Kennedy contributed to Marshall's point, saying, "There would have been a protest against the government ... instead of what it really turned out to be."[39] In an effort to continue to bridge the divide between the civil rights leaders and the Congress the attorney general addressed the Senate the day after the president's comments in that press conference.

On October 10, 1963, Robert Kennedy approved the first wire tap on Martin Luther King. He refused, at first, to install surveillance on his home in Atlanta.[40] He went ahead later to approve a request on King's home, with the caveat that they would revisit it in thirty days.[41] A document entitled "Communism and the Negro Movement" had been distributed widely, and Robert Kennedy took issue with it. He went to Hoover and said that it was "very, very unfair" to King and that it presented only one side. Kennedy was afraid that it would be leaked. He said he was concerned about the matter but said, "We wanted to obtain passage of legislation, and we didn't want to fail in the passage of legislation by a document which gave only one side." Hoover said fine and sent agents to obtain copies of the document.[42] In addition to King, Robert Kennedy approved wire taps on Bayard Rustin.[43] Despite Kennedy's defense of King, he approved the surveillance that would plague King for the rest of his life.

The issue with King and communists was not over yet. On July 29 Evans met with Burke Marshall and Robert Kennedy and presented a document entitled "Martin Luther King, Jr.: Affiliation with the Communist Movement." The report discussed King's relationship with Levison and even had King stating, "I am a Marxist." Of course the report came very close to the March on Washington, scheduled for August 28. In addition, Kennedy was trying to get the civil rights bill through Congress and stood by King in his letter to Senator Monroney. Kennedy noted that the while the reports were "disappointing — no hard evidence or documentation was presented to back up the assorted claims and characterizations." The FBI followed up with some other evidence against King, including the fact that many communist organizations were trying to infiltrate the March on Washington.[44]

"We must remove these injustices."

Robert Kennedy continued his statements before the Senate Judiciary Committee on July 18, 1963. He outlined the same topics as in his statement before the House. This statement, like the last, had a "total embargo" on it. Kennedy started his statement by saying, "We are in the midst of a great debate, — whether or not this nation, the champion of freedom throughout the world, can now extend full freedom to twenty million of our own citizens who have yet to achieve it." Kennedy stressed the importance of the legislation saying that there were parts of the nation where the National Guard were patrolling, keeping peace from racial strife. "This is what happens when long-standing legitimate grievances are not remedied under law. Great moral damage is done to individuals, to communities, to the state and to the very fabric of the nation." He went on, saying, "Our responsibility as a nation is most plain. We must remove the injustices."

In his introduction Kennedy stressed that Congress had the ability to act and that history was on its side. "In the first place, the congressional power is clear beyond question under the commerce clause. The suggestion that Congress should not exercise the commerce power because there is an overriding moral issue makes no legal or historical sense." Kennedy said, "It is because of the importance of the moral issues that Congress should act if it has power to act." That last statement embodies Robert Kennedy's position on the civil rights movement. If there was a legal reason for him to act on behalf of the civil rights movement, he seized it to its full potential. The moral reasoning was an aspect of this act, but overall he believed that the law should be the main reason for action. He said that child labor, minimum wages, gambling and prostitution "all raise moral issues too, and all have been dealt with by Congress under the commerce clause." In addition to the commerce clause Kennedy stressed that the Fourteenth Amendment was the reason why Congress should get involved. Once again, Kennedy stressed public education, voting, community relations service, a civil rights commissions, the use of federal funds and employment. Kennedy finished by saying, "The time is long past — if indeed it ever existed — when we should permit the noble concept of States' rights to be betrayed and corrupted into a slogan to hide the bald denial of American rights, of civil rights, and of human rights." Kennedy also said, "We have a need, and for this need there exists a remedy. Whether the remedy will be supplied is up to Congress."[45]

Robert Kennedy was not the only one with marching orders to make sure that this bill got through Congress.

The March on Washington for Jobs and Freedom was the pinnacle moment in the civil rights movement. It brought leaders from every aspect of the movement to the same platform, speaking with one voice. Roy Wilkins of the NAACP, John Lewis of SNCC and Martin Luther King for the SCLC were only a few of the many people who led this historic march. On July 2, 1963, several civil rights leaders met at the Roosevelt Hotel in New York City. A. Philip Randolph of the Brotherhood of the Sleeping Car Porters and his lieutenant, Bayard Rustin, had a lot to do with organizing the event. There was also Roy Wilkins of the NAACP, James Farmer of CORE, Martin Luther King for the SCLC, John Lewis for SNCC, and Whitney Young of the Urban League. Randolph made it clear at the beginning of this meeting that this was something he had wanted for more than twenty years and that Rustin, who was asked to leave the meeting by Wilkins, was the person who could make it happen. Wilkins had misgivings mostly because of Rustin's background as a communist. In the end Wilkins agreed that Randolph would lead the march, and there was a compromise with support from King and others that Rustin would be his deputy. However, Wilkins said, "You can take that on if you want, but don't expect me to do anything about it when the trouble starts."[46] The issue of communists penetrating the movement was real, and Wilkins was right to question Rustin. If the march was a not a success it would have had large implications for the movement.

Robert Kennedy was committed to seeing that the march was successful. Burke Marshall remembered, "As it came, as it developed, it was clear that it was awfully disorganized in the beginning of the summer, and the president had publicly endorsed it, more or less." With President Kennedy's statement from July 17 the march was linked to Kennedy's bill as well as to the administration's commitment to civil rights. "The attorney general wanted to make sure it was a success, and it was organized right," Marshall said. He went on to say that while Randolph had taken a great deal of credit and rightfully so, "The person that organized it, as a matter of fact, was the attorney general, who assigned it to John Douglas," who dealt with the march full time for at least four weeks. Douglas handled some of the logistics, which contributed to the success. "On making sure that there were enough toilets around, that there was food, that the character of the people who were coming was in close touch with the police." Marshall concluded, "And so I think that made a lot of difference, all that work."[47] Robert Kennedy agreed with Marshall, saying that until the Justice Department became involved, "It was very, very badly organized." He went on saying that the Justice Department kept track of the "people who were Communists and who might get involved around the country" and that they also worked with Roy Wilkins to determine who some of those individuals were.[48]

The March on Washington was a huge success. On August 28, 1963, people of all races marched on the Lincoln Memorial in support of jobs, freedom and Kennedy's civil rights bill. A CBS camera mounted on the top of the Washington Monument showed the crowd gathering around the reflecting pool. Some counted an upwards of 500,000 people surrounding the Lincoln Memorial.[49] In addition to the civil rights groups, Kennedy involved organized labor and white religious leaders. In an effort to keep the crowd controlled it was Robert Kennedy who favored the Lincoln Memorial rather than the Capitol. It certainly would help his case in Congress if he kept the demonstrators at bay. The reflecting pool, he believed, reduced the possibility of violence. In addition to that, Kennedy closed Washington's bars and liquor stores.[50] Many who spoke denounced the administration's efforts at civil rights reform. James Bevel of the SCLC said, "Some punk who calls himself the president has the audacity to tell people to go slow. I'm not prepared to be humiliated by white trash the rest of my life, including Mr. Kennedy."[51] The one speaker, however, who was asked to change his speech was the SNCC's John Lewis.

John Lewis's speech was seen as inflammatory and, some believe, had the potential to embarrass the administration. Washington's archbishop Patrick O'Boyle, who previewed the speech early, saw the remarks as "incendiary" and sent the draft to Burke Marshall.[52] Robert Kennedy read a copy of the speech and saw it as "inflammatory and [a] radical attack on the country and the president." Kennedy wanted Lewis to revise it.[53] In addition to Marshall, O'Boyle and Kennedy, Walter Reuther, the labor union leader, also believed that Lewis's speech went too far. Both he and Marshall edited the draft. Marshall, riding in a police motorcycle sidecar, brought the new version to Lewis at the Lincoln Memorial.[54] In addition to Marshall and Reuther working on the speech, other civil rights leaders met at the Lincoln Memorial to change the language because it did not represent the spirit of the march. Among those leaders was the Reverend Eugene Carlson Blake of the National Council of Churches, a white pastor who was arrested during the movement. He had particular objections to the language. The largest issue with the speech was the use of the terms "revolution" and "the masses," which clearly had a communist connotation. However, A. Philip Randolph defended the language, saying that he had used it for years. Next was the imagery of "Sherman's March" and "scorched earth" as the SNCC made its way through the South, nonviolently. King commented, "John, I know you as well as anybody. That doesn't sound like you."[55] Lewis remembered that Roy Wilkins was "having a fit." Wilkins believed that the SNCC just wanted to be different. He got in Lewis's face, saying that he was "double crossing" him. Lewis shot back, "Mr. Wilkins, you don't understand. I'm not just speaking for myself. I'm speaking for my colleagues in SNCC, and for the people in the Delta and in the Black Belt. You haven't been there, Mr. Wilkins. You don't understand." At that point Bayard Rustin got in between them.[56]

This speech had caused the most anxiety of the day, and A. Philip Randolph was determined that it not hurt the spirit of the march. He approached Lewis and said, "John. We've come this far together. Let us stay together." With that Lewis and James Forman sat with a portable Underwood typewriter and edited the speech. Lewis wrote later that he was angry after the edits, but "The speech still had fire." He used the word "citizens" instead of "masses." He believed that his message was "not compromised." Finally it was his turn. "Brother John Lewis," Randolph said after his introduction of Lewis to the crowd. Lewis remembered looking out at the "sea of faces" and feeling a "combination of great humility and incredible fear. I could feel myself trembling a little bit."[57] Despite his misgivings about the drama leading up to the speech, Lewis left his mark. "We will not stop," he said as he closed his speech. "If we do not get meaningful legislation out of this Congress, the time will come when we will not confine our marching to Washington." He continued, "We will march through the South, through the streets of Jackson, through the streets of Danville, through the streets of Cambridge, through the streets of Birmingham. But we will march with the spirit of love and with the spirit of dignity that we have shown here today." Lewis was still getting to say what he wanted: that this movement was something that needed to be addressed by the leaders of this nation and be taken seriously. He finished by saying, "We must say, 'Wake up, America. Wake up!!! For we cannot stop and we will not be patient."[58]

John Lewis came from a sharecropping family in the South. He was among those most affected by this racist attitude in the nation. His journey from Nashville in 1960 to the steps of the Lincoln Memorial in 1963 are a testament to the American dream. While there was still a great deal to be done — and he would play a role in those events — John Lewis embodied the spirit of the movement. His speech, like his actions, came from the heart of the angst of the civil rights movement, which was why his ascension to leadership was so important.

The next highlight of the march made history. Martin Luther King, Jr., prepared his speech in the Willard Hotel the night before. He wanted to pay homage to Lincoln so he started the speech with, "Five score years ago, a great American, in whose shadow we stand today, signed the Emancipation Proclamation." He continued to work on the speech, using some of the themes and language that he had used in other speeches from the movement. All night he worked at using the common refrain, "With this faith.... With this faith." King was not satisfied with this and gave his handwritten draft to Wyatt Walker to be typed the next morning.[59] When King finally made his way to the podium for his speech all the major networks were covering the event. ABC, NBC and CBS broadcast the speech live. He recited his prepared text verbatim until he had said, "We will not be satisfied until justice runs down like waters and righteousness like a mighty stream." King went off the prepared the text when he started his famous line, "I have a dream." From that moment, the crowd and King worked off each other. King's words had an impact on the people and the people shaped his next verse. He was able to bring in the phrase "with this faith" and used the song "My Country 'Tis of Thee" as a way to bring out the true meaning of the nation, thus linking it to the success of the movement and a promise to future generations to enjoy freedom and equality. He took the final line, "Let Freedom Ring," and linked it to parts of the nation, bringing home the notion that the people of the U.S. were all connected and this movement was something in which every American from New Hampshire to Georgia should have a stake. He finished by saying that when we finally "Let Freedom Ring ... we will be able to speed up that day when all God's children, black men and white men, Jews and Gentiles, Protestants and Catholics, will be able to join hands and sing the words of the old Negro spiritual. 'Free at last! Free at last! Thank God Almighty, we are free at last.'"[60]

Dr. King's speech was the highlight of a day that was already historic. Robert Kennedy remembered that President Kennedy watched "a good part of the march on television in Washington, and saw Martin Luther King speak. Oh, he made a helluva speech."[61] President Kennedy said to one of his aides in the White House, "He's damn good." When he met with the leaders of the march later that day, he welcomed King by saying, "I have a dream." Kennedy was impressed that King went off the text and valued a good line in a speech.[62] The meeting was more about the civil rights bill than a review of the march. Roy Wilkins tried to flatter JFK, calling him "politically astute." He was getting him ready to make a push for a stronger bill. Wilkins and then Randolph asked Kennedy to add a section banning racial discrimination in employment. The issue of employment was an epidemic to young African Americans. Randolph said, "I may suggest to you that they present an almost alarming problem — they have no faith in anybody white. They have no faith in the Negro leadership. They have no faith in God. They have no faith in the government. In other words, they believe the hand of society is against them."[63]

Kennedy stressed that the civil rights bill suffered from a great deal of resistance from many lawmakers. He had a count done during the meeting. Randolph said, "It's obviously going to take nothing less than a crusade to win approval for these civil rights measures." Kennedy agreed, but Randolph also pointed to Kennedy's importance in this fight, saying,

"Nobody can lead this crusade but you." He wanted Kennedy to take the message to the voters and bypass Congress. Kennedy responded, "I think it would be helpful if you gentlemen indicated as you would here that this is a matter that ... involves both parties." Kennedy pushed for civil rights leaders to lobby both parties, as it was difficult to get the Republicans on board with the bill. King said very little at this meeting as it was mostly about the politics surrounding the impending legislation. He did suggest that a "private moral appeal" might influence President Eisenhower to reach out to the Republican leadership. Kennedy replied, "No, it won't. No, it won't." The Reverend Blake, however liked the idea, and Kennedy sent him to Gettysburg, hoping it might pan out.[64]

In the wake of the March on Washington there were several civil rights incidents prompting action from the Kennedys. First, on September 2, 1963, Alabama governor George Wallace issued an executive order that prevented the opening of Tuskeegee High School, which was supposed to be desegregated. Much to the dismay of the local officials, Wallace surrounded the school with state troopers. All throughout the South, African American students were entering white schools, but in Alabama, Wallace stood firm and declared that he would not relent on his pledge to uphold segregation. There was a bombing of the home of Arthur D. Shores, an African American lawyer in Birmingham. Robert Kennedy ordered the FBI to investigate the bombing.[65]

Wallace continued sending state troopers to schools that were planned to be desegregated that fall. One police chief in Huntsville called his actions a "tyrannical use of power." On September 8, Wallace went on television to say that he would not longer interfere with the integration. However, the Justice Department had federal judges prohibit him from halting desegregation. With that order, determined to defy federal courts, Wallace called out the National Guard.[66] In the midst of fighting Congress over the language in the civil rights bill and on the heels of the March on Washington, President Kennedy had had enough. "It should be clear that United States government action regarding the Alabama schools will come only if Governor Wallace compels it," President Kennedy said in a September 9 statement. Kennedy said that there were 144 school districts that were desegregating peacefully. "In the State of Alabama, however, where local authorities repeatedly stated they were prepared to carry out court directives and maintain public peace, Governor Wallace has refused to respect either the law or the authority of local officials." Kennedy stressed, "For his own personal and political reasons — so that he may later charge federal interference — he is desperately anxious to have the federal government intervene in a situation in which we have no desire to intervene."[67]

President Kennedy put the responsibility on Wallace, implying that this was another tactic in this game of "cat-and-mouse" for human rights in the country.

> The governor knows that the United States government is obligated to carry out the orders of the United States court. He knows that the great majority of the citizens in Birmingham, Mobile, Tuskegee, and Huntsville were willing to face this difficult transition with the same courage and respect for the law as did the communities in neighboring states. And he knows that there was and is no reason or necessity for intervention by the federal government, unless he wishes and forces that result.

Kennedy finished by saying, "This government will do whatever must be done to see that the orders of the court are implemented — but I am hopeful that Governor Wallace will enable the local officials and communities to meet their responsibilities in this regard, as they are willing to do."[68] Kennedy followed this statement the next day by federalizing the National Guard units who surrounded the schools in those four cities.[69] Kennedy's actions made it clear that Wallace's charade was futile. Unfortunately, that would not be the last time that Alabama was in the news that month.

On September 15 a bomb exploded at the Sixteenth Baptist Church in Birmingham, Alabama, killing four girls. President Kennedy immediately sent Burke Marshall to Birmingham. In addition, he issued a statement the next day admonishing the climate that Wallace and other officials had fostered in that state, saying, "It is regrettable that public disparagement of law and order has encouraged violence which has fallen on the innocent. If these cruel and tragic events can only awaken that city and state — if they can only awaken this entire nation — to a realization of the folly of racial injustice and hatred and violence, then it is not too late for all concerned to unite in steps toward peaceful progress before more lives are lost." He recognized the role that African American leaders played in these events, saying, "The Negro leaders of Birmingham who are counseling restraint instead of violence are bravely serving their ideals in their most difficult task — for the principles of peaceful self-control are least appealing when most needed." He finished by saying, "This nation is committed to a course of domestic justice and tranquility — and I call upon every citizen, white and Negro, North and South, to put passions and prejudices aside and to join in this effort."[70]

Robert Kennedy remembered in 1964 that issues such as this bombing could have been prevented with better leadership. He acknowledged that it was Klansmen who set off the bomb, killing those girls, but there were others who were culpable. He said, "In Alabama it's George Wallace, the political and business leaders and newspapers. They can all deplore it. In the last analysis, I think they're the ones that created a climate that made those kinds of actions possible." Kennedy concluded, "Otherwise they wouldn't have occurred."[71]

Robert Kennedy continued his support for the civil right bill with several speeches. He spoke at the annual meeting of the Missouri Bar Association in Kansas City, Missouri, on September 27. He applauded the group, saying that all he knew about the group suggested "courage, high principle, and true engagement of the social realities of our time." He exclaimed that if the rest of the nation shared these ideals, "our nationwide problems in civil rights would be much less severe than they are." Kennedy went further with a discussion on the importance of testing the rule of law and the implications of court decisions. He focused on the *Brown* decision, saying that patterns in the world and America "pointed to the abolishment of the 'separate but equal' concept and reform established by the Brown decision was all but inevitable." He went on to say that the decision was what "the vast majority of the American public holds to be morally correct." Further, he contended that reversing that decision was "beyond the point of reason."[72]

Kennedy continued his message on the civil rights bill with a speech at the Conrad Hilton Hotel in Chicago on October 13. In that speech, which was a celebration of the 120th anniversary of B'nai B'rith, he stressed Franklin Roosevelt's four freedoms: freedom of speech, freedom to worship, freedom from want and freedom from fear. He contended, "Before these four freedoms are secure, we would add two new freedoms to the galaxy by which our course is charted — freedom to learn and freedom of opportunity." Kennedy's allusion to FDR's Four Freedom speech was an attempt to show Americans that the civil rights bill was meant to continue the notions of freedom for all. He said, "There can be no freedom from want without freedom of opportunity; there can be no freedom of opportunity without freedom to learn; there can be no freedom from fear unless each of the other freedoms is attained." He quoted Abraham Lincoln, who said, "Those who deny freedom to others deserve it not for themselves, and, under a just God, cannot long retain it." He exclaimed that if the civil rights bill was passed it would "go a long way toward removing inequities and injustices which are keenly felt by Negroes."[73]

Two days later, Kennedy addressed the House Judiciary Committee. He contended, "Every day of delay aggravates the problems of discrimination by hardening resentments and undermining confidence in the possibility of legal and peaceful solutions." He stressed, "The need for Congressional action and Congressional leadership is greater now than ever." He called the movement a "national crisis" and said that failure to act would have "tragic consequences."[74] He followed up those remarks with an address at the Annual Convention of the Theatre Owners of America.

On October 28, Kennedy continued his message that the civil rights bill was important for all Americans. While he was directed by John Kennedy to take the lead on this initiative, it was clearly something that he believed was important, and he was committed to seeing it through. He said to these people who owned and operated theaters in the South that the civil rights movement was "nationwide" and "something that must concern us all." He implore these owners, saying, "You know that the time is long past — if indeed it ever existed — when any opposition to civil rights could be argued on moral grounds." Kennedy said that the argument about whether or not the federal government had a role to play in private business was something that would "impede" the passage of the Civil Rights Act. He said that all social problems needed "responsible leadership at the community level." He stressed that they were respected in their communities and were "well qualified to be leaders." Kennedy acknowledged that there were many in the crowd who were pro-segregation. However, he wanted to be clear that the Civil Rights Act's "purpose it to assure that no man, woman or child in America will be discriminated against because of race, creed or color." He finished by saying, "If the disgrace of racial discrimination is to be purged from our land, in our time, it won't be a triumph of government alone. It will be the triumph of civil leadership in every American city and town — leadership of the kind so many of you have already shown — leadership by men responsive to the call for funda-mental human justice."[75]

The Kennedy brothers followed through on their promise to change the climate of the nation. Much of what they had done in 1963 was at the behest of civil rights leaders, but they also came into their own, establishing a strong voice for civil rights legislation and leading politicians into the fight for equality under the law. However, with that fight and these acts came political consequences. One such reality was that the South would be difficult to win in the next election. While polls had Kennedy picking up an additional 580,000 African American votes in the next election and showed an approval rating of 89 percent among African Americans, he lost ground with white Southerners.[76] Unwilling to lose the South, Kennedy started to campaign in those states. One of the cities was Dallas, Texas.

Toward the end of 1963, the Kennedy brothers were committed to civil rights reform. Their perseverance was something that sent new legislation to Congress. They were civil rights warriors and paved the way for others to continue that fight, ushering in change to America. Those actions changed the climate of the nation. The rights revolution in America was born from the civil rights movement. To be sure, the leaders of that movement played an integral role in the success and impact of its many actions. Robert Kennedy, however, was the linchpin that brought not only the Justice Department, but also the president as an ally in this movement. His commitment and determination made the ultimate difference that laid a foundation for other movements and brought America into a new era.

Epilogue: 1964 — Bobby and Ted

"His heart and soul are in this bill."

On November 22, 1963, John F. Kennedy was murdered in Dallas, Texas. This tragic event affected America in a multitude of ways. As the nation mourned, Robert Kennedy took up the torch passed on by his brother and assumed a leadership role for the nation and his family. The Kennedy assassination had a particular effect on civil rights legislation. James Hilty contends that it was very important to Robert Kennedy who got credit for the civil rights legislation. Robert Kennedy had hoped that the history books would credit him for "righting a terrible wrong and glorifying his brother's memory at the same instant with the passage of the act."[1] In the wake of the assassination, Robert Kennedy contemplated how the bill would get passed. Once president, Lyndon Johnson gave him a great deal of authority with the bill.

While it seemed that the bill would get passed in the House there was some consternation about the Senate. John Kennedy—and Lyndon Johnson afterward—both asked Robert Kennedy, "Where are we going to get the votes?" Robert Kennedy remembered in 1964 that President Johnson did not take an active part in the bill. "I had some conversations with him. I felt not only did I want to get a civil rights bill by, but I wanted to get it by for personal reasons, you know, because I thought that was so important for President Kennedy." In addition, President Johnson told the people in the Senate committee who were reviewing the law that they could not do anything without Bobby's approval. Johnson reiterated that to Robert Kennedy, saying, "I'll do on the bill just what you think is best to do on the bill. We'll follow what you say we should do on the bill. We won't do anything that you don't want to do on the legislation. And I'll do everything you want me to do in order to obtain the passage of the legislation." Burke Marshall contended that the reason Johnson was so giving was that "he didn't think we'd get the bill."[2] Robert Kennedy added that not only did Johnson believe that he could not get the bill passed, but also "he didn't want to be the reason, have the sole responsibility. If I worked out a strategy, if he did what the Department of Justice recommended, ... then, if he didn't obtain the passage of the bill, he could always say that he did what we suggested and didn't go off on his own." Kennedy also stressed that Johnson was a Southerner, and that had political ramifications. Also, their relationship was so "sensitive" at the time that Kennedy thought "He probably did it to pacify me."[3] This politician was different than John Kennedy. President Kennedy was willing to risk his own legacy at the behest of his brother, but Johnson was not going to do that.

While the bill was being debated in Congress, Robert Kennedy had to contend with the loss of his brother, which had an effect on both his personal and professional life. He had spent the better part of the previous four years with his brother. Their families spent time together and they worked together in many situations ranging from the Bay of Pigs to the Freedom Rides to the Ole Miss crisis to the Cuban Missile Crisis and Birmingham. Their relationship was unique in American history, and the sudden end to such a collaboration had many effects that continued to reverberate throughout the twentieth century. On November 22, 1963, he had received the phone call from J. Edgar Hoover at his home. The FBI director said, "I have news for you. The president's been shot." Later Hoover called back and told Robert Kennedy that John Kennedy was dead.[4] He said to Charles Spaulding, "God it's so awful. Everything was really beginning to run so well." Robert Kennedy spent the night in the Lincoln Bedroom. Sobbing, he could be heard saying, "Why, God?"[5] Of course, he was not the only one to lose a brother.

Edward M. Kennedy was an up-and-coming senator from Massachusetts. He occupied the same seat as his older brother before him, and had similar ambitions. Ted Kennedy was in the Senate on November 22 when the press liaison officer, Richard Reidel, said, "You'd better come over." The youngest Kennedy brother saw the news of the shooting over the Associated Press printer. He tried to call Bobby, his wife, anyone, but the lines were dead. When he finally talked to his brother at Hickory Hill, Bobby confirmed that their brother was dead.[6] On April 9, 1964, he decided to make his "maiden speech" before the Senate in support of the civil rights bill. "It is with some hesitation that I rise to speak," he started. "A freshman senator should be seen, not heard; should learn and not teach." Kennedy said in his memoirs years later, "It seemed to me that civil rights was *the* issue and this was *the* time." With that Kennedy launched into the morality of the issue, using his Irish heritage, as Bobby had done, as an experience that brought with it a certain amount of discrimination. He also discussed discrimination in federal programs, concluding that it was wrong to take African Americans' tax dollars if they were not allowed a voice in government.[7]

Ted Kennedy finished his speech with an allusion to his fallen brother. He quoted President Johnson, who said that no memorial or eulogy would honor the memory of John Kennedy more than "the passage of the civil rights bill for which he fought so long." With that he said, "My brother was the first president of the United States to state publicly that segregation was morally wrong. His heart and soul are in this bill. If his life and death had a meaning, it was that we should not hate but love one another, and that we should use our powers not to create conditions of oppression that lead to violence, but conditions of freedom that lead it to peace."[8] This young senator would shape his own legacy in the Senate.

Just after Ted Kennedy's speech to the Senate, on April 16 Robert Kennedy appeared on a panel discussion about the civil rights bill. The attorney general continued his support of the bill, contending, "There are no domestic problems that have a greater effect on all of us, whether we be white or Negro, than the civil rights problems that [are] facing the United States at the present time." He also said that it went beyond a domestic issue and was an international problem. He said, "How we treat our own people, how we treat a minority of our own population, is going to have an effect on what people think of us abroad." He went on to bring in the Vietnam War, which was just starting to get underway. He said that he had been looking at the casualty list from Vietnam and that were some African Americans from Southern states who had been killed there.

> The widow of one of them lives in Alabama. I was just thinking that if she brought her husband's body back and it was buried in Arlington across the river, and then she had to go back to Alabama, she wouldn't know what hotel she could stop at, she wouldn't know where she could stop at a

restaurant, she wouldn't know where she could stop for a restroom. When she gets back to her local community, she can't bring her children to a theatre. And yet her husband has just been killed in Vietnam on behalf of all of us.

This clearly affected Robert Kennedy. Of the widow and the fallen soldier, Kennedy said, "It just doesn't make any sense. It doesn't make sense to me and it certainly is not going to make sense to a Negro brought up under that system."[9] Robert Kennedy had found his voice, and it was comments like this that would follow him to his own candidacy for Senate and then the presidency.

When news of John Kennedy's assassination came over the television, Martin Luther King was home. He called to his wife, "Corrie, I just heard that Kennedy has been shot, maybe killed." While they were watching King said, " Oh, I hope that he will live, this is just terrible. I think that if he lives, if he pulls through this, it will help to understand better what we go through." When it was announced that Kennedy had died, King said, "This is what is going to happen to me. This is such a sick society." The assassination bothered King a great deal. It was greater than the act of one man and seemed more representative of a violent society. He believed that there were two John Kennedys — one before and one after Birmingham. King had thought there was going to be real progress in seeing civil rights as a moral issue and was unsure where the discourse was headed now.[10] In 1964 King would go on to win the Nobel Peace Prize for his efforts in nonviolence. His movement was not finished yet. In the next four years he continued his struggle for equality until his own assassination on April 4, 1968.

John Lewis was "devastated" when John Kennedy was assassinated. "For all his reticence in terms of civil rights, I believed that John Kennedy was the best hope we had for the White House," Lewis remembered years later. "I criticized him, yes, and he deserved that criticism. He needed it. Every politician needs to be pushed and prodded by the people he represents." Lewis found out about Kennedy's death while he was on a speaking tour for voter registration. "I felt sick. I didn't know what to do."[11] His speech that night was a eulogy to John Kennedy. Lewis went home and cried. He contends that there are still African American homes in the United States that have pictures of Jesus Christ, Martin Luther King and John Kennedy hanging on its walls. He wrote, "Kennedy represented hope and possibility to most of America, white and black alike, and when he died, that flame of optimism in all of us flickered just a little bit lower."[12]

On June 19, 1964, the Civil Rights Act of 1964 passed through the Senate with a vote of seventy-three to twenty-seven. Lyndon Johnson remarked later, "We may win this legislation, but we are going to lose the South for a generation."[13] On July 2, 1964, Lyndon Johnson had a signing ceremony. Martin Luther King looked on as Johnson signed the bill into law. Somberly standing among the elated crowd was Robert Kennedy. He no longer possessed the same seat of power that he once had with his brother. He accepted several pens from Johnson and distributed them to Marshall, Katzenbach and Doar.[14] Robert Kennedy would not remain attorney general for much longer.

On August 25, 1964, at Gracie Mansion in New York City, Robert F. Kennedy said, "The search for enduring peace and for enduring prosperity begun by President Kennedy and continued by President Johnson has successfully taken our country to many new frontiers. In these years we have made steady advances in human rights, economic growth, and leadership of the world toward peace." He announced in this statement that he intended to make himself available as a nominee for senator of New York. "I have made that decision because I think our country faces a fundamental political choice." He felt that there was an assault from the Republicans and contended, "No one associated with President Kennedy and with President Johnson ... can sit on the sidelines with so much at stake."[15]

Robert Kennedy was elected to the Senate and served the State of New York until his assassination on June 6, 1968. Killed only months after King, Kennedy's campaign was an effort to revitalize liberalism. He embraced a civil rights platform and crafted a voice separate from his brother John. Robert and Ted Kennedy served together in the Senate for only four years. Jack Newfield argued, "Because he had no fixed ideology, and could best comprehend himself in action, Kennedy forged his consciousness out of what he saw and felt in the rural South and the urban ghettos." Newfield goes on to write that the many civil rights struggles Kennedy witnessed shaped his philosophy more than anything else.[16] In the wake of Bobby's death, Ted took up the torch and paved the way for the disadvantaged. At the heart of his fight were the same principles that Jack and Bobby talked about in Georgetown that snowy day. The Kennedy brothers wanted to change the climate of the nation, and they did. Their vision started the nation on a new road of acceptance. In 2008, invoking Jack and Bobby, Ted Kennedy endorsed Barack Obama as a presidential candidate over Hillary Clinton. Obama went on to win the election and took office as the first African American president in 2009. In the crowd at a rally in Chicago the night Obama was elected was Congressman John Lewis of Georgia. Obama's election was a testament to all the hard work that the Kennedys and civil rights leaders endured during those tumultuous years of the early 1960s and beyond.

Chapter Notes

Preface

1. *By the People: The Election of Barack Obama,* directed by Amy Rice and Alyssa Sams, aired August 7, 2009 (HBO Films, 2009).

Introduction

1. Robert F. Kennedy, recorded interview by John Bartlow Martin, p. 90, January 29, 1964, and March 1, 1964, John F. Kennedy Oral History Project of the John F. Kennedy Library (hereafter JFKOHP).
2. Edmund S. Morgan, *American Slavery, American Freedom: The Ordeal of Colonial Virginia* (New York: W.W. Norton and Company, 1975), 6.
3. James T. Patterson, *Grand Expectations: The United States, 1945–1974* (New York: Oxford University Press, 1996), 20–22.
4. Robert F. Kennedy, recorded interview with Burke Marshall by Anthony Lewis, p. 342, December 4, 1964, JFKOHP.
5. Evan Thomas, *Robert Kennedy: His Life* (New York: Touchstone, 2000), 195.
6. Robert F. Kennedy, recorded interview by John Bartlow Martin, p. 91, January 29, 1964, and March 1, 1964, JFKOHP.
7. Philip A. Goduti, Jr., *Kennedy's Kitchen Cabinet and the Pursuit of Peace: The Shaping of American Foreign Policy, 1961–1963* (Jefferson, North Carolina: McFarland, 2009), 13.

Prologue

1. David J. Garrow, *Bearing the Cross: Martin Luther King, Jr., and the Southern Christian Leadership Conference* (New York: Quill William Morrow, 1986), 33.
2. Ibid., 38.

3. Ibid., 42–43.
4. Ibid., 47.
5. Ibid., 49.
6. Martin Luther King, Jr., "The Dimensions of a Complete Life," January 24, 1954, *The Papers of Martin Luther King*: http://mlk-kpp01.stanford.edu/index.php/encyclopedia/documentsentry/the_dimensions_of_a_complete_life_sermon_at_dexter_avenue_baptist_church/.
7. Garrow, *Bearing the Cross,* 17–18.
8. Ibid., 20.
9. Ibid., 22.
10. Ibid., 51.
11. Ibid., 54.
12. Ibid., 56.
13. Taylor Branch, *Parting the Waters: America in the King Years, 1954–1963* (New York: Touchstone, 1988), 160.
14. Branch, 161; Garrow, *Bearing the Cross,* 56.
15. Garrow, *Bearing the Cross,* 56.
16. Ibid., 57–58.
17. Ibid., 58.
18. Branch, 162.
19. Branch, 164–165; Garrow, 59–60.
20. Branch, 166; Garrow, 60–61.
21. Branch, 166; Garrow, 60–61.
22. Garrow, *Bearing the Cross,* 60.
23. Thomas, 51.
24. Ibid., 55.
25. James W. Hilty, *Robert Kennedy: Brother Protector* (Philadelphia: Temple University Press, 1997), 54.
26. Ibid., 64.
27. Ibid., 65.
28. Hilty, 66; Thomas, 59.
29. Thomas, 59.
30. Hilty, 67.
31. Ibid., 69.
32. Thomas, 61.
33. Hilty, 70.
34. Ibid., 72–73.
35. Ibid., 76.
36. Arthur M. Schlesinger, Jr., *Robert Kennedy and His Times* (New York: Houghton Mifflin, 2002), 105.

37. Ibid., 105–106.
38. Hilty, 83.
39. Edward Kennedy, *True Compass: A Memoir* (New York: Twelve, 2009), 40.
40. Thomas, 66.
41. *New York Times,* June 12, 1954, "Cohn threatens to 'get' Senator for gibe at Schine."
42. Hilty, 93.
43. Ibid., 94.
44. Ibid., 99.
45. Ibid., 105.
46. Ibid., 104–105.
47. *US News and World Report,* April 12, 1957, 77–79.
48. Schlesinger, *RFK and His Times,* 137.
49. Ibid., 143.
50. Doris Kearns Goodwin, *The Fitzgeralds and the Kennedys: An American Saga* (New York: St. Martin's, 1987), 791.
51. Ibid.
52. Ibid., 791–792.
53. Hilty, 106.
54. Schlesinger, *RFK and His Times,* 150.
55. Robert F. Kennedy, *The Enemy Within* (New York: Harper and Brothers, 1960), 36–41.
56. Hilty, 108.
57. Robert F. Kennedy, *The Enemy Within,* 41.
58. Schlesinger, *RFK and His Times,* 153–154.
59. Robert F. Kennedy, *The Enemy Within,* 43.
60. Burton Hersh, *Bobby and J. Edgar: The Historic Face-Off Between the Kennedys and J. Edgar Hoover that Transformed America* (New York: Basic Books, 2007), 171.
61. Schlesinger, *RFK and His Times,* 154–155; see also Hilty, 113–114.
62. Hilty, 111.
63. Schlesinger, *RFK and His Times,* 157.
64. Ibid., 159.
65. Ibid., 165.
66. Hilty, 130.

67. John Lewis, *Walking with the Wind: A Memoir of the Movement* (New York: Harvest, 1998), 11.
68. Ibid., 27.
69. Ibid., 31.
70. Ibid., 33.
71. Ibid., 34.
72. Ibid., 36.
73. Ibid., 37.
74. Ibid., 40.
75. Ibid., 41.
76. Ibid.
77. Ibid., 45.
78. Ibid.
79. Ibid., 47.
80. Ibid., 52–53.
81. Ibid., 53–54.
82. Ibid., 69.
83. Howard Zinn, *SNCC: The New Abolitionists* (Cambridge: South End Press, 1964), 5.

Chapter 1

1. Branch, 272.
2. Ibid.
3. Ibid.
4. Clayborne Carson, ed., *The Papers of Martin Luther King, Jr., Volume V: Threshold of a New Decade, January 1959–December 1960* (Berkeley: University of California Press, 2005), 368.
5. Ibid.
6. Ibid.
7. Branch, 306.
8. Ibid.
9. Ibid., 306–307.
10. Garrow, *Bearing the Cross*, 139.
11. Ibid.
12. Branch, 314.
13. Robert Dallek, *An Unfinished Life: John F. Kennedy 1917–1963* (New York: Little Brown, 2003), 268.
14. Zinn, 1–2.
15. Ibid.
16. Ibid., 2.
17. Ibid., 4.
18. Ibid., 5.
19. Ibid., 7.
20. Ibid., 9.
21. Lewis, 90.
22. Ibid., 91.
23. Ibid.
24. Ibid., 92.
25. Ibid., 92–93.
26. Branch, 274.
27. Lewis, 96–97.
28. Schlesinger, *RFK and His Times*, 294.
29. Lewis, 99.
30. Ibid.

Chapter 2

1. *New York Times,* October 8, 1960, "Kennedy Rushes to Campus Talks."

2. John Kennedy, "Speech to Howard University," October 7, 1960, John F. Kennedy Library (hereafter JFKL), http://www.jfklibrary.org/Research/Ready-Reference/JFK-Speeches/Remarks-of-Senator-John-F-Kennedy-at-Howard-University-Washington-DC-October-7-1960.aspx?sms_ss=emailandat_xt=4d3e5075f6be96ba%2C0.
3. Ibid.
4. Ibid.
5. Ibid.
6. Ibid.
7. Ibid.
8. Ibid.
9. *New York Times,* October 8, 1960, "Kennedy Rushes to Campus Talks."
10. Harris Wofford, *Of Kennedys and Kings: Making Sense of the Sixties* (Pittsburgh: University of Pittsburgh Press, 1980), 11.
11. Hilty, 171.
12. Garrow, *Bearing the Cross,* 143–144.
13. Ibid., 172.
14. Thomas, 100–101.
15. Hilty, 172.
16. Wofford, 18.
17. Ibid., 19.
18. Ibid.
19. Thomas, 101.
20. Hilty, 173.
21. Thomas, 101–102.
22. Hilty, 173.
23. Ibid.
24. Ibid., 174.
25. Ibid.
26. Thomas 102–103.
27. Ibid.
28. Ibid., 103.
29. Hilty, 174.
30. Ibid., 174–175.
31. Thomas, 100.
32. Hilty, 169.
33. Ibid.
34. Hilty, 174.
35. Ibid., 180.
36. Ibid.
37. Theodore Sorensen, *Kennedy* (New York: Harper Collins, 1965), 227.

Chapter 3

1. Robert F. Kennedy, recorded interview by John Bartlow Martin, p. 15, January 29, 1964, and March 1, 1964, JFKOHP.
2. Ibid., 16.
3. Robert F. Kennedy, recorded interview by John Bartlow Martin, p. 18, January 29, 1964, and March 1, 1964, JFKOHP.
4. John Seigenthaler, recorded interview by Ronald Grele, p. 307, February 22, 1966, JFKOHP.

5. Ibid., 310.
6. Arthur Schlesinger, *RFK and His Times,* 231.
7. John Seigenthaler, recorded interview by Ronald Grele, pp. 320–321, February 22, 1966, JFKOHP.
8. Ibid., 323.
9. Ibid., 323–324.
10. Ibid.
11. Schlesinger, *RFK and His Times,* 233.
12. Robert F. Kennedy, recorded interview by John Bartlow Martin, p. 18, January 29, 1964, and March 1, 1964, JFKOHP.
13. John Seigenthaler, recorded interview by Ronald Grele, pp. 325–326, February 22, 1966, JFKOHP.
14. Schlesinger, *RFK and His Times,* 233.
15. Schlesinger, *RFK and His Times,* 286.
16. Robert F. Kennedy, recorded interview with Burke Marshall by Anthony Lewis, p. 353, December 4, 1964, JFKOHP.
17. Ibid., 349.
18. Ibid., 372.
19. Schlesinger, *RFK and His Times,* 286.
20. Ibid., 287.
21. Robert F. Kennedy, recorded interview with Burke Marshall by Anthony Lewis, p. 368, December 4, 1964, JFKOHP.
22. Hilty, 3.
23. Ibid., 7.
24. Ibid.
25. Thomas, 45.
26. Ibid., 130.
27. John Seigenthaler, recorded interview by Ronald Grele, p. 329, February 22, 1966, JFKOHP.
28. Robert F. Kennedy, recorded interview with Burke Marshall by Anthony Lewis, p. 358, December 4, 1964, JFKOHP.
29. Ibid.
30. Ibid.
31. John Seigenthaler, recorded interview by Ronald Grele, pp. 336–337, February 22, 1966, JFKOHP.
32. Carl Brauer, *John F. Kennedy and the Second Reconstruction* (New York: Columbia University Press, 1977), 93.
33. Ibid., 94.
34. John Seigenthaler, recorded interview by Ronald Grele, p. 334, February 22, 1966, JFKOHP.
35. Ibid., 337–338.
36. Carson, *Papers,* 546.
37. Ibid., 549.
38. Ibid., 550.
39. Ibid., 568.
40. Ibid., 568–569.
41. Garrow, *Bearing the Cross,* 88.
42. Ibid., 84–85.
43. Ibid., 86–87.

44. Ibid., 97–98.
45. Carson, 19.
46. Ibid.
47. Ibid., 20–21.
48. Zinn, 33.
49. Carson., 23.
50. Ibid., 23–24.
51. Ibid.
52. Ibid., 24.
53. Zinn, 33–34.

Chapter 4

1. Theodore Sorensen, *Counselor: A Life at the Edge of History* (New York: Harper Collins, 2008), 220.
2. Ibid., 221.
3. Wofford, *Of Kennedys and Kings*, 98–99.
4. Branch, 384.
5. Lewis, 124.
6. John F. Kennedy, "Annual Message to the Congress on the State of the Union," January 30, 1961 (Gerhard Peters and John T. Woolley, *The American Presidency Project,* http://www.presidency.ucsb.edu/ws/?pid=8045).
7. Hugh Davis Graham, The Civil Rights Era: Origins and Development of National Policy, 1960–1972 (New York: Oxford University Press, 1990), 27–28.
8. Ibid., 27.
9. James N. Giglio, *The Presidency of John F. Kennedy* (Lawrence: University of Kansas Press, 1991), 159.
10. Ibid., 28.
11. Ibid., 38–39.
12. Nicholas Katzenbach, recorded interview by Anthony Lewis, pp. 34–35, November 16, 1964, JFKOHP.
13. Burke Marshall, recorded interview by Anthony Lewis, p. 43, January 13, 1964, JFKOHP.
14. Robert F. Kennedy, recorded interview with Burke Marshall by Anthony Lewis, p. 368, December 4, 1964, JFKOHP.
15. Ibid.
16. Burke Marshall, recorded interview by Anthony Lewis, p. 44, January 13, 1964, JFKOHP.
17. Ibid., 44–45.
18. John F. Kennedy, "Message for the Commission on Civil Rights' Third Annual Conference on Schools in Transition," February 25, 1961 (Gerhard Peters and John T. Woolley, *The American Presidency Project,* http://www.presidency.ucsb.edu/ws/?pid=8506).
19. Ibid.
20. John Seigenthaler, recorded interview by William A. Geoghegan, pp. 1–5, July 22, 1964, JFKOHP.
21. Ibid., 8–12.
22. Ibid., 42.
23. Ibid., 105.
24. Ibid., 300.

25. Robert Kennedy to Father Drinan, May 2, 1961, Robert F. Kennedy Attorney General Papers, General Correspondence, Box 9, Civil Rights, January 1961–June 1961, JFKL.
26. Address by the Honorable Robert F. Kennedy, Attorney General, to the University of Georgia Law School, May 16, 1961, Robert F. Kennedy Attorney General Papers, Speeches, Box 1, University of Georgia Law, May 6, 1961, JFKL.
27. Ibid.
28. Ibid.
29. Ibid.
30. Ibid.
31. Ibid.
32. Ibid.

Chapter 5

1. Raymond Arsenault, *Freedom Riders: 1961 and the Struggle for Racial Justice* (New York: Oxford University Press, 2006), 11–18.
2. Diane McWhorter, *Carry Me Home: Birmingham, Alabama: The Climactic Battle of the Civil Rights Revolution* (New York: Touchstone, 2001), 195.
3. Arsenault, 93–94.
4. Ibid., 98–99.
5. Lewis, 130.
6. Ibid., 138–139.
7. Hilty, 316.
8. Arsenault, 143.
9. Ibid., 145.
10. Ibid., 149.
11. Ibid., 150.
12. Ibid., 150–151.
13. Ibid., 151.
14. Ibid., 155.
15. Robert F. Kennedy, recorded interview with Burke Marshall by Anthony Lewis, p. 372, December 4, 1964, JFKOHP.
16. Ibid., 374.
17. Richard Reeves, *President Kennedy: Profile of Power* (New York: Touchstone, 1993), 123.
18. Schlesinger, *RFK and His Times*, 295; see also Arsenault, 164.
19. Reeves, 133.
20. Robert F. Kennedy, recorded interview with Burke Marshall by Anthony Lewis, p. 370, December 4, 1964, JFKOHP.
21. Ibid., 370–371.
22. Ibid., 372.
23. Hilty, 307.
24. Ibid.
25. Ibid., 318.
26. Arsenault, 169.
27. Ibid.
28. Schlesinger, *RFK and His Times*, 295.
29. Arsenault, 170.
30. Robert F. Kennedy to George

Cruit, May 15, 1961, Robert F. Kennedy Attorney General Papers, General Correspondence Box 10, Civil Rights, Alabama 1961, May 15–20, 1961, JFKL.
31. Burke Marshall, recorded interview by Louis F. Oberdorfer, p. 14, May 29, 1964, JFKOHP.
32. Robert Kennedy to George Cruit, May 15, 1961, Robert F. Kennedy Attorney General Papers, General Correspondence, Box 10, Civil Rights, Alabama 1961, May 15–20, 1961, JFKL.
33. Arsenault, 171.
34. John Seigenthaler, recorded interview by Ronald Grele, p. 432, February 22, 1966, JFKOHP.
35. Ibid., 435–437.
36. Ibid., 439.

Chapter 6

1. Arsenault, 179–180.
2. Lewis, 143.
3. John Seigenthaler, recorded interview by Ronald Grele, p. 440, February 22, 1966, JFKOHP.
4. Robert F. Kennedy, recorded interview with Burke Marshall by Anthony Lewis, p. 373, December 4, 1964, JFKOHP.
5. Lewis, 145.
6. Arsenault, 187.
7. Ibid., 190.
8. Ibid., 193.
9. William Doyle, *An American Insurrection: The Battle of Oxford, Mississippi, 1962* (New York: Doubleday, 2001), Apple iBook edition, 10.
10. Burke Marshall, recorded interview by Louis F. Oberdorfer, p. 1, May 29, 1964, JFKOHP.
11. Ibid.
12. Ibid., 3.
13. Ibid., 4.
14. Arsenault, 194.
15. Burke Marshall, recorded interview by Louis F. Oberdorfer, p. 7, May 29, 1964, JFKOHP.
16. Ibid.
17. Burke Marshall, recorded interview by Louis F. Oberdorfer, p. 6, May 29, 1964, JFKOHP.
18. Ibid.
19. Arsenault, 194.
20. Ibid., 195.
21. Ibid., 194–195.
22. Ibid., 197.
23. Ibid., 198.
24. Lewis, 149–151.
25. Ibid., 152.
26. Ibid., 204.
27. Burke Marshall, recorded interview by Louis F. Oberdorfer, pp. 15–16, May 29, 1964, JFKOHP.
28. Ibid., 16.
29. Robert F. Kennedy, recorded interview with Burke Marshall by An-

thony Lewis, p. 374, December 4, 1964, JFKOHP.

30. John Seigenthaler, recorded interview by Ronald Grele, p. 445, February 22, 1966, JFKOHP.

31. Arsenault, 204–205.

32. John Seigenthaler, recorded interview by Ronald Grele, pp. 444–445, February 22, 1966, JFKOHP.

33. Ibid., 446–447.

34. Ibid., 447.

35. Ibid., 448–449.

36. Arsenault, 205–206.

37. Ibid., 206.

38. Ibid., 207.

39. Ibid., 207–208.

40. Ibid., 210–211.

41. Lewis, 155.

42. John Seigenthaler, recorded interview by Ronald Grele, pp. 454–455, February 22, 1966, JFKOHP.

43. Ibid., 455–458.

44. Arsenault, 213–214.

45. Ibid., 214.

46. Lewis, 155.

47. Ibid., 156.

48. Arsenault, 215.

49. John Seigenthaler, recorded interview by Ronald Grele, pp. 458–459, February 22, 1966, JFKOHP.

50. Ibid.

Chapter 7

1. Robert F. Kennedy, recorded interview with Burke Marshall by Anthony Lewis, p. 377, December 4, 1964, JFKOHP.

2. Ibid., 384.

3. Ibid.

4. John F. Kennedy, "Statement by the President Concerning Interference with the 'Freedom Riders' in Alabama," May 20, 1961 (Gerhard Peters and John T. Woolley, *The American Presidency Project.* http://www.presid ency.ucsb.edu/ws/?pid=8142).

5. John Seigenthaler, recorded interview by Ronald Grele, pp. 460–461, February 22, 1966, JFKOHP.

6. Arsenault, 221.

7. All quotes from the wire to Patterson from Kennedy are from the *New York Times,* May 21, 1961.

8. Arsenault, 223.

9. Burke Marshall, recorded interview by Louis F. Oberdorfer, p. 25, May 29, 1964, JFKOHP.

10. Ibid., 225.

11. Ibid., 226.

12. Ibid., 227.

13. Ibid., 228–229.

14. Ibid., 230.

15. Arsenault, 232–233; see also Garrow, *Bearing the Cross,* 158.

16. Hilty, 324.

17. Robert F. Kennedy, recorded interview with Burke Marshall by An-

thony Lewis, p. 377, December 4, 1964, JFKOHP.

18. Ibid., 378.

19. Arsenault, 233.

20. Ibid., 385.

21. Arsenault, 233; Hilty, 324.

22. Robert F. Kennedy, recorded interview with Burke Marshall by Anthony Lewis, p. 378, December 4, 1964, JFKOHP.

23. Arsenault, 234–235.

24. Ibid., 235.

25. Ibid.

26. Hilty, 325; Arsenault, 237.

27. Hilty, 325.

28. Ibid., 386.

29. Ibid., 387.

30. Robert F. Kennedy, recorded interview with Burke Marshall by Anthony Lewis, pp. 378–380, December 4, 1964, JFKOHP.

31. Arsenault, 240.

32. Ibid.

33. Schlesinger, *RFK and His Times,* 298.

34. Ibid.

Chapter 8

1. Arsenault, 245–246.

2. Ibid., 247.

3. Lewis, 162–163.

4. Ibid., 163.

5. Arsenault, 250–251.

6. Garrow, *Bearing the Cross,* 159.

7. Arsenault, 252–254.

8. Burke Marshall to Joseph Patterson, May 22, 1961, Robert F. Kennedy Attorney General Papers, General Correspondence, Box 10, Civil Rights Memoranda, May 1961, JFKL.

9. Ibid.

10. Ibid.

11. Ibid.

12. Ibid.

13. Hilty, 323.

14. Robert F. Kennedy, recorded interview with Burke Marshall by Anthony Lewis, p. 387, December 4, 1964, JFKOHP.

15. Arsenault, 256–257.

16. Ibid., 257.

17. Ibid.

18. Robert F. Kennedy, recorded interview with Burke Marshall by Anthony Lewis, pp. 387–388, December 4, 1964, JFKOHP.

19. Ibid., 388.

20. Arsenault, 259.

21. Ibid., 261–262.

22. Ibid., 265–266.

23. Ibid., 266–267.

24. Lewis, 165.

25. Ibid., 166.

26. Ibid., 269.

27. Ibid., 275–276.

28. Ibid., 276.

29. Ibid., 271.

30. Ibid., 272.

31. Robert F. Kennedy, recorded interview with Burke Marshall by Anthony Lewis, p. 388, December 4, 1964, JFKOHP.

32. *New York Times,* May 25, 1961.

33. Ibid.

34. Robert F. Kennedy, recorded interview with Burke Marshall by Anthony Lewis, p. 388, December 4, 1964, JFKOHP.

35. Arsenault, 251.

36. Ibid., 271.

37. Ibid., 273–274.

38. Schlesinger, *RFK and His Times,* 299.

39. Ibid., 300.

40. Ibid.

41. Branch, 475.

42. Arsenault, 276.

43. Branch, 476.

44. John F. Kennedy, "Special Message to the Congress on Urgent National Needs," May 25, 1961 (Gerhard Peters and John T. Woolley, *The American Presidency Project,* http://www.pre sidency.ucsb.edu/ws/?pid=8151).

45. Ibid.

46. Robert Kennedy, *Voice of America* broadcast, May 26, 1961, Robert F. Kennedy Attorney General Papers, Speeches, Box 1, May 17–26, 1961, JFKL.

47. Ibid.

48. Ibid.

49. Ibid.

50. Edwin Guthman, *We Band of Brothers: A Memoir of Robert F. Kennedy,* (New York: Harper and Row, 1964), 156.

51. Ibid., 157.

52. Ibid.

53. Brauer, 152.

54. Ibid., 152–153.

55. Ibid., 153–154.

56. Arsenault, 292.

57. Ibid., 293.

58. Wofford, 157.

59. Ibid., 293–294.

60. Giglio, 166.

61. Ibid., 168.

62. *New York Times,* May 30, 1961.

63. *New York Times,* May 31, 1961.

64. Ibid.

65. Branch, 478.

66. Robert F. Kennedy, recorded interview with Burke Marshall by Anthony Lewis, pp. 388–389, December 4, 1964, JFKOHP.

67. Burke Marshall, recorded interview by Anthony Lewis, p. 53, June 13, 1964, JFKOHP.

68. Hilty, 330.

69. Ibid.

70. Carson, 37.

71. Ibid., 38.

72. Ibid., 389.

73. Ibid., 390.

74. Ibid., 390–391.

75. Ibid., 391.
76. Burke Marshall, recorded interview by Louis F. Oberdorfer, pp. 40–41, May 29, 1964, JFKOHP.

Chapter 9

1. Schlesinger, *RFK and His Times*, 300–301.
2. Robert F. Kennedy, recorded interview with Burke Marshall by Anthony Lewis, p. 394, December 4, 1964, JFKOHP.
3. Ibid.
4. Ibid., 395.
5. Ibid.
6. Ibid., 396.
7. Ibid. 397.
8. Ibid., 399.
9. Nicholas Katzenbach, recorded interview by Anthony Lewis, p. 2, November 16, 1964, JFKOHP.
10. Ibid., 3–4.
11. Ibid., 5.
12. Ibid., 9.
13. Ibid., 9–10.
14. Ibid., 10–11.
15. Ibid., 11–12.
16. Ibid., 13.
17. Ibid., 17.
18. Ibid., 17–18.
19. Ibid., 19.
20. Branch, 479.
21. Nicholas Katzenbach, recorded interview by Anthony Lewis, pp. 20–21, November 16, 1964, JFKOHP.
22. Branch, 479.
23. Ibid., 480.
24. Ibid.
25. Ibid.
26. Schlesinger, *RFK and His Times*, 301.
27. Ibid.
28. Ibid., 302.
29. Ibid., 303.
30. "Progress in the Field of Civil Rights: A Summary," Burke Marshall Papers, Box 16, Civil Rights Reports, January 20, 1961–November 20, 1961, JFKL.
31. Ibid.
32. Ibid.
33. Ibid.
34. Ibid.
35. Ibid.
36. Ibid.
37. Ibid.
38. Ibid.
39. Address by Attorney General Robert F. Kennedy at the National Conference of Christians and Jews Dinner, December 3, 1961, Robert F. Kennedy Attorney General Papers, Speeches, Box 1, National Conference of Christian and Jews, December 3, 1961, JFKL.
40. Ibid.

41. Ibid.
42. Ibid.
43. Carson, 57.
44. Ibid., 58.
45. Ibid., 59.
46. Ibid.
47. Ibid.
48. Ibid., 60.
49. Brauer, 154.
50. Carson, 60.
51. Garrow, *Bearing the Cross*, 182.
52. Branch, 540.
53. Ibid., 544.
54. Ibid., 545–546.
55. Ibid., 546.
56. Carson, 60; see also Brauer, 154–155.
57. Garrow, 185.
58. Branch, 551; see also Garrow, *Bearing the Cross*, 185.
59. Carson, 60.
60. Hilty, 332–333.
61. Hilty, 333; see also Brauer, 155.
62. Carson, 60.
63. Brauer, 168.
64. Carson, 60.
65. Ibid., 61.
66. Giglio, 170–71.
67. John F. Kennedy, "The President's News Conference," August 1, 1962 (Gerhard Peters and John T. Woolley, *The American Presidency Project,* http://www.presidency.ucsb.edu/ws/?pid=8799).
68. Carson, 61.
69. Ibid.
70. Zinn, 144.
71. McWhorter, 308.

Chapter 10

1. Martin Luther King, Jr., *The Nation,* "Fumbling on the New Frontier," March 3, 1962.
2. Ibid.
3. Ibid.
4. Ibid.
5. Ibid.
6. Ibid.
7. "Testimony by Attorney General Robert F. Kennedy Before the Judiciary Committee, House of Representatives, in Support of Legislative Proposals to Eliminate Abuses of Literacy Tests in Voting and to Abolish the Poll Tax," March 15, 1962, Robert F. Kennedy Attorney General Papers, Speeches, Box 1, March 14–24, 1962, JFKL.
8. Ibid.
9. Ibid.
10. Ibid.
11. Ibid.
12. Ibid.
13. Burke Marshall, recorded interview by Anthony Lewis, p. 64, June 13, 1964, JFKOHP.
14. Ibid., 65.
15. Address by Attorney General

Robert F. Kennedy Before the National Newspaper Publishers Association Morgan State College Baltimore Maryland, June 22, 1962, Robert F. Kennedy Attorney General Papers, Speeches, Box 1, National Newspapers Publisher, June 22, 1962, JFKL.
16. Ibid.
17. Ibid.
18. Ibid.
19. Ibid.
20. Ibid.
21. Address by Attorney General Robert F. Kennedy Before the National Insurance Association, July 26, 1962, Robert F. Kennedy Attorney General Papers, Speeches, Box 1, National Insurance Association, July 26, 1962, JFKL.
22. Ibid.
23. Ibid.
24. Ibid.
25. Ibid.
26. Ibid.
27. Ibid.

Chapter 11

1. Schlesinger, *RFK and His Times*, 313.
2. Ibid., 317.
3. Doyle, 67.
4. Ibid., 68.
5. Letter from James Meredith to the Justice Department, February 7, 1961, Burke Marshall Papers, Box 20, Ole Miss Integration, James Meredith February 7–May 15, 1961, JFKL.
6. Ibid.
7. Ibid.
8. James Meredith, *Three Years in Mississippi* (Bloomington: Indiana University Press, 1966), 51.
9. Burke Marshall, recorded interview by Anthony Lewis, p. 65, June 13, 1964, JFKOHP.
10. Ibid., 72–73.
11. Ibid.
12. Ibid., 74.
13. Telephone conversation between Robert Kennedy and Governor Ross Barnett, September 15, 1962, 2:15 P.M., Burke Marshall Papers, Box 20, Telephone Transcripts General, Sept. 15–20, 1962, JFKL.
14. Ibid.
15. Ibid.
16. Ibid.
17. Telephone conversation between Robert Kennedy and Governor Ross Barnett, September 17, 1962, 7:00 P.M., Burke Marshall Papers, Box 20, Telephone Transcripts General, Sept. 15–20, 1962, JFKL.
18. Telephone conversation between Robert Kennedy and Governor Ross Barnett, September 18, 1962, 12:30 P.M., Burke Marshall Papers,

Box 20, Telephone Transcripts General, Sept. 15–20, 1962, JFKL.

19. Ibid.

20. Telephone conversation between Burke Marshall and Governor Ross Barnett, September 18, 1962, 6:05 P.M., Burke Marshall Papers, Box 20, Telephone Transcripts General, Sept. 15–20, 1962, JFKL.

21. Ibid.

22. Telephone conversation between Robert Kennedy and Governor Ross Barnett, September 19, 1962, 1:30 P.M., Burke Marshall Papers, Box 20, Telephone Transcripts General, Sept. 15–20, 1962, JFKL.

23. Telephone conversation between Burke Marshall and Attorney General John Patterson, September 19, 1962, Burke Marshall Papers, Box 20, Telephone Transcripts General, Sept. 15–20, 1962, JFKL.

24. Telephone conversation between Burke Marshall and Attorney General John Patterson, September 20, 1962, 9:50am, Burke Marshall Papers, Box 20, Telephone Transcripts General, Sept. 15–20, 1962, JFKL.

25. Telephone conversation between Robert Kennedy and Attorney General John Patterson, September 20, 1962, 12:30 P.M., Burke Marshall Papers, Box 20, Telephone Transcripts General, Sept. 15–20, 1962, JFKL.

26. Burke Marshall memorandum, Summary of telephone calls to Tom Watkins, September 20, 1962, Burke Marshall Papers, Box 20, Telephone Transcripts General, Sept. 15–20, 1962, JFKL.

27. Telephone conversation between Robert Kennedy and Attorney General John Patterson, September 20, 1962, 3:15 P.M., Burke Marshall Papers, Box 20, Telephone Transcripts General, Sept. 15–20, 1962, JFKL.

28. Telephone conversation between Robert Kennedy and Attorney General John Patterson, September 20, 1962, 4:40 P.M., Burke Marshall Papers, Box 20, Telephone Transcripts General, Sept. 15–20, 1962, JFKL.

29. Telephone conversation between Robert Kennedy and Governor Ross Barnett, September 20, 1962, 4:53 P.M., Burke Marshall Papers, Box 20, Telephone Transcripts General, Sept. 15–20, 1962, JFKL.

30. Telephone conversation between Robert Kennedy and Governor Ross Barnett, September 24, 1962, 9:50 P.M., Burke Marshall Papers, Box 20, Telephone Transcripts General, Sept. 24–25, 1962, JFKL.

31. Ibid.

32. Ibid.

33. Ibid.

34. Ibid.

35. Ibid.

36. Ibid.

37. Ibid.

Chapter 12

1. Telephone conversation between Robert Kennedy and Governor Ross Barnett, September 25, 1962, 12:20 P.M., Burke Marshall Papers, Box 20, Telephone Transcripts General, Sept. 24–25, 1962, JFKL.

2. Ibid.

3. Ibid.

4. Ibid.

5. Ibid.

6. Ibid.

7. Ibid.

8. Ibid.

9. Ibid.

10. Burke Marshall, Memorandum of telephone conversation, September 25, 1962, Burke Marshall Papers, Box 20, Telephone Transcripts General, Sept. 24–25, 1962, JFKL.

11. Telephone conversation between Robert Kennedy and Governor Ross Barnett, September 25, 1962, 3:35 P.M., Burke Marshall Papers, Box 20, Telephone Transcripts General, Sept. 24–25, 1962, JFKL.

12. Ibid.

13. Burke Marshall to Robert Kennedy, Memorandum of telephone conversation, September 25, 1962, Burke Marshall Papers, Box 20, Telephone Transcripts General, Sept. 24–25, 1962, JFKL.

14. Telephone conversation between Robert Kennedy and Governor Ross Barnett, September 25, 1962, 6:10 P.M., Burke Marshall Papers, Box 20, Telephone Transcripts General, Sept. 24–25, 1962, JFKL.

15. Telephone conversation between Robert Kennedy and Governor Ross Barnett, September 25, 1962, 6:25 P.M., Burke Marshall Papers, Box 20, Telephone Transcripts General, Sept. 24–25, 1962, JFKL.

16. Branch, 647–649.

17. Telephone conversation between Robert Kennedy and Governor Ross Barnett, September 25, 1962, 7:25 P.M., Burke Marshall Papers, Box 20, Telephone Transcripts General, Sept. 24–25, 1962, JFKL.

18. Ibid.

19. Ibid.

20. Ibid.

21. Telephone conversation between Robert Kennedy and Governor Ross Barnett, September 25, 1962, 7:35 P.M., Burke Marshall Papers, Box 20, Telephone Transcripts General, Sept. 24–25, 1962, JFKL.

22. Ibid.

23. Ibid.

24. Ibid.

25. Burke Marshall to Robert

Kennedy, Memorandum of telephone conversation, September 27, 1962, Burke Marshall Papers, Box 20, Telephone Transcripts General, Sept. 27, 1962, JFKL.

26. Ibid.

27. Ibid.

28. Branch, 650.

29. Doyle, 102–103.

30. Ibid., 103.

31. Robert F. Kennedy, Memorandum of telephone conversation with Tom Watkins, September 27, 1962, Burke Marshall Papers, Box 20, Telephone Transcripts General, Sept. 27, 1962, JFKL.

32. Doyle, 95.

33. Telephone conversation between Robert Kennedy and Governor Ross Barnett, September 27, 1962, 2:50 P.M., Burke Marshall Papers, Box 20, Telephone Transcripts General, Sept. 27, 1962, JFKL.

34. Ibid.

35. Ibid.

36. Telephone conversation between Robert Kennedy and Governor Ross Barnett, September 27, 1962, 3:50 P.M., Burke Marshall Papers, Box 20, Telephone Transcripts General, Sept. 27, 1962, JFKL.

37. Ibid.

38. Ibid.

39. Ibid.

40. Telephone conversation between Robert Kennedy and Governor Ross Barnett, September 27, 1962, 4:20 P.M., Burke Marshall Papers, Box 20, Telephone Transcripts General, Sept. 27, 1962, JFKL.

41. Telephone conversation between Robert Kennedy and Governor Ross Barnett, September 27, 1962, 5:35 P.M., Burke Marshall Papers, Box 20, Telephone Transcripts General, Sept. 27, 1962, JFKL.

42. Ibid.

43. Telephone conversation between Robert Kennedy and Governor Ross Barnett, September 27, 1962, 6:35 P.M., Burke Marshall Papers, Box 20, Telephone Transcripts General, Sept. 27, 1962, JFKL.

44. Doyle, 116.

45. Robert F. Kennedy, recorded interview with Burke Marshall by Anthony Lewis, pp. 477–478, December 4, 1964, JFKOHP.

Chapter 13

1. Brauer, 188.

2. Telephone conversation between Robert Kennedy and Governor Ross Barnett, September 28, 1962, 1:35 P.M., Burke Marshall Papers, Box 20, Telephone Transcripts General, Sept. 28–Oct. 5, 1962, JFKL.

3. Ibid.
4. Ibid.
5. Ibid.
6. Ibid.
7. Ibid.
8. JFKL, Audio Files, Audiotape 24, Items 1–2A.
9. Doyle, 123.
10. Hilty, 342.
11. JFKL, Audio Files, Item 4A1.
12. Ibid.
13. Ibid.
14. Ibid.
15. Hilty, 342.
16. JFKL, Audio Files, Item 4C.
17. Ibid.
18. Ibid.
19. Ibid.
20. Ibid.
21. Ibid.
22. Ibid.
23. Ibid.
24. Ibid.
25. Telephone conversation between John F. Kennedy and Governor Ross Barnett, September 29, 1962, 3:16 P.M., Burke Marshall Papers, Box 20, Telephone Transcripts General, Sept. 28 — Oct. 5, 1962, JFKL.
26. JFKL, Audio Files, Item 4C.
27. Nicholas Katzenbach, recorded interview by Anthony Lewis, p. 92, November 29, 1964, JFKOHP.
28. Hilty, 343.
29. Burke Marshall, recorded interview by Anthony Lewis, p. 76, June 14, 1964, JFKOHP.
30. Schlesinger, *RFK and His Times,* 321.
31. Doyle, 126.
32. Brauer, 190; see also Steve Fayer, *Eyes on the Prize,* "Fighting Back."
33. Doyle, 127.
34. Burke Marshall, recorded interview by Anthony Lewis, pp. 76–77, June 14, 1964, JFKOHP.
35. Telephone conversation between Robert Kennedy and Governor Ross Barnett, September 30, 1962, 12:45 P.M., Burke Marshall Papers, Box 20, Telephone Transcripts General, Sept. 28 — Oct. 5, 1962, JFKL.
36. Ibid.
37. Ibid.
38. Ibid.
39. Burke Marshall, recorded interview by Anthony Lewis, pp. 77–78, June 14, 1964, JFKOHP.
40. Ibid., 77–78.
41. Nicholas Katzenbach, recorded interview by Anthony Lewis, p. 97, November 29, 1964, JFKOHP.

Chapter 14

1. Doyle, 55.
2. Ibid., 138.
3. Nicholas Katzenbach, recorded

interview by Anthony Lewis, pp. 98–99, November 29, 1964, JFKOHP.
4. Branch, 662.
5. Nicholas Katzenbach, recorded interview by Anthony Lewis, p. 100, November 29, 1964, JFKOHP.
6. Ibid., 101.
7. Branch, 663.
8. Doyle, 153.
9. Ibid.
10. Ibid., 155.
11. Ibid., 156–157.
12. Ibid., 157.
13. Ibid., 159.
14. Ibid., 161.
15. Ibid., 161–162.
16. Doyle, 149.
17. Nicholas Katzenbach, recorded interview by Anthony Lewis, pp. 101–102, November 29, 1964, JFKOHP.
18. Doyle, 162–163.
19. Nicholas Katzenbach, recorded interview by Anthony Lewis, p. 105, November 29, 1964, JFKOHP.
20. Doyle, 163.
21. Branch, 664.
22. Branch, 665.
23. Nicholas Katzenbach, recorded interview by Anthony Lewis, p. 109, November 29, 1964, JFKOHP.
24. Ibid.
25. John F. Kennedy, "Radio and Television Report to the Nation on the Situation at the University of Mississippi," September 30, 1962 (Gerhard Peters and John T. Woolley, *The American Presidency Project,* http://www.presidency.ucsb.edu/ws/?pid=8915).
26. Ibid.
27. Ibid.
28. Burke Marshall, recorded interview by Anthony Lewis, pp. 79–80, June 14, 1964, JFKOHP.
29. Ibid.
30. Nicholas Katzenbach, recorded interview by Anthony Lewis, p. 110, November 29, 1964, JFKOHP.
31. Ibid., 110–111.
32. Ibid., 111–112.
33. JFKL, Audio Files, Audio Tape 26, Item 1.
34. Ibid.
35. Ibid.
36. Ibid.
37. Ibid.
38. Ibid.
39. Ibid.
40. Ibid.
41. Ibid.
42. Robert F. Kennedy, recorded interview with Burke Marshall by Anthony Lewis, pp. 478–479, December 4, 1964, JFKOHP.
43. JFKL, Audio Files, Audio Tape 26, Item 1.
44. Robert F. Kennedy, recorded interview with Burke Marshall by Anthony Lewis, p. 485, December 4, 1964, JFKOHP.

45. JFKL, Audio Files, Audio Tape 26, Item 1.
46. Ibid.
47. Ibid.
48. Robert F. Kennedy, recorded interview with Burke Marshall by Anthony Lewis, pp. 479–480, December 4, 1964, JFKOHP.
49. Burke Marshall, recorded interview by Anthony Lewis, pp. 80–81, June 14, 1964, JFKOHP.
50. JFKL, Audio Files, Audio Tape 26, Item 1.
51. JFKL, Audio Files, Audio Tape Belt 4F, Item 1.
52. JFKL, Audio Files, Audio Tape 26, Item 1.
53. JFKL, Audio Files, Audio Tape 26A, Item 1.
54. Ibid.
55. Ibid.
56. JFKL, Audio Files, Item 4F3.
57. JFKL, Audio Files, Item 4F4.
58. Ibid.
59. JFKL, Audio Files, Item 4F5.
60. JFKL, Audio Files, Item 4F7.
61. JFKL, Audio Files, Item 4G2.
62. JFKL, Audio Files, Item 4G3.
63. Reeves, 363.
64. Ibid., 364.
65. Giglio, 174.
66. Ibid., 176.
67. Ibid., 177.

Chapter 15

1. Schlesinger, *RFK and His Times,* 326.
2. Address of Attorney General Robert F. Kennedy, Testimonial Dinner for Attorney General John Reynolds, October 6, 1962, RFK Speeches, Box 1, JFKL.
3. Address of Attorney General Robert F. Kennedy to the American Jewish Congress, October 28, 1962, Robert F. Kennedy Attorney General Papers, Speeches, Box 1, American Jewish Congress, October 28, 1962, JFKL.
4. Ibid.
5. Ibid.
6. Remarks by Attorney General Robert F. Kennedy at the Opening of Exhibit on the Emancipation Proclamation at the National Archives, January 4, 1963, Robert F. Kennedy Attorney General Papers, Speeches, Box 1, Emancipation Proclamation Exhibit at the National Archives, January 4, 1963, JFKL.
7. Ibid.
8. John F. Kennedy, "Annual Message to the Congress on the State of the Union," January 14, 1963 (Gerhard Peters and John T. Woolley, *The American Presidency Project,* http://www.presidency.ucsb.edu/ws/?pid=9138).
9. Address by Attorney General

Robert F. Kennedy at the 10th Anniversary Convocation, Center for Study of Democratic Institutions of the Fund for the Republic , January 22, 1963, Robert F. Kennedy Attorney General Papers, Speeches, Box 1, 10th Anniversary Center for Study of Democratic Institutions, January 23, 1963, JFKL.

10. John F. Kennedy, "Special Message to the Congress on Civil Rights," February 28, 1963 (Gerhard Peters and John T. Woolley, *The American Presidency Project*, http://www.presidency.ucsb.edu/ws/?pid=9581).

11. Ibid.
12. Ibid.
13. Ibid.
14. Ibid.
15. Ibid.
16. Ibid.
17. Ibid.
18. Branch, 699.

19. Robert Kennedy Interview on *Washington Report*, CBS News, March 3, 1963, Robert F. Kennedy Attorney General Papers, Speeches, Box 1, CBS News "Washington Report," March 3, 1963, JFKL.

20. Ibid.
21. Ibid.

22. Address to the Civil Rights Committee, New York City Central Labor Council, AFL-CIO, by Attorney General Robert F. Kennedy, March 9, 1963, Robert F. Kennedy Attorney General Papers, Speeches, Box 1, Civil Rights Committee New York Labor Council, March 9, 1963, JFKL.

23. Ibid.

24. Robert F. Kennedy, Address at Kentucky's Centennial of the Emancipation Proclamation, Freedom Hall, Louisville, Kentucky, March 18, 1963 (Dept. of Justice, http://www.justice.gov/ag/rfk-speeches.html).

25. Ibid.

26. Robert F. Kennedy, Message to the Speaker of the House, April 1, 1963, Robert F. Kennedy Attorney General Papers, Speeches, Box 2, April 2–25, 1963, JFKL.

27. Robert F. Kennedy, Address at the meeting of the University of South Carolina Chapter of the American Association of University Professors, April 25, 1963, Robert F. Kennedy Attorney General Papers, Speeches, Box 2, April 2–25, 1963, JFKL.

28. Ibid.

Chapter 16

1. Branch, 679.
2. Ibid., 683.
3. Ibid., 689–690.
4. Ibid., 691.
5. Ibid., 695.
6. Ibid., 700.
7. Ibid., 710.

8. Ibid., 711.
9. Ibid., 726–727.
10. Ibid., 727.
11. Ibid., 729.
12. Ibid., 730–731.

13. *New York Times*, April 13, 1963, "Dr. King Arrested at Birmingham."

14. Branch, 731.

15. Schlesinger, *RFK and His Times*, 328; Hilty, 349–350.
16. Hilty, 350.
17. McWhorter, 347.
18. Branch, 737.

19. Martin Luther King, Jr., *Why We Can't Wait* (New York: Mentor Group, 1964), 76.

20. Ibid.
21. Ibid., 77.
22. Ibid., 78.
23. Ibid., 79.
24. Ibid., 81–82.
25. Ibid., 86–87.
26. Garrow, *Bearing the Cross*, 246.

27. Schlesinger, *RFK and His Times*, 329.
28. Hilty, 350.
29. Garrow, *Bearing the Cross*, 249.
30. Reeves, 488.
31. Hilty, 350–351.
32. Hilty, 351.

33. Schlesinger, *RFK and His Times*, 329.

34. Burke Marshall, recorded interview by Anthony Lewis, p. 96, June 14, 1964, JFKOHP.
35. Ibid., 97.
36. Garrow, *Bearing the Cross*, 250.
37. Ibid., 252.

38. Burke Marshall, recorded interview by Anthony Lewis, pp. 97–98, June 14, 1964, JFKOHP.
39. Ibid., 98.
40. Garrow, *Bearing the Cross*, 253.

41. Burke Marshall, recorded interview by Anthony Lewis, p. 98, June 14, 1964, JFKOHP.

42. Robert F. Kennedy, recorded interview with Burke Marshall by Anthony Lewis, p. 494, December 4, 1964, JFKOHP.
43. Garrow, *Bearing the Cross*, 257.
44. Ibid., 259.

45. Robert F. Kennedy, recorded interview with Burke Marshall by Anthony Lewis, p. 495, December 4, 1964, JFKOHP.
46. Garrow, *Bearing the Cross*, 260–261.
47. JFKL, Audio Tapes, 86.2.
48. Ibid.
49. Ibid.
50. Ibid.

51. John F. Kennedy, "Radio and Television Remarks Following Renewal of Racial Strife in Birmingham.," May 12, 1963 (Gerhard Peters and John T. Woolley, *The American Presidency Project,* http://www.presidency.ucsb.edu/ws/?pid=9206).

52. Garrow, *Bearing the Cross*, 265.

53. Burke Marshall, recorded interview by Anthony Lewis, p. 103, June 14, 1964, JFKOHP.

Chapter 17

1. Schlesinger, *RFK and His Times*, 330–331.
2. Ibid., 331–332.
3. Ibid., 332.
4. Ibid.
5. Ibid., 333.
6. Ibid., 333–334.
7. Ibid., 334.
8. Ibid., 335.
9. Hilty, 357.
10. Hilty, 358.

11. Robert F. Kennedy, recorded interview with Burke Marshall by Anthony Lewis, p. 496, December 4, 1964, JFKOHP.
12. Ibid., 496.
13. Ibid., 497.
14. Ibid.
15. Hilty, 360.

16. Robert F. Kennedy, recorded interview with Burke Marshall by Anthony Lewis, p. 498, December 4, 1964, JFKOHP.
17. Ibid., 497.

18. Doris Kearns Goodwin, *Team of Rivals: The Political Genius of Abraham Lincoln* (New York: Simon and Schuster, 2005), 468.

19. Schlesinger, *RFK and His Times*, 337.

20. Robert F. Kennedy, recorded interview with Burke Marshall by Anthony Lewis, p. 518, December 6, 1964, JFKOHP.

21. Schlesinger, *RFK and His Times*, 519.
22. Ibid., 338.
23. Ibid., 338–339.
24. Ibid., 339.

25. Robert F. Kennedy, recorded interview with Burke Marshall by Anthony Lewis, p. 519, December 6, 1964, JFKOHP.

26. Robert F. Kennedy, Address to the North Carolina Cold War Seminar, May 17, 1963, Robert F. Kennedy Attorney General Papers, Speeches, Box 2, May 13–17, 1963, JFKL.

27. John F. Kennedy, "Remarks in Nashville at the 90th Anniversary Convocation of Vanderbilt University," May 18, 1963 (Gerhard Peters and John T. Woolley, *The American Presidency Project*).

28. Transcript, *Voice of America,* "Press Conference, USA," June 3, 1963, Robert F. Kennedy Attorney General Papers, Speeches, Box 2, "Press Conference USA" Voice of America June 4, 1963, JFKL.
29. Ibid.
30. Ibid.

31. Ibid.
32. Robert F. Kennedy, recorded interview with Burke Marshall by Anthony Lewis, pp. 519–520, December 6, 1964, JFKOHP.
33. Ibid., 520.
34. Ibid.
35. Ibid., 523–524.
36. Ibid., 524–525.
37. Ibid., 525–526.
38. Hilty, 365.
39. *Crisis: Behind a Presidential Commitment*, directed by Robert Drew, aired on October 21, 1963 (ABC News and Drew Associates, 1963).
40. Ibid.
41. Robert F. Kennedy, recorded interview with Burke Marshall by Anthony Lewis, p. 528, December 6, 1964, JFKOHP.
42. Ibid., 529–530.
43. Hilty, 366.
44. *Crisis: Behind a Presidential Commitment.*
45. Robert F. Kennedy, recorded interview with Burke Marshall by Anthony Lewis, p. 531, December 6, 1964, JFKOHP.

Chapter 18

1. Ibid., 539.
2. Schlesinger, *RFK and His Times*, 347; see also Victor Navasky, *Kennedy Justice* (New York: Atheneum, 1977), 99.
3. Robert F. Kennedy, recorded interview with Burke Marshall by Anthony Lewis, p. 542, December 6, 1964, JFKOHP.
4. Ibid., 543.
5. Ibid., 543–544.
6. John F. Kennedy, "Radio and Television Report to the American People on Civil Rights," June 11, 1963 (Gerhard Peters and John T. Woolley, *The American Presidency Project*, http://www.presidency.ucsb.edu/ws/?pid=9271).
7. Branch, 824.
8. *New York Times,* June 12, 1963, "Dr King Praises Speech as 'a Hallmark in History'."
9. Branch, 824–825.
10. Hilty, 369.
11. Ibid., 369–370.
12. *New York Times,* June 16, 1963, "Civil Rights: 'The Fiery Trial'."
13. John F. Kennedy, "Special Message to the Congress on Civil Rights and Job Opportunities," June 19, 1963 (Gerhard Peters and John T. Woolley, *The American Presidency Project*, http://www.presidency.ucsb.edu/ws/?pid=9283).
14. Ibid.
15. Remarks by Attorney General Robert F. Kennedy at Ceremonies Celebrating the 175th Anniversary of the Ratification of the Constitution, Independence Hall, Philadelphia, Pennsylvania, June 21, 1963, Robert F. Kennedy Attorney General Papers, Speeches, Box 2, June 21–26, 1963, JFKL.
16. Statement of the Attorney General Robert F. Kennedy Before the House Committee on the Judiciary Regarding H.R. 7152, the Proposed Civil Rights Act of 1963, June 26, 1963, Robert F. Kennedy Attorney General Papers, Speeches, Box 2, June 21–26, 1963, JFKL.
17. Ibid.
18. Ibid.
19. Ibid.
20. Ibid.
21. Hilty, 373.
22. Branch, 835–836.
23. Robert F. Kennedy, recorded interview with Burke Marshall by Anthony Lewis, p. 495, December 4, 1964, JFKOHP.
24. David J. Garrow *The FBI and Martin Luther King, Jr.* (New York: Penguin, 1981), 59.
25. Ibid., 60.
26. Branch, 838.
27. Ibid., 839.
28. Lewis, 206.
29. Branch, 839.
30. Hilty, 374.
31. Garrow, *The FBI*, 62–63.
32. Hilty, 376.
33. Garrow, *The FBI*, 65–66.
34. Hilty, 377.
35. Ibid.
36. John F. Kennedy, "The President's News Conference," July 17, 1963 (Gerhard Peters and John T. Woolley, *The American Presidency Project*, http://www.presidency.ucsb.edu/ws/?pid=9348).
37. Ibid.
38. Robert F. Kennedy, recorded interview with Burke Marshall by Anthony Lewis, p. 589, December 22, 1964, JFKOHP.
39. Ibid., 590.
40. Garrow, *The FBI*, 72.
41. Ibid., 74.
42. Ibid., 75.
43. Hilty, 393.
44. Garrow, *FBI*, 67.
45. Statement of Attorney General Robert F. Kennedy Before the Senate Judiciary Committee Regarding S. 1731, The Proposed Civil Rights Act of 1963, and S. 1750, July 18, 1963, Robert F. Kennedy Attorney General Papers, Speeches, Box 2, RFK's Answers to Questions on Civil Rights July 1963, JFKL.
46. Branch, 847–848.
47. Robert F. Kennedy, recorded interview with Burke Marshall by Anthony Lewis, p. 591, December 22, 1964, JFKOHP.
48. Ibid.
49. Branch, 878.
50. Hilty, 379.
51. Ibid.
52. Branch, 874.
53. Hilty, 379.
54. Ibid.
55. Branch, 879.
56. Lewis, 225.
57. Ibid., 226–227.
58. Ibid., 228.
59. Branch, 875–876.
60. For a good description of the "I Have a Dream" speech see Branch, 881–883.
61. Robert F. Kennedy, recorded interview with Burke Marshall by Anthony Lewis, p. 594, December 22, 1964, JFKOHP.
62. Branch, 883.
63. Ibid., 883–884.
64. Ibid., 884–886.
65. Brauer, 293.
66. Ibid., 294.
67. John F. Kennedy, "Statement by the President on Desegregation in the Schools of Alabama," September 9, 1963 (Gerhard Peters and John T. Woolley, *The American Presidency Project*, http://www.presidency.ucsb.edu/ws/?pid=9399).
68. Ibid.
69. Brauer, 295.
70. John F. Kennedy, "Statement by the President on the Sunday Bombing in Birmingham," September 16, 1963 (Gerhard Peters and John T. Woolley, *The American Presidency Project*, http://www.presidency.ucsb.edu/ws/?pid=9410).
71. Robert F. Kennedy, recorded interview with Burke Marshall by Anthony Lewis, p. 595, December 22, 1964, JFKOHP.
72. Address by the Attorney General Robert F. Kennedy at the Annual Meeting of the Missouri Bar Association, Hotel Muehlbach, Kansas City, Missouri, September 17, 1963, Robert F. Kennedy Attorney General Papers, Speeches, Box 2, September 25–27, 1963, JFKL.
73. Remarks by the Attorney General Robert F. Kennedy to the 120th Anniversary Dinner of B'nai B'rith, Conrad Hilton Hotel, Chicago, October 13, 1963, Robert F. Kennedy Attorney General Papers, Speeches, Box 2, October 13–15, 1963, JFKL.
74. Statement by Attorney General Robert F. Kennedy on H.R. 7152 Before the House Judiciary Committee, October 15, 1963, Robert F. Kennedy Attorney General Papers, Speeches, Box 2, October 13–15, 1963, JFKL.
75. Remarks by Attorney General Robert F. Kennedy before the Annual Convention of the Theatre Owners of America, Americana Hotel, New York,

New York, October 28, 1963, Robert
F. Kennedy Attorney General Papers,
Speeches, Box 3, Theatre Owners of
America October 28, 1963, JFKL.
    76. Brauer, 298.

Epilogue

    1. Hilty, 387.
    2. Robert F. Kennedy, ed. Edwin
Gutham and Jeffrey Shulman, *Robert
Kennedy in His Own Words: The Un-
published Recollections of the Kennedy
Years* (New York: Bantam Press,
1988), 210–211.
    3. Ibid., 211–212.

    4. Schlesinger, *RFK and His
Times*, 608.
    5. Ibid., 611.
    6. Edward Kennedy, *True Com-
pass*, 208–209.
    7. Ibid., 216–217.
    8. Ibid., 217.
    9. Excerpts from Remarks by At-
torney General Robert F. Kennedy at
a Panel Discussion "After the Civil
Rights Bill, What?," American Society of Newspaper Editors, 1964 Convention, Washington, D.C., April 16,
1964, Robert F. Kennedy Attorney
General Papers, Box 3, Americans Society of Newspaper Editors, April 16,
1963, JFKL.

    10. Garrow, *Bearing the Cross*, 307.
    11. Lewis, 244.
    12. Ibid., 245.
    13. Edward Kennedy, *True Com-
pass*, 217.
    14. Hilty, 388.
    15. Statement by Attorney General
Robert F. Kennedy, Gracie Mansion,
New York City, August 25, 1964, Department of Justice Website, http://
www.justice.gov/ag/rfkspeeches/1964
/08–25–1964.pdf.
    16. Jack Newfield, *Robert Kennedy:
A Memoir* (New York: E.P. Dutton,
1969), 40–41.

Bibliography

Secondary Sources

Arsenault, Raymond. *Freedom Riders: 1961 and the Struggle for Racial Justice*. New York: Oxford University Press, 2006.

Barrett, Russell H. *Integration at Ole Miss*. Chicago: Quadrangle Books, 1965.

Branch, Taylor. *Parting the Waters: America in the King Years, 1954–1963*. New York: Touchstone, 1988.

Brauer, Carl M. *John F. Kennedy and the Second Reconstruction*. New York: Columbia University Press, 1977.

Carson, Clayborne. *In Struggle: The SNCC and the Black Awakening of the 1960s*. Cambridge, MA: Harvard University Press, 1995.

Collier, Peter, and David Horowitz. *The Kennedys: An American Drama*. New York: Summit Books, 1984.

Dallek, Robert. *An Unfinished Life: John F. Kennedy 1917–1963*. New York: Little Brown, 2003.

Doyle, William. *An American Insurrection: The Battle of Oxford, Mississippi, 1962*. New York: Doubleday, 2001. Apple iBooks edition.

Garrow, David J. *Bearing the Cross: Martin Luther King, Jr., and the Southern Christian Leadership Conference*. New York: Quill/William Morrow, 1986.

_____. *The FBI and Martin Luther King, Jr.* New York: Penguin, 1981.

Giglio, James N. *The Presidency of John F. Kennedy*. Lawrence: University of Kansas Press, 1991.

Goduti, Philip A., Jr. *Kennedy's Kitchen Cabinet and the Pursuit of Peace: The Shaping of American Foreign Policy, 1961–1963*. Jefferson, NC: McFarland, 2009.

Goodwin, Doris Kearns. *The Fitzgeralds and the Kennedys: An American Saga*. New York: St. Martin's, 1987.

_____. *Team of Rivals: The Political Genius of Abraham Lincoln*. New York: Simon and Schuster, 2005.

Graham, Hugh Davis. *The Civil Rights Era: Origins and Development of National Policy, 1960–1972*. New York: Oxford University Press, 1990.

Guthman, Edwin. *We Band of Brothers: A Memoir of Robert F. Kennedy*. New York: Harper and Row, 1964.

Halbertsam, David. *The Children*. New York: Random House, 1998.

Hersh, Burton. *Bobby and J. Edgar: The Historic Face-Off Between the Kennedys and J. Edgar Hoover that Transformed America*. New York: Basic Books, 2007.

Hilty, James W. *Robert Kennedy: Brother Protector*. Philadelphia: Temple University Press, 1997.

Kennedy, Edward M. *True Compass: A Memoir*. New York: Twelve, 2009.

Kennedy, Robert F. *The Enemy Within*. New York: Harper and Brothers, 1960.

Kennedy, Robert. Edwin Gutham and Jeffrey Shulman, eds. *Robert Kennedy in His Own Words: The Unpublished Recollections of the Kennedy Years*. New York: Bantam, 1988.

King, Martin Luther, Jr. *Why We Can't Wait*. New York: Mentor Group, 1964.

Lewis, John. *Walking with the Wind: A Memoir of the Movement*. New York: Harvest, 1998.

McWhorter, Diane. *Carry Me Home: Birmingham, Alabama: The Climactic Battle of the Civil Rights Revolution*. New York: Touchstone, 2001.

Meredith, James. *Three Years in Mississippi*. Bloomington: Indiana University Press, 1966.

Morgan, Edmund S. *American Slavery, American Freedom: The Ordeal of Colonial Virginia*. New York: W.W. Norton, 1975.

Navasky, Victor. *Kennedy Justice*. New York: Atheneum, 1977.

Newfield, Jack. *Robert Kennedy: A Memoir*. New York: E.P. Dutton, 1969.

Patterson, James T. *Grand Expectations: The United States, 1945–1974*. New York: Oxford University Press, 1996.

Reeves, Richard. *President Kennedy: Profile of Power*. New York: Touchstone, 1993.

Schlesinger, Arthur M., Jr. *Robert Kennedy and His Times*. New York: Houghton Mifflin, 2002.

_____. *A Thousand Days: John F. Kennedy in the White House*. Boston: Houghton Mifflin, 1965.

Sorensen, Theodore. *Counselor: A Life at the Edge of History*. New York: Harper Collins, 2008.

_____. *Kennedy*. New York: Harper Collins, 1965.
Thomas, Evan. *Robert Kennedy: His Life*. New York: Touchstone, 2000.
Weisbrot, Robert. *Freedom Bound: A History of America's Civil Rights Movement*. New York: W.W. Norton, 1990.
Wofford, Harris. *Of Kennedys and Kings: Making Sense of the Sixties*. Pittsburgh: University of Pittsburgh Press, 1980.
Zinn, Howard. *SNCC: The New Abolitionists*. Cambridge, MA: South End Press, 1964.

Primary Sources

Carson, Clayborne, ed. *The Papers of Martin Luther King, Jr.* Volume 5, *Threshold of a New Decade, January 1959–December 1960*. Berkeley: University of California Press, 2005.
Katzenbach, Nicholas. Recorded interviews. John F. Kennedy Oral History Project of the John F. Kennedy Library.
Kennedy, Robert F. Recorded interviews. John F. Kennedy Oral History Project of the John F. Kennedy Library.
Marshall, Burke. Recorded interviews. John F. Kennedy Oral History Project of the John F. Kennedy Library.
Peters, Gerhard, and John T. Woolley. *The American Presidency Project*. Santa Barbara, CA: University of California (hosted), Gerhard Peters (database). http://www.presidency.ucsb.edu/ws.
Seigenthaler, John. Recorded interviews. John F. Kennedy Oral History Project of the John F. Kennedy Library.

Papers and Collections

Burke Marshall Papers. John F. Kennedy Library. Columbia Point, Boston, Massachusetts.
John F. Kennedy Library Archives. Columbia Point, Boston, Massachusetts.
Robert F. Kennedy, Attorney General, Papers. John F. Kennedy Library. Columbia Point, Boston, Massachusetts.

Audio Visual Sources

By the People: The Election of Barack Obama. Directed by Amy Rice and Alyssa Sams. Aired August 7, 2009. HBO Films, 2009.
Crisis: Behind a Presidential Commitment. Directed by Robert Drew. Aired on October 21, 1963. ABC News and Drew Associates, 1963.
Fayer, Steve. *Eyes on the Prize*. Episode 2, "Fighting Back." Directed by Judith Vecchione. Narrated by Julian Bond. Aired January 28, 1987. Backside Productions and PBS, 1987.

Index